The
Uneasy
Center

Paul K. Conkin

The *Uneasy* Center

Reformed Christianity in Antebellum America

The University of North Carolina Press

Chapel Hill & London

The paper in this book meets the guidelines for permanence and durability
of the Committee on Production Guidelines for Book Longevity of the
Council on Library Resources.

Library of Congress Cataloging-in-Publication Data
Conkin, Paul Keith.
The uneasy center : Reformed Christianity in antebellum America /
by Paul K. Conkin.
    p.   cm.
Includes bibliographical references and index.
ISBN 0-8078-2180-2 (alk. paper). – ISBN 0-8078-4492-6 (pbk. :
alk. paper)
1. Protestant churches – United States – History.   2. United States –
Church history – Colonial period, ca. 1660–1775.   3. United States –
Church history – 18th century.   4. United States – Church history – 19th
century.   I. Title.
BR520.C65   1995
280'.4'0973 – dc20   94-12292
                      CIP

99 98 97 96 95   5 4 3 2 1

Contents

Preface

For over thirty years I have devoted one-half of each semester in my fall intellectual history course to the evolution of Christianity in pre–Civil War America. This book is in large part a product of that teaching. For the last five years I have tried to add as much scholarly depth as possible to classroom lectures and to add the new material that seemed necessary to create a broad, synoptic history, one based on both primary and secondary sources. Given such a huge topic, I know many errors remain in the text, but I hope that the story is as truthful as long years of searching and reflection could make it and that the text is as clear and eloquent as the often complex subject matter allows.

I have not tried to tell the full story of religion in antebellum America. I chose what seemed clearly the most central and significant part of that story. What I have written is an account of Reformed Christianity in its glory years – from colonial plantings to roughly the end of the Civil War. By "Reformed," I mean those branches of Christianity that traced their modern origins to the reforms not of Luther but of Ulrich Zwingli, John Calvin, Martin Bucer, John Knox, Thomas Cranmer, and dozens of other architects of national churches on the European continent and in Britain. In the American colonies, and in the first century of national independence, these Reformed confessions made up, by far, the largest and most influential segment of Christianity in America. To use a spatial image, they occupied the center. To use a topographic image, they were the mainstream.

This Reformed center continually confronted religious competitors and in time suffered numerous internal schisms. By 1865 the churches in the Reformed tradition had steadily declined from near 90 percent of all Christians in 1776 to no more than 60 percent. With this came a diminution of relative influence on the larger culture, while internal factionalism further increased the unease felt by these confessions at the end of the sectional conflict. Yet, even as late as 1865 the Reformed denominations not only still enjoyed a numerical majority but also easily exceeded, in overall cultural and political and economic influence, all the other branches of Christianity combined.

In a worldwide perspective, the Reformed denominations in America made up only a small subclass of Protestantism. Protestant Christians were only one segment of the larger class of Christians, and of course Christians constituted only one of the major world religions. But in America this subclass almost defined the cultural meaning of "Christian" or even the meaning of "religion." This is because the paths of British settlement in America ensured the early dominance of Reformed Christians, most from the national churches of Britain (Anglican and Presbyterian) or from their immediate offspring (Congregationalists, Calvinist Baptists, and Methodists). Less numerous were non-English migrants from the French, German, and Dutch Reformed churches.

Reformed Christians never fully monopolized religion even in areas of British settlement. American Indians had their own varied religions. Roman Catholics came to Maryland, and unwanted Quakers immigrated to New England, New Jersey, and North Carolina. After William Penn opened Pennsylvania to all persecuted sects, Brethren or Anabaptist groups, Moravian pietists, and spiritualistic Schwenkfelders all migrated to America. Lutherans had first settled in New Amsterdam and New Sweden and then moved in increasing numbers to Pennsylvania. In the eighteenth century the whole Church of the Brethren moved to America, as did related congregations of Free Will Baptists from Britain. By the mid-seventeenth century, black slaves brought with them their own varied African religious traditions and soon blended them with Christianity. Finally, a few Jewish migrants settled in most of the colonies and slowly began to establish synagogues.

Most varieties of Christianity are now represented in America, including a few scattered congregations out of various Eastern and African traditions. But until the twentieth century, almost all American Christians were heirs of the church of the later Roman Empire. This church eventually and gradually separated into Greek (Orthodox) and Western or Roman Catholic wings. The paths of influence, and then of migration, ensured that a vast majority of American Christians, up until the nineteenth century, were in the Roman tradition. Even after the reforms by Luther and Calvin, and the great split in Western Christianity, the commonalities among Roman Catholic, Lutheran, and Reformed confessions remained most defining and most significant, at least from a broad and comparative perspective. Thus, in an introductory chapter, I have tried to trace the main lines of development in Western Christiantiy, an outline that some readers may need as a background for an understanding of Reformed Christianity in America.

No classification of Christianity in America will be useful for all purposes. But in order to clarify my Reformed center, I need at least to suggest who was not part of it. Here some of my judgments are challengeable, at least in some sense arbitrary. One clear tradition is that of the parent Roman Catholic church, a church largely excluded from most of colonial America but constituting the third-largest single confession in America by 1860 and thus the most threatening competitor of the Reformed mainstream. Although small in numbers in the colonial period, Lutheran confessions from Germany and Scandinavia grew rapidly in the nineteenth century because of waves of immigration. Lutherans were (and are) very close to the Reformed churches in doctrine and practice, as is the largest pietistic offspring of Lutheranism in America, the Moravians. Some of the Lutheran confessions in America overlapped at many points with their Reformed brethren. Yet, such was their historical background, their memories of early Reformation disagreements, and their ethnic loyalties that Lutherans have remained quite distinctive in America, clearly outside the Reformed mainstream. Notably, most but not all Lutherans in America were closer to Rome in doctrine and in worship than were Christians in any Reformed confession. Thus, using conventional but misleading spatial images, Roman Catholics and Lutherans were to the right of the Reformed center.

By the same imagery, all the other Christian confessions or sects in America were to the left of the center. I usually group these in nine classes based on distinctive doctrines and practices: the free will and separatist Anabaptist tradition (Mennonites, Amish, Church of the Brethren, Hutterites, Brethren in Christ, and other small offshoots of the original Swiss Brethren); spiritualistic and antinomian sects (American Friends, Shakers, and several small denominations); the adventist and corporealist tradition (Seventh-Day Adventists, Jehovah's Witnesses, Advent Christians); the Mormons (the Church of Jesus Christ of Latter-Day Saints and its Reorganized offspring); the American restoration movement (Disciples of Christ, Christians, and Churches of Christ); spiritualist and mind-cure movements (Swedenborgian, Christian Scientists, Unity); Holiness and Pentecostal churches (Church of the Nazarene, Assemblies of God, and at least a hundred smaller denominations); modern self-denominated "evangelical" denominations with both European and American, as well as Lutheran and Reformed, origins (Free Will Baptists, Evangelical Free Church, Christian and Missionary Alliance, Plymouth Brethren, and many others); and finally two such radically heretical offsprings of Reformed Christianity as to constitute a unique tradition, one with ancient doctrinal roots – Unitarianism and Universalism. When one adds these nine to Roman Catholicism, Lutheranism, and the Reformed tradition, one ends up with a dozen broad classifications of American Christianity, and even then numerous very small sects do not easily fit into any of the twelve classes. Given this variety, one moves back to the Reformed center with some appreciation of the wide array of Christian options present in America.

What do I mean by the "Reformed tradition"? In the heady days of Luther's reforms in Germany, those who identified themselves as Reformed did so to distinguish themselves on a few key doctrines and practices from Lutherans and, even more emphatically, from several emerging and radical sects. They recognized a commonality of doctrines, doctrines that in time many would identify with John Calvin, largely because of the influence of his church in Geneva and because of his writings, particularly his *Institutes of the Christian Religion.* Except in France, these Reformed Christians developed national confessions (Heidelberg, Belgic, Dort, the Thirty-Nine Articles, Westminster) and eventually gained state support. But as indicated earlier, in America I include in the Reformed camp not only those immigrants who still adhered to one of the national confessions but also those who dissented from some details of these confessions or of established practices but who remained in the same doctrinal tradition. For early America, this meant migrating English Puritans, who in New England adopted a congregational polity without any formal confession (they adhered doctrinally to Westminster), Particular Baptists or other Calvinist Baptists who accepted Westminster except for its permission of infant baptism, and finally the disciples of John Wesley, who nominally remained in the English church until his death and who, in America, accepted a revised confession based on the Thirty-Nine Articles.

This classification will confuse some people. The inclusion of Methodists departs from most conventional definitions of Reformed. Long before 1776 most Anglicans, in Britain and in America, had rejected what, by then, qualified as orthodox Calvinist doctrines. Only a minority of British Methodists, those under the influence of George Whitefield, remained self-confessed Calvinists. All who adhered to John Wesley, and all the early Methodists in America, joined Anglicans in what Wesley proudly proclaimed as an Arminian or anti-Calvinist doctrinal position. Within New England Congregationalism, at least a large and growing minority by 1776 had openly repudiated what they called Calvinism. Thus, my use of the word *Reformed* encompasses all Christians who traced their denominational origin to such reformers as Zwingli and Calvin or who continued to honor confessions within that tradition. It is not a term synonymous with Calvinism, at least as that label took on a precise and narrow doctrinal meaning in the seventeenth century. In fact, what helped distinguish Reformed Christians in America was their unending dialogue about salvation doctrines and thus their quite varied efforts to come to terms with a conventional or scholastic form of Calvinism. Therefore, Calvinism is a key subject in the following chapters, but it is not definitive. A growing share of Reformed Christians in America simply did not consider themselves Calvinists. Whether they were so or not depends, of course, on how one defines that loaded label. I believe one could frame a historical argument that the early Dutch Arminians, as they claimed, affirmed doctrines that were as consistent with an overall reading of John Calvin as were the selective doctrines ratified at Dort or Westminster.

Another troubling label is "evangelical." In origins, all the Lutheran and Reformed confessions proudly claimed to be evangelical, a term that distinguished them from the Roman church. By "evangelical," they meant to affirm as their only authority the word of God as revealed in scripture and as interpreted through the aid of the Holy Spirit, and also their belief that salvation (justification) depends on faith alone, which is a gracious or undeserved gift of God. These beliefs remained normative in all wings of the Reformation, however much they occasioned divisions over their exact meanings and implications. In this broad, Reformation perspective, all Reformed Christians in antebellum America were evangelical, although eventually a minority of Episcopalians (Anglo-Catholics) would protest such a claim.

In time, word use changed. In the eighteenth century, particularly after the Methodist revivals in England and a series of awakenings in America, certain British and American Protestants began to use "evangelical" as a distinguishing label of self-identity. They indeed believed they were returning to, or restoring, some of the heart themes of the early Reformation, but by now they used "evangelical" in a more restrictive sense. It now defined a subclass of Protestants. In the following chapters, I will try to capture the meaning they gave to "evangelical" and to adhere to a clear and precise definition of the term. To make the semantic game even more confusing, by the twentieth century the label has assumed, among many self-proclaimed "evangelicals," an even more restrictive or exclusive meaning. But my point here is that my subject – Reformed Christianity in America – differs from the class defined by eighteenth-century meanings of the word *evangelical*. Some Christians in the Reformed churches were evangelical, some not. Some were orthodox Calvinists, some not. And the subclasses, Calvinist and evangelical, did not fully overlap. Such insistently anti-Calvinists as the early Methodists were all evangelical by the eighteenth-century use of the term. Many rigidly Calvinistic Old School Presbyterians, although proudly evangelical by Calvin's use of the label, were antievangelical in the new American context.

With some regret, I here include only the story of the mainstream. Even though I had to subdue constant temptations to make more and more comparisons with the churches outside this tradition, I can assure readers that the other forms of Christianity were constantly in mind. My awareness of them helped shape much of this book, in ways perhaps not apparent to a reader. For the Reformed mainstream, I have tried to be comprehensive, even though no one can include every theme in such a broad synthesis. One mandate was to avoid what is all too tempting – an urban or northeastern bias. I have tried fully to include and integrate the South into my story, even as I have tried to remember that a vast majority of antebellum Christians lived in small villages or rural areas.

In subject, I have self-consciously tried to integrate four themes – theology, doctrine, institutions, and religious practices (primarily worship). I have not included any social analysis of church members, have not extensively evaluated the role of churches in the larger society, and have not moved very far into popular distortions or vulgarizations of normative beliefs and practices. These are all fascinating subjects, pursued with ever greater sophistication by able scholars. I simply could not do everything, and perhaps in what I chose to do I reflect what most fascinates me about religion in America. I hope others share that interest, share my belief that these aspects of religion are vital in what they reveal about the identity of Americans, and also my conviction that these aspects are a necessary prelude for informed inquiry into the social or folk history of religion.

I did not want to place too much emphasis on serious theology. Yet, about one-fourth of the following book involves theology. I define theology as an intellectually rigorous systematization of, or philosophical apology for, a theistic religion. Christian theology has always, from Paul on, been the work of Christian intellectuals. It rises above a simple statement of doctrines or simple defenses of such doctrines. One might use a fancy word and call it *metadoctrinal.* Of all Christian traditions in the early Republic, only those churches in the Reformed tradition had developed intellectual and philosophical traditions, and the needed academies and seminaries, that made possible reasonably sophisticated theological inquiry. As in so many areas of American culture, Reformed Christians enjoyed, for a time, a type of theological hegemony. I therefore devote two full chapters to the best of Reformed theology and incorporate theological themes into other chapters.

Doctrines are critical. This book fails completely if it does not clarify the normative or official or confession-based beliefs of each Reformed denomination and if it does not identify the points of internal tension and debate about these beliefs. In the pluralistic religious environment of America, the most important basis of denominational identity, and of competitive appeal, was doctrine, most of all those doctrines concerning the requirements of salvation. The Reformed denominations had to convince Americans that they best understood scriptures, or what God commanded, and thus offered more hope or assurance of redemption than other competing denominations. Each Reformed confession had to make this case against the other competing, non-Reformed traditions, but given the predominance of Reformed churches in early America, the most intense competition was within that tradition, such as the competition between rigid Calvinists and Wesleyan Arminians or between Baptists and infant-baptizing Presbyterians. Throughout this book, my most demanding challenge has been to present nuances of belief so clearly and so truthfully that, if the protagonists on all sides could come back to earth, they would be pleased by my descriptions.

Next to doctrines, institutions were the most important basis of identity and of conflict. Most basic was polity, or the way the various denominations governed themselves. In America, the Reformed denominations reflected the whole spectrum, from the congregationalism of New England and of Baptists, to a republican or presbyterian middle way, to the episcopal system of Methodists and Episcopalians. But institutions extend beyond polity, to mandated ways of selecting, training, and ordaining clergy, to mission programs, and to educational and benevolent organizations. In the early nineteenth century, para-church institutions, such as organized campgrounds and other supports for annual revivals, and above all Sunday schools, often assumed an importance equivalent to the organized church and its worship.

As much as possible, I have tried to understand various worshiping traditions. At times, liturgical conflict was as important as doctrinal conflict among the Reformed denominations, but one has to note that issues about the order and content of worship were rarely distinct from matters of correct belief. In the one, quite exceptional case of the Protestant Episcopal church, liturgy was the most important basis of denominational identity, and in the German Reformed church, it was long a catalyst of conflict and division. I have devoted one chapter to Reformed worship, and throughout the book I have given attention to liturgical issues whenever they were the source of identity or the basis of conflict.

I feel no need to defend the importance of a book on religion or, more specifically, Christianity in America. By such outward measurements as church membership and attendance, the United States ended the nineteenth century as a great deal more Christian than at its beginning. By the same indicators, at the end of the twentieth century, the United States promises to be more Christian than any other major, industrialized country. Church affiliation remains at around 50 percent, reported attendance at just under 50 percent, actual attendance on any Sunday at about 25 percent, and a full or deep commitment to confessional doctrines and practices at about 20 percent. It is doubtful that these loyalties were greater either one hundred or two hundred years ago. At least in a general way an overwhelming majority of Americans still affirm the core beliefs of the Semitic religious tradition (theism and divine providence). Churches remain vital institutions, serving as the primary social institution beyond the family for up to half of Americans. Christian symbols and Christian festivals or holy days remain central to the larger culture. Of course, these outward continuities may conceal an inner erosion of the most basic or distinctive Christian beliefs. Also, Americans are clearly divided in their evaluation of these facts: some applaud and some deplore the continued appeal and strength of Christianity.

Pluralism and adaptability are at the heart of continued Christian cultural ascendancy in America. The vitality of American Christianity has most often derived from new springs of belief and conviction, often among splintering sects, new religious movements, or intensely prophetic or spiritualistic minorities in older denominations. Here, and not in the mainstream, one finds the most intense piety or fervor, the most unconventional values, and at times the most active social involvement. Out of such vital springs has come the rich variety of doctrines, the different gods or conceptions of a god, and the different forms of worship and devotion that make Christianity so broadly appealing. Given the present variety, Christianity, in some of its expressions, can appeal to almost everyone.

Adaptability has been as important as diversity in broadening the appeal of Christianity in America. Most of the Reformed denominations not only have assimilated change (this is inescapable, and most so when people are not conscious of change) but also have made deliberate and adaptive modifications to accommodate shifts in the larger culture – in beliefs, in operative values, and in patterns of conduct. In perhaps no other country have the mainline churches (our substitute for national churches) been as able to retain as members, or deflect as potential critics, such a large proportion of its intelligentsia, including academics and scientists. In an era when the most vital and visible Christians are those who, in one way or another, stand outside the mainstream, it is easy to dismiss, or underestimate, the continued strength, and cultural ascendancy, of those who are still at least nominally in the Reformed center, those who are heirs of distant Geneva or of a less distant nineteenth-century form of evangelicalism. Today, these Reformed denominations are often latitudinarian in doctrine, ecumenical in outlook, and liberal in theology and doctrine. What such churches have lost in fervor, or clarity of purpose, or integrity of doctrines, should not conceal what they have thereby retained by their inclusiveness, by their openness to new intellectual challenges, and by their continued influence on elite culture. To a much greater extent that most people realize, members of the Reformed mainstream still own and govern America.

My approach has been deliberately sympathetic. I wanted to understand each confession, grasp why it had such appeal to converts, comprehend its internal integrity. I have no confessional agenda. I may reflect unrecognized preferences, reveal my own taste in religions. I am fascinated with all religions and in some respects am more fascinated with the sects outside the mainstream than with the churches within it. My effort to understand beliefs and preferences from an internal perspective, in the way adherents understood them, does not mean that I suspended certain types of judgment made possible by hindsight. I often identify confusions and circularities in doctrine or theology, critical problems in sacred texts, or moral compromises in social policy. I consider this a necessary component of honest description. What I hope is that I have been evenhanded in such judgments, that I have not played favorites.

I cannot begin to list all my debts. In ways that I cannot measure, students have forced me to think, and rethink, the content of this book. In 1990 I enjoyed a National Endowment for the Humanities University Fellowship that allowed me to enjoy fifteen months for undiverted work on this project. Colleagues in my department here at Vanderbilt have contributed specialized knowledge or made helpful corrections. More specifically, Margo Todd, an expert on English Puritanism, read and made very helpful suggestions on the sections dealing with the Reformation in England and Scotland. My family, as always, has forgiven me the inattention that came from my overabsorption in searching and writing.

The
Uneasy
Center

Pre-Reformation Christianity in the West

*T*he Reformed Christianity that moved to America with British colonists was a belated product of the Western church. Despite all the controversies that followed the attempted reforms of Luther, the resulting Catholic and Protestant wings of this Western church still shared most major doctrines, including those so basic as rarely to occasion controversy. Thus, the first task, if one is to understand Reformed Christianity as it flourished in early America, is to go back to earlier roots, to explore broad commonalities.

Christianity is in the theistic and providential Semitic family and is most distinctive among major world religions for its emphasis on doctrines or correct belief. It has an experiential dimension, sanctions various rituals, and mandates certain moral codes. But such is its diversity that the exact details vary from sect to sect. Teleologically, it is above all a salvation religion, as distinguished from predominantly enlightenment religions (Buddhism) or ecstatic religions, but in at least some of its expressions it has a place for ecstasy and wisdom. Organizationally, it has its sacred texts (it is a religion of the book, although no more so than Islam), its prophets, its temples and shrines, and plenty of organization.

Christianity is a complex religion. It, like Islam, was a daughter of Judaism. It had no clear date of birth, matured slowly, and has never been a static religion. The diversity of beliefs, values, and practices among avowed Christians obscures any core beliefs and values, if there are such. The early history of Christianity is in part hidden because of lost sources. Yet one can offer some broad characteristics of the type of religion that developed very quickly after the death of Jesus.

Jewish Roots and the Early Religion of Jesus

Early Christians, even when Gentiles, retained the foundational cosmology of the Jews. This was, and remains, the Semitic and theistic core of Christianity. The Jews gradually developed and refined their belief in a masculine, creative, and providential god. By the Hellenic period, some Jews had moved to a true monotheism, or a belief in only one god for all nations, although their religion retained tribal and exclusive elements. Early Christians kept the cosmology and, under the influence of Paul, dropped the tribal elements and advertised a new, transcultural, or catholic religion, a universality earlier preached by Deutero-Isaiah but rarely achieved by the Jews.

The early Jewish religion was communal, not personal. The Jewish god, Jehovah (an English rendition of Yahweh), dealt with the whole people of Israel, and the ordinary people suffered severe afflictions because of the failings of their leaders. But prophetic reformers, most notably Jeremiah, introduced elements of personal devotion and personal responsibility into the primitive religion. The Jews of the first Israel, up through the Babylonian exile (after 586 B.C.E.) of the intellectual and political leaders of a defeated Judah, did not believe in life after death or offer any type of salvation beyond this world. The benefits of obedience to Jehovah manifested themselves in national or personal prosperity, moral self complacency, and happiness. But after the captivity, and an enduring diaspora of Jews, aspects of other salvation religions began to affect Judaism. At least after Alexander's conquest of Palestine, a few Jews began to affirm a belief in a resurrection of the righteous to share in a future restored Davidic kingdom, one to be ushered in by a specially anointed servant of Jehovah, or what some sectarian and apocalyptic Jews referred to as a son of man or a messiah. This belief in a resurrection was first recorded and preserved in the apocalypse of Daniel, written around 165 B.C.E. The resurrection doctrine, and the belief in deliverance by a messiah, were widespread, even normative, among Jews by the time of Jesus. Thus, the early followers of Jesus reflected or adopted Jewish theism and the hope for a restored life in a coming kingdom.

Even in its earliest expression, Judaism was a religion of law and sacrifice. The Jewish tribal deity required adherence to his commands, eventually codified as written or oral laws attributed to the legendary lawgiver, Moses. These laws concerned all aspects of life: human relationships, rituals of cleanliness and holiness, and ritual sacrifices. Sacrifices were integral to many ancient religions, including those of Canaan, which most influenced the early Jews. In Judaism, sacrifices were acts of appeasement to Jehovah, or a ritual means of gaining absolution or forgiveness for disobedience or uncleanliness. The sacrificial animals assumed the burden of guilt from the individual. Soon, a special priesthood performed such atoning sacrifices on altars and, after its completion in Jerusalem, in the first Jewish temple. The sacrificial objects became gifts to the priests, part of their livelihood.

After the Babylonian conquest, widely dispersed Jews developed special religious services in synagogues. These involved not altar sacrifices but acts of celebration and the teaching of the law as now embodied in the Torah and in oral traditions. Instead of priests, special scribes or learned teachers (rabbis) presided at synagogue worship. Both the priestly and sacrificial aspects and the prophetic and moralistic aspects of Judaism would survive in Christianity. The Christian belief in an atoning savior continued the sacrificial aspects, whereas forms of worship in Christian assemblies reflected the synagogue heritage. The earlier role of both priests and rabbis helped define the duties of a Christian clergy.

Upon these Jewish foundations and precedents, early Christians built a distinctive new religion. It featured a new scheme of salvation related to the life, the status, and the teachings of Jesus of Nazareth. Jesus left no writings. No early descriptions of him have survived. The first extant literature about him is in letters written by Paul, but the first of these (to the Thessalonians) date from at least fifteen years after Jesus died. By then Christians had developed distinctive forms of worship. Paul did more than anyone else to order beliefs and practices and to provide an intellectual apology for the new religion. It would be at least another twenty years before other devout Christians would write biographies of Jesus (the author of the book now attributed to Mark wrote possibly as early as 70 C.E.). Thus, what we know about Jesus comes from these later biographies or from letters written by Paul or other early apostles in the emerging Christian church. The beliefs and liturgies of the new religion shaped their descriptions of Jesus, leaving forever clouded the way eyewitnesses perceived Jesus or how he viewed himself and his mission.

The one central, distinguishing belief of the new religion was that Jesus was the delivering messiah promised by Jewish prophets. However important the teaching ascribed to Jesus, his role and status was what was all important for a new salvation religion. Since the Greek word for Messiah was Christ, and since the new religion soon became primarily a Gentile religion, the disciples of Jesus gained the label "Christian." It literally meant one who acknowledged that Jesus was the Christ, the anointed one, the son of man referred to in Daniel and expected by Jewish sectarians. This messiahship was exemplified in a miraculous birth (Gentile Christians, drawing from gospel accounts, came to believe that Mary conceived Jesus through the work of God's spirit, not by a normal conception, and thus that she was a virgin at the time of his birth), in numerous miracles performed by Jesus, and above all in his resurrection on the third day after his unmerited execution and death on a cross. Thus, the minimal doctrine of Christianity became this one – that Jesus had a special divine role or identity and that, through his death and resurrection, he opened the way for a new form of reconciliation between God and humans. In a sense, early Christianity made up a new salvation cult, one of hundreds that developed in the Hellenistic world. Orthodox Jews rejected the messianic claim and correctly noted that Jesus did not restore the Davidic kingdom.

All Christians, by definition, believed that Jesus was the messiah. Beyond this acknowledgment, they disagreed, at times violently. Almost all Christians came to believe that his role was not, immediately, to establish any worldly kingdom, but by his sacrificial or atoning role to make possible a new spiritual kingdom or church, consisting of his faithful disciples. Jesus meantime had returned to his father but promised to come again and complete his kingdom, perhaps on a cleansed and perfected earth. Thus, early Christians did not drop the apocalyptic promise of Hellenistic Judaism but postponed it.

As far as scant records indicate, early Christians never agreed on doctrines or practices. Even Paul, who provides the earliest window on the embryonic church, fought bitter battles with other Christians, including the two leaders of the first church in Jerusalem, Peter and James. As the new religion spread beyond Palestine and among Gentiles, regional differences multiplied. The two early Jewish Christian sects – Nazarenes and Ebionites – reflected a form of Christianity that did not survive and did not provide a pattern for the Gentile church. The early Jewish Christians, from what we know about them, kept many Jewish traditions, including circumcision, worshiped on the Sabbath in a pattern closely modeled on the synagogue, had only one accepted gospel (a version of Matthew), believed Jesus was the son of Joseph (no virgin birth) and traced his lineage through the male line, and believed that Jesus was a man with a divine mission, not an incarnate or preexisting divine being, let alone a god. Such Jewish Christians apparently resented Paul, refused to accept his more Hellenic theology, probably rejected any doctrine of a separate soul or spirit, and affirmed not immortality but a future resurrection. This most primitive or Jewish form of Christianity would later offer a guide to certain Unitarians and Adventists.

Early Christian missionaries spread Christianity throughout the Roman Empire and into parts of Africa (Ethiopia) and Asia (Armenia) beyond the boundaries of the empire. Within two centuries, certain enduring Christian traditions shaped the original "orthodox" churches. Because of emerging differences, which would occasion the first six of seven great ecumenical councils (those that involved the whole church) over a period of three centuries, each of the orthodox traditions became distinct on often subtle issues of doctrine, worship, and polity. Only in the twentieth century would Americans directly encounter members of the ancient and enduring Oriental churches (Antiochian, Assyrian, Arminian, Coptic, Egyptian, and Ethiopian). None of these had any direct impact on the early history of Christianity in America. Thus, American Christianity, in its origins and maturation, reflected only one of the ancient traditions, that of the church that received recognition in the later Roman Empire and that matured its doctrines in the seven ecumenical councils (325 to 787). From this church would derive, in the West, the Roman Catholic church and, in the East, the Greek-influenced Orthodox churches.

From the church of the Roman Empire came all the modern, European state churches. They now make up four groups of churches (Roman Catholic, Eastern Orthodox, Lutheran, and Reformed). Members of all these traditions would eventually migrate to America, although except in Alaska, few Orthodox Christians arrived until the late nineteenth century. Since all these confessions (denominations in a pluralistic America) derive from the church of the empire, and all affirm the great doctrinal settlements of the councils, they are religious cousins. Much more than they realized, Reformed Christians in America still affirmed most of the central doctrines that matured in the early centuries of this Western church.

Because of the Catholic-Protestant dialectic, and what remained until the twentieth century divergent trends on both sides, Americans were not in a position to recognize the commonalities that were still much more basic than the fought-over differences. These commonalities reflect developments in the Western church up to the seventh century. In theology, they reflect the merging of Jewish prophetic and wisdom thought with Greek philosophy. In literature, they reflect three centuries of screening and evaluation that led to the New Testament canon. In polity, they reflect the maturation of a masculine and episcopal hierarchy. In doctrine, they reflect the hard-won and complex products of the great councils, including a trinity formula and a complex understanding of the human and divine traits of Jesus. In worship, they reflect the evolution of an ever richer and more elaborated pre-Eucharistic and Eucharistic liturgy.

It is not my purpose here to tell the full story of these developments. I want only to emphasize that the church resolved the most troubling issues in these early centuries. One could refer to the result as the great settlement. All the state churches of Western Europe, whether later designated Catholic, Lutheran, or Reformed, remained generally within the terms of this settlement, although such a claim has to be qualified for church government. Various sectarians challenged one or more aspects of the settlement (in polity, key doctrines, or liturgy), although few rejected the New Testament canon.

Canon and Polity

The deepest conflict in the church came early, beginning in the second century of the Christian era. This conflict helped stimulate the winning side to develop a canonical body of Christian writings, to establish an authoritative form of church government, and to establish orthodox (authorized and universal) doctrines. The sources are too skimpy to fill in the whole story. What survived is the product of the winning side in all the varied conflicts. Most of what we know about alternatives comes from the winners, those who condemned and in the process described or distorted the doctrines and practices of those who lost.

The label "Gnostic" (one who knows) has come to designate certain commonalities among the strongest or most appealing of the losing Christian sects. *Sect* is the correct term, for the early Christians had no legal recognition, faced local and severe but cyclical persecution from 70 C.E. onward, and therefore had to fight out doctrinal battles among themselves. As we now identify them, the great fathers of the church were those who fought and won in competition with Gnostic sects. Some now refer to the winning side as the great church or as normative Christianity.

From surviving Gnostic writings, including at least half of the identified gospels, letters, acts of apostles, and apocalypses that competed for canonical status, it is clear that Christianity would have been a very different religion had any of the Gnostic schools prevailed. Since the label is imprecise, with the identified Gnostic teachers quite varied, one has to deal with ideal types. Two commonalities encompass the largest number of "Gnostics": first, a rejection of the goodness of the creation and often a repudiation or subordination of the creator God honored by the Jews; and, second, a spiritualization or divinization of the Christ with a concomitant slighting or denial of his human traits. Gnostic sects (remember that all Christians belonged to sects) stressed a transforming conversion or rebirth, which often involved a special initiation and a preternatural knowledge of the truth (gnosis). Some sects were quite ascetic or perfectionist but stressed a type of insight or knowledge or a divine gift that transcended any moral codes or any religion based on law and obedience, making some Gnostics the original antinomians. Like all early Christians, they apparently stressed spiritual gifts, such as ecstatic speech and healing, resulting in a very experiential and warm religion that accompanied their repudiation of worldly values. In most of these ways, the Gnostics rejected traditional Jewish elements – a creator god, the substantive goodness of all creation, a prudential and ordered and moralistic devotional life, and hope for a perfected kingdom in this world.

One early impact of the Gnostics was to force the competing and, in the end, the larger and successful wing of the Christian movement to think about the literature used in Christian communities. In the second century (about 140), one of the more extreme sectarians, Marcion (whether he was a Gnostic depends on definitions), in effect established a canon for his followers. He began by rejecting the authority of the Jewish scriptures (or the only recognized scripture for early Christians) and recommended to his disciples only ten letters of Paul and one gospel (an early version of one now attributed to Luke – significantly, the gospel writer most closely associated with Paul). Marcion's Pauline preferences threatened to capture this apostle for a Gnostic form of Christianity, and possibly earlier Gnostics of like mind even influenced the content of II Peter (a late canonical book that ends with a warning about the difficulties of understanding some of

Paul's obscure passages, which the ignorant and unstable had misinterpreted to their own ruin).

By the time Marcion endorsed his minimal Bible for Christians, other congregations had circulated and used all of Paul's church letters and the presently canonized four gospels. They did not conceive these writings as scripture and thus were not always careful when they copied the writings (a source of divergent textual traditions that created great difficulties later when the church tried to decide on one correct Greek text for each canonized book). It would be another century before most Christians would identify any distinctively Christian writings as of the same sacred status as the Jewish Bible. But many of the heads of leading congregations (bishops) took up the challenge of Marcion and began a serious consideration of what writings the churches should use as guides to belief and worship. As early as 180, one of the leading patristic fathers, Irenaeus, defended the authority of all four now canonical gospels, Paul's letters, and other letters by apostles. He claimed that the authors wrote under divine inspiration. He believed these texts, and not a flood of new ones by Gnostic authors, alone reflected apostolic sources, were uncorrupted in content, and had correctly identified authors, or the "scholarly" criteria that would guide later debates over a New Testament canon. But behind the effort to identify proper readings for Christians were clear doctrinal criteria – a rejection of the otherworldly and antinomian themes in gnosticism.

The screening of a distinctively Christian literature continued for over two hundred years beyond Irenaeus. By 182 the church in Rome listed the writings it endorsed, a list that approximated the later canon (it included two books that were not later included and left out about six or seven that were). In about 220 Clement of Alexandria first referred to an "old" and "new" Testament, a distinction that began to place certain Christian writings on the same level as the Jewish books. By 250 Origen, the ablest early Christian theologian and Old Testament scholar, claimed a type of inspiration for the emerging New Testament, although he was not sure about the exact books to include in it. By then everyone accepted a core, including the four gospels, thirteen letters attributed to Paul (modern scholars believe misattributed for at least three and possibly as many as six letters), Acts, and I Peter. At least by then everyone had agreed on a large number of books that they would exclude, including many with Gnostic content. The remaining issue would be the doubtful or hotly contested books – James, Jude, II Peter, II and III John, Hebrews, and Revelation. Only in 367 did the famous bishop of Alexandria, Athenasius, command acceptance of the present twenty-seven books, and no others. Ecclesiastical councils endorsed his list in 363, 393, and 397. This did not settle the issue for all time. The Syrian church long rejected Revelation, and Luther and Calvin expressed their profound doubts about James. But, for most purposes, this difficult and particularly divisive issue was settled by the fourth century and as a result of a clear anti-Gnostic crusade. The New Testament canon became the least contested, and most influential, commonality among all the churches (no similar agreement would hold on an Old Testament canon, since Jews and later Protestants would reject as canonical approximately fourteen books or parts of books recognized by Roman Catholics).

The challenge of Gnostics, and of other soon stigmatized or heretical groups, created a clear need for some system of government in the church. The need for order, for authorized and uniform beliefs and practices, lay behind the development of various clerical orders. The detailed development of such a clergy probably took place at a different tempo in various geographical areas. The New Testament church, as described primarily by Paul, was not yet well ordered. It had no clear clergy, although congregations had offices – deacons to collect and distribute alms, and elders to instruct and discipline converts. In the era of persecution, congregations met in homes, often under the protection of affluent men and women, who in some sense filled the role of later pastors. Self-identified apostles served as missionaries, but it remains a bit unclear what gave men and women (both sexes seemed to go on missions, often as husband-and-wife teams) the title of apostle. Possibly it was charismatic gifts, since Paul spoke in tongues to convince one of his congregations of his apostolic authority. But even by the time of the martyrdom of Paul (about 65), leaders of local congregations began to emerge. They became the spokesmen of the church and by 100 were corresponding with each other over such issues as doctrine or useful literature. With conflict and fragmentation, the winning side in the sectarian battles began to emphasize order and hierarchical authority. Some of this concern was reflected in the letters to Timothy and Titus, attributed to Paul but in all likelihood written long after his death, letters that endorsed church order and helped the church provide a balance to his more charismatic and antinomian impulses (in this case, the Gnostic challenge led not just to a selection of a canon but possibly to the composition of a small part of it).

The ecclesiastical system matured in the second century. Local leaders in congregations exerted more and more authority. Soon the congregations had at least two levels of officials: the deacons (including women into at least the third century), who took care of alms and other practical forms of ministry, and the presiding officer, a position that gained several almost synonymous titles – bishop, priest, presbyter, elder. Since the two offices had the sanction of Paul and the emerging New Testament, they have remained common to almost all Christians (Quakers and other spiritualists rejected any offices at all). Out of these two orders emerged an episcopal system, but no one can fill in all the details. The presiding elder in congregations eventually needed assistants or helpers, those who had the training, or the type of ordination, that allowed them to preside at worship and administer the two great mysteries or sacraments of the early church, baptism and the Eucharist. This meant three clerical orders – a presiding elder or bishop, assisting presbyters or priests, and deacons. In time, the presiding elders alone claimed the title of bishop, a title that at first probably designated their administrative preeminence, not a higher spiritual order within the church. Whereas bishops normally presided at Eucharistic worship in the large congregations, presbyters did this in smaller congregations outside the large cities or presided at weekday worship services.

By the third century, in at least most Christian areas of the empire, an episcopal system was fully in place. It would become more rigid and uniform after recognition of the church by Rome and the delegation of more and more secular tasks to the church. In an episcopal or monarchical system, authority derives from the bishops at the top. They ordain elders and deacons, the two lower orders. Bishops gain their authority from other bishops, in a special type of ordination called consecration, one that involves the laying on of hands (a tradition of Jewish synagogues) and special anointing. By tradition, not by any clear scriptural authority, the great church came to accept the idea of apostolic succession, or a belief that the clergy, and particularly the bishops, had originally gained their ordination, and authority, directly from Jesus's disciples, meaning an unbroken line of spiritual authority within the church. This also accompanied the complete exclusion of women from the priesthood.

After the conversion of Constantine in 312, the ending of persecution, and full state recognition by 395, the governmental system of the church increasingly imitated that of the empire. Bishops in large cities gained extra administrative authority (not spiritual) and would eventually be called archbishops. The bishop of Rome had much influence, although at first not clearly more so than bishops in Constantinople and Alexandria. According to well-supported tradition, the disciple Peter had served as bishop in Rome and was martyred there. This, as well as location, gave the bishop of Rome a special position, leading to the origin of the papacy. Even before Constantine, the bishop of Rome had tried to exercise a degree of centralized authority; the emperors solidified such authority, although the papacy did not gain all its present spiritual authority until the nineteenth century. Finally, even in the second century, bishops in various geographical areas began to consult with each other, forming the first church councils. After Constantine's conversion and the end of persecution, and usually with the authority of emperors, bishops ostensibly representative of the whole church gathered in the great ecumenical councils, beginning at Nicea in 325. These councils provided a representative and legislative balance to the power of the pope in Rome or the patriarch in Constantinople.

With Luther and Calvin, the issue of a correct policy would once again divide the Western church. The reformers never argued that, on scriptural grounds, one could identify a single correct polity, but they believed scripture could not support the priestly system that had developed in the Roman church. They were open to regional variations in church government, and various Lutheran and Reformed churches opted for episcopal, presbyterial or republican, and congregational forms. Some Lutheran and Reformed Christians continued to believe in some version of apostolic succession, as in the English church. But for the most part Protestants rejected three clerical orders and accepted only deacons and elders. They believed bishops in the early church were presbyters, possibly with added administrative roles. Both in Lutheran Sweden and in Reformed England, the state churches opted for an episcopal order, with bishops who had governmental authority over the lower clergy and who received special ordination. But bishops did not necessarily have any superior spiritual authority, and thus the office was primarily administrative in function. Later, the Anglican church would divide over the status of bishops, with High Church advocates arguing for a scriptural and apostolic authority for bishops (they alone had the power to ordain priests), countered by Anglican evangelicals (and American Methodists) who applauded episcopacy as a useful system of government but who denied any special apostolic status to bishops (they were an optional element in church government; thus such evangelicals gladly recognized ministers in churches without bishops).

The Great Doctrinal Settlements

With recognized bishops and authorized councils, the emerging church of the empire could sanction something close to common doctrines. It tried to do just this, but with enormous difficulties. It could clearly stigmatize Gnostics and other sects and, after imperial recognition, even use coercion against dissidents. The great doctrinal settlements are much too complex for any detailed description here, but once again, what was so important later, and in America, is that the Roman church had already settled these most subtle issues, at least to the satisfaction of the Protestant state churches.

The central doctrinal issues all involved the status of Jesus and aspects of salvation doctrine. Even with Paul, who was clearly influenced by Stoics, Christian intellectuals began the process of assimilating the working beliefs of early Christians with Greek philosophy. Out of this came a conception of the Christ that had little to do with the life, or the teachings, of Jesus as remembered in the church. Late Platonists, in Plato's academy, or philosophers we now identify as middle Platonists (to distinguish them from the later Neoplatonists), had integrated aspects of Plato's philosophy (a realm of essences or ideas that had a prior status in reality to the realm of material objects or existence) with the Aristotelian idea of a self-reflective, divine mind whose perfection drew all things toward it (a teleological or prime mover). What such a pure mind thought would be the divine ideas celebrated by Plato. Such ideas, now associated with a mind, provided a model or blueprint or formal structure for all objects in the world. Some Stoics identified a type of world soul, or a formal foundation for the world itself, or what Greeks called "Logos." This Hellenic philosophy had already influenced Jewish intellectuals, particularly at Alexandria, and provided a ready-made theology for the church. The Logos, the realm of pure essences that provided a model for any possible world, could be associated with the idea of wisdom in Hellenistic Judaism, or with the messiah in Christianity. Particularly in the late or post-Pauline book of Colossians, and even more in the Gospel of John (possibly by an Alexandrian author), one finds a biblical assimilation of Logos and other late Platonic themes. In brief, some Hellenized Christian intellectuals viewed Jesus as a divine Logos, as the informing ideas that lay behind the created world. Given the Semitic theism, then the Logos was an emanation from, or the original creation of, a providential god. It was by, and through, these divine ideas that such a god was able to create the world and all the spirits that inhabited it, including angels, demons, and humans. Thus, the Logos was a mediator between God and the world. At such a cosmic level, the Christ was scarcely a person at all but was the soul of creation, or the truth that lay revealed in all things. Only figuratively was such a Logos the son of God, and the Logos theology had no place for a Holy Spirit. At times, early Christian theologians made the Christ the divine Logos (as in John 1); at other times, they understood the divine ideas to be the soul of Jesus.

Greek philosophy offered suggestive terms for conceptualizing a Christ, but it had little to do with the elevation of Jesus to divine status within the church. The evidence is slim, but it seems that Christians very quickly made Jesus out to be not just the son of God, not just a special prophet or teacher, but in some sense himself divine. We know that it was laypeople who persisted in praying not to Jehovah in the name of Jesus but to Jesus, even though the early bishops did not approve. The earliest hymns or liturgical prayers, some incorporated in the gospels and in Paul's letters, reveal this divinization, as do the very cosmic images of the Christ in Colossians or the Platonic (Logos and images of light) themes so omnipresent in the Gospel of John. Even before Paul taught in Corinth, Christians had probably developed baptismal creeds that included a three-part reference to Father, Son, and Holy Spirit. Thus, at the end of the gospel attributed to Matthew (almost certainly written before 100, but with the commission possibly a later addition), we find such a baptismal creed included in the great commission that Jesus gave to his disciples (go forth and make all nations my disciples and baptize all in the name of the Father, Son, and Holy Spirit).

What the church lacked was any clear or uniform understanding of the concept of a Christ, or the central and distinguishing doctrine of Christianity. Until the fourth century, and the end of persecution, various Christian intellectuals, often in the dialogue with Gnostic sectarians, tried to work out a logical understanding of issues that would never fully yield to any logical explication. As heirs of Jewish monotheism, how could Christians conceive of Jesus as a god and yet not fall into polytheism? And how could they conceive the Holy Spirit, the comforter who came to the early Christians at the day of Pentecost and already a part of baptismal creeds? In fact, almost all the controversies would involve Jesus, not the Spirit, which means that doctrines about the Holy Spirit developed in Christianity almost on the coattails of a complex Christology.

Up through the third century, the most able Christian theologian was the Old Testament scholar at Alexandria, Origen. He offered a vast, cosmic, and transcriptural account of God, creation, and redemption. Origin explained the rebellion of original, created spirits (later angels and humans), whose fall led a cosmic god to create the physical universe and to begin a long process of reconciliation through various historical eras. In Neoplatonic imagery, Origen foresaw the eventual restoration of all things to God (and thus the end of materiality and of any personal identity). The Logos was the main agent in this process of restoration. Jesus, as the Logos, was subordinate to, or from, the father God, but Origen believed that this Logos emanated eternally from God or was generated before time by God, as was also the Spirit. Jesus, the one unfallen spirit, has as his soul the divine ideas or Logos, the basis of all created worlds. This theology, although later declared heretical by the church, makes clear the divinity of Jesus, his eternal albeit subordinate status, and his embodiment of the truth that is in all things. Origen, by accepting the interim necessity of the material universe, and its integral role in God's cosmic plan, rejected Gnostic antiworldliness, but his was a strongly Hellenized and Platonic conception of world history and of the status and role of the Christ.

The issues about the Christ's identity first came to a head in the early fourth century, leading to the first ecumenical council at Nicea in 325. For over three centuries, until 681 and during the work of six ecumenical councils, the Western church struggled with this identity problem. In a sense, the accepted solutions were mediatorial, even at times politically mandated, compromises. But except in the case of sectarians and Unitarians, the solutions held and were never challenged by the major reformers (Christians never stopped debating the meaning of, or trying to find better rationalizations for, the received trinity formula). Once again, the big problems were well disposed of long before Christianity came to America.

Almost from the beginning, the church had a trinity. That is, Christians acknowledged Father, Son, and Spirit. The issue first resolved at Nicea was not to endorse a belief in a trinity (all sides agreed on this) but rather to find a formula that could express the proper understanding, or even make sense, of the three persons acknowledged at every baptism. The New Testament includes reference to the three persons but no such formula or doctrine. Up through Origen, despite the pressure of lay opinion on behalf of a fully divinized Jesus, the leading intellectuals in the church, under Hellenic influence and committed to logical consistency, had always given preference in being to God the Father and had thus, in some sense, subordinated the Son and the Spirit. Some had seen the persons of the Trinity as modes of, or expressions of, the one unitary God (modalism).

A successor to Origen at Alexander, Arius, further developed the views of Origen and unintentionally opened the deep controversies over the Trinity that lasted for a century. Arius, like Origen, believed that God created (or eternally creates) the Son, the first and greatest of the angels, and through him all other being. This divine Logos became incarnate as the Christ. Created but in all respects divine, he was the preexisting savior of humanity. The position was reasonably consistent both with the New Testament and with earlier Logos doctrines. It seemed to support a much higher conception of the Christ than most modalist doctrines. But Arius's own bishop in Alexandria rejected any subordination of Jesus, any belief that he was in any sense a creature, and thus launched a very divisive controversy in the church, particularly in the East. Constantine, in the first major intrusion of political authority into the doctrines of the church, asked for a council of the whole church to convene at Nicea (the first ecumenical council), largely to settle the Arian controversy.

The council finally approved a conciliatory formula – the first Nicene creed, one of the most important documents of church history. Ostensibly, the Arians lost, for the creed described the Christ as "of the same being" as the Father. When Arius rejected the formula, the church deposed him as presbyter. What followed was mainly confusion. Constantine, for political reasons, soon adopted an Arian view and eventually deposed and exiled a key defender of the Nicene formula, Athenasius, bishop of Alexandria (in a sense this was a family quarrel in northern Africa). For a period, Athenasius and most Western bishops upheld Nicea, while a majority in the East preferred Arianism as the best defense against modalism. Soon several revisions of the Nicene creed gained local support. When the last committed Arian emperor died in 378, the supporters of Athenasius finally prevailed and at the second great council, at Constantinople in 381, adopted a stronger revision of the Nicene settlement, or what most now identify as the Nicene Creed, one that became a part of worship in the church and served as the first written doctrinal statement of a universal or catholic church. It is most explicit on the nature of Jesus (begotten before all ages, true God from true God, of one substance with the Father, through whom all things were made, who came down from heaven, who was incarnate by the Holy Spirit and made man, and who died and was resurrected). The creed is less explicit on the Spirit. In what later became a point of controversy, it simply said that the Holy Spirit "proceeds" from the Father and, with the Father and the Son, is worshiped and glorified. The belief that the Spirit also is of one nature with the Father was not in the creed, although most within the church would make this inference. Either this creed, as slightly revised, or another related version (the Apostles' Creed) became the preferred baptismal creed of the church and a part of most liturgies.

The trinity controversies bared, and soon agitated, other related issues, most of all the nature of the incarnation. How could a god assume a human form? How could a god suffer and die on a cross? How could a god exhibit not only a human form but human needs, affections, and even the afflictions of the body? How could one conceive of Jesus as both a human teacher and yet a full god? The Gnostics, and even some Arians, emphasized the essential divinity of the Christ and thus saw his human traits as incidental. The Logos occupied or used the human form but was in no sense human. After Nicea, the issue came to a head because of at least three competing, and subtly different, concepts of the human-divine attributes of Jesus. Space allows no full airing of the issues, and what follows will so oversimplify the issues as to horrify those Christians who now adhere to each of the contending views.

In 428, Nestorius became bishop of Constantinople. He objected to a title often used in the church – Mary as mother of God. He argued that Mary was only mother of a man used, or assumed as a medium, by the Logos. This implied a rather sharp distinction between Jesus as God and the human traits of the Jesus who suffered and died (gods do not die). This dualistic view, or two identities, shocked other bishops, who asserted the single identify of the Christ. The third ecumenical council, at Ephesus in 431, tried to resolve these issues and did so by affirming a single identity in the Christ. When Nestorius refused to concede, he was deposed and exiled, and subsequently his followers formed a church in what was then part of Persia (the Assyrian church, often called Nestorian, which today has the title of Apostolic and Catholic Assyrian Church of the East). The followers of Nestorius thus accepted the results of only the first two councils (Nicea and Constantinople).

The single unified identity asserted by the Council of Ephesus seemed too sweeping to many. Some bishops took it to an extreme that would, subsequently, gain the label Monophysite. At the fourth ecumenical council, at Chalcedon in 451, the church worked out a mediatorial or compromise formula, reminiscent of the trinity formula approved at Constantinople a century before. It involved language inherently ambiguous, open to somewhat variant interpretations: "our Lord Jesus Christ is one and the same Son, the same perfect in godhead, the same perfect in manhood, truly God and truly man," or consubstantial to the Father in his godhead, with humanity in his manhood. Some moderate Nestorians applauded the formula and in a sense rejoined the developing church of the West. The elements of dualism in the formula pleased them. On the other hand, those who emphasized the complete unity or singular identity of the Christ were not happy with Chalcedon. These Monophysites prevailed in all the Oriental churches except for the Nestorian; the Armenian, Coptic, Ethiopian, and Syrian (Jacobite) Orthodox church confessions remain Monophysite, and affirm only the first three of the great church councils.

With the schisms reflected in Nestorianism and Monophysitism, the hope for one universal church expired. Instead of one church, there were now five or six, although each would claim catholicity. Although the churches centered on both Rome and Constantinople accepted the settlement at Chalcedon, and even today subscribe the formula there established, the Eastern churches leaned toward a more Monophysite interpretation of that formula, a subtle difference that would later contribute to the separation of the Western and Greek churches. The Eastern Emperor, Justinian, who briefly reunited the whole Roman Empire, sought a reconciliation between his church of the empire and the Oriental or Monophysite churches. In the fifth ecumenical council, at Constantinople in 553, he forced reluctant Western bishops to accept new language to make clear that it was the second person of the Trinity who suffered in the flesh and on the cross and who willed to become a man without losing his divine nature, or a neo-Chalcedonian formula. The formula did not win over the Monophysites, but it did bring the churches of the Eastern empire (the later Greek Orthodox churches) very close to the Oriental churches and later pushed them father from the Roman Catholic church in the West. In a sixth ecumenical council (at Constantinople in 680), the bishops rejected another compromise pushed by emperors in behalf of union with the Monophysites (the council rejected the doctrine of one energy and one will in the Christ). But despite this setback, such unity-oriented understandings of Chalcedon remained normative in the East, not in Rome.

Salvation Doctrines

On two issues – salvation doctrine and patterns of worship – the church of the empire never reached the near consensus it achieved on canon, polity, and the nature of the Christ. At least in emphasis, various salvation doctrines competed for acceptance, and no one plan of worship gained universal acceptance. This meant, in these critical areas, a broad or inclusive church, one that permitted a great deal of latitude for regional differences. This latitude prevailed in Roman Catholicism up until the time of the Reformation, meaning that most of the doctrines and practices that Luther and Calvin endorsed had been at least a part of the church all along or had been normative in the church up until the time of Augustine.

Christianity was a new salvation religion. This was its appeal. All Christians believed that Jesus, by his suffering or death on the cross, had provided a new means of reconciliation with God. Almost all Christians affirm the atonement, meaning that the death of Jesus had a sacrificial purpose – to remove the penalty for human pride and arrogance, for a human inability to obey God in spirit and in deed. Unable to be truly righteous in themselves, humans somehow come to share in the righteousness of the Christ. This reconciles them to God. It saves them from the penalties that justly attach to their flawed character and will and their self-serving conduct. Beyond this, Christians have not agreed. Dozens of different interpretations of the atonement, of the exact requirements of salvation, have marked the history of the church, and these divisions, more than on any other issue, have distinguished the various denominations of Christians in America.

One difference of emphasis, one tension in views of salvation, was present in the New Testament. This tension was between what might be denominated the hard and the soft views. Paul detailed the hard view in Romans, but in other letters he reflected a softer view. The book of Hebrews supports a hard view; the book of James epitomizes the soft view. The two positions are not necessarily in conflict; viewed in a certain perspective, they even complement each other. The hard view goes something like this. A sovereign God, for reasons of his own, in order to manifest his glory, allowed the drama of human rebellion and ultimately a partial reconciliation to take place. He is sovereign. All is from him. Humans, like the pots made by the potter, are subject to his will on all things. God chose to effect the reconciliation of some humans, and his chosen means to do this was through the incarnation, suffering, death, and resurrection of his son. Jesus, by his sacrificial death, fully atoned for the sinfulness of humans, in the sense that this sacrifice was sufficient to cancel or forgive all the evil that humans exemplify. But the atonement was conditional. Only those God chooses for salvation, only those who are able, through grace, to respond to him with trust and love, gain the benefits of the atonement. The church of the West fully concurred in this hard view (the atonement is conditional, not unconditional, and humans are incapable of gaining salvation by their own choice or effort). The initiative must be from God. Thus, it is by a gracious gift that anyone gains salvation, meaning both a loving life here on earth and some form of life beyond death (Origen and Neoplatonists usually believed this would not involve a preservation of the individual ego but some absorption back into the One, a position that the church rejected in behalf of some form of immortality and then a resurrection to a new life in a new kingdom). Some early heretics, notably the disciples of the British theologian Pelagius, rejected limited atonement and complete human inability. The Pelagians believed that Christ's death fully absolved humans of any inherent or innate guilt and thus reconciled all to God. The condition of salvation was then in human hands, for humans had the ability to respond to God in love and in obedience.

In Romans Paul clearly drew the implications of divine sovereignty. God chooses whom he will bless. Of course, God works through the human affections and, as at Paul's own conversion, overwhelms them with his majesty and beauty. Humans respond to God in trust and love. Their subsequent choices reflect such faith and, by that fact, reflect the highest possible standard of moral beauty or holiness. But still the initiative is from God. It is his choice, the work of his Holy Spirit, that brings one to the moment of faith. Thus, salvation is conditional on faith and is always a gift, in no sense desired or earned. For until the Spirit works in the human heart, no one can really desire God, let alone gladly and fully obey him. Only those elected to salvation desire God and serve God. Only such saints are truly virtuous, capable of good works predicated on the glory of God and not selfish ends. The Jews did not always understand this and fell into the heresy that good works, obedience, could bring them salvation. Indeed, truly good works save, but what the Jews did not realize was that no natural persons are capable of truly good works, and thus all have to rely on God, to trust in him, if they are to receive salvation (not gain it, for it is not a choice and not an achievement). This Pauline perspective informed the theology of Augustine and fanned the reforming zeal of Luther and Calvin. Note that, when conjoined with the role of sacraments in mediating God's grace, it was a quite orthodox position within the Roman church and, if correctly interpreted, remains such today.

The other, softer view of salvation might be termed quasi-Pelagian, since the Roman church always condemned Pelagianism and endorsed a conditional atonement. What distinguishes the soft view of salvation is emphasis more than substance, a human much more than a divine perspective. In the soft view, salvation, even though ultimately from God, still depends on obedience and good works. This perspective involves a more governmental conception of God and a more moralistic conception of Jesus and his ministry. It seems to allow more leeway to humans, to make them more responsible for their own salvation. Even Paul, in preaching to his churches, easily fell into this language, one of human choice and human action. Both he and Jesus talked of faith, at times, as if it were a choice, not an unmerited and irresistible gift. Jesus commanded people to love God and also their neighbors, as if love were an option, open to choice, something one could will.

In the Roman church, the soft and voluntaristic emphasis generally won out. How does one gain the unmerited grace of God? Cannot one do something, reform oneself, at least cooperate with the Spirit? What is God's means for being gracious to us? Such questions imply that salvation involves effort, duty, constant devotion – in effect, a type of religion of good works. In the developing Western church, the theologians kept alive the hard and rigorous understanding of Romans, most of all the Augustinians. In technical doctrinal terms, the hard view remained the most lofty position of the church. But in practice, the church so interpreted the demands of salvation as to assimilate a religion of good works, not mere moral works, for this was the type of heresy broached by Pelagius and a view that had doomed the Jews. In the church, as it developed by the time of Augustine, one was saved by the unmerited grace of God, but the original avenue of his grace was the sacrament of baptism. This sacrament either marked the time when God forgave infants or converts of their Adamic or original guilt or in itself was the formal means for such remission of sinfulness. It alone brought one into the church. By tying the grace of God so closely to sacramental obedience (even though it be by parents in presenting an infant), the church seemed to place the initiative in human hands, including the priests who administered efficacious sacraments. Of course, infant baptism was involuntary and thus in itself only opened a continuing drama of salvation. The child had to receive instruction, later confirm his or her faith, and work toward sanctification or loving obedience. But the church provided means to assist an individual in what became a pilgrimage toward the kingdom. Most important, in time all important, was the Eucharist, for in the Western church this gradually became not a communal meal but a reenacted and miraculous repetition of the sacrifice of the Christ, a sacrament that in itself distributed God's grace to those who participated, or even attended, this altar sacrifice, in what was an incremental, not instant or overwhelming, work of God's grace.

In the sacramental system of the church, the concern of members often shifted from salvation, or avoiding some form of eternal torment, to a nonscriptural concern with what happened immediately after death. The church, in its creeds, and despite the strong Hellenic influences, had retained the late Jewish emphasis on a resurrection, which in almost all versions of Christian eschatology accompanied some type of judgment and assignment to one's deserved fate. But until the resurrection, what happened? Most Gentile Christians easily accepted a belief in the immortality of the soul, in some cases even the preexistence of the soul (Origen) and in almost all cases its continued existence after the death of the body (later Adventists would reject such immortality, as did in all likelihood early Jewish Christians). It was one's fate in this interim period, after death and before the resurrection, that came to concern Christians who were within the church. This led the Roman church (but not the church at Constantinople), based on inferred and not direct scriptural authority, to fill in some of the details. The soul would survive and enjoy various levels of beatification according to one's prior devotion and faith. This quantified postmortem blessings and introduced an obedience-reward motif into Catholic eschatology, a motif that seemed both logical and fair. In this life one not only gained salvation but stored up merit that would help ease the transition to judgment and the kingdom. The intervening stage, called purgatory, was a time when disobedient and unfaithful Christians would do penance and, in a sense, pay the just penalty for unforgiven sins. And the sacraments, particularly the Eucharist, became avenues of grace not only for the living but also for the dead, as priests began to offer private Masses for people in purgatory. In such a moralized and legalistic context, it was easy to forget that salvation was unmerited and always a gift from God. The hard way of Pauline faith had become a slightly concealed form of Jewish legalism. It was these popular and legalistic forms of devotion, the resulting loss of a sense of God's initiative in salvation, the role of priests in mediating God's grace, and the closely correlated but nonscriptural aspects of worship that provoked the reforming zeal of Luther.

Worship

In the years after the death of Jesus, his followers gradually developed distinctive patterns of fellowship. Since the first Christians were also Jews, it is not surprising that in Jerusalem they continued to attend temple ceremonies or that both in Jerusalem and in areas of the Diaspora they continued their participation in synagogue services. Gradually, at first as a supplement to Jewish forms and then as a substitute for them, Christians developed their own special assemblies and practices. In so doing, they drew heavily on Jewish precedents. In their group meetings they came to revere practices that seemed appropriate for paying obeisance to and honoring their God and, above all, for celebrating and giving thanks for the ministry, the sacrificial death, and the resurrection of Jesus.

It is not clear whether all the early Christian communities adopted the same forms of worship. They probably did not. We know precious little about beginnings. The sources are few, and most are ambiguous in what they tell us. Early Christians confronted two models of worship in Hellenistic Judaism. One was the declining priestly tradition, centered on temple sacrifices. Such sacrificial motifs remained central in Christianity, with Jesus viewed as the sacrificial lamb that atoned for human sinfulness. In the development of the Christian Eucharist, priestly and sacrificial elements gradually became dominant and remained so until the time of Luther. The second tradition involved synagogue worship and, before that, the work of prophetic reformers. They had most emphasized righteousness and, after Jeremiah, a personal much more than a mediated relationship with Jehovah. The prophets began a ministry of sermonic judgment centered on the lectern or pulpit and on adherence to the moral components of the law, with less emphasis on priestly mediation and sacrifice. This less sacramental approach to Jehovah informed early synagogue worship, a type of worship devoted to reading and understanding the law and its demands. Soon the scribes or rabbis that presided in the synagogue became more important religious leaders than the traditional priests at Jerusalem. In the broadest sense, the priestly and sacrificial worship of the temple became dominant in the Roman Catholic church, whereas Luther and Calvin tried to revive the prophetic synagogue mode. Such issues of worship style correlated closely with doctrine and thus were at the heart of the Reformation critique of Roman Catholicism.

The New Testament provides precious little support for a rich and formal worship. The first descriptions of Christian worship are in the undisputed epistles of Paul (those he almost certainly wrote himself), with the most detailed in his letters to the large, troubled congregation at Corinth. He never described in detail an actual worship service, perhaps because no one pattern predominated even in his churches. What he attested to was a range of activities that took place at Corinth, apparently on Sunday. Christians of a Jewish heritage probably still adhered to Sabbath rules and thus could not have attended Christian services on the Sabbath. For them, and for Gentiles, Sunday was also the day of the resurrection, and at least by the mid-second century, Christians referred to it as the "Lord's Day" and thus vindicated it as the proper time for worship. In all likelihood the early Jewish Christian sects, centered in Palestine, incorporated Christian elements into a continued Sabbatarian pattern of worship. This means that one cannot, on New Testament grounds, even certify authoritatively the proper day of worship.

Paul wrote his letters to Corinth approximately twenty-five years after the death of Jesus. By then the early Christians had clearly developed certain customs. At Corinth they continued the Synagogue pattern – scripture reading, prayer, teaching, and what Paul referred to as psalms, hymns, and spiritual songs. They collected alms at Paul's bequest, to be used for the poor Christians in Jerusalem (he conducted a vast collection effort). They enjoyed spiritual gifts – prophesy, healing, glossolalia, and the interpretation of tongues. In fact, one could use Paul to justify modern Pentecostal services as well as, or better than, most highly formal types of worship, although the purpose of much of his description of gifts was to get the people at Corinth to moderate and order the more ecstatic parts of their worship. Someone baptized new members (Paul chose not to do this himself), and the congregation carried out baptisms for the dead. It is not clear whether they baptized infants or only adult converts, and nowhere is there an exact description of a Christian baptism. Indirect evidence suggests triune immersion, but full proof is lacking.

The Corinth congregation celebrated something that resembled the later Eucharist. On each Sunday it enjoyed a special fellowship meal (apparently families brought the food and drink), which had already gained heavy symbolic meaning related to memories of a final Passover supper Jesus had with his disciples. Paul provides the most ancient reference to this supper, meaning that it had already become very significant in the early church. It would be at least a quarter century before the composition of the three synoptic gospels, with their detailed account of such a supper, and possibly thirty-five years or more before the author of the Gospel of John would pen the strongest Eucharistic imagery (in Chapter 6). This means that the gospel writers were, in all likelihood, guided in their accounts by developed worship practices in their own Christian congregations.

Paul did not describe a sacrament (mystery) at Corinth. The congregation gathered for what seemed to be a full meal, comparable to later fellowship dinners or potluck suppers. But it was more than that. Paul offered instruction on the special meaning of this meal, tied to the words of Jesus (words of institution in later worship) at the original supper, and he preached warnings against abuse (engaging in gluttony, not providing food for the poor, and coming to the table when unworthy). In this way he gave the earliest insight into what would become the Christian Eucharist. Within the next century the churches would divide this meal into two institutions – the Agape or love feast (revived by John Wesley in the eighteenth century), and the Eucharist, by 150 C.E. already limited, at least in some congregations, to specially consecrated bread and wine.

From this Pauline grab bag later Christians could choose what they wanted to emphasize. Few sects ever affirmed the whole range of activities mentioned by Paul. Notably, most Western churches would eventually all but ignore the spiritual gifts, which seemed most important of all in the volatile and ecstatic Corinth congregation. Some later sects would add elements not mentioned by Paul, such as the washing of feet, based on what Jesus did before his final supper with his disciples, or special forms of greeting (the holy kiss). Except for the occasional baptism of converts, we have no New Testament record of other ordered Christian ceremonies, such as ordinations, confirmations, weddings, and burials, although some congregations may well have developed rites for the dead. In any case, they would soon incorporate special references to Christian martyrs into their services.

In the next three hundred years a whole series of innovations or elaborations transformed this early pattern of worship. Later Christian perspectives would vary widely about these developments. Some Christians, bent on restoring the New Testament church, would view almost all developments in worship after the first century as corruptions of an early and pure church. But less rigorous restorationists, such as Luther and Calvin, generally accepted the main lines of innovation up until the time of Augustine. It therefore makes sense to refer to the first-century church as the New Testament church and to the church that developed (matured or degenerated) from the second to the fourth centuries as the primitive church. Notably, today, most attempts at liturgical reform hark back to this primitive church.

Several developments, parallel to worship, helped make possible the forms of worship that competed by the fourth century. The New Testament canon provided the literary content of much worship. An episcopal hierarchy ensured clerical control over worship and gradually demoted the role of women, while the doctrinal settlements led to the great creeds utilized in worship services. The orthodox trinity formula, by establishing the full divinity of the Christ, enhanced the mystery and awe, and the sacrificial motifs, of the Eucharist.

What was still lacking, into the fourth century, was place. Christians, in interludes between persecutions, built a few meetinghouses before Constantine, but a majority had to worship in homes, caves, or catacombs. With official recognition this all changed. The larger congregations almost immediately began building houses of worship. At first patterned after Roman courts (a basilica, with a rectangular seating area and a semicircular platform or apse), these originally simple buildings would, through elaboration, become the complex churches of the Middle Ages, many built in the shape of a cross with up to half the interior (the chancel, with its altars, choirs, and pulpits) reserved for those who officiated at worship and with laypeople restricted to the nave.

By the fourth century the church of the empire did not have a uniform liturgy, but all the major rites shared common features. All made the Eucharist the center of worship. For reasons unclear, the church of the persecution had begun excluding all but baptized members from this sacrament, meaning a two-part service. The first segment, which was open to all and of particular importance for those preparing for conversion, contained the essentials of much later Protestant worship – scripture from both Testaments, prayers (either written or extemporaneous), psalms or anthems, a homily or sermon, and the recitation of creeds.

The secret service involved the steps in the celebration of the Eucharistic meal. By tradition, it began with an offertory or collection. Originally, this had meant all the alms as well as the bread and wine that the people brought to the front of the assembly or to the table; by the fourth century the collection was increasingly limited to the elements of communion, and in time it would be much elaborated, with processions and much fanfare. This was followed, at least in the Roman rite, by prayers of thanksgiving, by an explanation of the origins of the sacrament (institution), and then by what became the heart of the Eucharist in both the Roman and the Eastern rites, the prayer of consecration. In time this would be elaborated into several elements, including some responses from the audience, and could take a long time. By whatever doctrinal interpretation, including later Protestant ones, this prayer marked the transition from ordinary bread and wine to the sacramental elements, however understood as to their substance and their function. After the consecration, the priest usually made a ritual of the breaking of the bread before offering the bread and wine (the communion proper) to the people, who usually knelt before what the Roman church called the altar, a title that suggested the sacrificial meaning this church gave to communion.

Of the ancient rites, the one used at Rome was the most austere and simple. The Eastern rites, centered on Constantinople, were much more elaborate and awe inspiring and have continued with few changes from the fourth century to the present. Through time, even though the essential elements remained, the churches in the West added more and more items to both the pre-Eucharist service and the celebration itself, with some regional variations. By the Reformation, a High Mass in the Catholic church included over one hundred distinguishable rituals, or over three times as many as in the time of Augustine. In time, variable or supplemental elements became a part of the accepted liturgy. These included more and more prayers, various repeated responses, such as the Santus ("Holy, Holy, Holy"), Sursum corda ("Lift up your hearts"), Kyrie eleison ("Lord have mercy"), and psalms and canticles, often sung by a special chorus or choir. Consistent with the ancient synagogue tradition, in High Masses the scripture and prayers were all sung or chanted (plainsong) by priests and congregation. In addition to such liturgical elements, the worship soon included more and more pageantry and symbolism. Solemn processions, with the people standing, included entrance of the clergy and attendants, the movement of the scriptures to the pulpit, and above all the bringing of the communion elements to the altar. Punctuating much of the service were amens and signs of the cross. Adding to the color and the mystery were the increasingly ornate vestments adopted by the medieval clergy, the range of statuary, stained glass, and other works of art that graced major buildings, and the frequent censing (the use of incense also had synagogue origins, possibly originally related to a practical need to fumigate). The altar, originally a table for the Lord's Supper, became a more and more elaborate structure, graced by engravings and at times by an elaborate tabernacle and lighted by candles. Since the spoken or sung words that accompanied the Eucharist were in a soon nonvernacular Latin, and some uttered so quietly as to be unheard, even language took on a highly symbolic meaning, not a literal one.

No one argued that all these embellishments were of scriptural origin. Some had roots in the synagogue, some in pagan worship, some in the pageantry of imperial courts. The issue was whether they were appropriate in Christian worship, and on that issue Christians were, and remain, deeply divided. In the Reformation, liturgical reform often revolved around just how many of these nonscriptural embellishments would remain a part of Protestant worship. The most radical Protestants wanted to abolish all of them and go back to the simplicity of the New Testament. But the much deeper quarrel with Roman worship, by Luther and Calvin, involved the content and meaning of the forms, and also the degree of lay participation in worship. Here the worst corruptions, in their perspective, involved changes that came after the age of Augustine.

For the Roman church, the Eucharist was a sacrificial rite. The imagery – altar, officiating priest – made this clear. The consecration so transformed the elements as to be, in itself, a miracle. This was the understanding long before the church worked out the doctrine of transubstantiation (the miraculous transformation of bread and wine into the literal body of the Christ). In time this sense of a miraculous transformation, of a sacrifice reenacted, created so much awe and fear that medieval laypeople virtually withdrew from participation in the sacrament. The church eventually withdrew the cup (apparently out of fear of spilling the blood of Christ), with communicants receiving only a bit of bread on their tongue while at the altar. By the time of the Reformation, few laypeople received communion more than the required once a year, this often at Easter. This did not diminish the Eucharistic character of public worship; in some ways it enhanced it. But the Eucharist was now a performance, a spectacle, carried out by priests, soon with their backs to the audience when churches began moving the altar from in front of the pulpit to the east wall. This further switched the symbolism from one of a place to eat a meal to an altar for the performance of sacrifices. Even the remaining liturgical elements (those involving lay responses) were gradually replaced by choirs, to the extent that congregants in the nave were left to types of private prayer and devotion during the service. Symbolic rood screens (or in the Eastern church, real screens) separated the altar area from the nave, further distinguishing and distancing the special mysteries there enacted.

This withdrawal of the sacred, or its monopolistic control by priests, led the laypeople of Europe to demand what became a new ritual in the Middle Ages – the elevation of the Host. The officiating priest, after consecrating the bread, would hold it and its container high in the air, so the people could see it and be struck by the miracle of the body of the Christ in their midst. Soon, priests and the laypeople paraded the Host through the streets or attributed to it various miracles and healing.

Accompanying this sacralization of the Eucharist was an often almost magical understanding of its function. In its doctrines the church affirmed the sacraments as means or avenues of grace, with the Eucharist the central sacrament. The priest therefore took on the role of the ancient Jewish priests, who offered sacrifices in behalf of the people who gathered before the temple. The sacrifice was for a purpose – to forgive sins, to bring merit. This led to Masses performed for stated purposes, and often in return for gifts to the church, including many to aid the dead in purgatory. One accusation was that the church had turned the Mass into a sacrament for the dead, not for the living. In fact, in some areas of Europe priests largely lived on the earnings from private Masses for the dead. Since the sacrament was efficacious, totally apart from the faith of the one who presided, or of the audience that watched, it seemed to make salvation a matter of works. Thus, for Luther and Calvin, the sacrificial Catholic Mass became the central symbol of a corrupt church, for it involved priestly mediation rather than faithful participation by Christians, an almost mechanical religion of merit and good works, not faith, and so many elements of popular magic and superstition as to preclude sincere worship.

Such a critique of the Mass was not fair. Although they did not participate directly, generations of Christians had come to love the Catholic Mass, with its esthetic richness and sense of mystery. It often took decades for Protestants to wean their flock away from the old worship and particularly from the traditional Eucharist. Meanwhile reformers within the old church tried to change some of the most flagrant abuses or to increase the frequency of communion for laypeople (after the reactive and reforming Council of Trent, the pattern of lay participation did change, with the norm eventually becoming weekly communion by all faithful Catholics). But in no sense did the church retreat on the meaning of the sacrament. In 1570, at Trent, it for the first time made a common liturgy mandatory (with minor exceptions to accommodate regional differences and with special exemption for affiliated Eastern rites). In reaction to the Protestant emphasis on justification by faith, the church reiterated and solidified its sacramental tradition and its sacrificial understanding of the Eucharist and in this sense helped widen the developing gulf between Catholics and Protestants.

The Separation of Rome and Constantinople

On only one issue – the use of icons in worship – did the patristic church fall into such deep divisions as to require adjudication at a final ecumenical council, at Nicea in 787. In its deliberations, and decisions, one can already glimpse some of the divisions that would later separate the Roman and Greek churches. The word *icon* simply refers to any representation that takes the same form as the object represented; thus it is distinct from an index, which points to or refers to an object, or a symbol, that stands for an object but does not take the same form (it does not look like an original but causes one to think about the original). After state recognition, and the building of separate edifices, the Western churches rather quickly began to incorporate all types of visual imagery, some indexical (as in architectural spires that pointed toward heaven), some symbolic (as in the cross), and some iconic (wall paintings and statues). Most imagery radically violated the Jewish condemnation of any representations of divine objects. Particularly in the Eastern churches of the empire, some of the visual images became highly formalized (in the West, painting and mosaics were more realistic and naturalistic), or what many today associate with the term *icon*. These, by a type of consensual rule, took standard forms and depicted, often in abstract form, as well as symbolized, the great Christian truths. In time, a limited family of conventional icon types, each symbolizing some archetypical religious truth, became a vital part of church life in the East. The icon painters assumed a special vocation, took special training, and worked only after prayer and fasting. The finished icon received a priestly blessing or consecration before taking its place on the wall or the icon screen (separating the nave from the altar) of a church.

It was such icons, and the near worship of them, that a series of Eastern emperors, for a variety reasons, condemned. The second Nicea council achieved a final compromise settlement, one subject to varied interpretations. It condemned the worship of icons but allowed their veneration, much as Christians were beginning to venerate or even address prayers to saints. In practice, the churches of the West did not use icons, and later condemned them, while the Eastern churches made them a crucial component of churches and of both worship and private devotion. Icons, even today, mark the most visible difference between worship in Orthodox as compared with Roman Catholic churches. The Western churches kept their paintings and statues not as objects of veneration but as aids to devotion and adornments of sanctuaries. By the Renaissance the robust and naturalistic style of such imagery seemed a world removed from the conventional and abstract icons of the East.

In the vague Middle Ages, or the years from the last council in 787 to the intellectual renaissance that the Western church enjoyed after 1200, all the major doctrinal settlements remained unchallenged except by heretical sects, whom the church quickly crushed. But in the years after the second Nicene conference, the churches of the West, centered on Rome and the papacy, and those in the more politically stable Eastern empire, centered on the patriarch at Constantinople, steadily grew further apart in both doctrine and liturgy. Yet one cannot date one point of final separation. The icon issue rankled long after 787. In what is now France, a regional council in 794 condemned all icons, a position that, in practice, came to characterize all Western churches. Already, small and subtle doctrinal issues distinguished East and West. In brief and quite oversimplified language, the Eastern church retained a slight tinge of Arianism and clearly held to a neo-Chalcedonian or near Monophysite view of the Christ. Beginning as early as the sixth century, some Spanish churches began to modify the Nicene creed; they added the words ("from the Son") in the statement about the Holy Spirit – the Spirit now proceeded from the Father and the Son, not just from the Father as in the decision of the council or the position defended in the East. This new language went into a new creed often called Athanasian in the West (the final basis of the three creeds used in Western churches to this day, the Nicene, Apostles', and Athanasian) and into one that used Augustinian interpretations of the Trinity. A Frankish council approved the new version, with the *filioque* (from the Son), in 809. The pope accepted the doctrine but at first did not make a formal change in the creed used at Rome (under imperial pressures, the pope added it to the Roman Mass in 1014). By such a doctrinal innovation, the Western church eliminated the last vestige of subordinationism from its creeds.

Political issues had as much to do with periods both of union and of separation as did doctrinal and liturgical issues. The Roman Empire continued in the East until the Turks took Constantinople in 1453. This gave a type of stability to the church in the East, with neither doctrines nor liturgies changing very much from the fifth century onward. In the same period, political instability marked the West, with Rome steadily declining in all but symbolic status. The Western empire slowly disintegrated, after a series of Germanic invasions. Political power fragmented into local institutions, with only verbal gestures to the old idea of one unified empire. Charles the Great managed a bit of a revival, and of centralized leadership, after 800, and it was he who forced a Frankish council to adopt the *filioque*. After his empire splintered, Western Europe endured two centuries without any strong or centralized states, and in this interlude the papacy tried to fill the vacuum, with at least an assertion of clerical dominance and, under a few strong popes, the actual exercise of effective political authority over weak kings in the feudal states of Western Europe.

The "dark" ages are hard to define and in any case did not last long. Even before the pope crowned a new Roman Emperor in 962 (the origin of the Holy Roman Empire that lasted until Napoleon) and, in so doing, upheld the old dream of one empire and one church, one could glimpse the early development of a new, pluralistic nation-state system, one in which strong kings would gain ascendancy over the papacy, although they allowed the church its own lands (another nation-state), often bargained with the papacy, and at times clearly used it for their own ends. Before the nation-states were able to exert centralized power over large geographical areas, the church launched a series of crusades to Jerusalem. This brought Western and Eastern Christians together but fostered resentment, not unity. As early as 1054, when the pope tried to reassert his authority over the Eastern churches, his legates in Constantinople were rebuffed, and out of the conflict the pope and the patriarch excommunicated each other. Although often cited in textbooks, this was only a temporary separation, although icons and the *filioque* now stood in the way of any doctrinal uniformity. In a huge crusade in 1204, Western soldiers conquered and sacked Constantinople as if it and its church were pagan.

Only in 1261 did the Byzantine peoples drive out the Western troops and regain sovereignty, and not with friendly feelings toward Rome. In all but a political sense, the separation of the Eastern and Western churches was a fact. By liberation in 1261, Byzantium was already defending its eastern borders against the Turks and at times sought Western aid. Its delegates even acknowledged the primacy of Rome in 1274, in a frustrated attempt to buy aid. After the loss of most of Asia Minor, and of a large share of the Eastern churches, delegates from the fading empire again capitulated at the Council of Florence in 1439, the last time the Eastern church would formally acknowledge the primacy of Rome. In only a few more years Byzantium fell, and thus there remained no political reason for unity. Soon, the cultural gap helped extend differences in doctrine and liturgy. Even the great church of the empire was now two churches.

Reform Challenges

An intellectual renaissance began in the Roman church in the thirteenth century. This reflected the recovery of lost aspects of Aristotelian philosophy, the improvement of universities, and the growth of a scholastic dialectic. The theological position of the church became more contested and more rich. In particular, the moderate realism of Thomas Aquinas challenged the Augustinians within the church and in many respects reinforced the trend toward sacramentalism and a religion of constancy, devotion, and good works, as did new types of monasticism. With the Renaissance, the hierarchy gradually lost political power to the emerging, centralized nation-states of Europe but at the same time became more wealthy, more worldly, and regionally more corrupt.

What one has to emphasize before the time of Luther and Calvin is that the Roman Catholic church was diverse and latitudinarian. It varied in liturgy according to geography, from the liturgy followed in small local parishes presided over by unlearned priests, where even the Mass might be in the vernacular, to the great High Masses presided over by bishops in large cathedrals. Doctrinally, one could assume a rigorous Pauline or Augustinian position or join in the growing acceptance of Thomism. One could follow an ascetic life in a monastic order or reduce church life to the rites of passage (baptism, confirmation, marriage, final rites) plus annual participation in a single Mass on Easter, preceded by confession before a priest.

Luther, prodded by a heavy conscience to reform this vast and diverse church, ended up creating a revolution or civil war. He first reacted to obvious corruptions, those long recognized by other reformers within the church, such as the abuse of indulgences (grants of prior merit or pardon to ease one's suffering in purgatory), but the logic of his critique led him to a thoroughgoing criticism of a whole series of what he saw as wrong turns or unscriptural innovations made after the age of Augustine. He wanted to restore the church as it once had been, but note that this was not the New Testament church but the church that followed the first five ecumenical councils. He did not reject any of the council settlements. In doctrine, he wanted to resurrect the hard view of salvation preached by Paul and Augustine, to revive the full implications of justification by faith through grace. Liturgically, he wanted to abolish correlated corruptions, particularly the priest-dominated Mass, with its alleged efficacy in transmitting God's grace and its sacrificial motifs. In polity, he wanted to purify the now inflated and corrupt and wealthy papacy and to restore a simple priesthood that could minister to, not dominate, the Christian laity. He found the model for all these reforms within the history of the church. He wanted to be conservative and traditional.

Luther created new state churches in Germany, organized – as much as princes would permit – according to his conception of a proper church. Because he had to fight endless battles with the old church, it was inevitable that he would emphasize points of difference or make a display of even relatively minor innovations, such as his marriage. In other words, it was the dialectical relationship with Roman Catholicism that helped shape the Lutheran churches, as well as Reformed churches in Switzerland, Germany, France, the Netherlands, and Britain. The reaction within the Roman church was equally intense. What is critically important is to realize that what people now call, or miscall, the Reformation, had almost as much shaping influence on the subsequent history of Roman Catholicism as on Lutheran and Reformed churches. It was out of a complex dialectic that both gained their identities, fortified over the next three centuries. In reaction to Luther and other regionally successful reformers, the Roman church did indeed clean up many of its internal corruptions. Perhaps more important, in a defensive reaction at the Council of Trent, it began a move, one that lasted for two centuries, away from an inclusive and rather pluralistic church, to one much more carefully structured and uniform in liturgy, more dogmatic in doctrine, more centralized in government, and less accommodating in its increasingly Thomistic theology. It cleaned up abuses in its sacramental system but, much more than before, defended a sacramental, essentially incremental, approach to salvation, one carefully tied to the authority of church and priesthood. In time, these religious reactions would join with resistance to types of political liberalism, leading to the very defensive and conservative church of the nineteenth century.

The Lutheran reforms that became a rebellion, and the defensive reaction that led to a strict and rigorous and dogmatic Catholicism, opened a Pandora's box. In the midst of the new religious intensity, on both sides, and the new debates about critical doctrinal issues, and the inevitable insecurity of confused Christians about their own salvation, all the doctrinal compromises, even those seemingly settled in the great councils, had to stand new and critical scrutiny. It was in the ongoing struggles that followed this ferment, controversy, and doctrinal innovation that European Christians first moved to America. Unlike in Central and South America, all types came to what would become the United States, here to continue the old quarrels and quite soon to launch fascinating new ones. But an overwhelming majority of British Christians, and at least a large minority of continental Christians, who immigrated to colonial America were in the Reformed and not the Lutheran tradition. This implicates the special role of John Calvin and of something later called Calvinism.

John (or Jean) Calvin (1509–64), a humanist scholar with a superb legal but not philosophical mind, proved himself a very effective pastor and a lucid, logical, second-generation systematizer of early Protestant doctrines. In his homeland of France, he moved only gradually, after his university training, away from the Roman Catholic church. He spent most of his adult years as a refugee pastor, mostly in the small republic of Geneva and more briefly in Strasbourg. In a series of expanded editions he perfected his brief for an evangelical Christianity in his famous *Institutes of the Christian Religion* and supplemented this by printed sermons and commentaries. Well-ordered and clear, his writings did not constitute a tight, philosophical theology. He flirted with inconsistencies and all too quickly dismissed the most challenging questions as beyond all human competence, as best left to the hidden determination of a sovereign and in large part unfathomable God. Humans know all they need to know, particularly affecting their own salvation, but they are far from understanding in full the nature and purposes of God.

In most respects, Calvin was more systematic than dogmatic. He was willing to accommodate considerable differences within Reformed Christianity. He lacked the passion, and many of the personal weaknesses, of a Luther, although he could be very nasty to opponents. In time he was as influential for his pastoral achievement, for the church order he developed in Geneva, as for his doctrines. In fact, it is impossible to attribute to Calvin even one strictly novel or distinctive doctrine. Eclectic, always deferential to Paul and Augustine, Calvin would have applauded this retrospective judgment. He valued truth, not originality.

Many have said it: Calvin did not create Calvinism. But such a clever judgment may be as cheap as pointing out that Jesus never created Christianity. In a sense Calvinism, as much as other reasonably coherent doctrinal positions, developed out of controversy and the need for self-conscious intellectual weapons. Thus, a systematic Calvinism was largely a creation of the seventeenth century and became a useful reference point only when deep doctrinal divisions developed within the various Reformed churches. Calvinism came to designate, if not any distinctive doctrines, at least the relative stress placed on certain doctrines. Later, ordered versions of Calvinist doctrines, such as those legislated at Dort and Westminster (see chapter 1), took on some of the coloration of internal conflict. Calvin, in his generation, might not have stated the doctrines in the same way or placed the same emphasis on them. But, nonetheless, the later Calvinist formulas, even the most dogmatic or scholastic versions, were quite consistent with the teachings of Calvin. In this sense they were not corruptions, not even drastic oversimplifications, but were contextually selective, polemically useful arrangements of some of his teachings. Perhaps unfortunately, always confusingly, a doctrine called predestination would be at the heart of later Calvinist formulations, not because Calvin gave unusual stress to it but because this doctrine proved to be a test case.

Calvin did not create the Reformed movement. The tradition he joined began in Switzerland and in German states along the Rhine, led by such able reformers as Ulrich Zwingli and Martin Bucer. By the time that Calvin committed himself to a Reformed French church, several able ministers in Strasbourg, Zurich, Heidelberg, and other Protestant centers were already able advocates of an evangelical Christianity that was, doctrinally, very close to that of the developing Lutheran churches in Germany. These reformed confessions were most distinct from Lutheranism on certain points of belief (the nature of the divine presence in communion, the nature of confession and penance, the regenerative role of baptism, and later, the degree of human involvement and choice in regeneration) or practice (in contrast to Lutheran churches, most Reformed churches were less liturgical and sacramental and were less passive in their relationship to political authority). Under the guidance of a closely linked group of ministers, but supported and at times guided by active laypeople, the Reformed movement gained a dominating position in much of Switzerland, in the Palatinate and parts of the Rhineland, in scattered Huguenot enclaves in France, in the Netherlands, and finally in England and Scotland. Patterns of migration later ensured the dominance of these Reformed churches in early America, as contrasted to Lutheran churches and several small sects that were outside any of the national confessions.

CHAPTER 1

Reformed Christianity in Britain and

Colonial America

*B*ecause of the patterns of migration to early America, the largest number of colonists came from the state churches of Britain (Anglican and Presbyterian). Whether orthodox Calvinists or not, they traced their origins back to John Calvin, to his close associates, or to the church order he helped establish in Geneva. Such a tradition informed the four largest colonial denominations, all of British origin (Anglican, Congregational, Presbyterian, and Separate Baptist), and two much smaller continental transplants (Dutch Reformed and German Reformed). The backdrop to the transplantation of Reformed Christianity to America was the complex reformation of the English and Scottish churches.

Reform of the English Church

Protestant reforms within the English church came gradually, often in the midst of bloody conflict. The first break with Rome, under Henry VIII, involved legal issues of authority, not doctrines or rituals. From 1530 to 1534, Henry sought the support of the church for either an annulment of his marriage to Katherine of Aragon or a divorce from a wife who had not borne him a son. Frustrated in his attempts to gain what he wanted from the church, Henry in 1533 married Anne Boleyn and in 1534 declared himself sole head of the English church, thus breaking all ties to the pope. He forced most English churchmen to go along with this shift in polity and cruelly executed the few leaders who refused to support his divorce (the most famous martyr would be Sir Thomas More). At first, this break with Rome did not change the doctrines or forms of worship in the English church. Still a subject of debate among historians is the strength of the Roman church in 1534 and the degree that earlier English reformers, such as John Wycliffe, had gained covert followers and thus prepared the way for internal changes. It seems that the degree of dissatisfaction with the existing church, and the openness to the types of well-publicized reforms begun by Luther, varied from region to region in England.[1]

Henry seemed to relish his new religious role and was in sentiment a committed Christian. Influenced by several advisers tied politically to Anne Boleyn, he explored an alliance with Lutheran princes in Germany and in 1536 approved a Lutheran-influenced but moderate set of ten articles, which marked the first official move toward a more Protestant church in Britain. The articles affirmed justification by faith and referred only to the three sacraments accepted in the Augsburg Confession (baptism, Eucharist, and penance) but left in place most of the existing Roman liturgy. It is not clear how much, if any, effect the new articles, or a subsequent reduction in the number of holy days, had on local forms of worship and devotion. For those local congregations already committed to a broader reform agenda, the shift in 1536 at least gave them some leeway to revise beliefs and worship forms. In the wake of this first quasi-Protestant reform, Henry began dispossessing the monasteries, largely for financial gain and in retaliation for churchmen's increasing opposition to his policies.

After 1538, a period of reform virtually ended, with reaction the order of the day. Henry had been pushed further than he wanted by his most persistent evangelical advisers, Thomas Cromwell and Thomas Cranmer, while conservative churchmen had tried to salvage as much of the old doctrines as possible. Alliances with Catholic states also mandated moderation. The conservatives won most arguments after 1538. Thus Henry achieved a church only slightly reformed, and this more at a doctrinal than at a liturgical level. The English church retained communion in one kind (bread), transubstantiation, clerical celibacy, private Masses, and individual confessions before priests. In 1540 Cromwell, who had resisted enforcement of such conservative policies, was executed for treason. An intimidated Archbishop Cranmer salvaged as much of the early, and essentially Lutheran, reforms as possible. In 1543, a new formulation of doctrine, one enthusiastically approved by Henry, dropped any commitment to faith as the sole basis of justification (Henry wanted equal emphasis on works) and limited the reading of the English Bible to the upper ranks of society. In 1546, an ill Henry approved heresy trials against even moderate evangelicals, but in the final four months of his life he once again aligned himself with more evangelically oriented advisers, or those who would control the regency set up to govern for the new boy king, Edward. Also, throughout the period of reaction, Cranmer had retained his position as archbishop.

A new wave of reform came during the brief reign of Edward VI. It eliminated most remnants of Catholicism and produced a new, moderately Calvinist confession and a vernacular *Book of Common Prayer*. These changes reflected Reformed more than Lutheran sources, since they now paralleled the influential reforms under way by Calvin in Geneva. Cranmer corresponded with Calvin, and Calvin's earlier Reformed mentor, Martin Bucer, moved from Strasbourg to England in

1549 to teach at Cambridge and help guide Edwardian reform until his death in 1551. John Knox, in exile from his native Scotland, took refuge in England and contributed to the new reforms before moving on to Geneva to serve under Calvin as assistant minister, all in preparation for his return to Scotland in 1560 to assist the reformation in his home country. Thus, the more evangelical English bishops joined an international network of Reformed intellectuals.

What happened in the seven years of Edward's rule seemed, in retrospect, revolutionary. But the changes came by degree and were not without intense opposition; such were the radical shifts required at the parish level that it is impossible to gauge how deeply the ordinary people assimilated the new Protestantism. Edward approved a strongly Calvinist confession (Forty-Two Articles). A rapid turnover in bishops all but eliminated the conservatives and led to a young and able group of preachers and bishops. The leaders of the new order suppressed endowed prayers for the dead, ended Masses for the dead and condemned the purgatory doctrine, introduced a completely new communion service (both elements, plain bread, tables to replace altars, no elevation of the Host, and no corporeal presence), and ordered the use of an English Bible. The clergy could marry, images were no longer accepted in churches, and priests were now called ministers. Many papist ceremonies became illegal, such as ringing of holy bells, kissing altars, and clerical processions. At the very end of Edward's reign, the Crown ordered the confiscation of all vestments (except surplices) and plate. Of all the changes, the second prayer book, that of 1552, proved most important. It introduced a formal and prescribed and soon beloved liturgy, which, with limited later changes, remains the basis of Anglican worship today.

At Edward's premature death in 1553, Henry's eldest and Roman Catholic daughter, Mary Tudor became queen. She quickly moved the English church back to Rome, with the enthusiastic support of at least a large minority, and possibly a majority, in England who remained loyal to the old church. She married Phillip II of Spain and reestablished a Roman Catholic liturgy. Her religious policies drove the ablest Reformed ministers and nonconforming laypeople into prison, exile, or martyrdom (280 burned at the stake). Many escaped to European Protestant centers – Strasbourg, Frankfurt, Geneva – there becoming part of a network of Calvinist activists.

Mary's reign proved brief, to the despair of Catholics and to the joy of leading Protestants. Succeeding her at her death in 1558 was Henry VIII's Protestant daughter, Elizabeth, the last of the Tudor monarchs. Guided by ecclesiastical advisers, she slowly and against determined opposition worked out an enduring, although not unchallenged, religious settlement, which rested on a clearly Reformed confession – the Thirty-Nine Articles – and, more important in the long run, a revised *Book of Common Prayer*. Roman Catholics at first strenuously resisted this settlement, which helped push Elizabeth more fully into the Reformed camp. But she resisted pressures for more extreme reforms, and at least in many of the rituals prescribed in the *Book of Common Prayer*, and in the episcopacy, she retained several traditional, nonscriptural reminders of Romanism (vestments for ministers, the use of traditional pulpits, and leeway in the communion for a doctrine of real presence), as a part of a deliberate effort to form a moderate English church with the broadest possible appeal.

The Elizabethan settlement brought temporary religious peace to England. The Thirty-Nine Articles were deliberately general or broad, but they were not latitudinarian. They still represent one of the more elegant summaries of Reformed Christian doctrine, including the doctrine of election or predestination. The articles have remained, to this day, a quite acceptable guideline for a now minority of Calvinist Anglicans. In fact, they are alone fully acceptable to such Calvinists, for as a whole the English church outgrew, or came to ignore, but did not repudiate, what most Anglicans now view as a historically significant confession. But the articles could not encompass the religious spectrum in England, particularly former Catholics who, even if willing to sever connections with Rome, still loved the older, sacramental religion or resented the endless preachments, the moral rigor, and the abstentious life of the more zealous Reformed ministers. At the other extreme were those who wanted a more thorough cleansing of the old and corrupt church; who yearned for a presbyterian or even a congregational polity; who wanted a converted, zealous, and well-trained clergy; who despised all nonessential forms in worship; who affirmed with rigor such doctrines as complete depravity, divine election, irresistible grace, and the perseverance of saints; and who aspired to a serious, rigorous personal and social morality. In time, these divisions gained labels, such as Catholic versus Puritan, or High Church versus Low Church, or Arminian versus Calvinist. But the labels would never be very precise.

At the death of Elizabeth in 1603, Calvinist doctrine was not a major issue in England. The broad church itself was Calvinist, at least in profession, in the dominant voices in its universities, and in a majority of its bishops and clergy. Yet tensions remained. Already, a few congregations had rejected the authority of the episcopacy and as nonconformists had faced severe persecution. The Brownists or Separatists were one such small sect, half of whom fled their exile in Holland to found the small Plymouth colony in New England in 1620. Later Quakers would take nonconformity so far as enthusiasm. Within the church, the various factions, all with blurred boundaries, competed for power and preference. Somewhere on the continuum between sacramentally oriented, High Church advocates and overt nonconformists existed a spectrum of churchpeople who, eventually, would gain the elusive label of Puritan. The label first came into prominent use largely as a pejorative term, particularly after the High Church party gained preference under Charles I and his archbishop, William Laud. Laud tried to enforce strict conformity even at the parish level. Laud and his supporters tended to use the label "Puritan" in a very encompassing sense, so as to include most of his clerical enemies – those strictly Calvinist in doctrine, those evangelical or non-liturgical in practice, and those who favored a more decentralized system of church government, whether presbyterian or congregational.[2]

This spectrum of so-called Puritans included a scattering of ministers and lay-people, most to the northeast of London, who late in the sixteenth century despaired of a fully reformed state church. Thus they began writing and subscribing congregational covenants. They did not mean for such covenants to separate them from the larger English church but used them as the local foundation, or justification, of their church order. Members had to subscribe to such a covenant, and each covenanted congregation claimed a large degree of local autonomy – the right to pass on the qualification of members and even an asserted but never realized right to elect its own minister. This began a special free church tradition in Britain, one distinguished not so much by congregational polity (various Anabaptist groups pioneered in this) but by the special role of the congregational covenant. Such congregations joined to create their own special identity, and by subsequent revisions or rewriting of covenants, they could change that identity. The local covenant was not a creed or confession but an all-important bond of union that soon replaced all creeds or formal confessions. Although forming only one distinguishable segment of Puritans in England, these "covenanting" Puritans dominated the mass exodus to Massachusetts Bay in 1630–31 and gave a distinctive shape to New England. Because of their role, the word *Puritan* quickly gained a much more precise and self-conscious meaning in the new world than it ever had in the old.

Briefly, during the Long Parliament (beginning in 1640), Anglicans of all types, including Puritans and Presbyterians, united in a common confession (the Westminster). They already shared the authorized English translation of the Bible (today often called the King James Version). These two works subsequently became the most influential documents in American Christianity. Even to this day, the Authorized Version (including modern updates) remains the most used Bible, and the Westminster Confession remains a doctrinal bench mark, ever useful in measuring how much Christians, in all the Reformed churches, have moved from their seventeenth-century roots.

Both of the great seventeenth-century Reformed confessions (Dort and Westminster) were born out of internal controversy. They helped establish the enduring and, in many senses, polar references – Calvinist and Arminian. The Arminian label derived from a moderate, avowedly Calvinist churchman in the Netherlands,

Jacob Harmensen (Arminius), who remonstrated against the now dogmatic doctrine of double predestination (that God chooses those who are to be saved and those who are to be damned) and most other doctrines implicated by it. Such are the ambiguities of language that it is difficult, today as much as then, to clarify the exact issues at stake. But in a sense not acceptable to orthodox churchmen in England as well as Holland, Arminius gave enough choice to humans in resisting or responding to God's grace as to jeopardize the doctrines of double predestination and the irresistibility of grace. As his critics realized, the whole, linked, interactive Calvinist scheme of salvation was now at stake. Thus, the counter-remonstrants in Holland, joined by the then ablest theologian of the English church, William Perkins, tried to convince Arminius of his errors and, when this failed, tried to settle the doctrinal issues by consultation at a called conference at Dort (Dordrecht), where orthodox Dutch Calvinists met in 1618–19. This led to the formulation of a new Confession and to the soon oversimplified but much quoted five points of Calvinism, or TULIP (Total depravity, Unconditional election, Limited atonement, Irresistible grace, and the Perseverance of saints). James I, the first joint monarch of England and Scotland, sent to Dort five official English and Scottish consultants, all orthodox Calvinists. At this point international Calvinism seemed to rally around a doctrinal consensus. But it is worth noting that Arminius considered himself a disciple of Calvin, and in this sense the Arminian wing of the movement was also part of the historical Reformed tradition. In time, the winning side at Dort monopolized, or determined, the meaning ascribed to the label "Calvinist."

Charles I, even more than James, chose sides within the increasingly factionalized English church. He sympathized with both a High Church (emphasis on episcopal authority and on a liturgical or sacramental approach to salvation) and an Arminian position and made William Laud, who was most clearly identified with a High Church form of Anglicanism, bishop of London in 1628 and archbishop of Canterbury in 1633. Instead of the so-called Puritans destroying the broad settlement (some had tried), it was now the king and Laud who in fact rather quickly sabotaged it. For a brief period – only a decade – the High Church party prevailed in England and even in distant Ulster, where Presbyterians suffered the exile of all their ministers. Laud's attempt to impose a revised worship guide on the Scottish church led to revolt in Scotland (see below). In England, Laud deposed, or even imprisoned, those ministers who would not strictly conform to a now centralized episcopacy. For those on Laud's side, this was a period of reform, of sacramental renewal. In fact, Laud's doctrine of a real presence in the Eucharist, and his desire to elevate sacramental worship as at least a counterweight to Puritan preaching, reflected an often neglected emphasis of both Luther and Calvin, and in that sense righted a balance. But Laud moved too far in the other direction to win over a majority, although so many nonreligious issues became involved in opposition to an imperious Charles as to blur the distinctively religious aspects of a developing civil war.

The beginning of the end of High Church dominance came in 1640 when a financially beleaguered Charles had to convene what became the revolutionary Long Parliament. Very quickly, those on the Presbyterian or Puritan side of the church spectrum gained control and shifted the balance sharply back toward the other extreme. In 1643 the Parliament, in order to gain Scottish military assistance, abolished the episcopal system in both England and Scotland and replaced it with a republican or presbyterian polity. This Presbyterian settlement proved ephemeral in England but remained the basis of a separate and independent Church of Scotland.

To create a much needed confession for this united church, the Parliament sanctioned a great conclave of English churchmen, with Scottish participants, who met at Westminster periodically from 1643 to 1648. The Westminster assembly developed the confession that still bears its name, as well as a *Directory of Worship* and a short and long catechism, documents that would remain authoritative in Scottish Presbyterianism but not for long in the church that created them. The Westminster Confession was not clearly in conflict with the Thirty-Nine Articles, but it differed in emphasis. Given the perceived threat of Arminianism, it contained the strongest possible language in defense of divine sovereignty and of divine election to both salvation and reprobation. As much or more than even Dort, it reflected a fighting version of Calvinism, one that sharpened rather than muted points of conflict with Arminians. But for Presbyterians, for the strongly Calvinist factions in the English church, and for a smaller number of Baptists, it became the final arbiter of doctrinal issues (though not theological issues, for it left plenty of room for divergence at a more lofty philosophical level).

In the midst of the English revolution, and especially after the establishment of the Republic in 1649, efforts at unity and uniformity quickly gave way to near religious anarchy. Under Oliver Cromwell, a loose polity prevailed, one that allowed wide toleration for formerly dissenting sects. The excesses of some of the reformers prepared the way for the last great shift in religious sentiment – back to the episcopacy and to now overt Arminian doctrines, to the church restored by Charles II when he was invited back to the British throne in 1660. Charles enforced a strict conformity to a slightly revised *Book of Common Prayer* and banned clergymen who refused conformity to it. Charles, personally, favored Roman Catholicism and was baptized a Catholic just before his death. His unpopular brother and successor, James II, openly embraced Roman Catholicism, which was one reason for his deposition by Parliament in 1688. With this Glorious Revolution, the broad Protestant religious establishment was now secure and would remain in effect up to the present. Nonconforming groups gained at least freedom of worship by the Toleration Act of 1689.

A footnote to this final settlement would have importance in American religious history. In England, five bishops and four hundred clergymen refused to repudiate their former oath of allegiance to James and thus would not declare allegiance to the new monarchs, William and Mary. These nonjurors lost their position in the English church, becoming a special nonconforming sect within England and the only Anglican church within Scotland. It was to these nonjurors that American Anglicans turned after 1783 to gain the consecration of their first American bishop.

Reform in Scotland and Ulster

Church reform came more suddenly, and conquered more completely, in Scotland than in England. In Scotland the linkage to Calvin and Geneva was direct. John Knox, the ablest Reform minister in Scotland, and soon a symbol of its reformation, spent several exile years as associate pastor with Calvin in Geneva. The fullest impact of this experience would not be doctrinal. Knox's doctrines were consistent with Calvin's but also with those of a dozen other reformers. What the Scottish church most clearly copied was the polity and modes of discipline developed in Geneva. In the form of Scottish Presbyterianism, Genevan institutions moved to America with Scottish and, more often, Scotch-Irish immigrants.[3]

Scottish reformers never gained all their goals. The lords in Scotland first broke with the Roman church in 1560, invited Knox back to Scotland, and approved a new Protestant confession. But the general assembly of the new church was not able to work out a new form of church government until 1567. At the time of the break in 1560, the Scottish monarch, Mary Stewart (or Stuart), who had just reached maturity, was in France with her young husband, Francis II. She came home and, although tolerant in religion, refused to ratify the act of Parliament that repudiated Catholicism. She worshiped as a Catholic but allowed the local churches some leeway in both doctrines and worship. Meanwhile, she became a pawn in European diplomacy, in part because she had a claim to being next in line for the English throne. Through the help of Queen Elizabeth of England, Scotland deposed a queen who would not personally convert to Protestantism.

From 1567 to 1572 a series of general assemblies worked out the discipline of the Scottish church. In most respects, they followed Calvin's system at Geneva. But the reformers were not able to persuade the lords of Scotland to permit a fully self-governing church, leading to problems and divisions for the next two hundred years. The two main problems were prelacy and patronage. The leading reformers in Scotland accepted only two orders of clergy, plus doctors or teachers in the reinvigorated universities. Presbyterians used the title of bishop for all their ministers or presiding elders. Some were not opposed to a special use of the title to denote an administrative function. In the interlude under Mary, the local congregations had begun to establish a system of local government without any episcopal supervision. The lords, for political and purely economic reasons (control over the remnants of church property), and in particular later monarchs, did not want to surrender all religious authority to the presbyteries and synods of the church. Thus, despite all the opposition, the lords kept the power of nominating clerical appointments in much of Scotland (lay patronage), and the government retained an awkward system of archbishops and bishops (prelacy). In theory they were under the control of the general assembly of the church. In fact, they were often directly submissive to political authorities.

After 1567 Presbyterians were usually able to maintain a local church order patterned on that of Geneva. With limited success, congregations at least asserted their right to call their own ministers, or made life miserable for patronage appointees. In the congregation an order of deacons cared for worldly concerns. Elected lay elders joined with the presiding elder or minister to make up the main legislative and judicial body, the session (called the "consistory" in Geneva). At the heart of this Genevan system was church discipline – the constant monitoring of lay belief and behavior. The session served as a continuing grand jury and trial court. Its purpose was to keep nurturing the faithful, bringing to repentance the sinful, and using its powers to expel members so as to protect the integrity of the communion service. In Scotland, Presbyterians also demanded a literate membership, and both parents and preachers accepted an obligation to develop local schools to educate a population largely illiterate before the reformation of the church. Presbyterians also set possibly the highest professional standards in all Christendom for their clergy.

Until the reign of James, in the newly United Kingdom, the Scottish church chaffed at lay patronage and on occasion at heavy-handed efforts by the king to assert his power directly over the church. Yet the church was in practice self-governing; the unwanted bishops made up what was really a type of shadow government. James, although a nominal Presbyterian, worked to gain a more uniform national church. He began to use the anachronistic episcopacy in Scotland to this end, with plenty of opposition in Scotland. Charles I went much further. He, abetted by Archbishop Laud, attempted to convert the Scottish church into an episcopal one with a new group of canons in 1635, and in 1637 he imposed a new prayer book modeled on the English *Book of Common Prayer*. This led to a rebellion in Scotland, led by clergymen and an uncompromising general assembly, which rejected all Charles's "reforms" in 1638. In place of his new system, the assembly approved a new national covenant, one that upheld a presbyterian system but a church still under the patronage of a Christian monarch. Such defiance led Charles to organize an invasion army in late 1638. By then, an aroused Scotland had rallied to the new covenant (leading to the label "Covenanters" for the rebels) and easily assembled an army that intimidated the English, without any open battles. In 1639 Charles again sent troops, and this time the Scots not only repulsed them in an open conflict but pushed across the border into England. In this way, the Covenanters anticipated the Puritan revolution. They also finally gained the self-governing church they had wanted for eighty years.

Even more heady victories followed, but these quickly turned to ashes. At first, Scotland tried to remain neutral in the English civil war. But the commonwealth forces badly needed the help of an experienced Scottish army and bargained to gain it. In effect, the enemies of Charles committed the English church to a presbyterian polity, one common to both kingdoms. Both parties accepted and signed the Solemn League and Covenant to effect this goal. Briefly, the Scots seemed ensured not only of a free church at home but of a similar church in all Britain. Out of this agreement came the Westminster assembly (see above). What the Scots had not bargained for was the execution of Charles I (Scottish troops had released him to the English) and the type of Puritan regime that followed. What the majority of the English people never accepted was the Presbyterian creed and the system of government pushed on them by the Scots.

In Scotland, the English revolution led to various factions. A clear majority did not accept the Commonwealth and Cromwell and plotted to restore a monarch who would accept their covenant. A faction in Scotland coerced the young prince Charles, out to regain the throne lost by his father, to sign the Solemn League and Covenant, and then joined his army and its French supporters in what became a final and bloody showdown with the forces of Cromwell. Cromwell's armies, in effect, policed Scotland and, among other repressive actions, suspended the general assembly. This ended the brief experiment with a free church, although Cromwell was happy to allow the local congregations to continue as before. With the Restoration in 1660, Charles II was not about to honor his earlier commitment to the covenant, and thus during his reign and the brief one of his brother James II, the general assembly did not meet in Scotland. Charles also, under the pressures of his English cabinet, restored both prelacy and patronage. Under the resented control of bishops, the nationalistic Scots chaffed and resisted. Meanwhile, the Covenanters, as the upholders of the old covenants now labeled themselves, helped rebuild a vital church, one that gained added fervor from its resistance to Stuart policies. In outlying areas, Covenanter congregations defied the state church and worshiped or held their communions in the woods and fields. Even Charles II had to relent, and under the shadow authority of his bishops, he accepted most aspects of the earlier church government. But the more extreme

Covenanters rebelled, killed an archbishop, and thus began in 1679 a series of events that contributed to the Glorious Revolution of 1688.

Most Scottish Presbyterians hailed the ascension of William and Mary in 1688. In 1690 they regained their general assembly and now, finally for the last time, an enduringly independent church, one without bishops although not without continued lay patronage. The existing bishops, and Episcopalian clergymen, were able to retain their parishes if they accepted the new order. With the early merger of the Scottish parliament into the British one, the general assembly of the Church of Scotland became the greatest single symbol of Scottish nationalism. But not all churchpeople rejoiced at the new order. A few congregations, for a time without a single minister, would not accept William and Mary as proper, covenant rulers, since they supported episcopacy in England. These radical Covenanters soon formed a separate Reformed Synod in Scotland and sent immigrants both to Ulster and to the American colonies. In 1733, a second major schism would have a direct impact on America. Some very orthodox Calvinists, who deplored lay patronage, seceded from the state church and established an Associate Presbytery (later a synod). Unfortunately, both the Reformed and the Associate synods soon separated into multiple factions.

Almost as important in America as the Scottish reforms was an offshoot of the Scottish church – the Presbyterian Church of Ulster. It was by way of Ulster, much more frequently than Scotland, that Scottish Presbyterianism came to America. After brutal military campaigns, England gained control of the northern counties of Ireland by 1603. In 1607 James I offered major incentives to other English or Scottish planters, who gained much of the land in Ulster under a form of feudal tenure. These planters in turn welcomed, with lower rents and no feudal obligations, leasehold farmers, most of whom came from the nearby southwest of Scotland (County Galloway in particular), where land was poor and rents high. These were mostly Presbyterians, but for a time they were unable to establish congregations. To their good fortune, however, a handful of Presbyterian ministers from just across the North Channel refused to accept the role of bishops in Scotland and fled to Ulster after 1613, there to establish new Presbyterian congregations.[4]

Here, as in Scotland, early Presbyterian success only began a century of strife and confusion. In Ireland, Presbyterians never gained the status of an established church but instead existed by suffrage under an often struggling Anglican establishment, this in a largely Catholic country. Under Charles I and just after a period of stirring revivals, the Presbyterian ministers suffered such persecutions as to force them to flee back to Scotland. In 1642, with the Long Parliament ascendant in England, Presbyterian clergymen came back to Ulster with English troops to suppress an Irish rebellion. Here they were able to establish an informal presbytery. Under the Stuart restoration, and even under William and Mary, the Irish

Presbyterians suffered numerous disabilities but managed not only to survive but to grow, often through informal modes of evading the rules of the established church. The disabilities continued into the eighteenth century, and a much resented Test Act of 1704 had some small impact on the waves of Scotch-Irish migration to the American colonies. But it was the economic distress, crop failures, higher rents, and effective American promotion that best explain the largest exodus yet of Europeans to America.

Anglicanism in Colonial America

The first Reformed Christians to settle permanently in what is now the United States arrived at Jamestown in 1607. They were nominally members of the Church of England, although not until Virginia became a royal (rather than a company) colony in 1624 was the church legally established. From settlement until after 1642, Virginia was also, by most definitions of the elusive word, a Puritan colony. The earliest clergymen were of Puritan leanings. Even a few Separatist colonists came by special invitation, and after 1631 one rather cohesive settlement of avowed Puritans successfully solicited three Congregational missionaries to come down from the new Massachusetts Bay Colony to preach in private homes. The early Virginia rules on church attendance were as tough as any ever enacted in Massachusetts, and at least a few idealistic ministers nourished illusory hopes of a successful mission to nearby Indians. In 1642 a new royal governor expelled the Puritan preachers and from then on required conformity on the part of all clergy. In 1649 a colony of three hundred Virginia Puritans moved to Maryland, in part for religious reasons. From this point on, the church in Virginia would be jealous of its prerogatives and more resistant to dissenters (at first Quakers, later Presbyterians and Baptists) than in any other colony. After 1660, only a few identified evangelical or Calvinist ministers served the Virginia church, but Virginia Anglicans, as a whole, successfully maintained a large degree of lay control through elected vestries, generally opposed an American bishop, and by the American Revolution, favored a near presbyterian form of church government.[5]

Throughout the colonial period, Virginia remained the largest Anglican colony, with the most parishes (eventually over ninety) and clergy (eventually over fifty). In most Tidewater areas of Virginia, until 1750, the church had no real competitors except a few, much resented Quakers. But for a variety of reasons the Virginia church remained vulnerable if not weak. It was not as well supported as a smaller number of Anglican parishes around Charleston, South Carolina, and not nearly as committed or as well led as mission Anglican congregations in the Boston area and in Connecticut. Eventually, Anglicanism became the established religion in New York, Maryland, Virginia, the two Carolinas, and Georgia. This did not mean direct funding by the colonial governments but rather laws that required the organization of local vestries, the assessment of local parish taxes, and the assignment of glebe lands to the clergy. Thus, the terms of legal establishment pushed the support of the church on local institutions. Although the clergymen could and at times did use the courts to try to collect their promised salaries, they were constantly at odds with their own vestries, particularly in the South. Even the parish system did not work well enough to sustain a self-supporting church except in Virginia, South Carolina, parts of Maryland, and a few urban areas such as New York City and Philadelphia. For all of New England, for most of the middle colonies, and for North Carolina and Georgia, the English church was, in effect, a mission church, with its clergy largely assigned, and paid, by the Society for the Propagation of the Gospel in Foreign Parts (SPG), a missionary society founded in 1702 by Thomas Bray, an English clergyman back from frustrating efforts to supervise an understaffed church in Maryland. From 1702 until the American Revolution, the SPG sent over 585 clergymen, a majority of the total in colonial America.

By the Revolution, the Anglican church was, at least on paper, a national church. Even in distant New Hampshire and Vermont it had two or three scattered congregations, and it had proven an attractive alternative for a minority of New Englanders who craved a more formal or esthetic worship. In fact, by 1776 the church had a more devout membership in Connecticut than anywhere else, in part because there it had always had the legal status of a dissenting sect. It had faced sharp condemnation from the Congregational establishment, but it had attracted an unusually able leadership. To be an Anglican in New England, if not a recent arrival from England, required courage and zeal.

Except for such local enclaves as Connecticut, the English church languished in America. Only numerically was it a close competitor to the Congregational majority in the thirteen colonies. By 1776 it had approximately 480 parish churches or chapels (fewer than Congregationalists, Presbyterians, and diverse Baptists), but many of these were not active or served by clergymen. Thus, its nominal membership was large and its strongly committed or devout membership relatively small, as proved by the rapid defection of its members during the Revolution. The difficult and enduring question is why the English church, which seemingly had everything in its favor, fared so poorly in colonial America.

One answer is obvious. The New England Puritans, with their coherent, well-funded, and well-led congregations, practically excluded their parent church from New England. This meant that, for almost a century, Anglicanism was not a viable option for up to 40 percent of the colonial population. For over a generation, New England Puritans were able to exclude any Anglican congregation at all, and even up to the middle of the eighteenth century they denied tax support to Anglican congregations. Yet, ironically, as the Anglican church gained a foothold in New England, as it even attracted a major defection of Puritans in Connecticut, it came to match the Congregationalists in lay zeal and clerical leadership. Thus, what most demands an explanation was Anglican laxity and weakness outside New England.

One partial explanation involved leadership, particularly the lack of an American episcopacy, either a resident bishop for all the colonies or one in each Anglican colony. Over and over again the American church almost gained its bishop. The king and Parliament, at several points, came within an inch of such an appointment, but in each case backed off. The story is too complex for any brief account. But one necessary condition for this failure was effective American resistance, shrill and almost paranoid among New England Puritans, less insistent but more damaging among Anglican lay leaders in the South. Thus, throughout the colonial period the church was in effect part of the diocese of the bishop of London and was supervised loosely, if at all, by commissaries appointed by him.

Linked to this lack of direction from the top was the uneven quality of the American clergy. Since the church had no local bishop, any colonial candidate for the ministry had to travel to England for training and ordination (no simple matter, with approximately one in five candidates dying from disease or shipwreck). Few made this choice, meaning that most of the clergy came over from Britain, some as permanent settlers, others on limited missionary assignments from the SPG. Few of the ablest clergy in Britain volunteered for service in America, for obvious reasons. It is unfair to make sweeping judgments about the Anglican colonial clergy as a whole or to subscribe to the old image of a clergy given over to idle amusements or, worse, to graft or drunkenness. The letters back to the SPG reveal both the frustrations ministers faced and, among many, their dedication to their task. But, on average, the Anglican clergy lacked the zeal of the Baptist lay preachers and the native ability and the educational attainments of the Congregational and Presbyterian clergy. Some of the reasons for this lack reflected not just the problems of recruitment for the colonies but also the often corrupted recruitment process, and the low status, suffered by clergymen back in England.

Another obstacle was environmental. Outside of New England and a few coastal cities, the pattern of settlement in the colonies worked against an Anglican-type church life. The colonists moved onto widely dispersed holdings, to isolated farms or plantations. They sought the best land, meaning a very sparse population except along favored rivers, with inland settlements linked by poor or nonexistent roads. From Maryland southward, the increasing use of slave labor on tobacco and rice plantations meant an even thinner white population. Thus, the Anglican parishes were usually countywide, covering up to one thousand square miles, meaning that most of the population could not travel to a parish church and that the small number of potential parishioners available in most sections of the parish precluded scattered chapels. Not only was it difficult to gather a church but it was almost impossible to supervise Christian morals, to furnish such essential ordinances as baptism and marriage, to offer schools for all families, or to do much about those who chose to have no connection with the church or, later, to join dissenting sects. Young people had to travel to England for confirmation, which in the Anglican rites required a bishop. This meant that the Anglican church was largely supported by baptized but unconfirmed members (not a vital issue, but symbolic of second-class membership). Thus, whatever its reported membership, southern Anglicanism became a church of scattered towns and villages and also to a great extent a church of the landed elites. Its clergy moved in elite social circles and faced enormous difficulties in ministering to backcountry yeomen, to indentured servants, or to black slaves.

A final handicap involved a religious culture or style. In intent, the Anglican parishes were inclusive. In fact, they were not so, at least not in most of America. After the early, quasi-Puritan phase in Virginia, the church did not minister effectively to those who wanted a warm, evangelical religion, one keyed to a rebirth experience and to a demanding or even austere moral code. Thus, after 1660 the church had little appeal for large segments of the population, a failure documented by the ease with which evangelical sects recruited converts whenever they "invaded" Anglican parishes. One has to note exceptions, such as the popular Devereux Jarratt in Virginia, in outlook a virtual Wesleyan, who attracted one thousand worshipers to his Low Church parish. It was he who welcomed early Methodist societies and joined them in a wave of revivals just before the Revolution. But Jarratt, often resented by his Anglican colleagues, was the exception that proved the rule. He, almost alone, broadened the appeal of the church to encompass the spectrum of social classes in Virginia, or perhaps disproportionately cast its appeal toward the lower classes. That he alone moved so close to the evangelical extreme says worlds about the church as a whole. After independence, the denomination with greatest appeal in former Anglican strongholds proved to be the Methodists, who in a sense became the evangelical and dominant offspring of the colonial English church in America.

The lack of evangelical appeal involved more than doctrine. In fact, colonial Anglicanism was more open and inclusive on doctrinal issues than any other American church, except possibly the early Moravians. The church did not demand adherence to any confession, although in worship the people recited the traditional creeds of the church (Apostles', Nicene, Athanasian). One could be a Calvinist (after all, the Thirty-Nine Articles suggested that one should be) or an Arminian or some loose, probably illogical combination of the two. It is usually impossible to gauge exactly how eighteenth-century Anglican ministers decided on these issues. Perhaps many never decided at all. But, clearly, few held to a consistent Calvinist position, one now stigmatized by earlier Puritan excesses in Britain. What the church demanded, much more than correct doctrine, was uniform practice. The identity of the church rested on the use of the *Book of Common Prayer* in all scheduled worship services and for all special occasions, such as burials or marriages.

This was not a terribly restrictive requirement. *The Book of Common Prayer* provided minimal commonality in an otherwise latitudinarian church. The minister (or pastor, rector, presbyter, priest – the very choice among these labels, although they are roughly synonymous, suggests the internal differences) could do as he wished in the sermon, making it a minor or a major part of worship. Laypeople could develop a varied devotional life or could create, as did the Methodists, para-church institutions, such as societies and classes. They could, in informal meetings, indulge in extemporaneous prayer and singing and testimonies, all as supplements to the prescribed worship. Nothing in doctrine or in the liturgy excluded evangelicals from the Anglican church. And, in fact, both in England and in the colonies, the church did accommodate a range of religious styles. Beyond the common liturgy, Low Church Anglicans were able to distinguish themselves from the High Church coreligionists by a range of symbols – by using simple church architecture, by emphasizing a communion table and not an altar, by rejecting such Catholic carryovers as incense, by simplifying or eliminating special vestments worn by clergymen, by rejecting certain clerical titles, by emphasizing Calvinist themes or the Pauline scheme of salvation in their sermons, and by giving a greater informal role to laypeople in church government.

Rituals of worship are quite distinct from doctrine, and both can be distinct from permitted or normative levels of feeling and affection. Most inclusive churches – those that try to serve the religious needs of a whole population – blend the elements in an often complex mosaic. But even in colonial America the trend was always away from such a broad church mosaic and toward the specialized appeal of distinctive sects within a pluralistic religious mix. Early New England was anomalous – an exclusive, narrowly defined religion in a social context that permitted no options, no alternative doctrines. Anglicanism remained, in commitment, inclusive but in fact soon had a narrow, often class-based appeal and thus was continually threatened by invading dissenters. It rarely had the resources, or the political power, to protect its turf, and if it did, as in parts of Virginia, this left over half the population effectively unchurched. In this sense it created a religious environment that almost cried out for toleration and denominational pluralism. With the Revolution, the Anglican church almost collapsed, and in the pluralistic environment that followed it was barely able to survive. In its salvaged Episcopalian form, it was unable to compete successfully with the booming evangelical denominations.

Congregationalists

New England Congregationalists made up the largest body of Christians in colonial America. In 1776 they also enjoyed greater institutional strengths than any other American confession. This strength represented a latter-day dividend from the religious hegemony gained by early Puritan congregations over almost every aspect of New England life. In Massachusetts Bay, Connecticut, and New Hampshire, the early Puritan society was very homogeneous. Through careful screening and rigorous exclusion, the Puritans were able to maintain this homogeneity much longer than confessions in any of the non-Puritan colonies.[6]

New England Congregationalists joined Presbyterians as the most stalwart defenders of Reformed orthodoxy in America. By the eighteenth century, this meant a defense of what everybody by then called Calvinism. Distinctive in institutions, the American Puritans remained fully within the Reformed mainstream in all their avowed doctrines. It is difficult to distinguish their normative beliefs from those of Presbyterians, although, unlike Presbyterians, Congregationalists never formally subscribed to the Westminster Confession. By 1776 Calvinism had arguably become both a badge of identity and a burden to Congregationalists and Presbyterians. The burden involved what had become the one central doctrine of all avowed Calvinists – the complete and absolute sovereignty of God. It seemed increasingly difficult for people to believe that God, from before time itself, had willed the whole drama of human rebellion and partial reconciliation, that he had decreed whom among lost and depraved humans he would save. For those who believed themselves chosen, this divine sovereignty was consoling. At least in theory, the children of faith had complete security. God chose and God was never fickle. In fact, as demonstrated in all Reformed churches, the problem of assurance haunted almost all the supposedly persevering saints, who had difficulty resisting Arminian beliefs.

The Puritans confronted all these dilemmas. It is not at all clear that their solutions were distinctive. Perry Miller, in his enormously influential books on Puritanism, argued that Puritans used the idea of a covenant, and a "federal theology," to take some of the sting out of Calvinism. But roughly similar strategies marked the development of seventeenth-century Scottish Presbyterianism. In a sense, all Calvinists developed reasonable arguments, or rhetorical strategies, to help them find peace in a God-controlled universe. The concept of a covenant, although rooted in ancient Jewish history, did have special prominence among

English and Scottish churches and had an even more focal prominence among the Puritans, who came to New England largely because of the role of written covenants within their congregations and towns. Puritans could speak of the covenant of grace in near contractual terms and could thus seemingly erode the sense of inequality and distance between God and humans. But any rhetorical device was subject to abuse, and the history of Christianity is rife with strategies that, in time, helped undermine a vital piety. However arbitrary the ultimate choices of God, all Calvinists believed, along with all other Christians, that God worked rationally in his dealings with humans. He used means to bring his elect to salvation. Even though no human could resist the workings of the Spirit, the Spirit did not use physical coercion but rather seduced the will or affections. God wooed his elect. He did not hit them over the head. Thus, although the initiative was always God's, the human response to God was active and the relationship dialogistic and affectionate. This did not mean, of necessity, any human impiety, although this was an ever present danger.

In practice, the differences between Calvinists and Arminians often blurred. Both doctrinal positions could lead to a form of legalism. The leaders in all the major Calvinist confessions had to walk a narrow line between enthusiasm and legalism. The ever present issue was assurance. How could one be sure of one's salvation? The answer would seem to be simple. How can one know that they love someone? One knows internally by tender and solicitous feelings, externally by the conduct engendered by those affections. Thus, all evangelical Christians had a compelling reason to look for evidence of a love of God in both their feelings and their conduct. To Calvinists, the order was critical – only faith (trust and love) makes possible truly virtuous works, those performed for the correct reasons, for the love of God. No Christian could dispense with introspective self-examination. Outwardly, moral deeds proved nothing. But the absence of such deeds documented the absence of faith. In this sense, good works are necessary for salvation, for they are logically inseparable from faith. But only faith motivates such works. Puritan ministers, like Reformed pastors everywhere, tried not to externalize faith but to use external conduct as a final test of faith. Individuals had to examine their motives, and early Puritans certainly excelled in this. But the public could scrutinize only good works. Thus, in the public arena, in the necessary judgments made by congregations, in the exercise of church discipline, the warrant of faith had to be good behavior, conformity to accepted rules, obedience to God's law as revealed in scripture. It may well be, as Max Weber later argued, that Calvinist doctrines created such psychological tensions that Calvinists had to find assurance, even develop a sense of personal identity, by what they did, by deeds, and that Calvinism thus supported a higher level of active involvement, a more rigorous moral standard, than any other form of Christianity. Much in the history of

New England Puritans supports such a psychological insight, but so does much in the history of Scottish Presbyterianism.

By the Revolution, most latter-day Puritans still affirmed the older doctrines and still accepted the same demands on themselves. But already the internal strains had divided Congregationalists, and in very complex ways. From the second generation on in New England one could detect developing strains. Anne Hutchinson, although driven close to an openly enthusiastic position (a claim of direct, private revelations from God), well expressed what might be called an evangelical extreme. She, and her so-called antinomian associates, glimpsed in conventional Puritanism a trend toward legalism, toward a religion of works, and away from converting faith and a Spirit-filled devotional life, despite the fact that the early Puritan congregations demanded that all aspiring members relate, in highly personal language, the converting work of the Spirit in their lives. Originally hot, the Puritans were quickly becoming cold. From Hutchinson's perspective, the congregations were full of purported but in reality unconverted and hypocritical people, and this included most ministers. The complaint became a perennial one – that religion had become too intellectual, too rational, too legalistic, too conventional, too accepting of the world, too prosperous, too cold. Such concerns informed the journals of ministers, supported the doubts and anxieties of laypeople, and in time helped spur local revivals. After 1734, with the revivals led by Jonathan Edwards and then by George Whitefield, these concerns led to several schismatic congregations. Most Congregationalists who came to share such evangelical concerns remained within the church, but from within they soon launched a running critique of more liberal or rational factions, particularly those who dominated Harvard.

Even before the end of the seventeenth century, one can also identify an emerging "liberal" faction among the Puritan ministers. After the disturbing revivals of the 1740s, a few critical ministries openly preached Arminian, as well as Unitarian and Universalist, doctrines. They first engaged in the interminable skirmishes against an often caricatured Calvinism. In most respects they were at opposite poles from the revivalists (often called New Lights) and congealed as a group out of their criticism of revival excesses. Quite self-consciously, these emerging rationalists rejected the Calvinist God and substituted a much nicer, more benevolent, more friendly God. The same concerns that led them to repudiate the Calvinist God led many of them, eventually, to question other orthodox doctrines – the Trinity formula, eternal torment, or biblical miracles. Whereas the more evangelical Congregationalists appealed to people of all classes, and particularly to those on the lower echelons of society, the rationalist or Arminian or liberal or Unitarian wing appealed primarily to a New England elite, to people of wealth, social status, and educational attainment. But even the mainline Congregationalists, though still nominally Calvinist, by 1776 also suffered some of the stigma of an established, prosperous, even smug church. This opens up the most distinctive heritage of New England Congregationalism – their unique polity and their accommodation with civil society.

After 1783, the only American Christians who could still claim to be in a tax-supported church, rather than a sect, were Congregationalists in Massachusetts, Connecticut, and New Hampshire. They, alone, had special legal recognition, and they still received financial support from local governments. The fact that these establishments survived the Revolution, and in New Hampshire and Massachusetts the drafting of new constitutions, simply documents the institutional strength of these churches. In many smaller New England towns the legally designated parish congregation remained the only available church. Here the early Puritan monopoly survived, but now largely by choice, only incidentally because of legal favoritism. Ironically, even as Baptists and other sects opened a prolonged, and eventually successful, attack on this now almost anachronistic religious establishment, its defenders scarcely remembered that, at its beginnings, it reflected Puritan efforts to separate church and state, to end the overlap of functions and jurisdictions that marked the state-church system of Europe.

Puritan institutions were unique in the British empire. Because they brought along their own charter, and because of a period of trouble in England, the Puritans who first came to Massachusetts Bay, and subsequently to Connecticut and New Hampshire, were able to fashion their own institutions with little external interference. In Massachusetts, they quickly turned a corporate directorship into a provincial government and created a distinct form of town government. Out of distaste for the episcopacy in England, they abolished any semblance of it in New England and, with this, any traditional civil functions for a church. In effect, they abolished the church as traditionally understood. They worshiped in the town hall or meetinghouse, allowed no civil function whatsoever to congregations or ministers (even the performance of a marriage by a minister was illegal), had no church laws or church courts, and assigned no formal welfare functions to the congregation, such as education or poor relief. The town government took responsibility for all civil functions, including these with a religious content, but had no authority over congregational business. This functional separation joined with a blending of religion and politics and with a mutuality or complementary relationship between covenanted towns and congregations. As a civic obligation, in order to receive the benefits of public worship, the town used taxes to pay the minister, but he was selected, or discharged, by vote of the congregation. Attendance at worship was compulsive, required by statute. The local town officials (who in most cases were also members of the congregation) believed that it was desirable to maintain homogeneous, ordered communities, and in behalf of this goal they mandated, by law, overt adherence to correct doctrines as well as conformity to a rigorous, religiously based moral standard. In one sense, the towns established a religion but not a church. The church blessed the role of magistrates but in no official way intruded into town affairs. By custom, no minister held political office.

A congregation, except in the cities, was coterminous with the town. Early, compact settlement meant that almost everyone in New England had access to a church, and by law all were supposed to attend worship. Only the poorest or the most wayward towns failed to hire ministers. In few other Christian societies did a minister have greater prestige or greater leeway for leadership. Yet the minister served a free congregation and thus had no ecclesiastical authority. The autonomous congregation hired and fired ministers at will and admitted members to communion. The original congregations had no creeds or confessions but were linked by shared beliefs. The ministers made up the only learned profession, generally received the most education of any vocational group, were often well paid, but yet spoke with no authority beyond that justified by learning or piety. They had to meet the needs and expectations of their congregation, but at least in the early years they enjoyed enough respect to be able to make rigorous or unpopular demands on parishioners. Typical tenures were long, often for life. Able ministers became so closely identified with towns as to bestow on them fame or notoriety. In no other American church were the ministers as able, overall, or as influential. The ministers, often alone, linked small villages to the larger world of culture, and in time they, not laypeople, proved to be the innovators, not only in their questioning of the received doctrines but also in their openness to science and scholarship and in their attempt to suppress or moderate popular forms of superstition and magic. Since each congregation rested on its own covenant and had control over its own identity, Congregationalism in New England was always open to change, and this meant internal diversity through time.

In the heady days of migration, in the first efforts to reform old-world institutions, the Puritan congregations moved closer than any other Reformed church to a sectarian model. In the newly formed congregations, membership was very exclusive. Such congregations admitted to membership only individuals with relatable evidence of rebirth. Only such communicants could present infants for baptism. Such rigor, or purity, meant that up to half of adults, and soon large numbers of young people, were not communicants, not fully in the church, although they had to attend its services. Thus, the Puritans, briefly, tried to preserve a religious monopoly through rigorous screening, based on both correct beliefs and experience, or all the attributes of a voluntaristic sect. Until the new Massachusetts Bay Charter of 1691, the Puritans successfully warned away, or expelled, not only Quakers and Baptists but also most Anglicans. They lost their monopoly by 1700 and soon also the zeal required to exclude competitors. Even before this, most congregations had relaxed the screening of members or adopted a form of halfway membership. In the eighteenth century, Congregational churches were privileged competitors with scattered Anglican, Baptist, Quaker, Presbyterian, and after 1784, Methodist sects. They enjoyed what by now was a venerable tradition, special governmental support and taxes (slowly, other approved sects gained the right to divert members' taxes to their own congregation, but the taxes of the unchurched still went to Congregationalists), strong educational institutions such as Harvard and Yale, the talent and prestige of their ministers, and the political, social, and economic preeminence of their members. By then, they had replaced the early sectarian elements by most of the attributes of a broad, inclusive church, one that now encompassed an increasing diversity of doctrines. But some of the old order lived on, particularly in the small, conservative congregations that dotted the New England countryside.

Presbyterians

Until at least 1760 the Presbyterians made up the second- or third-largest Reformed denomination in colonial America (behind Congregationalists and about equal to Anglicans), although they had probably lost this rank to the Baptists by the time of the Revolution. The growth of American Presbyterianism increasingly involved Scotch-Irish migrants, members of the Ulster Presbyterian Church. But even before the massive immigration of Scotch-Irish to America in the eighteenth century, a few scattered English dissenters and a few Scottish Presbyterians had founded an infant Presbyterian movement in the American colonies. A few English Presbyterians moved to Connecticut, New York (Long Island), and New Jersey by 1700 and there formed small congregations. In fact, in Connecticut the boundaries between Congregationalism and Presbyterianism blurred, with ministers moving freely among congregations. By 1700, the Connecticut Congregationalists had quasi-Presbyterian synods; English Presbyterians rarely adopted the tight, centralized Scottish system.[7]

In 1706 seven scattered Presbyterian ministers founded the Philadelphia presbytery, the first in America. The convening minister, Francis MacKemie, was from Ulster and had organized Presbyterian congregations on the eastern shore of Maryland and Virginia by 1690. The presbytery grew rapidly, particularly as it added churches in Pennsylvania and New Jersey, most of an English or Puritan heritage. In 1716 the Philadelphia presbytery upgraded itself into a synod, with three regional presbyteries.

By 1730, abetted by a growing wave of Scotch-Irish immigration, the church had expanded to approximately thirty ministers. By then the clear majority of ministers had emigrated from Northern Ireland, some moving with whole congregations. In the years before the American Revolution, possibly as many as 150,000 (probably less, although the number is a point of continuing controversy) Scotch-Irish came to America, with the first large wave after 1717, the last just before the Revolution. After an early preference for New England, based on religious affinities and a failure to anticipate Puritan intolerance, a majority shifted to Pennsylvania, which offered complete religious liberty and excellent land. From Pennsylvania, the Scotch-Irish moved mainly west and south, soon making up at least half of the population in the piedmont and subsequently over half of the early migrants across the Appalachians.

Clusters of Scotch-Irish settlers continuously petitioned synods in Ulster or even in Scotland to send ministers to America. They never had enough, and ministerial shortages, tied to exceptionally high educational qualifications, would place an enduring limit on Presbyterian growth. Early tensions between English and Ulster Presbyterians soon involved doctrinal issues. Irish migrants desired the tight discipline of their home churches. English Presbyterians, centered in New England and New York, wanted a looser system of church government and did not gladly subscribe to the Westminster Confession. But as a whole, the American church remained orthodox in a century in which rationalist and latitudinarian views grew apace. Inroads of rationalism had much greater impact in Ireland and Scotland than in America, reflecting a perhaps understandable conventionalism among immigrants. In the one case of a clearly Arminian, almost deist minister, Samuel Hemphill, who came over to the Philadelphia church, the synod tried and expelled him without dissent, gaining thereby the undying contempt of Benjamin Franklin, who loved Hemphill's eloquent but largely plagiarized sermons. Eventually, the synod split, not over doctrines but largely because of the fervor that accompanied what many would call the Great Awakening.

The first Presbyterian leaders of a distinctive revival faction were William Tennent and his four sons. William established himself, permanently, at Neshaminy in Bucks County, Pennsylvania, where in 1735 he opened a famous academy and informal seminary for aspiring ministers. Soon called the Log College, it served a vital role in Presbyterianism, since the growing church could not continue to import all its ministers from Ulster and since too few native candidates could afford to attend Harvard or Yale. Soon a dozen or so Tennent students made up an especially fervent circle in the church, for they embraced a warm, experiential approach to religion. Gilbert Tennent, William's eldest and most gifted son, took an M.A. at Yale in 1725 and then ministered to a congregation in New Brunswick, New Jersey. His ability in the pulpit (the "Son of Thunder") and his fervor made him a leader of the most revivalist faction in Presbyterianism. His perennial tours throughout the colonies made him the most influential itinerant evangelist in America except for the English (and Anglican) preacher, George Whitefield.

Of all Protestant churches in America, the Scotch-Irish Presbyterians enjoyed the most suitable institutional setting for periodic renewals within congregations. They met in the summer months for four- or five-day intercongregational communion services. These provided the single most significant continuity between the eighteenth-century awakenings and both nineteenth-century camp meetings and protracted revivals within congregations. These joint communion services began with a day of fasting and prayer on Wednesday or Thursday and continued with intensive preparatory services on Friday or Saturday. Ministers carefully screened candidates for communion and distributed leaden tokens that admitted one to a communion table on Sunday (this very conspicuously identified those outside the church). The Sunday sacrament involved multiple settings at long, linen-covered tables, with this followed by thanksgiving services on Monday. People came from all nearby congregations, resulting in huge throngs of people, extensive home hospitality, outdoor preaching from platforms (called tents in Ulster and in America), and frequent all-night prayer services.

Through the 1730s and 1740s, the more experientially oriented Presbyterian ministers reported ever better attended and glorious sacramental seasons, as well as wonderful "Sabbath" services. Gilbert Tennent and other ministers reported thousands in attendance at some joint communions, where almost all the preaching necessarily took place outdoors. So did most of the preaching by George Whitefield when he toured the middle colonies in 1739. Notably, the welcome he received from Presbyterians was reversed by the hostility and ostracism he suffered from most of his fellow Anglicans. The more effective preaching, such as that by Whitefield, elicited an unprecedented display of feeling – weeping, groaning, swooning, and crying out for mercy. In Whitefield's description of one Presbyterian congregation, people were "pale as death" and others lay on the ground in the trance-like state first noted at Ulster communions as early as 1624.

In the midst of the most fervent revivals, the Synod of Philadelphia split (in sentiment by 1739 and by the expulsion of the revival faction in 1841). The expelled New Side organized a group of evangelical presbyteries in 1743 and formed its own New York Synod in 1845. Several divisive issues led to the separation, not the least being the status of the more extreme physical exercises. The group behavior of the Log College men soon alienated a majority of their ministerial colleagues.

The evangelistic New Brunswick presbytery licensed ministers who lacked the normal educational requirements but who confessed a plenitude of experiential piety. The old synod responded with such tough educational requirements for ministers as to challenge the Log College tradition. The New Brunswick presbytery asserted its autonomy in licensing ministers. Meanwhile, often in response to lay requests, many Log College men became temporary itinerants and preached in local congregations against the wishes of the local, or at least neighboring, clergy, sometimes deeply dividing congregations (the offended ministers soon saw "intrusion" as a major crime).

The climax of a developing split came in 1740. In a thinly veiled challenge to many older, established ministers, Gilbert Tennent preached his famous, published sermon "The Danger of an Unconverted Ministry." Although its vehement and overt attack on "cold and sapless" sermons that froze on the lips of ministers "not sent of God" best fit Anglicans and deists, many of his colleagues who lacked Tennent's fervor or pulpit style felt it was aimed at them. The incipient Old Side ministers, including about half the Scotch-Irish immigrant ministers, were incensed. They felt beleaguered as they tried to maintain professional standards of collegiality, traditional educational requirements for ministers, a more centralized church order, and more careful adherence to the Westminster Confession. Perhaps above all, they feared a new, more florid, less systematic style of preaching and, although not opposed to all aspects of the revivals, feared the effects the new preaching might have on weaker laypeople, who often cried out or fell down in convulsion-like fits.

The Old Side–New Side split aired, largely among ministers, some enduring tensions within American Presbyterianism, tensions that would lead to a second schism a century later (New and Old School). The Old Side ministers were Calvinist scholastics, anxious to maintain a Scottish church without change, concerned with correct polity and rigorous discipline, suspicious of all new means used to gain converts, horrified at the emotional and physical excesses of the awakening, and resentful of the New England Puritan influences on American Presbyterianism. The New Side ministers were often willing to subscribe to Westminster but desired some leeway in its interpretation. They sought, rather than resented, cooperation with other evangelicals, often looked to Puritans for allies, and were thus more inclusive or ecumenical in outlook. They too sought rigorous church discipline, but more in a moral than in a doctrinal sense. Above all, the New Side embraced the awakening and a purer and more affectionate type of religion. As time proved, the ever more assertive laypeople favored the New Side. The Old Side seemed stuffy, cold, and unresponsive to lay demands. Also, the Old Side failed in the recruitment of able ministers, lost several of its young ministers to the Anglicans, suffered from the incompetence or the immorality of too many of its existing preachers, and despite desperate efforts was never able to build its own college (the New Side launched the College of New Jersey at Princeton).

Both sides (the Old Side Philadelphia Synod and the New Side New York Synod) remained nominally orthodox in doctrine, and soon after the split both began softening their positions. Reunion occurred in 1758, largely on New Side terms. While the schism lasted, Presbyterianism spread rapidly to Virginia and the Carolinas. In most cases, the New Side led in missionary work, but not always. As a result of heavy Scotch-Irish immigration and growth to the west and south, the New England influence in the church steadily declined in the last half of the eighteenth century.

The Presbyterians first moved south by way of the great valley of Virginia, migrating along with German sects. Subsequently, they invaded the central areas of Virginia, against often determined Anglican opposition. Here the dominant early figure was Samuel Davies, a very young, brilliant, politically astute Presbyterian minister, whose role in southern Presbyterianism almost rivaled that of his admired friend, Jonathan Edwards, among Congregationalists in the Connecticut Valley (Davies joined colleagues in a belated effort to lure Edwards to Virginia in 1751 and would follow him in the presidency of the College of New Jersey in 1758, even imitating Edwards in his premature death in 1761 in that by now cursed presidency). Davies's first congregations largely reflected not the normal Scotch-Irish immigration but former Anglicans who embraced a more affectionate religion under the influence of Whitefield and other itinerant revivalists and who found a welcoming home in New Side Presbyterian congregations (later, most such evangelicals would embrace Methodism).

Davies brought to central Virginia the New Side emphasis on religious affections but blended this with a demand for rigorous intellectuality. He closely followed Jonathan Edwards and always argued that his literate, often prospering Virginia parishioners would not tolerate a religion based only on sentiment or feeling. From 1747 to 1755, Davies was able to organize about a dozen congregations around Richmond and to introduce his original English flock to the old religion of Scotland, including its extended communion services. He helped attract a half-dozen like-minded young ministers, who joined in a period of almost continuous revival and growth. By then, most new members reflected the heavy Scotch-Irish migration, not further conversion of Anglicans. Davies and his associated ministers deserve special mention in American religious history because of their success in converting blacks. Davies made this ministry one of his highest priorities and successfully solicited financial support, and plenty of praise, from Britain.

After 1750, Presbyterian families moved in large numbers into the piedmont of North and South Carolina. Here, in competition mainly with Baptists and not

Anglicans, they became the dominant church. From here they moved in large numbers across the Appalachians just after the Revolution, thus gaining the earliest dominance west of the mountains.

Baptists

The word *Baptist* denotes not a national church, not the name of a reformer, not even a distinct polity, but a specific doctrine and practice. Thus, a Baptist is one who rejects infant baptism and accepts as valid only the baptism of adult converts. In America, the label generally also referred to the method of baptism – immersion. Thus, Baptists can embrace various doctrines, as they have, and various forms of church government, although most in America have in fact chosen congregationalism. By this definition, the earliest Baptists in the American colonies were Puritans who, for scriptural reasons, rejected infant baptism. Roger Williams, along with another exile from Massachusetts Bay, John Clarke, founded the first two baptizing congregations in Rhode Island by 1640. By 1700 approximately ten scattered Baptist congregations existed in New England.[8]

The first organized Calvinist Baptist group migrated from England, largely to the Philadelphia area, in the late seventeenth century, with the first identified congregation dating from about 1688. These Baptists represented a small Particular Baptist association in Britain, one that subscribed in most respects, except baptism, to the Westminster Confession and that united in a loose, Presbyterian polity. Seven of these small congregations formed an enduring synod in Philadelphia in 1707. These Philadelphia Baptists were, in fact, baptizing Presbyterians, and were possibly more orthodox than most Presbyterians in their Calvinism. Particular Baptists (the "Particular" label refers to the Calvinist doctrine of a particular or limited atonement) generally rejected more emotional forms of revivalism and chose closed communion and a degree of isolation because of their baptismal doctrines. They did not expand rapidly (the Philadelphia Synod had only forty-two congregations and three thousand members by 1776). Meantime, various non-Calvinist (General or Free Will) Baptists established themselves in the colonies. These included not only English Free Will Baptists, many with earlier connections to continental Mennonites, but also the German Anabaptist denominations – Mennonites, Amish, and Church of the Brethren.

The most important colonial Baptist group, one destined to become the largest wing of American Protestantism by the late twentieth century, formed somewhat loosely during the eighteenth-century revivals. Over one hundred separating New Light congregations in New England eventually chose adult baptism, on what they believed to be sound scriptural grounds. These congregations founded no synods and at first not even loose associations. This lack of organization makes elusive their early history and has consistently won them less historical attention than their numbers justified. In the 1750s these New England Separate Baptists sent missionaries south, usually before organized missionary efforts by the Philadelphia Synod. They found their most inviting opportunities in the piedmont of Virginia and North Carolina, with their first organized association – Sandy Creek – in North Carolina. For the next half century, the history of Baptists in the South would be exceedingly complex, with major regional variations. In most areas of the Old South the Separate Baptists either absorbed or eventually merged with the less evangelical Particular congregations, generally then adopting a label often used by the Particular congregations, Regular Baptists. Across the mountains in Kentucky and Tennessee, these Regular Baptists always outnumbered scattered Free Will groups. Among southern and western Baptists the theological distinction between Arminians and Calvinists often narrowed, making doctrinal labels almost useless. But, clearly, a majority of Baptists, whatever their professed label, remained nominally Calvinist. In the nineteenth century these Baptist associations would split over associational ties, particularly a joint missionary organization formed in 1814. The majority or Missionary Baptists became the dominant denomination, although it split over slavery into northern and southern conventions in 1844.

This sketch of institutional history is a bit misleading. It suggests a denominational identity that never matured in the colonial period. The synod, and overt confessional commitments, of the Particular Baptists proved exceptional among Baptists in America. The pattern, by 1776, was independent, self-governing Baptist congregations, loosely grouped into regional associations. The associations had no legal status and no formal authority over congregations, which selected and ordained their own ministers and which determined the qualifications of members. An association had some influence over doctrine and ministerial standards largely because of its one weapon – refusal of fellowship. Baptist missionaries spread the faith by extended preaching tours, often forming new congregations in homes. Men who professed a call, who had some gifts for public speaking, won the right to preach to such congregations. Small, scattered congregations meant that almost all Baptist preachers worked as farmers or artisans and preached part-time, without a salary or more than meager voluntary offerings. Beyond local associations, congregations usually had no ties at all to a larger denomination. In parts of the South, blacks made up a large share of early Baptists, constituting a majority in some congregations. The white membership largely consisted of small farmers or mechanics. In the mosaic of American Baptists, almost every possible doctrine would eventually find local support.

Continental Reformed Denominations

The Reformed congregations that moved from continental Europe made up a quite distinctive branch of Calvinism in America. Three continental Reformed confessions sent immigrants to America. After the revocation of the Edict of Nantes in 1685, many members of John Calvin's own church, the French Reformed or Huguenot, fled to America. They established congregations, particularly in South Carolina and New York. But, in time, almost all these congregations, usually under pressure from Anglican establishments, converted to the English church. In the process, the Huguenots assimilated the English language but locally kept alive many of their French traditions. Only in Charleston, South Carolina, did a single separate Huguenot congregation survive. Partly because of clustered patterns of settlement and intense ethnic and linguistic identities, Reformed German and Dutch congregations resisted the lure of assimilation, although many Dutch Reformed Christians in the Hudson Valley joined Anglican congregations.

The German Reformed church in America began with the German immigrants whom William Penn welcomed to the new colony of Pennsylvania after 1681. The first identifiable German Reformed congregation arrived at Germantown in 1683, but early congregations lacked ministers or support from the Reformed states in Germany. As a result, such German Protestants had to provide their own leaders, the first of whom, John Philip Boehm, actually took his orders in the Dutch church, thus linking his church with the Dutch Reformed, a link that continued throughout the colonial era. Both polity and doctrines were almost identical. By 1747 the church had up to eighty congregations and had organized its first classic (comparable to a presbytery). Its members remained concentrated in Pennsylvania and Maryland, with only scattered congregations in New York, in the valley of Virginia, and in the North and South Carolina piedmont. During the great revivals the young church successfully resisted an effort by the Moravian leader Count Nikolaus Ludwig von Zinzendorf to merge all the Germanic churches in America. During the revolutionary era the church suffered the separation of a revivalistic Wesleyan group, the United Brethren, led by Philip Otterbein. The German Reformed church declared its own independence in 1791, but at that time it had only 22 ministers serving 178 scattered congregations, with strength only in eastern Pennsylvania. Consistently, the church had weaker congregations than those in the major English confessions.[9]

Only the Anglicans in Virginia and the Pilgrims at Plymouth arrived in America before the first Dutch Reformed minister came to New Amsterdam in 1628. The church grew only slowly, hindered by a lack of ministers and by administrative control from distant Amsterdam. In 1664 Britain took over New York from the Dutch but did not threaten the Reformed church, which by 1700 had about thirty congregations in New York, more than the Anglicans. The church soon suffered internal friction and, for a time, a virtual schism. All factions were nominally orthodox. The church recognized the Heidelberg Catechism, the Belgic Confession, and above all the scholastic and rigorous Canons of Dort. In the eighteenth century its Calvinism best resembled that of the Covenanters (Reformed) and Seceder (Associate) wings of Scottish Presbyterianism. The internal factions more nearly reflected issues of assimilation and of religious style than of doctrine. From 1730 on, the more conservative congregations in the Hudson Valley resented the more puritanical and revivalistic congregations that formed in New Jersey. The leader of the pietistic or experiential faction, Theodorus J. Frelinghuysen, was a German (many members of the Dutch churches came from areas of Germany close to the Dutch border) whose preaching stimulated early revivals in northern New Jersey. The divisions very closely paralleled those between Old and New Side Presbyterians, and in this case the more evangelical factions grew most rapidly and eventually dominated the church in its period of separation from Dutch control.[10]

Separation came in two steps. In 1772 the Dutch church in effect declared its independence from European control and formed its own independent coetus. Then, after the Revolution, it and at least seven other America confessions established an independent denomination. Its 1792 constitution (Standards) united approximately one hundred congregations in New York and New Jersey as the Reformed Protestant Dutch Church in North America.

IN SUMMARY, the churches in the Reformed tradition dominated American Christianity at the time of independence. But by then many within these denominations had moved away from Calvinist orthodoxy. The Anglican church still had room for Calvinists, but in fact they made up a minority in the American church. The Presbyterians still adhered rather firmly to their Calvinist confession. The strongest tradition of all – the Congregationalists – encompassed a prominent Arminian faction and broader doctrinal compromises that would soon erode much of its Calvinist traditions. Yet, up until 1776, a clear majority of American Reformed Christians had remained at least nominally Calvinist. The great revivals of the mid-eighteenth century almost entirely involved Calvinists and rested on distinctive Calvinist doctrines. The erosion had occurred not on the growing evangelical flanks but on the other flank – latitudinarian, rationalistic, intellectualist, and humanistic. But by the time of the Revolution this pattern was about to shift dramatically. A small faction within Anglicanism, the Methodists, would quickly offer the most effective challenge yet faced by Calvinists in America. In this case the challenge came from the evangelical flank, and more distantly from the Arminian stream of the Reformed tradition, and as an internal or intramural challenge it proved almost irresistible. Thus, to understand Reformed Christianity in the early American Republic, one must grasp the appeal of what became the prototypal evangelical denominations – those that claimed John Wesley as their mentor.

Methodist Origins

*I*n the United States the first half of the nineteenth century was, preeminently, a Methodist half century. A new church as of 1784, the Methodist Episcopal church grew by leaps and bounds after the great revivals at the turn of the new century. Not even the quite varied but largely Calvinist Baptist sects grew as rapidly. By 1850 the by-then divided Methodist denominations led all churches in total membership, while the two more traditional and, as of 1776, largest Reformed confessions – Presbyterian and Congregational – grew much more slowly and gradually faded from the numerical competition, although they retained their leadership in higher education, in organized benevolence, and in serious theology.

The Methodist Episcopal church was the major offspring of colonial Anglicanism. The Methodists organized their episcopal denomination five years before the Episcopalians, were from the beginning larger, and grew much more rapidly. This new and original American denomination recruited its members widely but had greatest appeal in areas that had been predominantly Anglican. It had a much broader appeal than the Protestant Episcopal church among the poor and among African Americans. More than any Calvinist competitors, the Arminian Methodists laid claim to that increasingly loaded label – evangelical. Thus, insight into Methodism, into what John Wesley wrought, is a convenient window into the new meanings American Christians would give to the word *evangelical.*

Evangelical Christianity: Some Definitions

As earlier within Roman Catholicism, the maturing Protestant churches confronted serious, at times almost fanatical, internal revitalization movements. Such were, in a sense, endemic to Christianity. Luther, Zwingli, and Calvin began such efforts within Roman Catholicism, but in this case reform led very quickly to schism and polarization. Within Protestantism, a series of internal reforms, or further efforts to purify state churches, often led to separation, but not quickly. The broadest, and related, labels for such reforms became, in time, Puritanism, pietism, and evangelicalism. By many, but not all, conventional uses, "Puritan" referred to loosely unified reform efforts within the sixteenth- and seventeenth-century English church, "pietism" to seventeenth- and eighteenth-century revitalization movements within the Lutheran churches of continental Europe, and "evangelical" to purification movements largely within eighteenth- and nineteenth-century Anglo-American Protestantism.

Several commonalities linked the three labels. In each case, the early purifiers adhered to their state churches. The varied advocates who gained the label "Puritan" all tried to extend the ongoing reforms in the late-sixteenth-century English church but adhered, in some ways more loyally than anyone else, to the Elizabethan settlement and the Thirty-Nine Articles. The early pietists, beginning with Philipp Jacob Spener, subscribed to the Augsburg Confession and accepted the authority of the Lutheran church but tried to go beyond issues of doctrine and ecclesiology to matters of the heart – to greater love, more charity, a richer devotional life. In the eighteenth century, and particularly in what many in America would call the Great Awakening or in Britain the Wesleyan revival, the ministers and congregations most involved with revivals, and with a more affecting or heart-felt religion, remained within their existing confessions and worked therein to effect changes. They began to lay a special claim to the favored label of the early reformers, "evangelical." In most aspects, they were the pietists of Anglo-America, concerned to revitalize existing churches – Anglican, Scottish Presbyterian, or Congregational.

In each case, these reforms led at first not to new denominations but to parachurch institutions – devotional societies, meditation or prayer groups, and types of lay ministry. Only in time did the reforms lead to separate sects. Out of Puritanism came several dissenting sects in Britain plus a locally dominant Congregationalism in New England. Pietism would spawn a series of sects, with the Moravian church the most important from the American perspective, in part because of its impact on John Wesley and English Methodism. Finally, some of the more evangelical congregations that formed during the eighteenth century revival split from Congregationalism, most as Separate Baptists, and from Anglicanism, most as Methodists. But in America as societies became separate sects, and then as sects slowly gained the institutional strengths and the public acceptance of earlier state churches, these sects in turn spawned their own purification movements and a new spectrum of denominations. The story kept repeating itself, and almost always, the new and more fervent sects outgrew the parent churches.

Neither Puritans, pietists, nor evangelicals ignored doctrine. They could not, for Christianity is a doctrinal religion. It requires correct beliefs as well as the experiences, the rituals, and the moral codes that follow from such beliefs. In time each movement gave birth to new confessions and distinctive beliefs. But in no case was doctrine the original occasion for reform efforts. Rather, it was a perceived failure on the part of the clergy, or laypeople, within the existing churches to live up to the requirements of their own confessions. The churches were, or had become, lax and accommodating. Religion had become conventional and thus shallow and undemanding. By the same token, it had lost its transforming, prophetic edge, even as it no longer bestowed an appropriate joy and fulfillment. Words are never quite adequate to convey this experiential quarrel with established churches, in part because the perceived laxities or compromises varied from one locale to another. The most general demand was always for a more vital Christianity, for a fuller and deeper religion. In later terms, these reformers wanted a total religion, one that shaped all aspects of life. From an outsider's perspective, Puritans, pietists, and evangelicals sought more repressive forms of communal life along with more consoling and fulfilling types of personal religious experience.

This quest for a fuller and deeper religion involved four defining commitments, or what became the operative meaning of "evangelical" by the second half of the eighteenth century. First was an emphasis on the necessity of a crisis-like conversion experience. Second was an effort to attain an affectionate or Spirit-filled devotional life. Third was an accepted responsibility to do all possible to gain converts for such a warm and fulfilling religion. Fourth was a demand for a very lofty moral standard, for personal and social purity or holiness.

This definition still leaves plenty of options for evangelicals and plenty of excuses for internal disagreement and controversy. Evangelicals could be Calvinists or Arminians or some hybrid of the two, adhere faithfully to traditional doctrines or flirt with various heresies, be highly liturgical or choose plain and simple worship, embrace a highly centralized episcopal form of church government or choose radical congregationalism, retreat from the sinful world or prophetically judge the world and try to transform it.

John Wesley and His Doctrines

The mature John Wesley perfectly fit the above definition of an evangelical. Incidental to this status, he was also a moderately High Church Anglican, loyal both to episcopacy and to the English monarchy, a modified Arminian in doctrine, and heretical in his most distinctive doctrine – Christian perfectionism. His Methodist movement was evangelical at its founding. Yet, until his death, the English Methodists were, by Wesley's own desire, just an evangelical supplement to the English church. Thus, in a sense, Methodism became the evangelical wing of Anglicanism.

Wesley's personal biography has been almost as much a subject of scholarly exploration as that of Martin Luther. He was born in 1703 in an Anglican rectory in Epworth, Lincolnshire, England. His devout mother, Susanna, was of dissenting heritage, devout, at one point daringly involved in what amounted to a preaching role in her parish when her husband was away. She was more brilliant and exciting than the father, Samuel, a High Church, always impoverished, but tender and poetic rector. Only after graduation from Oxford did John, along with his younger brother, Charles, become fully caught up in intensive religious concerns. Charles, in fact, took the lead in forming a prayer and fellowship circle at Oxford in 1729, a small group that consisted of only four or five members and that was not unlike the hundreds of other informal devotional groups and societies forming all over Britain. The increasingly serious young men visited sick people and prisoners and even tried to reform prostitutes; they gained a reputation, among more frivolous students, for their puritanical zeal. Eventually the group recruited, among several young men, a youthful George Whitefield, who soon became the most powerful preacher in both England and America. John, older than most of the other men and already ordained in 1725 as a clergyman and a fellow at Oxford, served as mentor to the younger men after the summer of 1729. In 1732, a critic apparently first referred to these very serious and pious young men as "Methodists," a term usually associated with their disciplined devotional life but possibly related to John Wesley's Arminian beliefs (strict Calvinists had earlier used the term to libel the "new" methods of Arminians).[1]

After his father's death in 1735, John rejected an opportunity to succeed him at Epworth. Instead, he and Charles decided to travel to the new colony of Georgia. Onboard ship, in the midst of violent storms, he met a group of ten calm, hymn-singing Moravian missionaries committed, as was he, to a mission among the Indians. This experience changed his life and helped shape the institutions that later became distinctive to Methodism.

In most respects, the Wesley brothers suffered a disastrous eighteen-month interlude in Georgia. Charles proved ill equipped to serve the colony founder, James Oglethorpe, as secretary for Indian affairs, whereas John's moral rigor and High Church style ill served him as a pastor in Savannah. He soon realized the futility of any major mission to nearby Indians. To add to his sense of failure, an aborted courtship and a seemingly retributive denial of communion to the young lady forced John to flee Savannah under threat of arrest. These bitter experiences, plus his growing admiration for the Moravians, helped push his own spiritual pilgrimage toward a climax back in London. There he joined a small Moravian-influenced congregation and would soon take a short pilgrimage to their original settlement at Herrnhut in Saxony. By now he was a convinced evangelical and henceforth preached the necessity of a recognizable rebirth experience. Meanwhile, he struggled with doubts about his own conversion. He could not identify the time of rebirth. An anxiously awaited sense of comfort came in 1738 at a little chapel off Aldersgate Street; this became, in his judgment, his conversion experience, although it was only one of a series of intense religious experiences (later

Holiness and Pentecostal leaders would interpret this as the baptism of the Holy Spirit).

Wesley soon decided to part with the Moravians. He found among them what he considered too many unscriptural practices as well as too much Calvinism. But as he began to form his own religious societies he would adopt almost all the Moravian innovations. Like the Moravians, he founded Methodist societies within the established church, not in opposition to it, and like the Moravian leader Count Nikolaus Zinzendorf, who served as an informal Moravian bishop even though still a Lutheran cleric, Wesley, as an Anglican divine, became in effect the first Methodist bishop. But unlike the Moravians, who generally adhered to the irenic and mild predestinarianism of the Augsburg Confession, Wesley remained consistent with a majority of latter-day High Church Anglicans in affirming a free will position. On this issue he and his good friend and colleague George White-field ultimately divided, with Whitefield's Calvinist disciples eventually forming a small Methodist movement in Wales but eventually slipping into independency in England.

Wesley first dared address an open-air audience before a Newgate hanging. Then, in 1739, Whitefield persuaded Wesley to join him in field preaching in Bristol. Whitefield, just back from his trip to Georgia, thus involved Wesley in a developing revival. For the first time, Wesley confronted agonized crowds who, under deep conviction of sinfulness, swooned on the ground, exhibited various convulsions, or cried out in complete despair. These "physical exercises" would be an occasional outcome of his preaching for the rest of his career, but the greatest fervor occurred in the years around 1740. Although Wesley at first remained in the shadow of Whitefield, he gradually realized that even if he did not have Whitefield's magnificent voice, he did possess a near equal ability to move audiences. Thus in 1739 Wesley began what amounted to the first Methodist itinerancy; for the rest of his life he traveled all over Britain (an estimated 250,000 miles) in extended preaching tours, soon so planned as to allow him to visit, and supervise, a growing number of Methodist societies.

In the sense of my earlier definition, Wesley's Methodist movement was prototypically evangelical. This is true even though he remained an Anglican and quite formal or liturgical in his preferences for Sunday worship. Wesley proudly proclaimed himself an Arminian, although his doctrines differed at essential points from that of the Dutch remonstrants and thus from Arminius and his version of Reformed doctrine. By his proclaimed Arminianism, Wesley wanted to highlight his repudiation of several closely related and distinctive doctrines of self-denominated English Calvinists. This repudiation did not mean that he could not cooperate with Calvinists. On the essentials of conversion, holy living, and evangelical witness, he and such Calvinists as Whitefield were as one, even as both considered themselves good Anglicans (Whitefield much more consistently adhered to the Thirty-Nine Articles). Wesley did not always grasp the subtleties of a now scholastic and often rigid form of Calvinism, and thus he often sparred with caricatures. But he could not believe in the most harsh versions of the doctrine of complete depravity, not in the wake of Jesus' atoning sacrifice.[2]

Wesley's atonement doctrine, and his elusive beliefs about Christian perfection, provided a unique doctrinal stance for early Methodists. In time, aspiring Methodist preachers had to be experts on the atonement. This was the key doctrine that made them distinctive among other evangelicals and thus the major source of intramural doctrinal wrangling among Anglo-American evangelicals. A brief statement cannot do justice to Wesley's conception – the enduring Methodist conception – of the atonement. But it is a key to the whole complex of Methodist doctrines.

In his conception of fallen humanity, Wesley remained one with confessional Calvinists. Adam's sin led to complete depravity. The children of Adam retained no goodness, no ability to respond to God in love. Thus, unlike Arminius, who believed fallen humans retained at least a faint echo of an earlier goodness and reason, Wesley painted their plight in the darkest colors. But he compensated for this by a very un-Calvinist interpretation of the atonement. He believed that Jesus, in his death, fully atoned for Adam's sin and, in effect, made righteous all humans. Since the sin of Adam was imputed to all humans, so the righteousness of the Christ was now imputed to all humans, without condition. He referred to this as a type of general or preventive grace; it made possible salvation but in itself was not sufficient for salvation. Depravity thus lost its sting. Since all people received this general grace, then children were born free of sin. They were ensured of salvation. Infant baptism, which Wesley endorsed, did not remit any original sin but rather served as a pledge by parents to rear their children in righteousness and gave hope for a later rebirth experience.

This conception of a complete atonement moved Wesley very close to the Brethren or true Anabaptists, such as the Mennonites, and led enemies to call him a Pelagian. The prevenient grace of God did not ensure salvation for adults. It erased the curse of Adam but did not atone for willful disobedience. But it gave to all adults the ability, the means, to respond affirmatively to God, to nourish and cultivate the seeds of salvation already present at birth. In one sense, this need to cultivate righteousness was a lifelong responsibility. Yet, Wesley emphasized a special regeneration or rebirth as a necessary step in the life of a Christian. All adults sin, not by any necessity tied to depravity but because of weakness. Thus, adults find themselves in a condition of disobedience, of evil habits and dispositions. They, unlike infants, need a special work of grace (saving grace), one given through the Spirit at the time of regeneration. But even here the saving grace only reinvigorates a seed of salvation gained, vicariously, by Jesus' sacrifice, and although it brings temporary forgiveness and purity and the promise of additional gifts from the Holy Spirit, even the grace of regeneration does not ensure ultimate salvation (Wesley rejected the doctrine of perseverance).

Wesley retained the Calvinist emphasis on salvation as a gift, not as something earned by individuals. Perhaps more than any other theologian, he focused this sense of a gift back on the sacrificial death of Jesus and what he effected by it. The atonement thus became the huge, looming, all-important event for Methodists. Because of this general or complete atonement, all humans, in a sense, moved into the great ark of salvation. The righteousness that they inherited from the atonement was a moral righteousness, one embodied in free choice, in a human ability to cooperate with grace, to improve on it, to grow in righteousness even to perfection, but this righteousness was equally an ability to reject grace, to leap out of the ark of salvation. Given this perspective, salvation remained, always, conditional on the human use of grace, on the degree to which people responded to it, used it, perfected it. This meant, practically, that human salvation depended on obedience and devotion, day by day, year by year. One could be faithful in the church at one time but not necessarily forever. Thus, more than almost any other Protestant theologian, Wesley emphasized the path to sanctification or holiness.

Wesley rejected most implications of the doctrine of predestination, including the idea of a fully arbitrary election. He followed many earlier Arminians in his belief that God did foreknow those who would be saved, because God also knew they were the ones who would be faithful. God chose to save not all humans, not those whom he selected arbitrarily, but those who he knew would improve on the gift of the Christ, would render full obedience and complete love. Thus, salvation is a joint decision of God and humans, although ultimately completely dependent on God. Methodists gladly proclaimed their message of free grace and free will. In order to gain these appealing doctrines, they gladly gave up the most consoling aspect of Calvinism (the perseverance of the saints) and tried to deal with those who experienced regeneration and then fell back into a damning disobedience ("backsliders," in the Methodist idiom). Methodists were concerned not just with bringing the saving word to sinners but with helping wayward brothers and sisters return to the fold. They had the most urgent reasons to attend, daily, to the spiritual welfare of those within the church.

To Wesley's critics, such as Whitefield, these doctrines seemed to mean a return to a gospel of works, to a type of Christian legalism, and to a Catholic rather than a Protestant scheme of salvation. Wesley saw, in the Calvinist alternative, a doctrine of fatalism. Here is not the place to work out the complex, elusive issues that led to such a seeming doctrinal impasse among the two main emerging doctrinal streams in Anglo-American evangelicalism. But it is clear that Wesley indeed struggled to keep good works within the equation of salvation, not as a necessary product or outcome of faith but as an integral, causal part of the scheme of salvation.

Out of his Anglican roots, Wesley retained a concern for constancy and devotion and personal holiness, for a life of service within the church. He saw in Calvinism, perhaps wrongly, a threat to all this. Even his Arminianism meant a mild doctrine of perfection, one similar to that held by Mennonites. One could not remain in the church if one did not turn to God in contrition whenever one sinned, with sin having for Wesley a preeminently moral and not an ontological meaning (it is disobedience rather than the source of such disobedience). The church did not require a blameless life, one immune to temptation or the weaknesses of the flesh, but rather such a consciousness of the demands of holiness that a Christian who temporarily yielded to temptation would be intensely penitent and thus turn to God for a promised forgiveness. In this sense, any Christian was, at any one time, perfect, for if one had unforgiven sins one could not be a Christian, not for the period one remained impenitent. Anyone was subject to damnation who died with unforgiven sins. In a quite literal sense, one's salvation was always at stake. Almost all Christians at least momentarily lapsed from grace, but in such a way as to invite a prayerful and restorative transaction with God. But a pattern of disobedience, without guilt and repentance, literally took one outside the church. In the early Methodist societies, evidence of such an ongoing lapse led to severe discipline by the society, climaxing in expulsion.[3]

Wesley's most distinctive, confusing, and controversial conception of perfection went well beyond such a requirement of penitent restoration after willful misdeeds. He believed that Christians could, through time and constant moral effort and with the help of the Spirit, move from regeneration, and thus the secure promise of salvation for those who remained faithful, to complete holiness or sanctification, to the perfection realized by all Christians at the moment of death or at the resurrection. In his early Methodist movement, Wesley preached a generalized doctrine of perfection, one not clearly tied to any second, conversion-like, or instantaneous experience. After about 1760, when highly experiential attainments of holiness became widespread in his societies (a perfectionist revival), Wesley began to preach the possibilities of such a second step, although he never confessed the attainment of such holiness himself. Although Wesley wrote more about perfection than any of his other doctrines, and came to see it as the most distinctive emphasis within Methodism, his exact position remained elusive, even to his closest friends. He seemed rather frequently to shift his emphasis or slightly to change his conception of holiness. By *holiness* he meant not an absence of human weakness or ignorance, or mistakes based on these, and not even the absence of temptation, but a perfect and complete or even childlike love of God and thus the ability to resist all temptation and avoid sin, in the sense of willful misdeeds. He at times defined Methodist holiness not as an escape from human ignorance or weakness but as a state in which one would not voluntarily transgress any known law of God. The attainment of such holiness need not be uncertain or problematic but could be marked by an intense sense of joy and liberation, by an experience comparable in its emotional intensity to an earlier conversion.

Wesley saw even sanctification as reversible. People could lapse from holiness. At times, he seemed to conclude that most sanctified Christians would at times lapse, meaning that holiness was usually an ephemeral and temporary state. These qualifications raised logical problems, for it seems odd that a person blessed with holiness, with an all-consuming love of God, could somehow fall into disobedience. But he dared not claim the opposite, for this would have meant a form of antinomianism – that one so blessed by the Spirit could by definition do no wrong, however much one seemed to defy human moral codes. The holiness doctrine (the second step or complete sanctification) both confused and inspired early Methodists. It was a source of confusion and doctrinal controversy among Wesley's disciples. Yet, it would give a distinctive flavor to early Methodism in America, even as, by the late nineteenth century, it proved the most divisive doctrine in the church, both because its exact meaning remained unclear and because a growing number of Methodists chose either to ignore it or to repudiate it. The doctrine provided the foundation for a concerted Holiness movement within American Methodism in the mid-nineteenth century and for the separation of Holiness churches by the end of the century. These would, in turn, inspire one wing of the twentieth-century Pentecostal movement.

Methodist Institutions

Institutions, even more than doctrines, distinguished the early Methodist movement. In a sense, the Methodist movement grew up within a church and always owed several characteristics to such a unique origin. As Wesley joined in the great revival, after 1738, he preached not only to a growing body of followers in his two original societies, in London and Bristol, but also to throngs of people who met in open fields wherever he traveled. He rejoiced in the harvest of souls saved, but he worried about their continued nurture. His Arminianism, if anything, heightened his concern about retention, whereas his belief in Christian holiness gave added significance to the type of discipline or methodical growth that should follow conversion. In normal times this nurturing would take place within the parish church. But not then, not in England. Few Anglican bishops, or local rectors, welcomed the new revivals and their perceived excesses. Many openly opposed Wesley or even countenanced mob opposition to him. At the same time, Wesley believed that few established clergymen were born-again Christians, men full of grace, and thus he condemned the lack of evangelical concern in almost all the established churches. Finally, and this was itself an indictment of Anglicanism, the majority of his converts were artisans or wageworkers, people who were already massively deserting the established church. Most did not attend its services. Some had joined dissenting congregations. Wesley condemned all the dissenting groups, as well as Presbyterians, as roundly as he criticized the laxity of his own Anglican church. He never liked rebels, in religion or politics, and never emotionally accepted the extent to which he was a rebel himself. Given these realities, Wesley had no alternative but to create institutions to succor his converts. To do this, he created a uniform, highly centralized spiritual empire in his united Methodist societies.[4]

The established church remained important to Wesley, although at vital junctures he was more willing than his hymn-composing brother, Charles, to undermine that church. Eventually, he kept only the most nominal tie to Anglicanism, although he never admitted any formal break. In theory, but soon not often in practice, Wesley's converts were supposed to remain members of their parish churches. In fact, he admitted into his societies many who were either dissenters or without their own church, an inclusiveness that belied his protestations that his societies were mere supplements to the church. The Methodist societies soon had functional substitutes for many aspects of church life, but except where an ordained minister presided, as in Wesley's London congregation, they never met at times that competed with the normal parish worship service. Wesley also refused, except in a few exceptional cases, to allow any of his lay leaders to administer the sacraments (several defied him on this issue), a function reserved only for ordained clergy. Wesley loved the formal and ordered worship of his church, keyed to the *Book of Common Prayer*. Since he never rejected this, he felt free to go far in the other direction in various organized activities within his societies. That is, informality could replace formality, extemporaneous confessions and prayers could replace written ones, and rousing new hymns could replace the traditional psalms. What he perhaps did not anticipate at first, and later reluctantly accepted, was that for most Methodists the new forms of devotion became sufficient in themselves. What Wesley saw as supplemental to formal worship became a new worship alternative (for a more detailed examination of Methodist worship, see chapter 6). This break from the old church was apparent long before his death, but Wesley still sustained the myth that his societies were no more than devotional supplements to the church. It is clear, by the liturgy that Wesley prepared for the new American Methodist Episcopal church in 1784, that had his societies been full-fledged churches, or had they separated and accepted a dissenting status and thus taken full responsibility for the weekly worship service and for the sacraments, Wesley would have created very different institutions.

The word *society* was in common use for informal, voluntary devotional groups within the English church, but the Moravian precedent most influenced Wesley. A society was, in effect, a Methodist congregation, one originally formed among converts after a successful local preaching tour by either Wesley or one of his more effective lay preachers. The society, if strong, soon contracted rooms for meetings or built a meetinghouse, since almost no prelates would allow society members to use parish churches. The facilities were usually spartan, utilitarian, and not architecturally distinguished (in part a matter of limited funds). Some of these societies were very large, with over one thousand in Wesley's original London society (the Foundry). Yet, membership was as restrictive as in an exclusive club. At first, Wesley closely examined everyone who asked to join and determined if they had an authentic experience of God's grace and if they were willing to live a holy life. He even issued membership cards to admit them, reminding one of later Marxist cells or possibly the communion tokens widely adopted by Scottish Presbyterians. Since the societies were not churches, Wesley could easily adhere to the exclusivity typical of small sects and yet not sacrifice the Anglican idea of a broadly inclusive membership. The societies met, often early on Sunday morning, to sing and pray and hear sermons, in effect moving indoors the outdoor type of preaching services originally begun by Whitefield and Wesley. Unlike the familiar and repetitious elements of church worship, or the sacramental focus of High Church Anglicanism, these society meetings were thoroughly evangelical in the sense that the people gave thanks for their often recent conversion, tried to nourish the disciplined but involving devotional life that promised to keep alive the glow of conversion and lead even to sanctification, and committed themselves, at every meeting, to do all they could to win over the unsaved. In this sense, they duplicated the worship in Moravian churches.

Leadership was critical to Methodism. Like the Jesuits, or the later, Wesley-influenced Salvation Army, Wesley rejected any form of democracy or congregationalism. He opted for centralized control, or a form of monarchy much tighter than in the Anglican church. In effect, as an ordained clergyman, Wesley created a British-wide parish under his direct control (his movement soon spread to both Scotland and Ireland). He felt himself the pastor of every local society and tried, as much as human energy allowed, to keep direct control over all of them and to visit each of them as often as possible. But he could not minister to what quickly became dozens and then hundreds of societies (four hundred by his death). Without any prior planning, a group of laymen, and later a few laywomen, soon took on a leadership role in the new societies, a role related to their effectiveness in exhorting. Wesley, always reluctant to yield power, rather quickly tried to gain control over these local leaders. In 1743 he worked out an elaborate set of rules (the first Methodist Discipline) to govern them. In 1744 he began to meet annually with those he recognized as Methodist preachers, at what became known as the Annual Conference. In effect, these ministers were his servants. Most had common school education, many were able artisans, and a few had some university training. But Wesley chose them because they were called, pious, loyal, and effective. Since he, or the few ordained clergy in his movement, could not supervise all the societies, these unordained lay exhorters became, in effect, the Methodist clergy. Wesley tried to improve their qualifications; he gave them advice at Annual Conferences and recommended they read an unending series of books and tracts that he wrote (over four hundred in his lifetime), some written largely to guide his preachers. He kept tight reins. He screened carefully and dismissed any that lacked the level of piety and zeal and obedience that he demanded. He discouraged marriage among his preachers (he belatedly and unhappily married himself) and expected them to work at a level of near poverty. Although some lay preachers remained with their families and ministered to a local society, these preachers never gained full status under Wesley's system. They did not attend his Annual Conferences. His real preachers were all itinerants. That is, they traveled continuously, some all over Britain in the pattern of Wesley, making them what people would later call evangelists. But the main body of his itinerant ministers served set circuits, moving as infrequently as every two months to widely dispersed societies in the early days of the movement, later serving a more compact and linked group of societies.

The most distinctive Methodist innovations were at the congregational level. Methodists joined Moravians in reviving practices of the primitive church, such as love feasts and watch-night services. Above all Wesley loved the singing of hymns, at a time when the Anglican church did not use hymns in regular worship. Methodists believed in testimonials and in mutual scrutiny and support. The main institutional basis of this became the class meetings, another institution borrowed from the Moravians. After 1742, in each sizable society, Wesley required members to join a class, a mutual support group of about twelve people headed by a leader. These class leaders were not accounted preachers. At first they were scarcely more than stewards, responsible for collecting small offerings. Yet, in time they became the real ministry of Methodism, although only corporals in Wesley's spiritual organization. The class leader gathered the class, often in homes, at least once a week for prayer, Bible reading, personal testimony, discipline, and detailed group attention to any problems or needs of the members. The leader also met with members of his class as often as possible during the week, even in their homes, there teaching them and, in a sense, spying on them. Careful scrutiny preceded admission to a class, and expulsion was prompt for the wayward. In these para-church institutions, from the society down to the class, a functional egalitarianism muted or softened the hierarchical and thoroughly masculine power structure of the English church. Even Wesley, who would never have admitted women to the priesthood, allowed a few very able women to serve as Methodist preachers and, frequently, as class leaders. At the class level, all Christians testified as equals. This meant a level of involvement, and leadership roles, that women enjoyed in no other branch of Christianity except the Quakers and Shakers.

The early Methodists did not join the Moravians in devoting a large share of their resources to foreign missions. They mainly worked to proselytize the unchurched, or the underchurched, in Britain. Again, their quasi-church status, and lack of an ordained clergy, helped defer foreign missions. But at home, up to a third of the preachers spent most of their time in evangelism, and even local congregations tried to minister to those outside the societies. This involved more than soul winning. From the time he was mentor of the young men at Oxford, Wesley was service oriented. The Methodist societies joined Quakers in ministering to prisons and workhouses and did as much as possible to ameliorate terrible social injustices in Britain. Particularly for their own poorest converts, the classes collected alms, thus redistributing their often meager wealth. In hard winters some societies established their own workshops, where women could earn enough to buy needed food and fuel. Implicit in much Methodist preaching was an intense antipathy to wealth and finery, as well as to all the diversions of the world (theater, horse racing, games of chance, dancing, drunkenness). In this sense, at least, Methodism was a class-conscious movement, although Wesley remained very much a Tory in his personal politics.

Methodism in America

Although Methodist preachers spread the movement to Ireland, they made no particular effort to expand Methodism to the American colonies. Whitefield provided a continuous link between the great revivals in America and Britain, even as he helped rally a small, evangelical faction in colonial Anglicanism. But less than a dozen Anglican ministers took an active role in the revivals, while a majority condemned them. The benefits of revival accrued largely to evangelical factions in Presbyterianism and Congregationalism and to separating Baptist congregations. Notably, in Virginia, those Anglicans most taken by Whitefield, and most influenced by the revivals, separated from their parish churches and eventually joined with the Presbyterians. Even in the late 1740s they seemed totally unaware of the new Methodist movement in Britain. Yet, by 1760 several members of Methodist societies had emigrated to America. By 1765 or before, a Methodist preacher, Robert Strawbridge, formed a Methodist society in Maryland and even built a meetinghouse. Strawbridge scarcely yielded authority to a distant Wesley and violated Methodist rules by administering the sacraments. Within the next few years Methodist laypeople organized societies in New York, Pennsylvania, and Virginia. Apparently for the first time, a society member in New York City wrote Wesley in 1768, begging him to send experienced leaders to the new world.[5]

In 1769 Wesley responded by sending his first two missionaries to America. This marked the surprisingly belated opening of a Methodist mission in the colonies. Subsequent pairs of missionaries followed (Francis Asbury came in 1771), with the first conference of ten Methodist preachers held in 1773, on almost the eve of the Revolution. Wesley's motives in sending over his own men included keeping the movement under his control, keeping its practices in line with those in England, and keeping it within the Anglican church. Thus, no early American Methodist preacher could, by Wesley's rules, even marry couples. Yet, only a rare established clergyman aided the early Methodists, and only in Virginia did a notoriously Low Church or evangelical Anglican minister, Devereux Jarratt, actively cooperate with the Methodists, helping trigger the only extensive Methodist revival before the War for Independence. By 1773 the isolated societies reported a total membership of only 1,160. Because of spectacular revival successes in Virginia and North Carolina, this number ballooned to 8,673 by 1779. By 1784, the total doubled to approximately 15,000, and by then 83 lay preachers ministered to societies in 36 organized circuits (the Methodists in America had at least a third as many circuits as Wesley had back in England). By then the preachers were in a sense orphaned, with none ordained, none legally enabled to administer the sacraments, and almost none able to appeal to sympathetic Anglican clergymen. Even those Anglican ministers who had remained in America during the war had an unclear legal status at war's end.

In one sense, the Revolution aided Methodist growth. With so many Anglican parishes in disarray or without clergy, American-born Methodist lay preachers filled the vacuum. The tightly knit societies, and the circuit system, provided most of the benefits of organized religion to people who would otherwise have had no church connection at all. But in other ways the war impeded growth. Wesley spoke out strongly against the colonial cause, and all recently arrived Methodist missionaries, except for Francis Asbury, left the colonies. American patriots early identified Methodists with royalist sentiments and subjected their ministers to harsh loyalty oaths. The pacifist sentiment of several ministers also invited charges of treason. Yet, the number of societies expanded. In 1779 they divided into two geographically based conferences. Such growth made clearer the anomalous status of the societies in America. Could they remain under the direct control of a distant Wesley, and why should not their ministers, in a new republican America, assume the role of an ordained clergy? In fact, a few ministers openly rebelled against the system, organized a presbytery, and ordained themselves. A much larger number defied Wesley by administering the ordinances of the church to their members, who had no possible access to ordained clergymen.

By war's end, Francis Asbury was the recognized but beleaguered leader of Methodism in America. A nonordained bishop, he loyally tried to follow all of Wesley's commands. Thus, without complete success, he tried to discipline his ministers and, in particular, prevent them from administering the sacraments. Asbury, and by implication Wesley, faced very difficult choices. They had to bend in some way to the impervious demands of both ministers and laypeople, demands for a proper church with its own ministers and sacraments. Many also wanted a church that was more democratic and less centralized than the one controlled by Wesley. In effect, Wesley so responded to the American demands as to keep a centralized or episcopal church, but to gain this goal he had to compromise his earlier commitments and create an autonomous American church – the first Methodist church in the world and the first independent episcopal church in the United States.

The Methodist Episcopal Church

Wesley agonized about his orphaned American brethren for years. To the despair of his brother Charles, he decided on a radical course, one quite inconsistent with his former convictions. Assuming for himself the authority normally held only by bishops in the Anglican church, he ordained two of his own preachers as the first Methodist clergymen in the world, although the ordination was to be effective only in America. To justify his seeming usurpation of ecclesiastical authority, he in effect adopted the ecclesiastical position of Scottish Presbyterians, as well as most churches in the Lutheran and Reformed traditions, and denied any scriptural authority for the episcopal hierarchy as it existed in England.

The Reformation had reopened issues of polity and clerical authority. The early Roman churches soon adopted a hierarchical priesthood, and a very paternal one. This entailed three orders – deacons, elders or priests, and bishops. The word *order* is important, for it denotes the origin of the authority – in a special ordination of individuals who qualified for ascending levels of authority in the church. A person normally would receive ordination first as a deacon and then as a priest and then finally a special consecration as a bishop. In time the Roman church raised the ceremony of investment or ordination to the level of a sacrament. In this episcopal system, the order of bishops was apart from and above that of elders. The bishops had the special authority over congregations that was exercised by the early apostles. The major reformers rejected this three-ordered pattern and usually reduced it to two, deacons and elders. Luther and Calvin kept an ordained clergy but recognized no special order of bishops. This does not mean that Protestant churches did not use the title "bishop." Many did. Scottish Presbyterians used the title interchangeably with "teaching elder" or "Presbyter" and at ordination gave the title to all their clergy. In other Protestant churches or sects the title came to refer to special administrative or supervisory duties, those carried out by ordained clergymen. The major exception to this two-order system among Protestants was the English church, which retained an episcopacy similar to that of Roman Catholicism. This was Wesley's heritage, which he loved.

Wesley now acknowledged, all too conveniently according to his critics, that the primitive church had only two orders. This meant that the early bishops had a special administrative role, not a special or higher status. By implication, this was true of bishops in England, but Wesley did not push this conclusion. His object was to prove that the power to ordain lay, necessarily and originally, in the presbyters of the church and not exclusively in an order of bishops, although if a church had bishops (higher administrators), good order suggested that they properly ordain all priests, as in England. But American ministers had no bishops. They had never had a resident bishop, and now the Revolution had destroyed all their ties to the Church of England. English bishops had their authority from the king, who was head of the church, but he could have no authority over American ministers. This is what Wesley meant when he spoke of his poor ecclesiastical orphans in America. How could he give them the spiritual fathers they so deeply craved? If English bishops had been willing (they were not), and had the American preachers had the required educational requirements (they did not), Wesley could have persuaded Anglican bishops to ordain his priests in America. In the absence of this, all he could do was ordain them himself, thus creating a Methodist church to replace the Methodist societies.

As a presbyter with special administrative authority over the Methodist societies in America, Wesley now conceived of himself as their bishop. These societies had, by default, become functioning churches. He explained all of these legal technicalities in a letter to his preachers in America. In England, in September 1784, he and a clerical colleague, secretary, and perhaps aspiring heir apparent, Thomas Coke, ordained the first two Methodist preachers – on one day as deacons, on the next as elders – but only for the American Methodist church. He then sent them, along with Coke, to the United States, where they would meet their American brethren at the famous Christmas Conference of 1784, which founded the Methodist Episcopal church. But, ecclesiastically, this church began with this first ordination. Since in England only bishops ordained presbyters, the two men remained lay preachers whenever in England. Subsequently, Wesley also ordained

Methodist clergy in Scotland, where there was no episcopacy, but he then condemned one of these elders who baptized while in England (he was an elder in Scotland, merely a lay preacher when he crossed the border).

In his final innovation, Wesley performed a ceremony fraught with ambiguity. In the episcopal system, bishops received their appointment from the church head: the bishop of Rome for Catholics, the king of England for Anglicans. Wesley, in a sense, now claimed this office for the new American church but dared not go so far as to appoint or ordain a bishop for America. Thus, according to his new scriptural understanding, he chose to create what technically would be a nonepiscopal church for America. Wesley appealed to a providential calling and "set apart" Coke to be a "superintendent" of the new church. He did not even invite his subsequently horrified brother Charles to the ceremony. Except in title, he scrupulously followed a traditional ordination ceremony, including the laying on of hands. He did not "consecrate" Coke, did not denominate him a "bishop," and he made clear that he wanted the American church to use the title "superintendent," not "bishop," as a further certification that what he created was an administrative office, not a higher clerical order.

Coke and his two ordained companions, Thomas Vesey and Richard Whatcoat, carried out their assigned tasks in America. What is unclear is at what point in the Atlantic Ocean Vesey and Whatcoat moved up from lay preachers to ordained elders, and when Coke rose from elder to "superintendent." Even before the Baltimore conference, called for December 24 by the overjoyed preachers in America, Whatcoat assisted Coke in communion services, the first authorized administration of a sacrament by any Methodist preacher who did not have Anglican ordination. Coke also shared with his American brethren Wesley's letter, which explained what would happen in Baltimore, and presented them with a package of documents carefully prepared by a now eighty-one-year-old Wesley. Wesley carefully abridged the Thirty-Nine Articles of the English church, eliminating not only those that referred to the king but also those with the most clearly Calvinist doctrines. Instead of endorsing the *Book of Common Prayer* as a guide to worship, he sent along a derivative but simplified order of worship or liturgy. The Americans already had the final document, a recently revised *Book of Discipline and Polity* to guide ministers. Of the documents, this one proved most useful. In time the order of worship would help stimulate a liturgical revival among some Methodists, but it was largely ignored in the early church. Much more than Wesley realized, the existing American societies had functioned as full churches, despite the absence of the sacraments, and the more informal worship of the societies (hymns, prayers, preaching) long remained the norm in American churches. In other words, Wesley's attempt to engraft a formal church style on the societies did not take. The Articles, with slight emendations, remained the formal

Confession of the church, but the new church was never very confessional in its posture, and the Articles, broad and general in content, no more served as a creed or test of membership than did the Thirty-Nine Articles back in the English church. Subsequently, the writings of Wesley served more often as a doctrinal guideline.

At the Baltimore conference, approximately sixty, mostly young American preachers formed the new church. Coke, assisted by Whatcoat and Vesey and apparently one neighboring German Reformed minister, ordained a few of the young men as deacons (a first step toward becoming an elder or priest), while others continued on trial as apprentices. More critical, Coke ordained twelve or thirteen as elders, the original ordained clergy of the church. On three successive days, and by the intent of Wesley, Coke ordained Asbury first as deacon, then as elder, then as assistant superintendent. Asbury would not accept this ordination until his ministers had elected him for the position. By insisting on such a clerical election, Asbury placed the final authority of the new church in the General Conference, not directly in the bishops. This strategy foiled the intent of Wesley – to retain the appointing role for himself and thus to keep the American church closely under the control of the English movement. Neither in 1784 nor later did the American church adhere to Wesley's ecclesiastical scruples. They named their new church the Methodist Episcopal church, and in organization they fully conformed to an episcopal, not a republican, model. Against Wesley's recommendations and then his outright orders, both Coke and Asbury soon used the title of bishop, and Coke, by his own understanding, ordained Asbury rather than "set him apart." The church would continue the three orders of the Roman church, whatever the American clergy believed about the pattern in the primitive church (such issues seemed unimportant in America).

With great joy, the preachers returned home. In one sense, not much had changed. They largely ignored the liturgy and the Articles. They could now marry couples, baptize infants, and celebrate communion, though this would not be the weekly communion that Wesley had recommended. These more formal and sacramental aspects of church life, which had not been a part of the earlier societies, had less significance in Methodism than in the competing Reformed churches. Baptists certainly elevated baptism to a more critical position, whereas the Presbyterians were most distinctive for their extended summer communions. But the relative unimportance of liturgy and ordinances meant that, in worship as in other aspects of church life, the new evangelical motifs could completely dominate early American Methodism. From the founding, the central emphasis of Methodists would be on regeneration, on attained holiness or spirituality, and on effective revival techniques.

Asbury did almost as much to shape the American church as had Wesley in shaping the English societies. He became the dominant bishop even before Coke decided to spend much of his time back in England or in mission work. Asbury chose a tightly centralized governance for a rapidly expanding church. From 15,000 in 1784, the new church expanded to a recorded 57,631 (each preacher had to render full statistical reports to Asbury) in 1790 and, in the midst of the great revivals, to about 120,000 in 1805, or more members than back in Britain. For America such explosive growth was unprecedented. The organization helped. Locally, nothing much changed. The congregation long remained a "society" by name, and it met in a "meetinghouse." The foundation of the local society was the class system, with both lay leaders for the classes and lay exhorters or preachers for the whole congregation. Some local lay preachers would eventually seek ordination, but not without serious thought and almost monastic zeal. As lay preachers, they had only the congregation to please. But by that very fact they had no power, no right even to be delegates to governing conferences of the church. Even ordained ministers who gave up their itinerancy became second-class ministers, without membership or votes in annual conferences, all of which highlights the special polity, and clergy, that made Methodism so distinct in America.[6]

Even before the founding conference, Methodist ministers met in annual conferences. These continued, with new conferences added almost annually in periods of greatest growth. After Baltimore, the whole church met again in 1785, in what then became only a quadrennial general conference. Only bishops and ordained ministers could serve as official delegates to these general conferences, which, above all else, elected bishops. Laypeople had no formal role in Methodist church government at any level. In the early years, Asbury or his associate bishops presided, if at all possible, over all general and annual conferences. In time the borders of annual conferences coincided with those of a state, or a division of a state, and thus roughly paralleled a diocese or synod in other polities. At the annual conferences, the ministers rendered their reports and received their preaching assignments. All ordained ministers in good standing were itinerants, as was Asbury, who for thirty years spent almost all his time traveling the roads and trails of the new Republic.

"Itinerant" gained a special meaning in Methodism. It meant a minister on the move. Given the scattered rural pattern of population in America, the societies, except in three or four cities, were widely dispersed. Thus, each of the limited number of ministers had to serve several, mostly small societies (or stations), traveling on set schedules to each one and often meeting each one less than monthly. The number of ministers remained inadequate for the task, not because of a lack of education (the church required no formal training and roundly condemned seminaries) but because of the enormous commitment of time and energy required of any of Asbury's preachers. Unmarried himself, he so opposed marriage among his preachers that few risked his condemnation; if they did marry, their families suffered deprivation and often abject poverty while a largely absent father rode circuit or to distant conferences. This was a ministry that spent most of its time not in the study but on horseback. If a preacher could not afford a horse, he walked. The itinerants also moved as often as every three months from one circuit to another. Asbury believed in frequent rotations.

Methodist itinerants never served the full role of pastors or ministers. They still had the one old Wesleyan assignment – to save souls. An ordained minister also married, baptized, and buried his ever-changing flock, as well as preached powerful sermons. Itinerancy and rotation had one benefit for the busy ministers. Three or four carefully developed, tested, or memorized sermons could serve as their only repertoire for years, for they might never preach more often than that at any one station. After presenting their prepared sermons, they could always move on to completely impromptu exhortation (preaching "at liberty" or as the Spirit moved, a practice followed by Wesley). But the continuous rotation, often to new circuits hundreds of miles from their homes, if they had any stationary homes, meant that itinerants could not establish a lasting pastoral relationship with their flock. This was not their role. Also, they had no time to develop a local following or to engender factions or divisions. This was intentional. It left the ministerial function (most preaching, Bible training, visitation, counseling, and the discipline of members) to laypeople, to class leaders and lay preachers or the growing number of "settled" and thus stigmatized ministers.

At a more local level, Methodists formed districts (within annual conferences and comparable to presbyteries) and circuits. Because Asbury alone could not supervise the whole church, at least not after the great revivals, and because even well into the nineteenth century the church seemed reluctant to have more than three or four bishops at a time, the more detailed training and supervision of ministers soon devolved on an ordained minister who had supervisory but not assigning authority in each district, a position originally referred to as "ruling elder" and later as "district superintendent." Until Methodists were willing to establish seminaries, and this was for many conferences long after the Civil War, the district superintendent had to assume responsibility for whatever formal literary and biblical instruction the church offered its candidates for the ministry. In sparsely settled areas the district might be as large, geographically, as more compact conferences, and in these cases Asbury, or later bishops, tried to meet with district conferences that roughly paralleled annual conferences.

At the bottom of the hierarchy were the circuits. These were the "counties" in Methodism, the lowest unit of government and, to many, the jewel of the whole Methodist system. As ministers were able to form new congregations, the annual conferences kept creating new circuits. The circuit was a linked group of congregations, in as compact a geographic area as possible, served by one or more ministers. In much of America, including all early circuits west of the mountains, one harried minister had to serve a whole circuit, or up to as many as ten congregations. But, in time, at least a young minister on trial would help with the work in larger circuits. The ministers in a circuit set up schedules of travel and thus preached two or three times each week at set stations, with some time left over for other ministerial duties in more compact circuits. Usually, all the congregations in a circuit met together in quarterly conferences, attended not only by their own minister (or ministers) but also, if possible, by the district superintendent, by ministers from nearby circuits, and often by invited Baptist and Presbyterian ministers. For laypeople, who could not afford to travel as observers to distant annual conferences, and there hear sermons by their bishop, a quarterly conference could be the highlight of their church year. These conferences often involved fervent revival-type preaching by rotating ministers, much personal evangelism, plenty of swooning and shouting, and great hymn-singing, all of which climaxed in a communion service. After 1801, these conferences joined with, or consolidated into, the Methodist camp meetings, another institution more eagerly embraced by Methodists, and more carefully structured for evangelical purposes, than in any other denomination. By 1810 most circuits had their own developed campgrounds, with tents or cabins, and there scheduled one or more encampments or retreats each summer.

American Methodists took the lead in camping. Back in Britain, this institution remained marginal. After Wesley's death in 1791, his British congregations soon dropped all pretense of being part of the Anglican church. Most followed a liturgy comparable to the one Wesley had prepared for his American church. As a whole, British Methodism continued to be more formal in worship, even as its membership (artisans and wageworkers) remained more class-based than in America. After the great revivals of 1800–1801 in America, and the rapid spread of the new camp meetings, an amazing product of American Methodism, Lorenzo Dow, took the forms of preaching, the revival hymns, and the camping of American Methodism to England, where they had broad appeal. One of his disciples, expelled from the English Methodist church because of camp meetings and undignified singing, formed in 1808 the Primitive Methodist church. It alone conducted summers camps in Britain. In time, a few of its members migrated to America, creating one of the smallest Methodist bodies in America.

In America the new Methodist Episcopal church was not unique in its evangelical commitments. Most closely related were two originally small, Pennsylvania-based, German-speaking, but thoroughly Wesleyan denominations (Philip Otterbein's United Brethren and Jacob Albright's Evangelical Association). They shared all Methodist doctrines and institutions. Briefly, in the 1790s, a schismatic group (the Republican Methodists) led by a Methodist minister, James O'Kelly, repudiated the tight centralized control by Asbury and tried, without enduring success, to introduce representative institutions into the Methodist conferences (later achieved by an enduring Protestant Methodist church). Beyond this, plenty of Baptist, Presbyterian, and Congregational congregations, and a sprinkling of German and Dutch Reformed, Lutheran, and even Episcopalian groups, qualified fully as evangelicals. What remained distinctive about the Methodists was that they in all their institutions reflected so fully and completely an evangelical style. In the more traditional and Calvinist denominations, the evangelicals always faced internal opposition.

The Methodist Style

All the details in the world about Methodist beliefs and institutions still leave out the heart of the issue. What was it like to join a Methodist society in 1800? What was the inner texture of church life that so appealed to people? What was unique in Methodist religious culture? One common, but still largely external, approach to these questions is to ask what class of people became Methodists, and why. The fluidity of class lines in America, compared with Britain, makes an answer more difficult. In Britain, Wesley clearly appealed, most powerfully, to nonelites and often to people near the bottom of the social and economic hierarchy. He attracted a few wealthy and socially prominent disciples, mostly women, but even here one senses strong maternal motives, a desire to join a movement that could aid, reform, or redeem the underclasses. In America the Methodist movement appealed across a larger spectrum, with regional variations. Like all religious entrants into America, the early Methodists had to find their audience. Rarely did the Methodists try to invade, or directly convert, well-established Congregational, Presbyterian, or Baptist families. Instead, they cooperated in evangelical efforts but at the same time argued issues of doctrine and practice. The competition could be verbally sharp, but salvation was not at stake, and the Methodists had no reason to invade such misdirected but tolerant neighbors. Methodism had limited appeal in these confessions, at least until the pluralistic mixing west of the mountains invited movement back and forth among the denominations, either because of conviction, marriage, or convenience. Thus, the large clusters of Scotch-Irish settlers remained largely Presbyterian, and most New England Congregationalists stayed home, spiritually, even when they moved to Ohio.[7]

The original, well-targeted constituency for Methodism were those people, up to half the population, who did not fit comfortably within the older churches. This potential constituency resided in all the states, but by far the greatest numbers lived in the areas formerly dominated or, in parts of the South, even monopolized by the English church. This constituency also included a scattering of unchurched people, often low in the economic order, who did not fit in the by-now intellectualized and even fashionable Congregational churches, or the few Presbyterian congregations, in New England. Here, as elsewhere, the Methodist missionaries had to proselytize among the outsiders, as in near-frontier Maine, or among those whom even Asbury at times admitted the other churches had not particularly wanted – people less educated, less affluent, or more flagrantly immoral or slovenly. From New York south, excluding much of Pennsylvania, the Methodists confronted a large population of people, either English or African in origin, who never felt at home in the existing churches – indentured servants, tenants or farm laborers, some reasonably secure yeomen who simply liked their religion hot, and above all slaves. Many had been tempted toward an evangelical religion in the mid-eighteenth-century revivals but had never had any denominational option until the Methodists came. By 1800, about 20 percent of all Methodists were black, and in parts of the South the percentage rose to 50 percent. Its highest rate of growth would be from Maryland south, with notable strength west of the mountains. In the West it appealed more broadly across class lines, not because of some elusive frontier (no church could establish itself at the very edge of settlement) but because of the promiscuous patterns of settlement. Ethnic lines blurred more often than in the earlier seaport settlements, and the confusing mix presented opportunities for any sect able to take advantage of the flux and the resulting religious estrangement or alienation. The Methodists had zealous missionaries, and almost ideal institutions, to exploit this opportunity. Its circuit system multiplied the reach of its clergy, and its fervent evangelical style seemed to meet the needs of the largest share of the population. Here their converts cut across varied ethnic backgrounds. Even Scotch-Irish settlers, ill served by Presbyterianism, converted to Methodism, which also appealed widely across economic classes. That is, some Methodists in Kentucky and Tennessee became part of the local gentry, not in the same proportion as did Presbyterians but at least as often as among the Baptists.

Two images fit early-nineteenth-century Methodists. One is of utterly serious, censorious, abstemious, puritanical folk, bound by "thou shalt nots" and served by almost illiterate, often ranting ministers. The other image is of joyful folk, given to a warm religious style, plenty of zestful gospel hymns, and much shouting, along with testimonies and love feasts and well-ordered camp meetings. Of course, both images fit, at least to some extent. They even complement each other. Good Methodists were indeed serious folk. They took religion seriously. And they were censorious, at times to the point of a repressive legalism. Good Methodists had to eschew the world, its temptations and its pleasures. Every "civilized" amusement drew their condemnation, and their life could seem bereft of both beauty and intellectual culture. They had to dress plainly, live abstemiously, read only the Bible or devotional literature, eschew the theater or horse racing. Of course, the obverse of such moral rigor was an unusual concern, unmatched by any other sect except the Quakers, for the poor and disabled, an early and unambiguous denunciation of slavery (in 1784 the new church denied membership to slave owners, a position it soon modified), the earliest and strongest commitment to temperance, and a rather widespread antiwar or pacifist conviction at least among its ministers.

Even as they forbade worldly pleasures, or artificial stimulants and intoxicants, the Methodists aspired to nothing less than holiness. They tried to gain a perfect love of God, with the peace and joy and serenity this entailed. They advocated a hot religion, hotter than in any other major denomination in the early nineteenth century. The level of feeling, or affection, or emotional intensity, was high in almost all their services. Every meeting was, in a sense, a revival meeting. Weeping, shouting, and swooning was a normal part of the tortured road toward conversion, joined by a type of religious happiness, a glow that could erupt in almost ecstatic shouting in normal worship services and not just at camp meetings. Added to this intensity was the challenge, and the promise of holiness, of the second step. By 1800, Methodist itinerants, in their annual reports to Asbury, carefully compiled statistics on the number who experienced sanctification, along with the number who became new converts. All aspects of modern Holiness churches and much of modern Pentecostalism were present in early Methodism.

No other American denomination was so well situated to exploit the wave of revivals that swept most of America from 1800 to 1805. The Methodists were, in a sense, always working for a revival. They had already accommodated, in some sense even adopted and ordered, a range of physical exercises (cries, shouts, various convulsive motions, and falling and fainting). The most famous and most boisterous of the great revivals occurred at Presbyterian communions, such as those in central Kentucky. The Methodists, as yet, had not developed an institution so adapted to four- and five-day, intercongregational meetings as the traditional Scottish communions. But they joined in these Presbyterian revivals as well as organized smaller revivals of their own. Then, as Presbyterians, and some Baptists, split into warring factions, not strictly over revivals (no one opposed them) but over the permissible limits for physical exercises, or the role of ministers in inciting or moderating such exercises, or over the Arminian doctrines that seemed to sprout in the midst of all the emotional excesses, the Methodists, who found nothing unusual in most of the exercises and who were already professed Arminians, simply moved in and captured the largest share of converts. This happened in the trans-Appalachian West and in much of the older South. The Methodists, in almost all the West and the South, moved in one decade from the third-largest denomination (behind the Presbyterians and Baptists) to the largest. They also were first to appreciate the full potential of the camp meeting, and made it largely a Methodist institution, particularly in the Northeast.

Success soon posed dilemmas. It always does, but most of all among evangelical Christians. Preserving a religion that is pure, full, and deep, and at the same time one that is expanding, prosperous, and respectable, is not easy. Implicit in Christianity, and not just in its evangelical form, is an always impossible challenge – to love a god totally, to obey him (or her or it) always. Maybe no one, ever, rises to such a challenge. Maybe it is impossible. And perhaps no one, over a long period of time, can remain close to this goal, in the sense that one feels close to it. No doubt, evangelical Christians felt closest at times of conversion or, if they joined Wesley in affirming the holiness doctrine, at the moment when they felt themselves sanctified. But in the months and years that stretched beyond such climactic and intense moments, could they retain the love and the self-complacency? As a confirmed fact, most could not. Every great revival was followed by a later declension. By admitting the possibility of backsliding, Methodists at least explained the declension and were able to develop institutions to cope with it. From the class meetings to the love feasts and watch-night services, to worship on Sunday, to their glorious conferences, to the almost obligatory summer retreat or camp, they enjoyed continuous group support, which helped them to live, at least outwardly, the type of Christian life that was consistent with love and obedience. Other denominations had comparable supports, ranging from the traditional Catholic celebration of the Eucharist to the washing of feet among Brethren or Moravians, to the public baptisms by Baptists, and to the healing, holy dancing, and speaking in tongues among Shakers, but in no confession were these ever sufficient, and thus the continued complaint of all Christians has been the very personal sense of declension.

The Methodists soon compromised. They first compromised moral purity by a series of incremental accommodations to slavery and then eventually split North and South because of that institution. By Asbury's death in 1816, the rigors of itinerancy had led to mounting, and soon successful, demands for a more settled ministry. Gradually, the class system declined or gave way to a pale substitute in organized Sunday schools. The great camps easily moved from converting institutions to prosperous resorts for those seeking a vacation, with only a thin religious or educational justification.

As Methodists prospered, serious Methodists, dutiful and abstemious, could hardly avoid worldly success (unless they were blacks). They then compromised more and more with the world. By mid-century their ministers divided, and argued, over such amusements as the theater or card games. In time the "liberals" seemed always to win out. Women and men donned fashionable dress. From the beginning, American Methodists embraced education and established both academies and a scattering of denominational colleges, although they remained far behind the Presbyterians. These establishments posed no clear threat to piety, yet even before the Civil War, Methodists hotly debated the next step – seminaries for their ministers, not to dispense with a called ministry but to serve it. And the "liberals" won in time, although the Methodists never developed as prestigious seminaries, or produced as many serious theologians, as their Calvinist competitors. They had a late start. Closely connected with a better-trained clergy, the doctrine of holiness began to lapse in the larger, more fashionable churches until, once again by the Civil War period, Methodists fought divisive battles over this issue. And, in the denomination, the nonholiness factions eventually won. But along the way, such liberalizing trends spawned schisms, even as later mergers would spawn recalcitrant holdouts. Both the Wesleyan and the Free Methodist churches separated, in part, because of compromises on slavery, whereas a Protestant Methodist church rejected a tightly centralized polity. By the end of the nineteenth century, the holiness faction was in open revolt and soon splintered off into several denominations.

More critical than such outward signs of progress, and accommodation, were the internal shifts. Evangelical Christianity offered a redemptive promise – both in the quality of experience and joy in this life and in a life after death. The promise depended on a rejection of all the competing lures, and temptations, of a non-Christian society and thus of a syndrome of alternative values. The Wesleyan movement reflected an indictment of an established church that, to a large extent, had joined that world. In it one gained salvation too easily, and too gradually, without a terrible, frightening confrontation with one's own selfish and rebellious nature. By infant baptism, by instruction in church doctrine, and by a routine confession at confirmation, one moved easily, without any personal crisis or authentic conversion, into a comfortable church, which, instead of offering the challenge and the hard discipline and the spiritual support that led one toward holiness, provided benevolent moral guidance, offered a cheap cosmic insurance policy (really a false sense of security), and generally sanctified the secular pursuits that occupied most of one's time and concern. The church had joined and generally blessed the world. It made few demands. Everything was too easy, God too obliging. The conventional rituals, the traditional forms, the beautiful sanctuaries, the refined music, and the polished and literate sermons all stood as evidence of a captive, not a prophetic or redemptive, church. Such fashionable churches easily became an adjunct of established society, a consolation to those with wealth, power, and social preeminence. The church became respectable, even fashionable, so much so as effectively to be closed to the meek and the poor, to society's losers and outcasts, and to those who were lowly in spirit and who knew themselves to be sinners. In its beginnings, Wesley's movement was a counter to all this. He preached a full and deep religion that could never be at ease in the world. Thus, Methodism could measure its decline by the extent that it won acceptance by the larger society.

CHAPTER 3

Theological Foundations

Samuel Hopkins, long-time minister at Newport, Rhode Island, and America's most famous living theologian in 1800, survived to welcome the nineteenth century. He was eighty years old in 1801, infirm from a recent stroke and in many senses a living anachronism. Shaped by the revivals of the 1740s, a close friend and former student of Jonathan Edwards, he lived long enough to greet a new wave of revivals that climaxed just before his death in 1803. But Hopkins, a rigid, honest, realistic Calvinist, found little to console him even in reports from the new revivals. In a farewell sermon, probably presented to his elderly, dwindling congregation at Newport, Rhode Island, in 1801, he noted an "apparent" revival of religion among the few authentic Calvinists left in America but argued that it had not touched the majority of people, those corrupt either in religious principles or in practice. Apart from the revivals, worldliness and selfishness prevailed generally, while the great moral curse of America, slavery, made a lie out of all national ideals and lay, like an overwhelming burden of guilt, on Newport, which had based its prosperity largely on the slave trade, on the blood and sufferings of poor Africans, in violation of every law of God and man.

Hopkins had tried to stop the erosion of an older and purer faith. In the darkest days of the previous decade, in 1793, when either religious rationalism or religious disinterest had seemed all but to extinguish evangelical Christianity in America, Hopkins had published the first formal, systematic theology produced in America, the two-volume *System of Doctrines Contained in Divine Revelation.* Greeted even if rarely read by serious evangelicals, this publication ran directly counter to the dominant intellectual trends of this rationalistic decade. Even before this publication, Hopkins had become famous, not for his theological contributions but for his impossibly strict, narrow, dogmatic, and cruel version of Calvinism, that "one-hoss shay" later ridiculed by Oliver Wendell Holmes. Yet, when he died, almost everyone acknowledged that he was the most worthy successor of Jonathan Edwards, the elder spokesman for a cluster of approximately one hundred Congregational and Presbyterian ministers who continued to espouse Edwardian principles. These ministers represented the only reasonably coherent theological movement yet born in America and thus the first distinctive theological contribution of the dominant Reformed confessions in America. Appropriately, when Hopkins was much younger, an older Calvinist critic of some of his polemical essays had dubbed his theology the "New Divinity." The name stuck.

Hopkins was not clearly more able than some of his closest allies, such as Joseph Bellamy or Nathaniel Emmons, but he was the first to write a systematic apology for the second-generation Edwardians. It was his system, much more than the writings of other New Divinity advocates, that came to symbolize what seemed, to many liberal Congregationalists, a near caricature of an impossibly strict older Calvinism, whereas to strongly confessional Presbyterians or Dutch Reformed ministers it seemed a horrible example of a corrupted and humanized Calvinism. To a few German Reformed theologians at Mercersburg, Pennsylvania, it seemed to offer philosophical support for the highly individualistic, nonconfessional, nonchurchly, and nonsacramental heresies that had always characterized Puritanism. Thus, Hopkinsianism became a constant reference in doctrinal and theological debate for at least four decades, the first theological system in America to have so much direct impact on factional controversies in avowedly Calvinist denominations.[1]

In his theological writings, Hopkins tried to develop a persuasive apology for a received doctrinal tradition. He increasingly called this tradition Calvinism and believed the Westminster Confession a worthy summary of its main tenets. But his version of Calvinism derived from New England Puritanism and, more particularly, from the work of his theological mentor, Jonathan Edwards. In 1800 Hopkins remained the greatest living symbol of Edwardian Christianity in America. But to so identify him, as well as to understand the unique themes of the New Divinity, one must wrestle with the intimidating theological and philosophical achievements of Jonathan Edwards. Edwards held such a commanding position for two reasons – his brilliance as a Christian apologist, and the fact that four or five of his immediate disciples, including Hopkins, were able to take the lead in, even almost monopolize, the training of theologically serious ministers in late-eighteenth-century America. As the training of ministers slowly shifted, in the early nineteenth century, from tutorial work with older ministers, a type of apprenticeship, to study in theological seminaries, these Edwardians alone had a developed theological perspective and even a method of doing theology. Thus, Jonathan Edwards remained the primary reference point for early American seminaries, almost all supported by churches in the Reformed tradition. This raises a question, one that does not yield easily to an abbreviated answer: what did Jonathan Edwards achieve?

Jonathan Edwards

Jonathan Edwards (1703–58) added no new doctrines to Reformed Christianity. He followed dozens of able apologists in all the early Reformed churches, including several brilliant defenders of English Puritanism. In his perspective his task was not to change any of the basic doctrines but to find new ways of stating and defending them against new forms of subversion in the eighteenth century. He brought to this defense superb logical skills, combined with a great sensitivity to religious experience and a keen esthetic insight.[2]

Edwards was not sectarian. The product of New England Puritanism, he was never an apologist for, or even deeply involved with, distinctive Puritan institutions. Thus, his defense of a rigorously pious but warm and affectionate religion transcended denominational differences. In his psychological and ethical insights he transcended even the Reformed tradition, and in his more narrowly doctrinal polemics, such as *On the Freedom of the Will*, he spoke for all the Reformed and even Lutheran confessions. In his early, and late, ontological speculations, he addressed such broad issues, including the foundations of theism, as to transcend even Christianity. This generality, breadth, and philosophical sophistication made him, arguably, the most accomplished philosophical theologian thus far produced by any of the Reformed denominations. And, contrary to later images of him, he was not an isolated, neglected, largely frontier thinker but an intellectual who read widely, corresponded with able European thinkers, and was, appropriate for any theologian, reasonably conversant with the latest intellectual trends in both philosophy and the sciences.

Edwards distinguished himself in four areas – in probing the nuances of religious experience, in marshaling arguments in defense of divine sovereignty and against types of Arminianism, in utilizing an idealistic ontology in his understanding of God and of the Trinity, and in merging morality with esthetics. Each deserves explication.

Edwards first gained fame for his sensitive, even awe-struck description of a remarkable revival in his own congregation at Northampton, Massachusetts, in 1734. His *Faithful Narrative* became a literary classic, was widely read in Britain, had a direct impact on John Wesley, and launched in America a special literary genre (detailed, moving, even converting accounts of great revivals). Subsequently, Edwards engaged in a prolonged polemical controversy over the authenticity and beneficial effects of his and subsequent revivals in New England. He believed the revivals were the work of the Spirit, despite some unwanted excesses that he condemned. This defense required that he clarify the affectional elements in Christian commitment. In one sense, his commendation of a religion of the heart, of a love of God so genuine and full as to be moving and affecting, was unexceptional, almost beyond challenge by Christians. But his celebration of deep feeling was a backhanded method of condemning a cold, unmoving, lifeless form of religion, a Christianity compromised by a humanistic form of impiety. Edwards moved from a defense of the New England revival to a broader treatise on religious affections, a defense of affectional religion and a manual of self-examination. The book became a widely read devotional guide, distinguished in this genre by a sensitivity to the internal nuances of faith as well as to the necessary, outwardly visible, moral fruits of a selfless love of God.

Edwards, as few other theologians, struggled for complete piety, for an unqualified love of, or trust in, a sovereign deity. His more soaring conceptions of God – as an eternal ground, as a divine mind fully immanent in all its expressions – informed his defense of divine omnipotence and of the doctrine of election. In his *Freedom of the Will* he developed one of the most powerful philosophical polemics ever written, a classic reference for anyone puzzled over the issues of human freedom. In the book Edwards drew a series of careful distinctions, most importantly between physical and moral determinism. Like all Calvinists, he denied any physical necessitarianism, although all purely physical events had natural causes and, at a proximate level, permitted a deterministic model of explanation, but ultimately all physical events were contingent, their very existence dependent moment by moment on the mind of God.

Human choices are not a part of the physical processes of nature. Yet, Edwards argued that they have their own order, again one consistent with the orderly thought processes of God. Humans are able to consider options and to choose among them. This means that they are free. But even human choices are caused. In later jargon, we would say that at least they have necessary conditions. Edwards argued even more: that a person's developed preferences, or moral taste, one's affections or one's likes and dislikes, provide sufficient conditions for any choices one makes (not for the success of the action that follows). Thus, although physical options are present, they may relate to but do not determine any human choice. At the same time all human choices are morally necessary and predictable. To know a person's character is to be able to predict her choices. What Edwards did not explore is the complications present when various goods are open to choice and when individuals cannot at first decide. His contention – that people always choose what appears to them the greatest good – still holds. After days of agonizing indecision, a person may finally choose between two or more options, and it is little more than a tautology to argue that when one chooses, one always chooses the greatest apparent good. Possibly most of the meaning present in assertions of human freedom, even affirmations of something called a "free will," simply refers to the process, the period of indecision, and the personal change or growth that occurs during this time. For in such cases the occasion for growth, for becoming a different person, seems largely internal, part of a complex mental process. The rather muddy idea of self-determination, of one's having some choice not only about what one wills but also about what will one has, may relate closely to this agonizing period of inaction, to the quandaries of moral life.

Unfortunately, Edwards did not pursue these often phenomenological issues. He would have been impossibly prescient, ahead of his time, had he done so. Instead, he wrote a devastating critique of the intellectually absurd and morally dangerous beliefs defended by some English Arminians. These people professed to believe in free will, by which they meant that neither physical compulsion nor moral determinants lay behind human choices. As Edwards restated their views, he seemed almost to have fun identifying their absurdities. For Arminians – in order, they said, to retain human responsibility – disassociated choice from developed character, from preferences, from all reasons for choosing one option over another. Such a freedom entailed an absurdity – accidental or uncaused choices. One was free only when nothing determined choice or when one not only wanted an object but wanted to want it (this leads to an infinite regress). Furthermore, Edwards demonstrated that this Arminian view – only a choice rooted in free will is subject to praise or blame – led inevitably to a full suspension of moral judgment, for on clear examination all human choices have moral determinants. They reflect developed character. They exemplify final causes or reasons. Edwards, therefore, stressed that the only proper subject of praise or blame is the character of a person. A good person, by moral necessity, acts morally. And either we praise him for it or we cannot praise him at all. Edwards applied this point to his God. God, because of his character, does only good deeds, and it is for his character we praise him, or else we cannot praise him at all, since he does good necessarily. On these issues, Edwards's logic was impeccable. Whether he was fair to his Arminian foes, or to Arminians who may have relied on other arguments, is not as clear.

Even as a youth, Edwards somehow convinced himself that ultimate reality was mind-like. Later, influenced by English Neoplatonists at Cambridge, and possibly by John Locke's *Essay Concerning Human Understanding*, Edwards used idealistic and Neoplatonic motifs in his more philosophical theology. This meant that, to him, the best image of God was that of an all-inclusive mind, whose ideas were emanations outward, or modes of self-expression, or a form of self-edifying communication. Edwards often used images of light, or an overflowing of being, to express this aspect of God. The divine ideas of such a mind provided him, like many earlier theologians, with a rationalization of the Logos or Son of God, whereas the love and spirit of mutuality that obtained between a mind and its thought, or between a figurative father and son, provided an image of the Holy Spirit. Thus Edwards defended traditional trinity formulas. Also, what humans perceive as the creation is a further expression, or an effulgence, of God, distinguishable because it is finite and contingent, but ultimately an extension of God, not completely other than God. By these distinctions, Edwards retained a God who is distinct from his creation but fully involved in it, a God immanent in all being.

This conception of God transformed more traditional images of a creator god who made all things and then governed their behavior. Edwards's God moves out into all things, even as he can, if he wills, withdraw his light, cease his self-glorifying communication outward, stop certain forms of thinking, and in effect instantly abolish the world of cohering ideas that humans perceive as a physical universe. In this sense, divine creation is continuous, not an act in past time. And the physical universe reflects not rational intent at some point of creation but the rationality (the harmony and symmetry and rhythm) of God's own thought. It was these idealistic motifs that had least impact on Presbyterian and other Reformed theologians, or on those who continued to affirm the traditional dualistic ontology that gained, in the nineteenth century, most of its intellectual weapons from Scottish commonsense realists (Charles Hodge at Princeton would later see Edwards's idealism as a betrayal of the common sense of Calvin and his immediate successors and as a standing invitation to the forms of pantheism that dominated so much German theology in the age of Friedrich Schleiermacher).

Such an idealistic, and immanental, conception of God was suffused with esthetic content. The whole of being is harmonious, mutually supportive, beautiful. Such terms abound in Edwards's talk about God and in his personal devotions. Such metaphysical commitments colored Edwards's quite orthodox defense of Pauline-Augustinian-Calvinist doctrines. For example, irresistible grace took on new meaning. The divine mind, when actually confronted by humans, when perceived in all its beauty, when grasped in an immediate and moving way, as if by a sixth or supernatural sense, is so winsome that no person can do other, morally, than respond to such a sensibly present God in consent, trust, or love. Inevitably, the glory of God becomes one's greatest perceived good, and all other goods diminish in significance and appeal, for none of them have such perfect symmetry, consent of parts, unity, delightfulness, sweetness (the characterizations go on and on, and none are adequate). By characterizing irresistible grace in such direct, sensible, and esthetic terms, by making it a matter of an alluring object, not a coercive influence, Edwards defused most images of an arbitrary God pushing salvation on passive humans. But at the same time Edwards retained the heart of Calvinist orthodoxy – ordinary humans, without special illumination from the Holy Spirit, without a divine initiative, never really perceive or grasp the loveliness of God and thus do not, morally cannot, respond to him in faith or choose what is consistent with his will. The proper insight, the required perception, is always a gift. And what lies behind the response to such insight – the reciprocating love – is never, in itself, an object of choice, for love is not a choice but the parent of our choices, just as the will is not chosen but chooses. Once gifted with grace, humans can do no other than love God. Their affections, their choices, are now dramatically different than before. Anyone who has seen God is truly transformed.

Edwards drew on these theological insights in his moral theory. In a late, posthumously published book, *The Nature of True Virtue*, a book that had a decisive influence on Samuel Hopkins, Edwards defined true virtue, or the highest form of virtue, as a type of beauty. In the language of his idealistic ontology, which he usually used in this very abstract philosophical treatise, true virtue is the beauty reflected in a moral being's consent to all being, or to being in general. In Christian terms, the only true virtue is the beauty given off by Christians who love God and choose, in all things, what is consistent with his will and thus his self-glorification. In one sense, this was only an update on Jesus' two commandments – love God with your whole heart and mind, and love your neighbor as yourself. It also reflected the moral implications of justifying faith, as Paul or Augustine or Calvin used the word. Edwards recognized other, lower, partial forms of virtue. But all lower forms, even the most universal forms of human sympathy, reflected self-love and not love of God. Insofar as human ethical commitments embrace a large, even a universal human community, they at least suggest or prefigure true virtue, but even then an immense gap separates such lower virtue from true virtue, simply because these lower forms embrace wholes that are infinitesimal when compared with the totality of being. Yet, in most cases, the more universal human ethical systems command the same action as true virtue, meaning a convergence of deeds. At the level of the heart the chasm remains – all wholes short of God, when affirmed as the object of one's highest commitments, reveal only a partial beauty, which viewed from the perspective of God's beauty becomes only another form of ugliness. Even well-ordered parts, when not congruent with, conformable to, the whole, are blemishes on, obstacles to, perfect unity and wholeness. In a sense, Edwards did not advocate selfless or sacrificial behavior as a norm, for consenting action, that consistent with God's will, means that Christians still choose the greatest apparent good and reap the appropriate consequences that accrue to all who so choose.

The Nature of True Virtue was not a practical guide to morality, a fact that concerned Samuel Hopkins. Essentially, it reflected a very Platonic merging of the true and the beautiful, more an exercise in esthetics than in moral philosophy. Only in the broadest sense did it indicate a practical ethic – one that required a commitment to fuller and broader communities. It was also a very abstract devotional statement, another way of celebrating the sensible and affecting attributes of God as contrasted to the merely intellectual aspect tied to his mere existence. But it cohered with all Edwards's theology in being absolutely theocentric and in drawing sharply the enormous gulf, not of belief but of affection, that separated born-again Christians from all other people.

Although Edwards's theology proved very compelling in its logical rigor and esthetic sensitivity, it so raised the ante, so emphasized God's self-love and self-glory, and so stigmatized non-God-centered human concerns and preferences, as to raise a disturbing question – is anyone really a Christian? Of course, Jesus' strange command (strange in commanding what is never a choice) to love God fully also provoked such a question. Implicit in Edwards was the same command, but in his case his theological qualifications made very clear that such love is ultimately a gift, never originally a choice. Only God chooses. Thus, for all humans untouched by God's irresistible grace, true virtue – the love that reconciles and redeems – is never a moral option, never perceived as a compelling good. But even for those who claim to be Christians, the agony of self-examination may be an ordeal that leads inevitably to anxiety if not despair. Do they have the appropriate love? If honest in self-analysis, does anyone find such love? Edwards, at times, nourished his own doubts.

Edwards would have a mixed legacy in American theology. His battle against Arminians, his logical clarification of the issues involved in the debates over free will, became favored weapons of Calvinist apologists throughout the nineteenth century, among Presbyterians and Baptists as well as Congregationalists. Even Presbyterian clergymen in the frontier West often turned to Edwards for ammunition against Methodists or against other Arminians in their own midst. His writings on religious affections, his guides to self-examination, continued to sell to lay audiences into the twentieth century. His philosophical idealism anticipated major theological trends in nineteenth-century Germany theology, not exactly but at least suggestively. His more Neoplatonic images, and his sense of a beautiful unity behind the fragments of ordinary experience, matured in Ralph Waldo Emerson. Finally, his moral theory, particularly his emphasis on complete benevolence, provided central motifs for his students and immediate disciples, the founders of the New Divinity, particularly three young men who lived in his home and learned directly from the master – Jonathan Edwards, Jr., Joseph Bellamy, and above all Samuel Hopkins, his literary executor. But few bought all of Edwards's ideas. Traditional Puritans in New England and Orthodox Presbyterians in the middle colonies resisted his more abstract and more idealistic motifs, which led them to use the dismissive title "New Divinity" with the sense that it was neither acceptable nor traditional. Above all, in the late eighteenth century, in an age of humanism and rationalism, neither his American opponents nor, in the fullest possible sense, even his avowed disciples could stand the strain of such a theocentric worldview. In various ways they compromised it, making it easier, and in so doing made God more obliging toward humans.

Rationalism and Humanism

For both Calvinists and Arminians, the greatest perceived threat to Christianity in the eighteenth century was what they always called "deism." Minsters used the label very loosely, with Calvinists often assigning it to more latitudinarian Episcopalians or emergent Unitarians. In America, as in England, no one offered a precise definition. If deism means a non-Christian form of natural or rational theism, such as that espoused by Thomas Paine, then at best only a few thousand Americans ever professed such a religion. These committed deists, who joined in a few local societies and who indulged some very complex theological debates among themselves, were small in comparison with the hundreds of thousands of Americans who were largely indifferent to any of the competing religious claims. But orthodox Calvinists believed, with some justification, that the continuum of belief, from that of the first Arminian revisions of Calvinism to rationalism and deism and on eventually to atheism, was all of a piece. Each step represented an inevitable progression whenever Protestants rejected a logically coherent Calvinist position. They could not easily admit a Roman Catholic contention – that the progression began with Luther and Calvin, with a break from the traditional doctrines of the church. To admit this would have been to concede the Roman Catholic argument that the Reformation itself marked the first step toward atheism.

The word *reason* clearly became fashionable in the eighteenth century. Thus, from different quarters came the allegation that Roman Catholicism and evangelical Christianity were both irrational – meaning that they were internally inconsistent, empirically unsupported, or intuitively unbelievable. The criterion of rationality could be logic, fact, or intellectual taste. Obviously people believed their own position, in religion or elsewhere, to be rational, and the charge of "irrational" took on many of the attributes of demagoguery. This is not to claim that the issues were all meaningless. One indeed may be able, by almost universally accepted logical conventions, to point out contradictory aspects of belief, and such was the complexity of Christian doctrines that any sophomore could find some contradictions in almost any confession. And to the extent that any version of Christianity rested on, or entailed, empirically resolvable claims about nature or about human history (all forms of Christianity did this), then it was in order to ask Christians to justify such factual claims by conventionally accepted methods.

The major threat to evangelical Christianity came not from avowed deists but from self-professed Christians who moved only partway to a rational religion, often by way of a primarily moralistic religion. In effect, humanistic theists retained the Semitic cosmology but eliminated most of the Christian superstructure, except possibly a lingering respect for Jesus as a moral reformer. In America few went this far, but many, like Thomas Jefferson, tried to disinfect Christianity of its superstitious and culture-bound particularities. This effort eroded away most of the hard doctrines of Christianity – human depravity, an atoning Christ, justification by faith through grace – and substituted a consoling, human-centered religion. God was now a benevolent creator. He wanted to redeem all humankind. The one critical condition of redemption was obedience, doing good. The principal requirement of obedience was adherence to the golden rule and the ten commandments. Jesus set the example when he demonstrated the magnitude of God's love. The reward for virtue, for imitating Jesus, was some form of reward after death. The church provided instruction in obedience and provided a supportive community for all Christians. This all meant a simplified Christianity. Compared with it, the old Calvinist doctrines seemed obscure or fatalistic, well equipped to lead to dogmatic intolerance. The old doctrines either were beyond human understanding or at best were clear only to a clerical elite.

It was this decay of the old doctrines that confronted Edwards's disciples, particularly Samuel Hopkins. In a context of widespread rationalism and moralism within even traditional Calvinist churches, Hopkins tried to use Edwardian insights to build new fortifications for Pauline Christianity and to offer practical applications for evangelical benevolence. He suffered the consequences of such a strategy. Contemporaries found in his argumentative and complex essays an extreme form of Calvinism, and indeed, Hopkins explored in greater detail than Jonathan Edwards, and perhaps more honestly, the full implications of divine sovereignty. For Edwards, as for most Christian theologians, the overwhelming problem tied to God's omnipotence was not a qualified conception of human freedom (Edwards moved through these issues with ease) but the problem of evil, or at least what humans perceived as evil – natural calamities, the obvious fact of perverted human preferences, and the grave social maladies that so agitated Hopkins. Naming the proximate source of these moral evils – sinfulness in humans – or attributing it to an agent – Satan – did not cancel the hard truth: God made it so. For Edwards, an idealistic ontology, the immanence of God, and a very esthetic conception of evil (ultimately nonconsent, alienation, or ugliness) entailed a theodicy, but one so theocentric as to finesse the problem as most people had to confront it. If one, by faith or love, so merges one's will with that of God that the finite human perspective loses all force and meaning, it is easy to affirm that all is good, that all works for God's glory. In the transports of faith, one has no need to ask why God did it so, or why he unchained a rebellious angel, Satan, or why he ordained the fall of Adam and Eve. These are nagging human questions, responses to the claims of a human ego, and are essentially impious in their implied challenge to God's justice, at least as humans understand justice. In the words of Paul, who can question the great potter who, for his purposes, decided to make flawed as well as perfect pots? Certainly not the flawed pots.

In the late eighteenth century it was almost impossible for any theologian to finesse the issue of evil, particularly any Calvinist theologian. The problems evaporated if one affirmed a finite and limited God, in a universe apart from God, and in a world inhabited by many demigods who, admittedly from a weak position, nonetheless were in a position to bargain with God, to contend with him, to join in his causes, or to rebel against him in alignment with God's enemies. Given the unequal power of God and humans, humans were in the position of subjects, and it was in their own interests to obey God. But nothing could be farther from Edwards's immanent God, or all-sustaining mind, than such a monarchical and finite deity. Hopkins wrestled with the problem of evil and did not blink at the implications it imposed. He went further than Calvin dared, further than Edwards ever clearly moved, and admitted what was logically inescapable: God permitted sin to come into the world. Sin cannot be exempt from providence and God remain God.

This position was not one calculated for popular appeal. The historian, Joseph Haroutunian, in an enduringly provocative autopsy of a dying Calvinism, argued that even Hopkins and his New Divinity colleagues, as they tried to give a pious response to the problem of evil, so framed the questions and answers as to betray their own cause. They asked (in the context, their critics would hardly let them escape the question) exactly how the apparent evil that God permitted was not really evil in the longer perspective but served some higher purpose. It is not surprising that they framed their response not just in terms of how it all conduces to God's glory, for in their perspective this issue was beyond all human understanding, but also in the only meaningful way given the human concerns that motivated the question – how does apparent evil work to the benefit of our universe or the ultimate benefit of humans? Possibly the only pious answer is that it may not. God's ends may not coincide with natural good or human hopes. But for a Calvinist to concede this, or to end the debate by such a conjecture, was to lose the battle for people's minds in the eighteenth century. Thus, by accepting the humanistic assumptions that gave sense to the question, Hopkins by necessity lost the war even when, by good logic or effective appeals to the realities of human history, he seemed to win the skirmish.[3]

When cast in such human dimensions, the old orthodoxy could not survive. Its solutions were forced, contrived, and easily challenged. A child could suggest better ways (that is, from the perspective of human conceptions of equity and justice) for God to have planned human history. Even the atonement, the glorious and central doctrine of evangelical Christians, documented the sheer horror of God's way, self-glorifying or not. He not only loosed the devil and allowed Adam to eat the apple and set the terms of mortality as punishment but also allowed his own son to suffer on the cross in order to redeem some of the humans that he cast from the garden of innocence. His choices led to an endless story of suffering, and for what purpose? Put in such literal terms, God was a mean fellow indeed, even a bit sadistic, for he seemed to get his kicks either from the human suffering of those he chose to damn or from the love affirmed irresistibly by those he deemed to save.

It is unfair to indict Hopkins for such literalism. But in his theological system he did make some telling concessions to a more humanistic age, and in ways he never intended he began, or possibly continued, such a process of reinterpreting Calvinism as to make it more human-centered and benevolent. This reinterpretation, in New England, would culminate in the theology of Nathaniel Taylor and Horace Bushnell, both of whom gained direct inspiration from Hopkins. Thus, ironically, Hopkins would soon suffer from two quite divergent images. In the popular mind, he was the prototypal Calvinist – harsh, dogmatic, and unbearably censorious. But among old Calvinists in New England, and particularly among traditional, confessional Presbyterians, he appeared as a clever dialectician, one who subtly subverted evangelical doctrines and enticed Christians into needless and even impious efforts to fathom the ultimate secrets of God. He thus began a slide down a slippery slope to humanism and rationalism. "Hopkinsianism" soon became a bad word at Presbyterian Princeton Seminary, among conservative Dutch Reformed Christians, and later among Old School Presbyterians. In his essays, and his completed system of theology, Hopkins provided ammunition for both these assessments.

Samuel Hopkins

Hopkins was born in 1721, the son of a prosperous farmer in Waterbury, Connecticut. A dutiful child, he in effect grew up in the church, with no early or clear conversion experience, or a missing step that became significant to his later theology. As a first son, he had the privilege of attending Yale. At the end of his undergraduate years in 1741, he became involved in the great revival of religion and heard sermons by both George Whitefield and Gilbert Tennent. These revivalists helped plunge him into despair and guilt and led him to doubt that he was a born-again Christian. Out of his agony came eventual comfort and peace, gained in intense religious experiences that, at the time, he did not consider a conversion but that later, as a minister, he reflectively identified as the moment of regeneration, although he remained somewhat vague about the time. He eventually argued that a Christian need not know the time of rebirth (a retrospective judgment in any case) but need only gain, largely through the moral fruits of regeneration, the assurance that such had occurred. The awakening led Hopkins into the ministry, although for years he was not fully confident of his own salvation. After hearing a sermon by Jonathan Edwards, Hopkins decided to apprentice to him and lived much of the time from 1841 to 1843 in Edwards's household at Northampton.[4]

As an insecure young minister, Hopkins gained a pulpit at Great Barrington in western Massachusetts. He would remain there until 1769, when he resigned because of lack of financial support from his still small, struggling congregation. His location was significant in American theological history, for it placed him next door to Jonathan Edwards after Edwards lost his own pulpit at Northampton in 1750 and took, at Hopkins's urging, a position at the Indian mission at Stockbridge. In all visible ways, Hopkins was not a successful minister. His preaching was dull, his sermons were abstract exercises in theology, and his moral demands were so rigorous that few could meet his standards. His meager salary forced him to spend much of his time farming. In many years the town did not even pay him his due. He remained a quite obscure minister, with no publications until after Edwards died at Princeton in 1758. But from 1751 to 1757 he and a neighboring minister and soon his closest friend, Joseph Bellamy, met with Edwards in a type of continuing theological seminar at Stockbridge. As other scholars have noted, this was the first and, in caliber of professor and students, the most distinguished theological seminary in American history.

By Edwards's death, Hopkins and Bellamy were prepared to assume leadership in the continuing battle between about a dozen of Edwards's disciples and the increasingly self-denominated Arminians or, in their own favored term, the liberals. Both men published polemical essays in 1759, with the same theme. Hopkins made this clear in his title, which pronounced sin as an advantage to the universe. Both he and Bellamy, with somewhat difference emphases, argued that an omnipotent God willed that sin exist but that its existence contributed to God's glory and to the greatest general good of the universe. Of all conceivable worlds, this was the best. In this argument Hopkins helped establish a theodicy, a way of reconciling the ways of God with the apparent existence of evil, that would distinguish New Divinity theologians all the way down to Nathaniel Taylor and the New Haven theology of the mid-nineteenth century. Both he and Bellamy would, at times, use the theme of moral government to establish their claim. Taylor would make this theme the basis of his whole theological system.

In his last years at Great Barrington, Hopkins carried on an almost continuous pamphlet battle with the liberals. His opponents used the word *liberal* to identify a broad or catholic position, one that was inclusive rather than dogmatic or exclusive. In opposition to this form of liberalism, Hopkins took such bold and uncompromising positions as to embarrass most of the orthodox. His polemics helped establish a somewhat distorted image of Hopkins as the most rigorous and extreme Calvinist in New England. Behind his careful arguments, and logical consistency, Hopkins was actually making several unrecognized concessions to rationalism and humanism, concessions that at least hinted at more to come in such latter-day disciples as Taylor.

The issue that focused the polemical battles was regeneration. Hopkins, as a faithful disciple of Edwards, deplored the old halfway covenant (which allowed unconverted but morally acceptable parents to present infants for baptism) and, again following Edwards, denied any true virtue or benevolence in the unsaved and any grounds for hope in any action taken by the unsaved. He emphasized a complete disjunction between the selfish motives of the unregenerate and the complete benevolence that marked a Christian; he denied any efficacy in any of the means of grace (God often worked through such means but he alone could move the heart of a convert) and insisted on the necessity of almost superhuman moral achievement as the most appropriate conformation of regeneration (but not perfection). This was all good Edwardian doctrine and was in fact consistent with Calvin. But in the New England context, in the eighteenth century, such rigor had fallen into disfavor. Most ministers drew less sharply the disjunction between saved and unsaved, placed more emphasis on the means of grace, saw the road to salvation in more evolutionary terms, and were not quite so rigorous in their demands for holiness. Opponents saw in Hopkins a conception of regeneration that left sinners helpless and passive until God acted. This, joined with his somber personality, his frequent jeremiads, and his abstract sermons made him, as he sometimes ruefully admitted, a symbol of a caricatured and cruel form of Calvinism.[5]

In 1769 an unemployed Hopkins accepted a call to the First Congregation of Newport, Rhode Island. But the enmity of the liberals, the suspicions of old Calvinists, almost led the congregation to withdraw its offer. He was finally settled in 1771. If Hopkins had a golden period, it was the next five years. He now had a sophisticated audience, some of whom liked his theology. He developed a cooperative, although not close, relationship with a more powerful preacher, Ezra Stiles, who was pastor of the larger and growing Second Society. In Newport he had the opportunity to edit and publish Edwards's posthumous works, to write the first biography of Edwards, and to publish a more practical sequel to Edwards's *Nature of True Virtue*.

In Newport, Hopkins also confronted a compelling moral and social evil. This allowed him, for the first time, to move from moral theory to courageous advocacy. Newport was the center of the triangular trade, exchanging its distilled rum for African slaves for sale in the West Indies or along the American coast. In fact, to the despair of Hopkins, Newport largely owed its prosperity to the slave trade. He almost immediately launched a crusade against the trade, ministered to more blacks than any other minister in New England, denied membership to anyone involved in the trade, trained two blacks for mission trips back to Africa (the Revolution disrupted this plan), and soon advocated immediate and unqualified emancipation, although he believed that most blacks would choose colonization back in Africa. In his antislavery effort he followed in the footsteps of Quakers but easily fitted the issue to traditional Puritan themes. Thus, he saw this curse as a horrible blemish on Americans, a mockery of their claim to be a covenanted people. Until his death he confidently predicted God's judgment on the young nation. It did not deserve freedom when it denied such to the Africans.

The British occupied Newport for three years during the Revolution. Hopkins fled the city and held temporary pastorates elsewhere while the British ravished his Newport meetinghouse. When Hopkins returned to Newport in 1780, he was never able to put it all back together again. In the religiously cold eighties and nineties he ministered to a very small, aged congregation, largely made up of a few people, most women, who admired his theological system. The story was a sad one. An uncompromising Hopkins now seemed an antique survival of a past age, almost comical in his seriousness, his denunciatory jeremiads, and what his neighbors saw as his rigid form of Calvinism. He kept the faith, wrote essays and books, and in 1793 completed his theological magnum opus. He kept up his anti-slavery agitation and was, in his antique ways, the most famous man in Newport.

In a farewell sermon (he anticipated death), possibly written in 1801, Hopkins gave a rare, personal testimony. He appropriately apologized for the personal references and for departing from his usual discipline, one that required him to preach the gospel and not tell stories. By then he was pessimistic about the course of history, consoled only by his vision of a millennial age that was most likely to begin by 2000. He condemned all the apostasies of his age – the departures from Calvinist (his term) doctrines and from holiness and morality. He condemned all the compromisers – the liberals, Unitarians, Universalists, and even moderate Calvinists. In descending order, he looked at the world (few true Christians), America (cursed by slavery), New England (once the glory of Christianity but now cursed by every heresy imaginable), Newport (damned for its ill-gotten wealth and a resumed slave trade), and his own feeble, beloved, and faithful congregation, a saving remnant in the final, awful age when the seventh vial of Revelation was being poured out. This was only a prelude to divine wrath and destruction, which a dying Hopkins, crippled by a stroke, seemed to relish, for the millennium lay just ahead. In these last sermons a beloved disciple, a black man Hopkins had trained for the African mission, helped steady him in his pulpit. When he died in 1803, many assumed that this was also the death of an older, now repudiated Calvinism. Few shed a tear at its passing.

What his disciples, as well as his enemies, overlooked were the more novel and the more humanistic elements in Hopkins's mature theological system. His was a position in a lineage that stretched from Edwards to Hopkins and Bellamy to Timothy Dwight to the New Haven theology of Nathaniel Taylor to liberal forms of Congregationalism in the late nineteenth century. Hopkins, when understood in this developing tradition, anticipated not Hodge and the Princeton theology but a continuing series of more liberal and modernist revisions of evangelical doctrine, revisions made to fit new contexts and new intellectual influences. In this tradition Hopkins was a revealing but not a highly original or gifted theologian. He was not broadly learned, was on most critical issues completely dependent on Edwards, and yet was not always a perceptive interpreter of his mentor. Hopkins had more than his share of moral fervor, but he lacked the philosophical and esthetic subtlety of Edwards. He seemed completely oblivious to late-eighteenth-century biblical scholarship and to new challenges from the natural sciences, particularly geology. He read traditional books, did not have access to a major library, and was more unquestioning and naive in his use of biblical texts than Edwards had been a generation earlier. In fact, his very limitations as a scholar and philosopher are what allowed the elements of originality and the doctrinal compromises that made his system so revealing.

The Hopkinsian System

Hopkins, in most respects, offered a rather coherent restatement of scholastic Calvinism, keyed closely to the Westminster Confession. Unlike Edwards, who usually tried to move to a rather general, ontological level of understanding, Hopkins set as his task a more detailed, scriptural vindication of what he took to be the Edwardian outlook. This tactic, or the stating of a position and then an extended excursion through the Bible to justify it, made Hopkins vulnerable in ways that Edwards avoided. His proof texts were so clearly selective, or so arbitrarily interpreted, and so challengeable by others playing by the same rules, that they had to seem, even in a more credulous age, as sophistic as authoritative. Thus, his more distinctive interpretations were much more governed by aspects of personality and taste, and by the dominant concerns of an age, than Hopkins ever knew or would have admitted. This also contributed to the new departures evident in his developed system.[6]

Hopkins, like Bellamy, began serious theology with a theodicy, with justifications of the ways of God. This was the most central theme in Hopkins and even in the unfolding of the New Divinity movement. The two Edwardians were bold in daring to begin here, and in the honesty with which they dealt with issues that even Calvin finessed or evaded (in *Institutes* Calvin lapsed from a fully sovereign god only in his denial that God is in any sense the author of sin or of what, in a foreshortened human perspective, seems evil, a responsibility that he assigned fully to Adam). Hopkins asserted all the Calvinist superlatives about God, but his controlling characteristic is not so much power as holiness and righteousness, just one of many means that Hopkins used to give a compelling moral tenor to his theology. Given that God is holy and righteous (the implied circularity is part of the game), Hopkins drew on Edwards's moral theory to establish that God cannot do evil. All that he does is good or ultimately conducive to good.

Hopkins's key term for describing God was benevolence or love. He has a perfect goodwill, and he wills only that which is consistent with the general good, with the good of the whole. This means, by necessity, that what he does is always in behalf of his own glory and happiness, because God is the perfect being and the necessary end of all moral choice. This conception of a fully benevolent or loving god defines the terms of human reconciliation to God – a reciprocal love, or benevolence to being in general, a theme drawn directly from Edwards. Thus, Hopkins spent much time trying to establish that love, or benevolence, is the implied meaning of faith, although faith may begin with knowledge of God and trust in God. In making love the central meaning of faith, he moved a bit back toward the Roman church and away from the Reformers, who kept belief and consent at the center of their definition of faith. By stressing love or benevolence, Hopkins tried to entangle faith with holy living, at times to the point of so incorporating good works into faith as to almost nullify the role of belief. The faith that regenerates, although given by God through grace, is above all a love and benevolence that entails not primarily some sentiment or feeling (Hopkins did not deny these) but joyful obedience.

The presuppositions establish the case – God does only what, in the larger picture, or in the long term, maximizes good. The best way to picture this benevolence, and thus a pervasive theme in all the New Divinity theologians, is to describe God as a perfect sovereign or moral governor. Somehow, in ways not known by humans, the fall of Adam and the depravity of humans work to a good purpose. So also does natural evil. Hopkins was not nearly as ready as Nathaniel Taylor to speculate about all the ways that evil serves good ends or to stipulate what anyone committed to a moral system had to do in order to sustain such a system. But like a later Taylor, Hopkins was sure that God did not enjoy the punishment necessary to sustain justice. Thus, whatever the amount of evil and sin in this world, it was only what was minimally necessary for the good of the system as a whole, good for God and good for his universe. In a sense unfathomable, the introduction of sin into the world had to be conducive not only to God's glory but also to the maximum amount of human fulfillment and happiness. Here Hopkins was not very speculative but hinted that the fall of humanity led to a glorious plan of salvation, to the incarnation and sacrifice of the Christ, and to a form of redemption, tied to a reciprocal benevolence, that was more free, voluntary, and glorious than was possible for any dutiful citizen of Eden. It is therefore good that Adam did what he did (not necessarily good for Adam but for the general good of the whole) and that God chose to create moral agents in his own image. The strong humanism that typified Hopkins came through here and in his insistence that humans stood highest in God's regard, even above the angels. The redemption of some (Hopkins believed most) humans was the purpose that lay at the center of all history. One implication of this theodicy is that God did indeed choose to have evil, choose to have sin, choose to have humans like ourselves, but that this choice was a good choice, not an evil one.

It was in the context of moral government that Hopkins explained and defended the eternal decrees of God. He added nothing new to Edwards's analysis in *Freedom of the Will*. He argued, with an increasing sense that no one could comprehend his logic, that divine providence, including election of some and not others to salvation, was fully consistent with human freedom and responsibility. Like Edwards, he backed away from any literal imputation of Adam's guilt to his descendants and instead stressed a commonality of identity. Human depravity simply means that all humans prefer self over God, and always so choose. Because of such a flawed character, or corrupt will, they are enslaved to sin and, short of some transformation of character, some new will, are incapable of loving or obeying God, in spirit as well as in deed. This clarifies the need for a divine initiative in salvation, an initiative that may involve events over time, that may involve such means as the preaching of the gospel, and that always involves the will and affections, the working of the Spirit within the heart, and not any mechanical transaction. Even the eventual choice of God, enabled by the Spirit, is a true and thus voluntary choice and one that entails a subsequent life of God-affirming choices. Such regeneration transforms one's moral character, and loving deeds become the prime proof of such regeneration. Always for Hopkins, the proof of the pudding was in the eating, not in appearance.

Nothing in these views was new. Nothing was inconsistent with traditional Calvinist confessions. But one issue made Hopkins uneasy. He had all the right answers, but it is clear they did not quite settle his doubts. The troubling issue, even for Paul, had been God's choice of some undeserving humans for salvation and not others who were no more deserving. Hopkins tried to get God off the hook, and in this he moved much closer than he wanted to John Wesley and Arminian Methodists. Like all Calvinists, he stressed over and over again that no human deserves redemption. By their own will and choices, humans separate themselves from God and thus are guilty. Those who are graced with the ability to love God are peculiarly blessed, clearly undeserving, and can only render fervent thanks. Their good luck does not make it worse for those rejected. But why are some left out? Hopkins stressed that God saves every person he can, consistent with the general good and with his duties as a moral governor. It is as unfair to ask for more as it is to complain about the system. But Hopkins was still troubled, in part because of the fact that friends and loved ones might be among the damned. Would this not create sadness even in the kingdom and thus destroy the glory and happiness that was the end of the whole system? (Here his questions duplicated those of the biblical Salathiel in his long dialogues with an angel in the apocryphal book of II Esdras.)

At this point Hopkins conceded more than his Calvinist system would seem to permit. In one of the few slips from internal consistency (his system is full of circular arguments but is internally coherent), he speculated that God chose those whom he passed over because of good reasons unknown to us – because of different natural capacities, or different circumstances, that made them less beneficial to the kingdom. It was best for the whole system that he pass them over. Hopkins never suggested that those chosen were morally better than those rejected; he never suggested any special moral deficiency in the damned (depravity is complete for all), but still he attributed to God some criteria of selection, as had Edwards before him and as had even earlier Calvinists. He felt burdened to demonstrate that God was not arbitrary, but to the despair of good Calvinists he seemed to make something intrinsic to some humans the basis of God's choices. Even apart from any strictly moral criteria, Hopkins seemed to admit that, according to God's purposes, some humans were better situated than others or had certain needed attributes lacking in others. This was indeed a hole in the Calvinist dike, one expanded to a tunnel by Nathaniel Taylor.

Hopkins remained quite conventional on the role of the Christ and on the atonement. His governmental emphasis gave a legalistic cast to the atonement (the sacrifice of the Christ alone revealed God's horror of sin and thus made possible forgiveness based on attributed and not realized righteousness, yet without undermining moral government or God's commitment to justice). The method upheld law. In his understanding of attributed righteousness, Hopkins adhered to his usual moralistic bent. It was the righteousness of the Christ that justified humans before God, since they could not render such righteousness in this life (like all Calvinists, and unlike Wesley, Hopkins saw sanctification as a goal but not a possibility before death). But once regenerated, the Christian had a central obligation to move as close to Christ's perfect love or benevolence as possible. Hopkins would accept no compromises, no relaxation of moral rigor.

Hopkins became famous for an extreme demand for disinterested love of God as the standard for Christians. He was often quoted, or slightly misquoted, as demanding that Christian love required that one be willing to be damned for the glory of God (not a new point of view, for even Wesley said much the same). Jokes abounded about this harsh side of Hopkins. What Hopkins did argue is that a fully consenting and benevolent person would not want to be saved, or want anyone else to be saved, unless this was consistent with the glory of God. Benevolence implied even this degree of self-denial. Of course, anyone so self-denying was, by definition, at one with God, and if God had decreed the salvation of anyone, such would be among the elect. And the unsaved, almost by definition, were too self-serving to desire God's glory. So, in fact, no one would ever be in a position willingly to be damned for God's glory, although in a sense all humans who faced certain damnation contributed to God's glory by their damnation. Hopkins only used such language to set a standard for love of God.

On more practical issues, Hopkins was very conventional and often parochial. He endorsed congregational polity and two ordained orders, not three, and he rather surprisingly argued that, in all likelihood, there had been an unbroken line of ordained elders from the early apostles, even though this lineage passed through a corrupted Roman church. Since he had continuously warred with his own congregations, he wanted to establish the special authority of ministers. He approved only a male priesthood; he wanted consideration and even attention to the concerns of women but would not allow them any role in the ministry or in church government. Yet his closest admirers in his churches were women members, and in one case an unmarried woman became his confidante and soul mate. He was not sacramentally oriented and seemed to take rather lightly the Lord's Supper. It was indeed symbolically important, but he felt that it need not be celebrated very often. He was rigid in his emphasis on a Christian Sabbath (the first day of the week) and spent an enormous amount of time refuting those Christians who believed that Christians should worship on the last day of the week. He also spent much of his labors refuting Unitarians, Universalists, deists, and other heretics. In these polemics he was parochial, self-serving, and at times blatantly unfair to his opponents. But on two issues he took a quite original stand – infant baptism and the millennium.

The baptism of infants touched on issues that seemed very personal and important to Hopkins. It is important to remember that he never experienced a clear, crisis-like conversion, even as he, unlike most evangelicals, never remembered many youthful indiscretions. In the later words of Horace Bushnell, Hopkins grew up in the church and never felt himself outside it (not even when he doubted his conversion). He cherished revivals and revival conversions but never believed this was the normal, or best, way to sustain the church. This again reflected his moralistic bent, his tendency to move quickly from the esthetic or sentimental aspects of Christian love to its payoff at the level of conduct. He joined Edwards and the other New Divinity ministers in rejecting a halfway covenant or any covert system of salvation by good works. Yet, he wanted to pack as much of the moral imperatives of good works into the Calvinist scheme of salvation as possible. Infant baptism, tied to the concept of covenant relationships, gave him a means to do this. Incidentally, few other Calvinists ever accepted his views on infant baptism, either his rigid insistence that it be limited to children of clearly redeemed parents or his belief that it gave a covenant guarantee of salvation to children of devout and dutiful parents.

Calvinists always had to struggle with the problems of infants who died before an age of accountability. Were they damned for a lack of faith, since faith involves elements of belief and choice? Or did God, in his mercy, extend grace to them, automatically if they died before their inherent depravity eventuated in its awful fruits? Hopkins did not offer an answer for the unbaptized children of sinful parents, but his normal pessimism suggested a harsh verdict. He had a seemingly consoling, but in actuality a guilt-inducing, answer for church members. He believed that righteous parents had an obligation to present infants for baptism, on the basis of their sincere confession of faith. Analogous to Jews who circumcised male infants, they thus brought their child into the covenant of grace. But it was a conditional covenant. God, in his ultimate wisdom, had indeed decreed, before time began, that infants fortunate enough to have faithful parents, those that exerted every possible effort to rear children in the ways of the Lord, were among the elect. Such children were in the church at baptism, and as soon as they could understand what this meant they could profess faith and come to the communion table, apparently without any crisis-like conversion or any one remembered moment of rebirth (this moment would have been at whatever time, usually unrecognized, when they could affirm faith). This, in effect, represented a form of baptismal salvation conditioned on the performance of parents. If such baptized infants later repudiated the faith, this was, to Hopkins, evidence that the parents had failed in their duties, although such failure did not mean the parents were unsaved, just derelict, possibly as a result of human weaknesses. For Hopkins, as a parish minister, and one very concerned with "his" church children (he held special classes for them at Newport), this doctrine was a powerful club with which to beat parents and keep them on their toes. One can only wonder how much guilt it created on the part of parents who tried their best but still saw their children stray from the church and proper righteousness. In a much more benign context, this conception of baptism supported Horace Bushnell's later emphasis on Christian nurture in the family and congregation and his sense that a continuum of growth in knowledge and piety was more normative than was a period of sinfulness followed by an explosive conversion.

In his eschatology, Hopkins affirmed what had become conventional in the Hellenized Western church. He emphatically rebutted corporealists, those who denied the existence of a separate soul or spirit. Thus, he believed that, at death, the spirit of the redeemed joined Christ in the heavens and, in a type of bliss, awaited the judgment and the resurrection of the body. Evil spirits suffered in the interim. At the judgment, these separate souls reunited with highly spiritualized bodies, the blessed to live in a new heaven and earth forever, the cursed to face eternal torment, but a torment proportionate to their sins (a non-Calvinist position but a consistently moralistic and legalistic one).

Typical of a more irenic emphasis that was widespread even among Calvinists in the eighteenth century, Hopkins always affirmed that a vast majority of humanity would be saved, even to the ratio of one thousand saved to each person lost. The scriptures made clear that in the time of Jesus most humans would be lost. It never gave the ratio for all time. Yet, Hopkins was a gloomy judge of his own age. In it an even smaller proportion of humans seemed headed for glory. The testimony was all around – the church was in decline, the world increasingly going to the devil. Thus, Hopkins's empirical observations warred with his conception of a God who so planned the universe as to maximize good. In the abstract it was easy to argue that God had condemned only the number necessary to sustain a moral government or to uphold justice. In fact the saving remnant seemed to shrink each year. Hopkins resolved these dilemmas by a rather unique conception of prophetic history and the coming millennium.

In his gloomy last years, Hopkins spent more and more time struggling with the more apocalyptic sections of the Bible. This upsurge in interest in prophetic books, and in last things, flowered in England as well as America. His speculations make clear that he was a good Protestant. The mark of the beast referred to modern Roman Catholicism; the pope was the anti-Christ. As he read the veiled predictions in Daniel and Revelation, he came to some firm although speculative conclusions about the course of world history. He concluded that the church was entering the darkest times before its redemption. World history was moving toward a final climax, when God would destroy all the evil kingdoms. Some prophetic signs had not yet appeared, but Hopkins concluded that the world was entering a final era of horrible declension, with the true church reduced to a saving remnant (to Hopkins, this remnant was primarily made up of Calvinists). This devolution, well under way by the turn of the century, would climax by the end of the nineteenth century. God's vengeance would follow, until he had all but eliminated evil by the year 2000. Since Hopkins believed, quite literally, in a creation around 4000 B.C.E., he believed that in 2000 history would enter its seventh millennium and that plenty of biblical evidence suggested this would be the one thousand glorious years predicted in Revelation, or the promised millennium. He was not exact about dates, and it was not his intent to prejudge God but only to point out the evidence that suggested such a timetable. As he neared death, this was about the only consolation he had. Despite all the troubles, the glorious age of the church was nigh.

Hopkins does not easily fit into later, neat, and at times rather silly distinctions between pre- and postmillennialism. He joined most premillennialists in seeing a terrible period of trouble and apostasy just before the advent. Yet, he preferred a spiritual and not a governmental interpretation of this advent. Jesus would not literally come to earth to govern, but his spirit would so dominate the world that the church would achieve unity and then convert all nations. This would be the golden age of the church, preceding the judgment and the resurrection that would come at the end of the thousand years, themes close to Edwards and most post-millennialists of his day. After the desolations, only a small human population would remain alive, but in the millennium this population would grow explosively, as an era of peace and righteousness finally allowed humans to fulfill the mandate to Adam, to subdue and replenish the earth. Hopkins did not fear a huge population but looked forward to billions and billions of people, which the earth could support if humans used it responsibly, which they could do when wars ceased. His preference for billions and billions seemed to reflect not a love for crowded cities but a desire to increase the number of the redeemed. Perhaps, for an old and gloomy Hopkins, only such huge numbers, more than had inhabited the earth in all previous generations, could sustain his belief in a God who damned only the numbers necessary to sustain his moral government and the general good. Up until 1800 the largest proportion of humans had seemed among the damned. In 1800 almost all were. In the best of all possible worlds, and over the whole scope of time, it seemed unfair and unlikely that the vast majority of humankind would be damned. All those future Christians in the seventh millennium would right the balance, redeem God's wisdom and righteousness in staging the whole show, and make the eventual heaven a much more populous place than hell.

HOPKINS was a lesser thinker than Edwards. But in the early nineteenth century, America produced no abler theologian and no one as influential. The new century would be a rich one for at least competent theology. Soon the country would be deluged with an enormous volume of theologically charged articles and books. The problem faced by present scholars is charting a clear boundary between doctrinal controversy and serious theology. Every denomination had its own apologists and soon its own periodicals. Who, among all the controversialists, deserved the label "theologian"? After 1800 an increasing number of theologically oriented ministers moved into the new divinity schools and theological seminaries. A few effectively transcended narrow denominational concerns. By 1850 serious theological and scholarly controversy had become almost entirely an academic game, and by then America had several able, professional theologians, with Charles Hodge, Nathaniel Taylor, and Horace Bushnell the most talented and influential (for their contributions, see chapter 7).

Both Taylor and Bushnell were in the direct lineage that led from Edwards to such immediate disciples and students as Hopkins and Bellamy, to Edwards's grandson, Timothy Dwight, and then to his student and disciple Nathaniel Taylor, who in turn taught and directly influenced Bushnell. Thus, Hopkins participated in the largest and most influential theological tradition in American history. Hodge, at Princeton, helped mature the second-most influential tradition, at least within the Reformed tradition: the Princeton theology. Less noticed generally at the time, but quite well received in Europe, was the third major Reformed theological tradition in America before the Civil War, the theology of John Nevin and Philip Schaff at Mercersburg, a theology centered on the corporate church and its sacraments (see chapter 5). From the perspective of Hodge, even an admired Edwards began the erosion of Calvinist orthodoxy, but the full and destructive implications of this erosion first became clear in Samuel Hopkins. To a large extent, the Princeton theology matured in a dialectical encounter with the successors of Hopkins, with both Taylor and Bushnell being prime targets of Hodge's jeremiads. Thus, Hopkins has a unique role in the history of American Reformed theology, for more than any one else, he provided the transition from Edwards to the divisive theological controversies among Reformed thinkers in the nineteenth century.

CHAPTER 4

The Age of Evangelical Hegemony

*I*n the early Republic, evangelically oriented Christians gained their greatest cultural hegemony. Only after 1830 did the major evangelical denominations confront a strong counterbalance in immigrant churches (Lutheran and Roman Catholic), in nonevangelical trends within older Reformed denominations (Episcopal, German and Dutch Reformed, Presbyterian, and Congregational), and in new, growing, and distinctive American varieties of Christianity (Disciples, Adventists, and Mormons). For a brief time it had seemed that four largely evangelical denominations – Separate Baptists, Methodists, Presbyterians, and Congregationalists – might gain an enduring monopoly on American Christianity. It was not to be. By around 1830, it was already clear that the center would continue to erode in an increasingly heterogeneous America.

Mainstream evangelical Christians gained power and influence within a particular cultural and religious environment. They exploited a developing form of religious pluralism, or free competition, which involved a very complex relationship between church and state, religion and politics. They profited from waves of regional religious awakenings featuring new revivalistic institutions. In these revivals, the Methodists and the Baptists, the most uniformly evangelical denominations, won the largest prizes in the overall religious competition. Evangelicals, recognizing the increasingly feminine appeal of Christianity in America, worked hardest at converting and retaining male members. Because of patterns of settlement, racial divisions, and revival success, the more evangelical denominations gained a virtual monopoly among both blacks and whites in the Deep South. Finally, evangelicals enjoyed the returns from several institutional innovations, ranging from camp meetings to several forms of cooperative benevolence to enduring and very significant Sunday schools.

One must return again to that troubling word *evangelical.* It gained a rather narrow meaning in the late eighteenth century – an emphasis among Protestants on a crisis-like conversion experience, on a very experiential devotional life, on the winning of converts, and on a very rigorous standard of personal and social purity or holiness. By 1800, the proponents of such a spiritual Christianity consistently used the label for themselves and proudly added the label to their periodicals and organizations. But such was the prevalence of the term, and such the continuing ambiguity of it among scholars, that the label too easily invites vacuous comparisons.

As most often used by contemporaries, "evangelical" seemed to encompass an overwhelming majority of American Protestants. It is thus difficult to fill in the other side. Who were the nonevangelicals? In part, the very inclusiveness of the label may serve as evidence that one side had all but won out in the religious competition. Those who made the label a mark of self-identity certainly believed they so used it to distinguish themselves from a majority of Americans, although, by their perspective, not necessarily a majority of Christians. They tended to make authentic Christianity and evangelical synonymous. To them, the label excluded not only the churches outside the Reformed tradition, such as Roman Catholics, Unitarians and Universalists, and the Anabaptist sects, but also all Episcopalians, Presbyterians, Congregationalists, and German and Dutch Reformed who emphasized Christian nurture over a vivid rebirth experience, who substituted a humanist moralism for spirituality (that is, for guidance by the Holy Spirit), who rejected revivals and did not devote themselves to the saving of souls for Christ, and who compromised their Christian profession by all manner of compromises with worldly values, fashions, or amusements. But all these "lukewarm" or heretical Christians did not constitute the main body of nonevangelicals in America, for they were not as significant, not as numerous, and perhaps not as convertible as the nearly two-thirds of Americans who were unchurched, unsaved, or not yet responsive to the gospel. Thus, self-proclaimed evangelicals felt themselves to be a minority class of born-again and spiritual Christians.[1]

American Denominationalism

Even by 1800 the United States, as a whole, enjoyed or suffered an unprecedented degree of religious pluralism when compared with other countries within Western Christendom. No other nation had to accommodate as much sectarian diversity. Regionally the religious mix varied in America. In rural towns in New England, and in a few tidewater counties in the Old South, one denomination remained dominant, often without effective competition. Rhode Island and Pennsylvania had all along been at the opposite pluralistic pole. But the greatest diversity developed in new settlements, in backcountry New England, in upstate New York, in the southern piedmont, and finally across the Appalachians. Migration patterns and local isolation made possible relatively homogeneous religious enclaves even in the West, but such were the methods of land sale and the patterns of economic enticement that fertile and extended regions west of the Appalachians almost always attracted settlers from every eastern region and sect. On moving, Presbyterians or Methodists or Dunkards from homogeneous eastern communities suddenly found themselves settled, almost promiscuously, among people from strange churches or with no churches at all. Sects mingled and had to compete. Traditional Christians, well versed in their own doctrinal traditions, mixed with people with no doctrinal sophistication at all. Thus, in new settlements the diversity of the nation as a whole became a reality at the very local level.[2]

Not in 1800, not even in 1860, did Americans enjoy or suffer a complete separation of church and state. The majority opposed such, and possibly still does. At first in such settings as Pennsylvania, then nationally with the federal constitution of 1787, Americans worked out a very intricate legal accommodation with religious diversity. The solution was more than mere toleration yet something short of religious equality or state neutrality. The original 1787 constitution did not mention religion. Since it was an enabling charter, and since it gave to Congress no authority to legislate on religious issues, the new federal government could neither establish a state religion nor exercise control over the religious life of Americans. The First Amendment simply reaffirmed these limits – the federal Congress could not establish a religion or, most important at this time, interfere with existing state establishments, and it could not limit the free exercise of religion by individuals. The drafters of the constitution wisely wanted the new federal government to remain aloof from sensitive religious issues, for they appreciated the religious differences from state to state.

No state, in its original constitution, denied religious tolerance. None granted full equality for all religions or set up a wall of separation between church and state. Three New England states continued tax support for a favored church, Congregationalism or, very briefly in Massachusetts from 1825 to 1833, for some Unitarian congregations. All the states provided for certain disabilities on religious grounds, at least for atheists, and over half placed some disabilities on Roman Catholics. The antiestablishment clause of the First Amendment amounted to a pledge that the federal government would not restrict such religious disabilities or preferences at the state level. Ironically, today the same clause prevents state establishments.

The three state establishments quickly became anachronisms. But the several constitutional disabilities, and state favoritism for theistic beliefs, endured, soon joined by strong blasphemy and Sabbatarian laws. These rested on broad popular support. The trends in the early nineteenth century, the period of greatest evangelical dominance, were all toward more formal or informal restrictions on those far outside the religious mainstream, although effective minorities fought against such threats as Sabbatarian legislation. Institutionally, church and state in the early nineteenth century were not as functionally separate as they had been in early Massachusetts. A few states even fully delegated civil functions to the churches (marriage, for example) or subsidized schools or eleemosynary institutions owned or sponsored by churches. Yet, with some degree of scrupulosity, the states embraced the idea of sectarian equality. In principle, if not in practice, the states tried not to pick favorites, at least in the sense of not favoring Methodists against Presbyterians or Baptists over Congregationalists (the Baptists led the fight against an establishment in New England). Thus, public policy endorsed open and free competition among Protestant denominations. At times unintentionally, public policy clearly favored not individual sects but the dominant evangelical or at least Protestant mainstream, a favoritism quickly grasped, and condemned, by Roman Catholics, by dissenting smaller sects, and by non-Christians.

This quasi or limited separation of church and state reflected political realities. The vast majority wanted to push no closer toward separation or full state neutrality. It is possible to separate church and state, although not, in many contexts, without some threat to an often competing value – the free exercise of religious belief. For example, governmental recruitment and pay of Christian and Jewish military chaplains abets "free exercise" but, however strenuous the efforts to represent all sects, still favors theistic religions or those that utilize a clergy. What is almost incomprehensible, at least in nations within the Semitic religious tradition, is a separation of religion and politics. Christians, almost by definition, give religious sanction to moral (and thus policy) positions. It makes no sense to ask Christians to dispense with religious commitments when they vote or hold public office. Religion, if serious, involves all aspects of life. Any state action may have powerful religious implications, particularly since the certification and enforcement of certain moral standards is the major purpose of any government. And here is the ever-present dilemma. If a culture is religiously heterogeneous, with divergent but religiously sanctioned moral standards (think of abortion), then almost any state action necessarily has the effect of favoring one religion over another. It is possible to segregate certain distinctively "religious functions," such as forms of worship, and to adopt a public neutrality toward them, but to many believers these may be largely peripheral to moral positions commanded by their faith. Thus, even though state governments tried, in the early nineteenth century, to be neutral, to treat all sects equally, they faced an impossible task. Given this, it was all but inevitable that the values of the dominant religious mainstream would prevail in legislation governing alcohol, public schools and their curriculum, behavior on Sunday (evangelicals incorrectly referred to this as the Sabbath), or slavery. It was equally inevitable that religious minorities, particularly those farthest from the mainstream, would feel repressed within what they saw as an informal evangelical establishment.

By 1820, the members of the four major denominations enjoyed, in most areas of America, such a preponderance of power and influence as to be able to set norms and standards for the whole society. Locally, evangelicals could control elections and thus influence or control legislation. Not that born-again church members ever made up a majority in America. But a preponderance of respected, socially prominent, economically successful, politically involved citizens were evangelical Christians. Many individuals, even if not actually communicants, were part of extended evangelical communities (those who were in the families of church members, who attended church services, who to some extent shared evangelical beliefs, and who, at some stage in their life, might become church members). Thus, whenever evangelicals reached a consensus (frequently at the local level, less often nationally), their will was likely to prevail. When evangelicals embraced temperance, and by 1830 complete abstinence, they were able to erect local laws to forbid the manufacture or sale of alcohol beverages. On most issues they faced often strenuous opposition from nonevangelicals and sometimes, in the more controversial areas of public policy, suffered the effects of being a numerical minority. Fortunately, or unfortunately, evangelicals never achieved a consensus on many divisive issues (slavery is the prime example) and thus had to waste their energy on intramural conflict.

Notably, American evangelicals, even in their heyday, never formed a Christian political party or faction. In New England, the Federalist party in its declining years was almost a Congregational party. By 1840, in much of New England and the Middle West, the Whig party had gained the allegiance of an overwhelming majority of evangelicals, but it remained a broad-interest party with several constituencies. The sectional interest of the South stood in the way of any national, evangelical political party or alliance. The class and economic appeals of the Jacksonian Democrats often had irresistible appeal for Methodists and Baptists, particularly in the South. After all, religiously anchored moral issues made up only one determinant of party allegiance and voting performance, but in many areas outside the South, religious views correlated with party allegiance better than any other identifiable variable.

Except for the anachronistic establishments in New England, the label "church," in its fullest traditional sense, did not fit American denominations. These were all volunteer organizations, with equal legal status, distinguished from each other by their various names – their "denominations." By certain sociological criteria – historic roots, intellectual assets, social respectability – some denominations came closer, in both status and function, to traditional state churches than others, allowing a carefully qualified use of the terms *church* and *sect* in America. But the normal American pattern would still involve multiple and competitive churches or sects at the local level.

The principle of nonfavoritism to any of the main competitors meant that governments could not for long maintain unchallengeable cooperation with churches in the two vital areas of education and public welfare. This meant a narrowed institutional role for churches in America. The equality of denominations reinforced the already strong bias of most evangelical denominations (Congregationalists, Methodists, Separate Baptists) against ecclesiastical traditions, clerical authority, a formal or corporate church life, and a sacramental or liturgical form of worship. New revival techniques, even a new revival culture, soon came close to severing salvation from church membership. Literally, in the revivals of the early nineteenth century, people believed themselves to be "saved," fully redeemed Christians, even before they submitted themselves for baptism or became members of any congregation. Such "unchurched" Christians might, in some cases, and against ministerial advice, never make up their minds about which "church" they wanted to join. At least at the level of popular understanding, this often meant such a demotion of the status of "church" as to approach its trivialization. Such a trend was never unchallenged. Not only immigrant Lutherans and Roman Catholics but also conservative voices within the Reformed camp, including Episcopalians, Presbyterians, and members of the German and Dutch Reformed churches, resisted many forms of revivalism, emphasized the role of the corporate church, and retained traditional forms of worship (see chapter 5).

American Revivalism

This leads to a second, critical characterization of early-nineteenth-century evangelicals – revivalism. No word, not even *evangelical,* is more elusive and ambiguous than *revival.* In its most general and traditional sense, it meant a period of renewal among church members, or numerous conversions among nonmembers, most often youth, within congregations. In almost all Protestant churches, these times of renewal were cyclical, tied to such varied necessary conditions as ministerial leadership, generational tension, external threats or crises, or the complex dynamics of lay devotional life within congregations. After the widespread awakenings of the 1740s, the word *revival* increasingly denoted regional, national, or even international periods of quite general or widespread fervor and renewal. The prevalent use of such metaphors as "spreading waves" suggested the imitative aspects of such revivals.[3]

By 1800, the word *revival* increasingly distinguished a special, emerging Protestant institution – a planned, organized series of evangelical services keyed primarily to the salvation of sinners, secondarily to the renewal of those already in the church. Some of these organized "revivals" or "revival meetings" involved outdoor, intercongregational camps or retreats; others involved an at least annual, planned series of in-church services, conducted at least in part by visiting ministers or by an emerging new clerical specialist: the professional evangelist or revival preacher. To some extent, these in-church revivals also involved neighboring congregations, at least as visitors. These "revival meetings" slowly became the normal, and in some denominations almost the exclusive, occasion for conviction and conversion and thus for the recruitment of new church members.

The institutional roots of such planned, organized revival meetings went far back. In fact, one can find some precedents or analogies among pre-Reformation Catholics, such as retreats at monastic centers or itinerant missionary efforts by priests. More immediate and direct precedents came out of Scottish Presbyterianism and English Methodism. By 1620, Presbyterians, both in Scotland and in Ulster, began using their distinctive, four- or five-day communion service as an early version of a revival meeting. Periodically, the sacramental seasons became so intense or unruly that people lingered all night, with prayer, song, exhortations, and all manner of physical exercises (crying out, convulsive movements, swooning). Communion rituals clearly separated the saved and unsaved and brought enormous pressures on those who shared the belief system but were still outside the church, particularly youth. By the climax of such communions in Scotland in 1742, when up to thirty thousand people attended two summer sacraments near Glasgow, it seemed as if almost all conversions now took place in conjunction with these sacraments. In this sense, the summer communions, which moved almost weekly from one congregation to another, became a form of Presbyterian "revival meeting." As soon as Scotch-Irish immigrants were able to establish churches in America, they resumed the great Scottish communions and used them for the same purposes. By the 1740s such sacraments became the institutional base of a great awakening in almost every presbytery in the middle colonies (Whitefield preached at such communions both in Scotland and in the colonies) and then, by the 1750s, in Presbyterian revivals in Virginia. Such "set aside" interludes in church life, quite separate from Sunday worship, with people lured away from the place and the pressures of daily life, with a carefully structured and intensely absorbing atmosphere or environment, with outdoor preaching "tents," and with sermons especially adapted to the occasion, became the harvest time for Presbyterians.

This emerging institutional context joined with slow and subtle changes in the private religious experience of individuals. The conversion experience became, at least in part, a public experience, something that reached a climax at these sacraments. Presbyterians were very circumspect in judging others, even in making precise estimates about numbers converted. But in the eighteenth century the more evangelical congregations accepted subtle changes in their ritual of conversion, in assumptions and expectations about a very turbulent, even at times devastating, process that led from an original conviction of sinfulness, occasioned by hearing the word and by the prompting of the Holy Spirit, through often long periods of weeks or even years of ongoing introspection and personal struggle, until sooner or later one found release or what Presbyterians usually called "comfort." This marked the end of the process, the moment of rebirth. Thus, the great Presbyterian communions could have two desired effects. They could be God's means for initiating a period of conviction, for launching a personal spiritual process or crisis, one soon somewhat stereotyped and recounted in numerous conversion narratives. For others, already under conviction, these sacraments could bring the process to a climax, although not until a final peak of personal agony.

The most important innovation in the morphology of conversion would be a gradual abridgement of the amount of time that normally elapsed between conviction and comfort. Concomitant with this sped-up process and the intensification of the experience that accompanied it was the transfer of almost all the steps into the public arena. In other words, the whole process could now take place during a week-long revival, whether that meant a Scottish-style sacrament, a planned retreat or encampment, or a summer revival meeting within a congregation. By 1800, this abridged, intensified, and public version of conversion had almost replaced earlier, extended, intermittent, and mostly private transactions between God and his deviant children.

In many ways the Methodists contributed more to nineteenth-century revival institutions than did the Presbyterians. Early Methodist itinerants became the prototype of later, specialized evangelists. Whitefield and Wesley made their contribution not as parish ministers but, at first, as field preachers and then as itinerant revivalists. Among Wesley's early lay preachers, the most talented itinerants preached not within set circuits but all over Britain, wherever Wesley sent them. They entered new territories, preached in the field, and focused their whole effort on the "saving of souls." Since they were laypeople, not responsible for formal worship or sacramental duties, they could orient both their mission preaching and their preaching within organized Methodist societies toward the conviction of sinners. The new, rousing Methodist hymns and the extemporaneous prayers could also serve the same goal.

The other Methodist institutions, such as love feasts and the all-important class meetings, were not converting institutions but were nurturing devices for the saved. Yet even these helped train laypeople for evangelical work within their own families or in their own neighborhoods. In this sense, these institutions helped build morale for Wesley's salvation army. Every Methodist was supposed to testify, in certain contexts exhort, and in all contexts do all possible to lead others to Christ. The success of Methodist classes inspired other Christians to work out parallel institutions. Baptist and Presbyterians, by the eighteenth century, formed their own socials or societies, or what in time became prayer circles or prayer meetings, as well as mutual support groups. In time all the evangelical churches realized that the success of a revival rested not so much on the preacher or preachers but on lay preparation and involvement. This lay involvement meant not only participation in songs and public prayer but also direct persuasion, even pleading, with sinners, a type of ministry that quickly moved in large part from the private to public sphere. By the time of the great western revivals of 1800–1801, both Presbyterians and Methodists not only encouraged lay exhortation but began to gather (in a few cases carry) those people who were under deep conviction to designated sites, where laypeople could pray, and plead with them, console them, and engage them in prayers or hymns. Since one conspicuous place to gather the deeply afflicted was the front pews, where mourners sat at funerals, this site became known in the West as the "mourner's bench." Later, when Charles Finney perfected the technique, he called it, more precisely, the "anxious bench." Notably, such lay evangelism, now fully apart from traditional worship services, provided new and widely accepted roles for women.

For early Methodists, evangelical efforts pervaded all their religious services. But even they, gradually, began to distinguish between normal worship services and special evangelical occasions. In America they had no institution as serviceable as the Presbyterian sacraments, but they had their own annual conferences, where the itinerant ministers gathered with bishops or presiding elders to conduct church business. These included soul-searching testimonies by the preachers, a heightened sense of brotherhood among the hard-working itinerants, and the inspiration and zeal needed to carry them through their next assignments to a circuit. These annual conferences always featured worship and communion services for lay audiences. Methodist families often traveled one hundred miles, camping en route, to hear their bishop deliver the climactic sermon at the annual conference. The crowd, the special environment, and the power of the preaching made this a converting time, or a revival.

Even closer to the Presbyterian communions were the quarterly conferences held in most Methodist circuits. These were essentially intercongregational lay conferences, with extensive home hospitality for those from distant congregations. Ministers from nearby circuits came and preached, in rare times a bishop might attend, and Methodists often invited nearby Presbyterian and Baptist clergymen. These conferences became, in effect, mass revival meetings. The conference usually began on Saturday. The limited business meeting took little time, since the circuit would have no more than two or three ministers or, in remote areas, only one. On Sunday, a typical quarterly conference began with a morning love feast, with testimonials serving as the prominent feature along with the bread and water. After this came communion and then the preaching. For many rural Methodists, this was the only sacramental occasion they knew, further linking the quarterly conference with the intracongregational communions of Presbyterians (often overlooked is the fact that almost all early revivalism in America had a strong sacramental component). The preaching was deliberately directed at soul saving and usually had to be from an outside tent, since the crowds almost always exceeded the capacity of the meetinghouse. Physical exercises and conversions were routine at such conferences and at some the preaching extended beyond Sunday into the early weekdays. After the turn of the century, as camping became enormously popular, most Methodist circuits merged their quarterly conference into planned summer camp meetings, held at their own developed campgrounds. These provided a carefully contrived, in a sense artificial, environment perfect for new evangelical techniques. It was the culture of the quarterly conference that blended so easily into organized camps and that helped make camping much more popular among Methodists than among Baptists and Presbyterians.

The Baptists also developed early prototypes of revival meetings, although their radical congregationalism precluded formal conferences. Some Baptist congregations remained independent, with no associational life at all. But most congregations joined local associations, which held joint meetings at least annually. Some of the first records of family camping in America involved Baptists who attended such association meetings, which featured fervent preaching, communion services, and baptisms, or institutional forms very close to Methodist quarterly conferences. In addition, throughout America neighboring Baptist congregations often gathered along streams for mass baptisms, another occasion for a convicting form of preaching by multiple ministers in an outdoor setting.

Despite the precedents of George Whitefield or Gilbert Tennent, the widespread revivals of the 1740s did not lead to an enduring and separate evangelical ministry. Most ministers in the evangelical denominations had to accept frequent assignments away from their congregations. They visited and preached in areas without ministers, or moved to frontier areas to help gather congregations, or traveled as visitors to Presbyterian sacraments, Methodist conferences, or Baptist associations. The Presbyterians and Methodists both came to appreciate ministers especially skilled in such mission work and thus more often selected them for extended periods away from their home congregations. But almost no one worked full-time as an evangelist. Informally, some "called" ministers without pulpits undoubtedly tried to make a living by their own self-appointed itinerancy, as did some individuals during the revivals after 1740. After the turn of the century, increasing numbers of ministers gained their reputation primarily from their revival preaching, and some probably spent at least half their time on the revival circuit, although most still had a home congregation or a circuit assignment. Neither Baptists nor Congregationalists as yet had any mechanisms for ordaining nonsettled clergymen; congregations, not the denomination, ordained their ministers. Even Charles Finney, who for several years made evangelical work his vocation and thus gained the deserved reputation as one of the most influential evangelists in American history, held two different pastorates in New York City. But by 1810 Congregationalists and Presbyterians in New England were at least able to appoint a few full-time missionaries, largely to work with Indian tribes at frontier posts but some to work with weak congregations, often by holding planned revivals. Such denominational evangelists soon joined an even larger, but less ordered, group of free-lance revivalists, men (and a few women) who specialized in revival preaching (or, in the twentieth century, in radio and television preaching). Such specialists were part of a new and distinctive, although as yet unordered, profession, one that would have enormous impact on American Protestantism.

These new revival institutions came to maturity at the beginning of the new century, but it is easy to overemphasize innovations and ignore continuities. Likewise it is easy to use such labels as Second Great Awakening to obscure the diversity of revivals in the new century. The great Presbyterian communions took place every year, and in any year a few would be fervent enough or productive enough to gain local recognition as a time of revival. After 1787, incited by new religious concerns among students at Hampden-Sydney, a wave of Presbyterian revivals, tied to the great summer sacraments, spread from southern Virginia into the Shenandoah Valley and into the Carolina and Georgia piedmont. Almost all the architects of the revivals in Kentucky and Tennessee from 1787 to 1805 experienced conversion, or completed their ministerial apprenticeship, during this revival. Among the converts in North Carolina was one James McGready, in many ways the father of Presbyterian revivals in the West, and also Barton W. Stone, pastor at Cane Ridge congregation in Kentucky at the time of the soon legendary communion of 1801. But on close inspection, one finds accounts of regional revivals at almost any time – among New England and New York Baptists at the end of the Revolution, among some Congregationalists in the early 1790s, among Baptists and Methodists in Virginia just before the Revolution and again around 1801. What has helped obscure the prevalence of revivals, even in the purportedly "cold" nineties, is that most did not spread very far. They remained local or regional and erupted only sporadically.[4]

At the turn of the century, as in 1740, the eruptions were more widespread, more closely linked to each other, and more explosive than ever before. James McGready and four Presbyterian colleagues, joined by one Methodist, utilized the familiar Scottish communion, plus organized prayer meetings and other devices, to stimulate a series of great summer sacraments that began in 1797 but climaxed in 1800 and 1801 in the Cumberland area of Kentucky and Tennessee. These might have remained local events, in an isolated near-frontier area, except for the deliberate and effective publicizing by McGready and others. Essential to this publicity were two or three newly formed eastern evangelical or missionary journals, each eager to publish news not only from all sections of America but also from Britain and from foreign mission outposts. By 1800, editors were beginning their very important, often neglected role in American religious history.

The so-called McGready revivals (he perhaps unintentionally overemphasized his role and understated that of his colleagues) involved some innovations, although one can exaggerate them. Most of the revivals, largely in Logan County, Kentucky, and Sumner County, Tennessee, were quite traditional. In the climactic summer of 1800, for example, at least nine Presbyterian congregations in the Cumberland Basin held their annual, scheduled communions, a tradition now almost two hundred years old. At least seven ministers cooperated in the joint services, including one very charismatic Methodist. Devout families traveled, as they had for generations, to attend as many of these festive occasions as possible, enjoying the normal home hospitality provided by hosts. Already, in sparsely populated areas of America, attendance often involved heroic efforts, such as one or two days of travel, camping in wagons along the way, and possibly something close to camping in the barns or yards of host families. Even at the most famous of these Cumberland communions, at Gasper River in July 1800, it is not clear that the tradition of home hospitality broke down, although the number of visitors, some from one hundred miles away, surely taxed local resources. When the host minister, John Rankin (not James McGready, as usually reported, although he of course came and preached and served tables), arrived for the scheduled, opening Friday session, he was surprised to find twenty to thirty wagons encamped on a gentle slope near the meetinghouse.

Apparently no one had planned this encampment. The individual families chose this alternative, it seems, not because of necessity but because they wanted to be close to the action. Such was the intensity of these communions, as already demonstrated at the Red River Church a month earlier, that the people continued on the grounds way into the night, long after formal services had ended. It was, therefore, convenient to camp on the grounds in order not to miss some of the exciting events. It is not clear that all the campers were committed to a revival. By now, these sacraments were objects of wide interest and attracted growing numbers of spectators (some of whom quickly ceased to be casual spectators). From then on, increasing numbers of campers came to such sacraments in the Cumberland and, beginning in the spring of 1801, to several of the fifty or so great communions held during the season in the more populous central basin of Kentucky. But, as yet, these meetings largely involved de facto camping, tied to wagons or canopies erected beside them, without any careful planning, any camp rules, and any prepared tents or cabins. Nonetheless, the accounts of the Gasper River camping spread like wildfire. Rankin took the news back to former congregations in North Carolina. Within two or three years Christians all over America were building camps, some motivated not only by religious goals but also by a local spirit of boosterism or even by entrepreneurial expectations.

According to the participants, the Logan County sacraments involved an unprecedented excitement and innovative physical exercises. They were probably wrong on these judgments. They did not know, in detail, about the great Scottish communions almost a century earlier. At Red River, for the first time in the West, for possibly the first time in two decades anywhere in America, large numbers of participants, devastated by their sense of sinfulness, fell to the floor, some in a complete coma. This massive falling came to distinguish not only the Logan County sacraments but also those in central Kentucky in 1801 and, in the next two years, in the Carolinas and Georgia piedmont and in the Red Stone Presbytery of Western Pennsylvania and Virginia. To some extent, all Presbyterians enjoyed a period of renewal, although in central Virginia and from Maryland into New England without as many, or as extreme, physical exercises. Crying, shouting, and various convulsive movements (some later caricatured as jerks) accompanied the falling. In 1800 the falling and other exercises followed scheduled services and, except for involuntary crying or shouting, never interrupted the actual serving at the communion table. The wildest night at Red River followed the impromptu, uninhibited exhortations of a visiting Methodist. Largely because of their sacramental institutions, the largest crowds, the wildest exercises, and the most national publicity all involved Presbyterian revivals, but at least a majority of the Presbyterian clergy in the West, all of whom participated and all of whom rejoiced at a long-awaited and prayerfully solicited revival of religion, tried to maintain order, to downplay the religious significance of the more extreme exercises, and to restrain a few of their colleagues who, if anything, helped to trigger the more extreme reactions. Internal division over the exercises, over the proper role of ministers during the revival, and over doctrinal compromises that seemed to accompany the revival soon split the Presbyterian church in the West and helped slow its growth. Ironically, the Presbyterians reaped few of the benefits from revivals that largely began within their own congregations.

The climax of the great western revival came at Cane Ridge, in the prosperous central bluegrass county of Bourbon in early August 1801. This famous sacrament was exceptional, not in kind but in scale. An unprecedented number of ministers and congregations made plans to attend and participate in this meeting, carefully planned and publicized by the host minister, Barton W. Stone, with unprecedented cooperation by Methodists and so scheduled as not to compete with any other nearby communions. Thus, local observers realized that Cane Ridge would be historic in scale, which led many observers to write detailed narratives or letters about it, resulting in extensive coverage in the new, evangelical press. At least ten

Presbyterian congregations shared in the communion and eighteen Presbyterian ministers attended and either preached or served at one of the multiple table settings or ministered to the hundreds who were soon in distress. At least four Methodist ministers, and one black Baptist minister, also preached. Hundreds of laypeople exhorted. Attendance probably reached ten thousand on Sunday and possibly exceeded twenty thousand over the six days of almost continuous preaching and exhorting (from the meetinghouse and three outdoor stands or "tents"), all of which ended in part because of shortages of provisions for people and horses. Almost everyone who lived in the area, from the governor of Kentucky to slaves, at least visited Cane Ridge, most at first as mere spectators. By most estimates, one thousand people fell during the six days, about the same number as those who took communion on Sunday. Thousands more were caught up in milder exercises. In fact, even the most casual observers were often afflicted, possibly without religious significance.

Cane Ridge was climactic, but it did not end such sacraments. No later one, in part by design, was as large, but those led by a small minority of "New Light" ministers were much wilder. The exciting summer communions continued, with only slightly less zeal, in 1802 and 1803, although by then the Presbyterians were deeply divided. Stone and five other ministers with a Cane Ridge background led a revolt within the Kentucky Synod. The wilder New Lights provided a fertile ground for Shaker recruitment in the West. The milder rebels from Calvinism, under Stone's leadership, created an early Christian or restoration movement in Kentucky.

Presbyterian sacraments in Kentucky gained the well-deserved attention of the country. But this attention, and all the controversies about the meaning of the physical exercises, diverted attention from smaller, equally intense revivals among Baptists and Methodists in their conferences or association meetings and most often for Baptists in protracted meetings in individual churches. These denominations never split because of the revivals. They simply reaped the returns during a period of explosive growth for both denominations in Kentucky, Ohio, and Tennessee. In the Carolinas and Georgia, the Presbyterian communions provided the institutional format for a series of great union meetings from 1801 to 1803, some of which approached Cane Ridge in scale and fervor. These rather quickly involved planned, organized camping. Here, more than in Kentucky, the Presbyterians were joined by Baptists, Methodists, and a few ministers from Episcopal and German Reformed churches, which meant more cooperation but less focus on the Presbyterian sacrament.

What is not often noted is that, although these revivals always subsided locally, they never really ended in America. For Methodists and some Presbyterians, they rather quickly merged into organized camp meetings and became annual affairs.

Physical exercises were simply part of the new revival culture, ever present but soon stereotyped and scarcely remarked. Only in cyclical periods of great fervor, often following years of local declension or coldness, did the more extreme exercises recur, as they did in the mid-1820s in a series of nonsacramental revivals conducted by Charles Finney in upstate New York. Once again, swooning marked the most extreme reaction to the intense feeling and emotion provoked by the ever-powerful drama of salvation.

What gives some credence to the concept of a national Second Great Awakening was a series of revivals in new England, primarily among Congregationalists, that paralleled those in the West and in the piedmont. Even as McGready observed the first stirring in Logan County in 1797, scattered ministers throughout New England began to report revivals within their congregations. These became general by 1801 and included a brief, much publicized awakening among Yale students stimulated by the preaching of college president Timothy Dwight. The success of well-placed Congregational evangelicals helped conceal earlier and continuing periods of revival among New England Baptists and Methodists, rapidly growing denominations in New England but ones that trailed the Congregationalists and Presbyterians in the competition for wealth, status, and educational achievement. The revival among Congregationalists revived older Puritan themes of sin and redemption, served as a counterbalance to the growing liberal or Unitarian faction in the church, led to two new evangelical journals, and contributed directly to the founding of a thoroughly evangelical seminary at Andover. It indirectly helped stimulate a theological renaissance among Yale faculty members, and as in the West, this revival suffered no clear ending, for in each year after 1800 the evangelical journals received reports of revivals from some of the towns and congregations. But neither in New England nor in the country as a whole were the later revivals ever quite as general as in 1801. Cycles were never again in phase, meaning that local memories of great revivals during the rest of the century have quite varied dates, although the well-publicized Finney revivals in the late twenties and early thirties, and a well-publicized urban revival movement in 1858, led by businessmen and including leading Episcopalian laymen, have led some scholars to stress three nineteenth-century awakenings before the Civil War.

The label Second Great Awakening obscures too much even when applied only to the first decade of the century. Among Congregationalists in New England and New York, among Presbyterians in Pennsylvania, Maryland, and central Virginia, and among a scattering of Episcopalians and German and Dutch Reformed congregations, the reports of revival revealed rather sharp regional and denominational differences. Most of the revivals in the older, traditional congregations took place in the meetinghouse and under the leadership of a parish minister. In those congregations, almost no reports listed the more extreme physical exercises. In part because of the often inflated stories from Kentucky, and eastern horror at western excesses, ministers, if anything, tried to moderate and then downplay the level of feeling or physical response and used their pulpits to guide and moderate the emotional extremes. Thus, the reports of new England revivals, in the same journals that carried letters about Cane Ridge, emphasized the solemnity and the seriousness of the work, or by implication its authenticity and durability (no empirical data proves that in fact tamer conversions outlived wilder ones). The evidence also suggests that, although those Congregationalists who espoused and led revivals certainly emphasized the crisis-like conversion, they did not expect it to take such dramatic or explosive forms as in the revivals in the West. These regional and denominational differences suggest that claims of a great, nationwide awakening may conflate too many religious phenomena, or rest on too many ambiguities in the word *revival*, to retain much descriptive value.

Despite differences, much remained common to, even definitive of, early-nineteenth-century revivals. This included a continuous emphasis on a vivid rebirth experience, on somewhat varied institutional means of facilitating these conversions, on an abridgement of the time involved in moving from conviction to conversion, and on a shift of such conversion experience from the private to the public sphere. Such shifts did not require any doctrinal revisions. The new forms of revivalism could be congruent with conservative Calvinism or Wesleyan Arminianism. It depended on how one understood what happened. But the new emphasis did mean that conversion was more manageable, more open to human techniques. Calvinists could understand these as God-ordained means, effective only through his choice and under the guidance of the Holy Spirit. But, no doubt, the clear human contrivances used to facilitate revivals, together with Finney's emphasis on the ease and reasonableness of the human response, abetted free will beliefs.

One final commonality is less easily documented but is supported by a growing flow of new gender-oriented research. Women members increasingly predominated in every nineteenth-century denomination for which we have membership lists. Their preponderance increased in periods of religious decline, indicating that adult males were much more susceptible to declension and thus made up a prime target for fervent evangelical efforts. It is not possible to do more than speculate about this feminine shift. Since it was even more marked in more conservative or liturgical congregations, the trend was clearly not a result of greater female susceptibility to warm, revivalistic methods or a very spiritual type of devotional life. Perhaps a threatened clerical profession deliberately adopted new revival methods in a desperate effort to regain male allegiance, an allegiance that greatly affected the profession's income and prestige. Maybe changing norms for men and women (including an increased emphasis on female duties to preserve and foster moral values in children) reflected increasingly separate work patterns, at least in cities and towns. It is possible that more carefully defined and separate gender roles – separate spheres – among the middle class abetted female religiosity even as such changes tempted males to seek both status and fulfillment in secular occupations. The evidence so far suggests that the nearest approach to balanced male-female membership came during or in the wake of successful revivals in the more clearly evangelical congregations. This, again, means that the major variable in membership involved men, not the more faithful women, who remained in the churches through thick or thin. From this perspective, the new revival methods reflected efforts, at times desperate efforts by wives and mothers, to find a means to win husbands and sons back to the church.

Denominational Competition

The new revival techniques seemed to favor the Methodists over all other denominations. To a lesser extent, the same techniques favored Baptists and Presbyterians over Congregationalists. Congregationalists, at least if one deducts the separating Unitarian congregations, lagged farther behind their three evangelical competitors in each decade, growing more slowly than the overall population. By 1820, after two decades of spirited revivals in almost every area of America, the Methodists had probably caught up with all varieties of Baptists in total membership (in 1800 the Baptists probably had more members than any other tradition). Starting with a small base of only an estimated 15,000 members at the time of their Christmas Conference in 1784, the Methodists had an estimated 2,700 congregations by 1820 with an estimated 200,000 to 300,000 members.[5]

It is impossible to determine exact numbers of church members in the early nineteenth century, or even today. All estimates have to depend on unreliable reports from the churches themselves. But if the Methodists had even 200,000 members in 1820, the total population within the range of influence of Methodist congregations was close to one million out of a national population of just over ten million. Contemporary Presbyterian and Methodist ministers generally multiplied the number of communicants by five to encompass all those who made up part of an extended church family. This included all children, all lapsed or unconverted youth or adults who were part of church families, and even families who had no communicants but who nonetheless attended services and remained potential converts. By 1820, the Presbyterians had less than 100,000 members in only 1,700 churches. The Congregationalists had fewer congregations but a slightly higher estimated membership, which reflected the larger size of well-established town congregations in New England and possibly also the less restrictive membership qualifications in many of the more liberal congregations. As one moves from the screening rigor of the Methodists and Baptists to such inclusive, and usually not evangelical, churches as the Episcopalians, membership figures tended to converge toward the total church population (in 1820 the struggling Protestant Episcopal church had just over 15,000 members). Until the Civil War, most membership statistics for Roman Catholics included the whole number of baptized people, including infants. The often cited and, to Protestants, frightening transition around 1850, when Roman Catholics reportedly became the largest American denomination, is challengeable on many grounds. At that time the number of Americans within the larger orbit of either the Baptists or the Methodists easily exceeded active, adult Roman Catholics (around 1,000,000 in 1850). In 1860 the Baptists had five times as many congregations (over 12,000) as did Roman Catholics (2,500); the Methodists (20,000) had close to eight times as many.

The relative success of the Methodists, and to a lesser extent the Baptists, is easily explained, at least with the benefits of hindsight. The Methodists as a whole, and a large share of Baptists, embraced new revival institutions with enthusiasm and without the internal factionalism that haunted Presbyterians and Congregationalists. The tight Methodist episcopacy, tied to the itinerant and circuit system, gave the Methodists a competitive edge among unchurched populations, particularly those in new areas of settlement. Bishop Francis Asbury built, in a quiet literal sense, a tightly disciplined salvation army. The Separate Baptists had nothing as centralized and efficient, but its missionaries exploited its simple, congregational strengths. Unencumbered by any denominational requirements, traveling Baptist preachers could stage a local revival, baptize the converts at the nearest creek, and form them into a Baptist congregation, one that might gather for months or years in a private home. The congregation could quickly recruit, from among its more fervent or eloquent converts, a young man who felt the call to preach – without any delay for formal instruction or certification by any church hierarchy. But despite these advantages, Methodists and Baptists did not usually displace Presbyterians or Congregationalists, and they did not gain disproportionately from the increasing movement of individuals among Protestant denominations (intermarriage was the primary cause of this, with religious taste or simply matters of propinquity or convenience secondary causes).

In the jumbled mix of populations in the West, the Methodists competed with Baptists and Presbyterians to organize the earliest churches. Here, a head start could be critical. In rural areas the local population simply could not support two or three competing congregations. If the Methodists organized the first congregation, then in all likelihood the community would remain Methodist for the next century. Individuals living near the unmarked boundaries of rural villages might have a choice – go west to the Baptist church, east to the Presbyterian. Most people did not have such an easy choice. Undoubtedly, after the original distribution of churches, migrating families often made choices about land purchases in part because of religious preferences. But thousands of rural Americans had to accept an unwanted choice. Thus, former Baptists might attend the only reasonably available congregation, be it Presbyterian or Methodist. They might never join; their children probably would. The early start, of course, did not ensure success in the competition. Large numbers of midwestern or Kentucky Baptists converted, in mass, to the early Christians and Disciples. Rebellious ministers sometimes defected, carrying with them most of their congregation into strange new denominations, such as Universalists, Mormons, Disciples, and even Shakers. But the major congregational shifts came later in the nineteenth and in the twentieth centuries and would reflect the divisions of liberals versus conservatives, fundamentalists versus modernists.

The great revival of 1800–1805 split the Presbyterians in the West. In 1802 the Kentucky Synod, in recognition of the rapid expansion of congregations in the Cumberland area of Kentucky and Tennessee, created a new Cumberland Presbytery. In a pattern already begun in its parent Transylvania Presbytery, the new presbytery quickly relaxed the normally rigorous Presbyterian requirements for the licensing and ordination of ministers. Requiring only limited literary instruction, it licensed young men who had no classical learning (no Latin and Greek). By the language of the time, this meant they were illiterate, although all had an English education. Also, to overcome widespread doctrinal qualms among several young men, most of whom converted in the great communions of 1799–1801, the presbytery allowed them to take exception to the doctrine of double predestination, or to subscribe the Westminster Confession only "insofar as it agreed with Scripture." Within two years the presbytery had licensed or ordained seventeen young men, most converted or inspired by the McGready revivals. By such flexibility on training and doctrinal conformity, this new presbytery made a bid to compete effectively with both Baptists and Methodists and in fact expanded more rapidly than any other presbytery in America.

What followed was a complicated story. Thomas Craighead, a longtime, quite rationalistic Presbyterian minister in the Nashville area, was horrified at both revival excesses and the relaxation of normal educational requirements for ministers (he was more of an Arminian than any of the young men). He and a few sympathetic colleagues protested the new presbyterial methods to the Kentucky Synod, leading in 1805 to a special, and unsympathetic, synod commission appointed to adjudicate the problems in the new presbytery. After hearings, with doctrinal slippage soon a more important concern than educational attainment, the commission commanded each of the young men to submit to a doctrinal examination. Their mentors, including the now venerable James McGready, advised the young men against yielding to what everyone in the Cumberland saw as an illegal inquisition. On their refusal to submit, the commission suspended all the young men from the ministry and brought charges of either heresy or insubordination against the five older ministers, including McGready, who had organized the great communions of 1800.

After several attempts to find a basis of compromise, and three considerations of the issues by the Presbyterian General Assembly, the synod prevailed. It abolished the Cumberland Presbytery and refused to license any of the young preachers. Eventually, McGready adhered to the old church but still defended the young men. One of the five older ministers, John Rankin, joined the Shakers. Two others, William McGee and James McAdow, backed the young rebels, who were now led by the able, socially prominent Finis Ewing, a powerful preacher, a friend and later patronage appointee of Andrew Jackson, and a bitter enemy of Thomas Craighead.

In 1810, Ewing, another of the young men, Samuel King, and the now ill McAdow met in Dickson County, Tennessee, to form an independent Cumberland Presbytery. McGee soon joined the new denomination. It grew to a synod in 1813, approved a confession in 1814, one with many Arminian compromises, and formed a general assembly in 1829. In polity it remained Presbyterian, in doctrine hybrid, in style as evangelical as Methodists. In its confession, one modeled in most details on Westminster, it retained the perseverance of saints but rejected or modified the traditional Calvinist doctrines on depravity, election, atonement, and irresistible grace. On these issues it was at least as close to Methodism as it was to Dort and Westminster, but it reflected a somewhat confusing American version of the doctrines of the Dutch remonstrants. The Cumberland Presbyterians utilized rural circuits, much as did Methodists, formed camp meetings, and emphasized revival techniques.[6]

Denominational growth just after 1800 took, roughly, the following patterns. Congregationalism remained dominant among the established, landowning, or commercial Yankee families, both in new England and in enclaves in Ohio and farther west. The Congregationalists either had almost no appeal, or never developed effective methods of proselytizing, beyond this Yankee population. The Presbyterians proved tenacious and, given their institutional constraints, were effective evangelists. In the centers of Scotch-Irish settlement they held their congregations, at least if one includes the Cumberland Presbyterians. Even in areas of earliest Presbyterian penetration west of the mountains they were quite successful in resisting the lure of Methodists and Baptists. A few East Tennessee counties dominated by Presbyterians before 1800 kept a Presbyterian majority throughout the century. Baptists were as equally tenacious and more flexible in expansion than Presbyterians, who simply could not recruit and train enough ministers to meet the demands of their own former parishioners who moved west, let alone compete with Baptists and Methodists in convening and organizing churches in areas of new settlement.

After 1800 one can identify enduring centers of Congregationalism and Presbyterianism. One can also chart the necessarily gradual expansion of Presbyterianism, at a pace not much beyond the natural increase of its heavily Scotch-Irish membership. The important new trend was the almost unchallenged success of the Methodists, and in some areas the Baptists, in capturing the larger share of migrants, of both British and African descent, in almost all the growing territories and states west of the Appalachians. Eventually, a religious atlas would reveal this success. Outside early Congregational and Presbyterian enclaves, either Baptists or Methodists organized the largest numbers of churches among British settlers in a band across central and southern Ohio, Indiana, and Illinois, in Kentucky and Tennessee, and most overwhelmingly in areas of the South and Southwest open to settlement after 1800 – in Missouri, in Alabama and Mississippi, in northern Louisiana, and later in Arkansas and Texas.

In the South, Methodist and Baptist dominance involved a very successful ministry to blacks and the creation of biracial churches. This meant that, by emancipation, nine out of ten black Christians were Methodist or Baptist. Unlike in the northern tier states of the Old Northwest, where non-British migrants (German, Irish, Scandinavian) helped establish a very different denominational mix, with Lutherans or Roman Catholics often in a majority, in the Deep South, largely because of the deterring effect of slavery on European immigration, the population remained religiously homogeneous, with a dominant white, formerly British owning class, some with lingering allegiance to Episcopal and Presbyterian churches but most either Baptist or Methodist. The underclass, made up of Africans and more impoverished whites, was even more concentrated in Baptist and Methodist congregations. Today, the largest numbers and most faithful adherents of the revivalistic, born-again evangelical Christianity of the early nineteenth century are the descendants of mid-American and southern Methodists and Baptists, both black and white. They have moved east and north and west. They now live everywhere, including wherever blacks have settled, and they are now denominationally diverse, since later schisms helped spin off new varieties of Baptist churches and numerous Holiness and Pentecostal denominations that derived from Methodism.

The disproportionate feminine appeal, and values, of a warm, evangelical Christianity created special problems in the South. One of the ironies of evangelical Christianity was that, even as it seemed to conquer the South, it appeared in many ways least fitted to that section. Outside the border states, where Presbyterians, some Episcopalians, and the Restoration churches contributed to a religious pluralism that almost matched that of the North, the Deep South became overwhelmingly Baptist and Methodist. Presbyterians declined in relative strength and, in parts of the South, in real numbers during the period after 1837. To an increasing extent the more formal and intellectual Presbyterian form of evangelicalism became a refuge of affluent and socially prominent whites, including many prominent slave owners, who enjoyed or suffered the same status as did Episcopalians in some of the tidewater areas of the Old South. This meant that the predominant Baptist and Methodist forms of evangelism in the South would enjoy less of the intellectual resources, the theological sophistication, and the political clout enjoyed by Presbyterians and Congregationalists in the North. Southern evangelical Protestantism thus remained Low Church, egalitarian, revivalistic, intensely communal, localistic, and biracial. These traits helped it survive in a culturally alien environment. But what was unclear, until the Civil War, was whether evangelical religion was a countercultural alien or was on the way to becoming *the* culture of the South.[7]

Much in the antebellum South seemed inconsistent with Methodist and Baptist spirituality. The slave system, even apart from its injustices to blacks, created enormous temptations for white male owners – in arrogance and false pride as well as great cruelty and sexual exploitation of black women. The lag in public education left a large share of the white population with limited literacy and with an accompanying crudeness in manners and naïveté in religion. A non-Christian culture of honor and shame survived in the masculine South and provided motives that often overpowered an evangelical ethic of morality and guilt. Southern white males were jealous of personal honor, quick to defend themselves, and thus given to violence, even when cloaked in the code duello among those who continued the affectations of gentlemen. Clan and family loyalties remained strong in the South, leading to personal vengeance and in some areas a dearth of public authority and public order. Hunting and violent sport prevailed. In such a secular and macho setting, the churches faced an impossible task in domesticating white men, in engendering on male youth the virtues of the Sermon on the Mount. Young white men grew up in the ambivalence of two competing ethics and were pulled in both directions. In times of revival, they might embrace the church and its morality. Yet, it was hard to turn loose of the old habits, resulting in the strain and tension of being an evangelical Christian in the South. Good Methodists and Baptists, or at least women in these churches, tried to domesticate and discipline the men of the South, but with limited success. Thus, a pre-Christian and anti-Christian ethic often prevailed, or in effect forced compromises in Christianity itself.

The Civil War aided the evangelical cause. The dislocation, suffering, and death created the stimulus for religious revivals, many in the camps of Confederate soldiers. The antislavery crusade before the war and the role of northern churches in reconstruction afterward made reunification with northern churches almost impossible. The loss and humiliation of the war led to such defensive reactions as the cult of a lost cause, to an overly defensive attempt by whites to justify a distinctive, southern culture, and to the beguiling idea that the South remained more loyal to the old-time religion than the North. In the aftermath of war, the southern economy collapsed. Incomes remained at only half the national average. Schools closed. A generation grew up with either no public schools or inferior ones. Blacks suffered more deprivation than whites. Literacy rates declined for whites, while a majority of blacks either remained illiterate or gained only the most rudimentary education. The churches suffered from ill-educated ministers who served rural white congregations or the now-separating black congregations. Southern Baptists and Methodists struggled to build colleges and even seminaries, but the result of their effort would be institutions markedly inferior to the best northern institutions. The scattered academies and colleges established for blacks, largely through the efforts of northern churches, were also inferior. In such a context, southern evangelical religion changed little into the early twentieth century. Southern Baptists and Methodists resisted new intellectual innovations, froze in place the older revival methods, and widened the gap between southern and northern branches of the same traditions. At the same time, this atavistic but warm evangelical religion met the desperate needs of blacks and whites, provided the only available leadership opportunities for blacks, and continued to provide a weak brake on southern violence in the worst of times.

Evangelicals faced competition everywhere, although least of all in the Deep South. In time, all the mainstream evangelical denominations, except perhaps Southern Baptists and small northern branches created by pre–Civil War splinters, backed away from evangelicalism as I have defined it. Here the definitional problems multiply and become almost unmanageable. But, briefly and too simply, from the late nineteenth century to the 1920s, a liberal majority among Congregationalists, northern Baptists, Presbyterians, and Methodists moved back toward earlier Reformation and Catholic roots. They so blurred or diluted the conversion experience as, virtually, to move back to a type of Christian nurture, to instruction and confirmation. They replaced an affectionate or spiritualistic emphasis with a more moralistic one, at times even a more ritualistic or sacramental one. They converted much of their outreach or missionary zeal from soul saving to humanitarian reform. They slowly gave up their austere, even ascetic, and repressive quest for moral purity and thus slowly accommodated worldly arts and amusements. In this sense, these liberal Protestants converged toward Episcopalians and even Roman Catholics.

Before this erosion from within, evangelicals faced powerful competition from nonevangelicals. The most successful competition came from new, nonevangelical denominations with many areas of doctrinal and cultural overlap with evangelicals. The major example here would be the various Christians and Disciples. Even today, in its liberal manifestation (Disciples of Christ), this movement is fully competitive with Baptists, Presbyterians, and Methodists in a stretch from Ohio across southern Illinois and Illinois; in its more conservative manifestation (the Churches of Christ), it is a viable competitor of Baptists and Methodists from Kentucky and Tennessee to Texas.

Denominational Cooperation

Evangelical erosion and later schisms within the four great evangelical denominations created more, not less, diversity within American Christianity. Such changes gradually dissipated any threat (or hopes) of evangelical consensus. But before this happened, the dominant evangelical denominations, and the culture they supported, were like a great magnet. It was hard for nonevangelical denominations, including ethnic ones, to resist this culture, to maintain a separate integrity. This is a story that does not fit here but lies within the complex story of American Lutherans, American Friends, and even the very separatist and traditional Anabaptist sects. In each case, dynamic internal factions adopted evangelical beliefs and rituals, including revival meetings. The impact on their confessions varied, but to note this capitulation to evangelical beliefs and techniques is to document, in yet another area, the degree of cultural hegemony enjoyed by early-nineteenth-century evangelicals.[8]

As significant in the long term as the new revival techniques were institutional changes in the evangelical churches. Absent, at least until 1830, were strong, well-funded, centralized denominational bureaucracies. Of the big four evangelical denominations, only the Methodists had a tight, episcopal polity, but its two or three bishops (Asbury and William McKendree were most significant early in the new century) had no central headquarters. They rode on their own circuits to annual and district conferences. Methodists met, nationally, only every four years in their general conference, which left the regional annual conferences as the dominant centers of Methodism. But early in the century these conferences had almost no bureaucracy, not even a resident bishop, and no funds for any extended educational or missionary activities. The Presbyterians, although with a less hierarchical polity, had more of a center. After the reorganization of the old Philadelphia–New York Synod in 1788, with a slightly modified confession, the church assembled in an annual general assembly, which served as the highest court and legislative body. Since the general assembly met in its early years most often at Philadelphia, this became a home for the denomination's early publishing, educational, and missionary agencies.

Baptists and Congregationalists had no formal denominational machinery. The Congregationalists joined in statewide associations in New England, associations that eventually assumed the functions of a denomination but strictly on the basis of voluntary support from congregations. In 1801, the Connecticut Congregationalist Association approved the Plan of Union with the Presbyterians (the other New England associations soon approved it). This represented an effort by the two denominations to prevent competition in the West. The plan ended up favoring the Presbyterians, for a majority of western Congregationalists chose the tighter Presbyterian policy, but at the same time, and in part because of these preferences, several presbyteries from New York and the upper Midwest took on a Congregational cast – less strictly Calvinist in doctrine, less rigorously confessional, more under the sway of New England theological fashions, and often more receptive to new revival techniques (see chapter 8).

The same patterns slowly emerged for Baptists, but with more confusion. At will, local Baptist congregations joined local associations, which at first amounted only to an often annual meeting of ministers and laypeople, with purely advisory recommendations to the congregations. Some congregations chose not to participate in any association, whereas a few sent delegates to more than one. Until 1814 only the old Philadelphia Synod had any national status, and at best it represented a minority of regional associations. In 1814, spurred on by the success of a handful of Baptist foreign missionaries, Baptists from all over the country rallied in support of a new general missionary convention. This voluntary convention long served as the major national organization of Calvinist Baptists, but for years it was little more than a fund-raising agent for missions. Regrettably, joint support for foreign missions split the church throughout the South, leading to mission (the source of the later label, "missionary Baptists") and antimission (primitive) factions. By 1830 the New England Baptists were already distinguishable from their southern counterparts because of their greater willingness to join in cooperative efforts with other Calvinists, their stronger educational institutions, and at least some openness to new biblical scholarship. But only the slavery issue would fully split missionary Baptists north and south, a schism not yet healed.

Given the relative weakness of church government, plus several shared goals, it is no wonder that representatives of the four largest evangelical denominations joined forces in over a dozen educational, missionary, and reform organizations. The climax of such interdenominational "benevolence" came around 1830. By then the often resentful Baptists and Methodists began to move these formerly joint efforts within their own denominations. The cooperative effort never fully displaced denominational dominance in publications and higher education. Each major denomination sponsored (but did not subsidize) periodicals, which advocated the doctrines of the sect but which were often entrepreneurial ventures by ministers or laypeople. All denominations struggled to build their own academies and colleges. In the new century the mainline evangelical denominations slowly withdrew from elementary education, leaving this function to the emerging public schools. For the churches this was a wonderful arrangement, for such was the dominance of mainline Protestants on school boards and among teachers that "public" schools, in most of America, meant schools that reflected evangelical assumptions or schools that often joined in a functional alliance with local churches.

The evangelical denominations realized that if they were to have educated ministers, they had to retain control over academies and colleges. Also, the limited public support for higher education left a compelling need that, in most areas of America, only the churches could fill. In higher education the Congregationalists and Presbyterians had a head start. By 1800, Congregationalists had the strongest colleges in America (Harvard, Yale, Dartmouth, Williams) and continued to establish new colleges between 1800 and 1830 (Amherst, Middlebury). The Presbyterians had as their pride and joy the College of New Jersey at Princeton, where they added a theological seminary in 1812, one that became the custodian of the traditional Calvinism of Dort and Westminster. In addition, they built new academies and colleges almost annually, soon almost dominating higher education from New York to the west and south. They added seminaries at Hampden-Sydney in 1812 (Union, which subsequently moved to Richmond) and Auburn in Ohio in 1821. The Presbyterians first established colleges across the mountains (what became Tusculum and Maryville in Tennessee and Transylvania in Kentucky, although they subsequently lost control of this university). Other Reformed denominations had their flagship colleges – the Dutch Reformed at Queens (Rutgers), Episcopalians at William and Mary, Columbia, and Kenyon. The Baptists trailed but in the early nineteenth century began strenuous efforts to catch up. New England Baptists had an early college at Providence (it gained its permanent name of Brown in 1804), whereas southern Baptists established struggling institutions (what is now Furman University in 1825 and Mississippi College in 1826).

The Methodists lagged. On principle, they repudiated theological seminaries and had none before 1830. From the formation of their church in 1784, Methodists had struggled to build academies and colleges, with often dismal early results. But in the new century they did well numerically, although not in quality. Before 1830 they had dozens of small academies, most pretentiously called colleges. Only in that year did they establish an enduring institution with some pretensions to quality – Randolph-Macon in Virginia, followed a year later by Wesleyan in Connecticut. After 1830 the Methodists founded new colleges, most small, many ephemeral, at least annually, and probably had a hundred by 1860. Yet, even by the eve of the Civil War, Methodism had few notable scholars, few of their own as college presidents, no theological seminary, and no institution that qualified as a true university (Drew would be first in 1860). This meant, as some Methodists lamented, that Calvinists had a near monopoly on quality education in America.

The first large, interdenominational publishing, benevolent, and missionary associations developed in England and then spread to the United States. In Britain these associations had strong evangelical support, meaning in this case from the Low Church wing of Anglicanism and from better-established independent churches. The first major benevolent organization, the Society for the Suppression of Vice, matured during the French Revolution and joined a concern for moral purity with fears of French infidelity and political anarchy. The society tried to promote temperance, eradicate prostitution, and protect the Christian Sabbath. Other ministers or lay leaders soon formed missionary, bible, and tract societies and dominated an early Sunday school movement. In Britain, such organized benevolence involved affluent people and was targeted at the "lower classes," particularly in the new manufacturing areas of Britain. What remained constant in all the efforts was what distinguished these initiatives from those of earlier Calvinists – an almost maudlin sentimentality. Beginning with Hannah More's repository tracts in the 1790s (such as *The Shepherd of Salisbury Plain*), tract societies, and then Sunday schools, inundated the masses of Britain with tear-jerking stories of poor but pious children doomed to early death, with deathbed scenes usually at the climax. A typical novelette, *The Dairyman's Daughter*, inspired people for over a century in both Britain and America. These tracts were intended not only to reform morals, even to lead to conversion, but also to replace romances or novels as popular reading material for the masses.

In the United States, organized interdenominational associations usually began locally or at a state level and then, by a series of mergers or unions, formed a national organization. But the national name, and the claim, usually exaggerated the scope of such organizations, since in most cases the South was only marginally included. And the denominational inclusiveness varied widely from one association to another, with Congregational and Presbyterian domination the rule and with only limited Methodist and Baptist participation or none at all in a few organizations. As in Britain, many of these societies (Bible, Sunday school, temperance) drew support from nonevangelicals, including Episcopalians and Unitarians. The early leadership for such associations, which paralleled a boom in secular societies, clubs, and fraternities, came from more established clergyman or prominent laymen in the eastern cities, from Boston, New York, Philadelphia, and Baltimore. To this extent, the organizations began with an elitist or paternalistic slant, for they reflected the desire of established American Protestants to deal with the perceived evils of America, evils that they identified either with the poor classes in the few American cities or with the imagined shortcomings of Americans in the

South and West. Such class identity led several historians, in the 1960s, to characterize these societies as an evangelical empire or united front, an instrument of class control.

Two of the largest societies in America primarily published and distributed literature. The American Bible Society (1816) and the American Tract Society (1814 in New England, nationally in 1825) both had state and local affiliates. The Bible Society tended to be most inclusive, since few Protestants could oppose its main aim – to publish Bibles, to sell them at subsidized prices to all who could afford them, and to give them to the destitute, so that all Americans had the "word of God." In Britain the Bible Society even briefly distributed Roman Catholic versions of the Bible. In a pluralistic America, perhaps to the surprise of many Protestants, even the distribution of Bibles was not immune to controversy. This was because of an issue that Protestants usually ignored – the proper canon. The parallel twentieth-century controversies would be over the proper English translation of the Bible. Roman Catholics used modern, English versions of the Latin Vulgate, a Bible first translated into Latin by Jerome. As his guide to what Christians by then called the Old Testament, he used the original Greek version of Hebrew scriptures, or the Septuagint. After the destruction of the Jewish Temple in 70 C.E., Jewish teachers or rabbis finally agreed on a Hebrew canon, one that reflected such stringent selection criteria as to exclude over one dozen books or parts of books included in the Septuagint. In addition, Jerome included two late Jewish books that had a wide acceptance among early Christians. Jerome recognized the lower status ascribed to some of these writings by Jews, and in this sense he included them as only quasi-canonical for Christians. The leaders of the Reformation – Luther and Calvin – accepted the Jewish canon and thus demoted and set aside the contested books as useful but not authoritative. In reaction, the Roman Catholic church, at Trent, made the acceptance of an equal status for these books a matter of church dogma. Early Protestant versions of the Bible, including the English Authorized or King James Version, always included these books but set them off in a separate Apocrypha. By the nineteenth century, English and American publishers, supported by decisions by several evangelical denominations, left out this part of the Bible, and thus Protestants gradually lost familiarity with these readings, including some of the jewels of Jewish literature. By 1830 the canon controversy in America added new fuel to Protestant fears of Roman Catholics (they did not even have the right Bible). It also meant that even the distribution of Bibles could not be free from sectarian controversy.

The tract societies had a more clearly sectarian purpose. They tried to inundate the country with sentimental and clearly evangelical literature, which had as its aim the improvement of morals and the conversion of sinners. But like the Bible societies, the tract societies operated much like large publishing houses. They used funds from the sale of their pamphlets and novelettes, combined with gifts from both the lowly and the rich, to create a national sales organization. Full- or part-time representatives of both the Bible and the tract societies spread throughout the country. In particular, such traveling representatives or colporteurs visited local churches, often successfully requesting time during the worship service to make their pitch for support. In their eastern headquarters, and at annual conventions, the officers and employees of the two societies met in a combined business and devotional context and took on some of the para-church functions that distinguished early Methodist societies. The tract societies, in effect, joined their efforts with those of domestic missions (led after 1826 by the American Home Missionary Society) and even foreign missions. The Bibles and tracts were the main tools of home missionary efforts.

Until 1810, missions usually meant domestic efforts to convert Native Americans or unchurched whites in the West. The American Education Society (1816) was an adjunct of this cause, for it provided scholarships to prepare young men for the ministry and for missionary assignments and in a few cases helped subsidize schools for this purpose. The growing enthusiasm for foreign missions dated back to the turn of the century, when new evangelical or missionary magazines carried reports of British missionaries from far-flung parts of the world. But American denominations at first did not have the means to do more than offer meager support for a few devoted missionaries among the American Indians. In 1806 a group of pious young men from Williams College decided to devote their lives to foreign missions and, after training, traveled to India with support from the Congregational and Presbyterian American Board of Commissioners for Foreign Missions. One of the first missionaries, Adoniram Judson, was a Baptist, and his reports and appeals helped influence the formation of the General Missionary Convention, the first national Baptist organization. But the total number of foreign missionaries never numbered over a dozen or so in the period before 1830, and even these mission efforts effectively split the Baptists and drew hostility from the emerging Christian-Disciples movement. Unlike Bible distribution, or advocacy of moral reform, missionary activity could not, at least for long, transcend doctrinal differences. Thus, the separate denominations all soon had their own missionary societies, many organized and operated by churchwomen.

More general reform activity invited denominational cooperation but always contained the seeds of conflict. Overlapping with the boards that operated publishing and missionary societies were those that served in temperance, peace, Sabbatarian, and antislavery societies. From the perspectives of most evangelical Christians, these were the important moral issues of the century. Temperance reform (here the Methodists led the way) moved from an early emphasis on moderation to a commitment to total abstinence and legal prohibition (Temperance

Society, 1826; American Temperance Union, 1836). Thus, one of the perennial themes in the tracts was the evils of alcohol and the terrible social burden of alcoholism, themes reflected in another series of sentimental pamphlets. Given the patterns of alcohol consumption in the early Republic (the highest in all American history), this crusade seemed fully justified, although in all but a few local contexts it failed to gain its legal goal of complete prohibition. The crusade as a whole, joined with dozens of mostly secular health crusades, dramatically reduced alcoholic consumption in America, largely because of the shifting behavior of evangelical Christians. Temperance reform involved most evangelicals and drew support from nonevangelical Protestants and even Roman Catholics.

The other issues never gained as much broad support. Peace reform thrived in times of peace but in America floundered on the developing sectional controversy. As a whole, evangelicals won their local battles for stringent Sabbatarian laws, but not without intense opposition, which peaked after 1830 as a result of immigrant, ethnic opposition. Finally, slavery was a type of dynamite for the churches. Most evangelicals, even in the South, joined in the early but highly illusioned colonization campaign (missionary aspirations in Africa often coincided) but after 1830 would split over organized antislavery and abolitionist issues.

The Sunday School

Of all interdenominational institutions, Sunday schools had the most lasting impact on American religion, including considerable impact on Roman Catholics and Jews. The schools had this effect because American Protestants converted early Sunday schools into institutions never dreamed of by the founders of the movement.[9]

An organized Sunday school movement began in Britain around 1780. The idea was not new and was rather simple – to set up literacy classes for working-class children on Sunday. Precedents for this existed even in America. In the 1750s, Samuel Davies and a few Presbyterian colleagues established Sunday classes for both black children and black adults in central Virginia. For centuries, ministers had conducted catechism classes for youth and, as a corollary to these, often focused on literacy skills, particularly for children who had enjoyed little or no instruction.

Self-consciously organized American Sunday schools began in Philadelphia and in Pawtucket, Rhode Island, in the 1790s. These involved paid instructors who concentrated on literacy, with the religious element restricted to the literature read in the classrooms. In Philadelphia, a First Day Society tried to design schools to cope with the decay of an earlier apprenticeship system and with the unruly and unregulated behavior of children on Sundays. The founders were established businessmen, religiously eclectic, with Episcopalians, Roman Catholics, Quakers, and even a Universalist (Benjamin Rush) joining with Presbyterians. Except for the most generalized religious content, the instruction was nonsectarian. In Pawtucket, Samuel Slater hired teachers to offer Sunday instruction to his youthful factory workers, initiating a form of factory paternalism. In each case these Sunday schools reflected an early attempt to offer a minimum of education to poor children. Sunday was the only time these children could attend classes. Such schools lasted in a few cities into the 1820s, and literacy instruction remained a secondary focus in some Sunday schools until the states established a viable public school system. Gradually, the churches relinquished responsibility for elementary education and converted Sunday schools into very different institutions.

By 1800, individual congregations or clusters of congregations began to establish their own Sunday schools. Inevitably, however broad the targeted populations, these had a religious although not necessarily a sectarian purpose. Early in the new century, locally organized Sunday schools varied widely. Some still hired teachers; an increasing proportion recruited usually youthful volunteers. Some continued to include literacy training with indoctrination; others were upgraded catechism classes still taught by ministers. In a few cities and states early public school commissioners, struggling for funds, subsidized Sunday schools as a cheap way of gaining literacy among the masses. Whatever their format, these evangelical church schools emphasized the religious side of instruction. The approximate goal was biblical understanding and moral reform, with the ultimate goal being conversion. Increasingly, the organizers of such schools, and the youthful teachers within them, were women. Most early urban schools would remain outreach or mission schools; that is, the organizers aimed them at children, or in a few cases also adults, who were not part of the church and lived in nearby poor neighborhoods. In a few northern cities these targeted populations were free blacks. Thus, the schools often met in rented buildings in the poorer neighborhoods. Even the teachers, although unpaid, might be non–church members, even in some cases unconverted but idealistic youth (volunteering to teach in the Sunday school dramatically increased the odds of subsequent conversion).

In these early years the Sunday schools were not yet part of any denominational structure. Some union schools drew support from several congregations. Lay leaders, not ministers, dominated these local Sunday school societies or union associations. In 1824 a majority of these union societies (with 723 schools) joined in the American Sunday School Union, and it is likely an even larger number of mostly nonunion schools remained unaffiliated. According to estimates in 1832, about 8 percent of all eligible children in the United States were in affiliated Sunday schools, and in the headquarters city of Philadelphia this percentage soared to 20 percent.

The American Sunday School Union supported the formation of Sunday schools. It did this by effective advocacy and by the publication of a large repertoire of Sunday school literature, ranging from teachers manuals and youth magazines to tracts to whole libraries of acceptable reading material. Still ahead were the millions of quarterlies, with their coordinated lesson plans, that would eventually make up one of the largest publishing efforts in American history. Hired agents of the union traveled about the country, spreading the gospel of Sunday schools and, not incidentally, creating markets for union literature. The union gained most of its goals. By 1832 every state had Sunday schools, and one state, New York, had 2,708. The schools, as yet, were sparse in the Deep South but were strong in Kentucky and Tennessee. The union was evangelical but as unsectarian as possible, although it was at first dominated by Congregationalists and Presbyterians. It tried to keep Sunday schools free of direct denominational control and, in some cases, of ministerial domination. When all the denominations eventually adopted or incorporated their Sunday schools, the union tried to maintain its preeminent role as a publisher.

Gradually, the Sunday schools changed functions. Even by 1830 congregations began to move the schools fully within their churches and to extend the classes to children of church members. Either separately or soon in common classes, the mission children blended with home children. This democratized the schools but undoubtedly converted them from a largely missionary function to one of institutional development. The Sunday school classes replaced the older catechism classes. And in the more evangelical denominations (Methodist, Baptist), and particularly in rural areas, churches soon added adult classes. In Methodism, Sunday schools gradually replaced the earlier class system.

In rural America (80 percent of the total), the Sunday school became an effective competitor to the traditional church and its worship. The local head of the Sunday school (almost universally called the superintendent) at times displaced ministers, particularly circuit ministers, as the most important leader of the local congregation and held a more powerful position than elders and deacons. Agents of the union nourished such an institutional dominance. In areas with irregular or infrequent worship services, the Sunday school met every week, with opening exercises that were a substitute, often a favored substitute, for the "preaching" service. Such Sunday schools often represented the only Sunday gathering, and these gained a privileged position throughout rural America. Just as Methodist societies eventually became churches, so now Sunday schools became, for up to half of American Protestants by the mid-nineteenth century, the only type of weekly religious service they knew or cherished. Ministers often resented Sunday schools and recognized in them a threat to their status and their authority. The para-church role of Sunday schools forced denominations to "capture" and then use them for sectarian purposes. Beginning with the Methodists, all the evangelical denominations eventually took over the work of the American Sunday School Union, including publishing. After the Civil War, the most influential representatives of a central denomination were the authors who spun out the millions of pages of Sunday school literature, literature used by congregations all over America. These often anonymous men and women became more powerful arbiters of biblical understanding, of correct doctrines, and of moral standards than the clergy.

Sunday schools also provided excellent new opportunities for lay leaders. Teachers met in training sessions, held their own devotional exercises, became deeply involved with their children, and could exert a major influence on youth. Dedicated teachers become local heroes. Youthful teachers met, courted, and married each other. Here, even more than in the developing missionary societies, women gained leadership roles – not at the top, for they rarely served as superintendents, but as teachers and as delegates to Sunday school conferences. They also wrote tracts or trained new teachers in local institutes. They became involved in pedagogical theory and often moved back and forth from public schools to Sunday schools. This lay involvement, and women's leadership roles, very clearly separated the Sunday schools from traditional Protestant worship, in which women had a largely passive role.

AFTER 1830 the most uniformly evangelical denominations entered a more perilous era. The period of interdenominational cooperation was almost over. Not only slavery but also a host of other issues (foreign missions, the pew system, instrumental music, Masonry) would trigger schisms. Emerging new and nonevangelical denominations, often keyed to one distinctive and appealing doctrine (universal salvation, the early advent) seduced evangelicals. Perhaps more important, the relative homogeneity of the population began to erode with the new waves of immigrants from Ireland and Germany. The small Roman Catholic church, heretofore a competitor more in fantasy than in fact, began to grow exponentially with each decade. Even a Protestant America, not just an evangelical one, soon seemed threatened. Within the evangelical mainstream, particularly in Congregationalism and Presbyterianism, the very substance of evangelical Christianity seemed to erode as new intellectual influences, new forms of scholarship, and new scientific theories seemed to undermine the Pauline scheme of salvation and Calvinist doctrines. Finally, even beliefs that largely transcended the ravages of eighteenth-century rationalism – such as the foundational Semitic cosmology – were now under siege as a result of philosophical challenges or new geological and biological knowledge.

CHAPTER 5

Outside the Evangelical Consensus

*T*hroughout the early nineteenth century, a significant minority of congregations that derived from the Reformed tradition either rejected or moderated the beliefs and preferences of American evangelicals. This nonevangelical group included the moderate and High Church wings of the Protestant Episcopal church from its founding in 1789, important factions within both the German and the Dutch Reformed churches, and a significant and growing minority of Presbyterians and Congregationalists. In many ways, those who resisted an evangelical style were prophetic, for they led the way in what became, after the Civil War, a general movement away from evangelical commitments among a majority of mainstream congregations, particularly in the North. To some extent, these congregations dispensed with, or ceased to emphasize, a crisis-like conversion, substituted rituals or more formal worship for an earlier warm and simple style, watered down or rejected revival techniques, and so compromised with worldly fashions and amusements as to undermine any ideal of moral purity or holiness.

From the eighteenth century on, some American Anglicans rejected the most critical leg of evangelicalism – the necessity of a rebirth experience. This rejection accompanied an emphasis on growth and nurture within the church, on the centrality of the sacraments and moral attainment, and on a more formal, sacramental, or liturgical conception of worship. This usually paralleled a rejection of the most distinctively Calvinist doctrines in the Thirty-Nine Articles and an emphasis on the more catholic and inclusive doctrines reflected in the *Book of Common Prayer*. In a loose way, we now refer to this as a High Church party in the always divided Anglican and later Episcopal churches. Within the German Reformed church, two able theologians at its seminary in Mercersburg, Pennsylvania, moved to much the same position. In the American context, this emphasis on nurture in the church, rather than a dramatic conversion, meant a rejection, at times a scathing condemnation, of the more popular and emotional forms of revivalism.

Some conservative Presbyterians and Congregationalists who rejected new revival techniques still considered themselves evangelical. They believed in the necessity of justifying faith and a rebirth experience. These conservative evangelicals made up a reasonably coherent alternative in American Protestantism, one best exemplified by the Old School Presbyterians (see chapter 8). The most vocal opponents of revivalism among Congregationalists eventually separated into a separate fellowship – the American Unitarian Association (1825). Since the early Unitarians moved far toward a form of Christian rationalism, or soon adopted a radical form of philosophical idealism, they moved completely outside the Reformed mainstream.

Conservative or traditional Presbyterians continued to use the word *evangelical* much as had Luther and Calvin. It denoted the role of the Word and the Spirit in the church, but not such unwanted modern and often American innovations as the anxious bench or an overly sentimental devotional life. Such conservative evangelicals were orthodox and confessional. They adhered to such traditional confessions as Westminster, supported an academic and intellectual concern for correct doctrines and for well-trained ministers, and often accepted a philosophical critique of many aspects of modernity. The denominations that best reflected this tradition were the varied and schismatic Associate and Reformed branches of Scottish Presbyterianism (the Covenanters and Seceders), conservative and later Old School Presbyterians, and the Christian Reformed Church (see below). But despite these reactions to popular evangelicalism within the Reformed and nominally evangelical denominations, the most coherent nonevangelical Protestants in early-nineteenth-century America were in the Protestant Episcopal church, the only Protestant confession in which evangelicals were usually a minority, although a large and influential minority.

The Founding of a Protestant Episcopal Church

The American Revolution left the Anglican church in the United States without a head and, at least in theory, without a legal clergy. Its ministers had all sworn their allegiance to the English monarch. Of the two hundred or so clergy in America in 1776, up to half remained loyal to this oath and thus backed the British cause. Others tried to remain neutral, while in Virginia and South Carolina the majority probably supported the patriot side. In the northern centers of the church – New York, Connecticut, the Boston area – almost all the clergy, who had sharpened their identity in reaction to the Congregationalists, were Tories as well as High Churchmen. These ministers, in many cases, fled to Canada or back to Britain, often receiving a hero's welcome because of their prior suffering at the hands of patriots. At war's end, all New England outside Connecticut had only five remaining clergymen; North Carolina, Georgia, and Pennsylvania had only one each. Only Maryland, Virginia, and South Carolina retained as many as twenty clergymen. Connecticut had about seventeen, but most of these were now embarrassed because of former Tory sentiments. Not all these ministers were able to function effectively; some were old, some were ill, and some had only minimal qualifications.[1]

In these dire circumstances the remaining Anglican clergy, joined by laymen, began gathering in state or regional assemblies or conferences. They sought legal strategies to establish what they, by an early consensus in Maryland and then throughout the South, chose to call the Protestant Episcopal church. Even the label involved efforts to find enough commonality to make an American church. The "Protestant" in the title pleased southerners, many of whom would have preferred a church without bishops, whereas "Episcopal" pleased High Church advocates in Connecticut.

The road to a new American church proved treacherous. It took six years to do all the work. This meant that the Methodists gained a head start, forming their more centralized episcopal church in 1784, five years before the Episcopalians. Anglicans in Connecticut led the way to an American church. They elected a former loyalist and High Church spokesman, Samuel Seabury, as their bishop-elect and sent him off to England in 1783 to seek consecration. Maryland also elected an aspirant bishop, William Smith, but he did not make a planned trip to England. When Seabury arrived, he found that bishops in England had no authority to consecrate him without requiring an oath of allegiance to the king. Only an act of Parliament later removed this requirement. After almost a year of complex but unsuccessful negotiations, Seabury gave up on a regular consecration and traveled to Scotland in 1784 to receive his orders by authority of nonjuror bishops. He returned to Connecticut to assume almost monarchical control of his church, in effect creating what turned out to be a short-lived denomination in New England. He tried to establish a virtual Laudian church and manifested his authority by ordaining deacons, not only for Connecticut but also for other nearby states.

Meanwhile, the rest of the church, usually without Connecticut involvement, tried to move ahead. Conventions in New York and Philadelphia in 1785 led to a drafting committee, instructed to write a constitution and revise the *Book of Common Prayer*. The committee completed a surprisingly presbyterian constitution. It provided for a triennial general convention with lay and clerical delegates from each state convention (also constituted by laymen as well as priests), provided for one elected bishop in each state, and made the bishops only ex officio members of the general convention. The committee left much of the *Book of Common Prayer* intact, except for references to the king, but made several changes to appease Low Church and southern factions. In part because of a small Arian-leaning congregation in Boston (King's Chapel, which later joined the American Unitarian Association), the first American draft excluded the Athanasian and Nicene creeds, leaving only a modified Apostles' Creed (it did not include any reference to Jesus' descent into hell). This draft did not include any mention of baptismal remission and made the sign of the cross optional in baptism. These changes, all calculated to please evangelicals, were unacceptable to Seabury and the Connecticut church. Finally, the convention asked the English church to consecrate its first elected bishops, and to support this appeal it secured letters of support from sympathetic governors and the active intervention of the American minister in London, John Adams, who had in the past been a bitter critic of any American episcopacy. In the new voluntary context, almost no one opposed an American Episcopal church, and most Americans seemed to see cooperation by the British in gaining such a church as a symbol of attained nationhood.

An assembly of bishops in England wanted to help. They petitioned Parliament, as it turned out successfully, for an enabling bill, one that allowed them to consecrate only three bishops (this was all that was needed to establish an American succession), who were to have no ecclesiastical authority in Britain. This began the process that led, later, to several independent national churches in the larger Anglican family. But the English bishops did not like the prayer book changes or the diminished authority of bishops, and they made consecration conditional on a reconsideration of these issues. In Wilmington, in 1786, another American convention revised the prayer book, dropping most of the deletions except for the Athanasian Creed, and on several doctrinal points tried to appease Seabury with a more High Church stance. Already, in behalf of national unity, and to gain the support of Connecticut, several American leaders in the developing church, most notably a young and able William White of Philadelphia, had decided to recognize Seabury's irregular consecration. Thus, the emerging church sent only White (Pennsylvania) and an evangelically inclined Samuel Provoost (New York) to England. There, the Anglican bishops conceded the disputed issues and ordained the two, thus making possible the creation of a legally separate but sister denomination in America.

After the two bishops returned to America, the new but still very weak church assembled at its founding convention in Philadelphia in 1789. Only twenty-two clergymen and sixteen laymen attended the first sessions (so different from the conference of the optimistic Methodists five years earlier). The prayer book revisions helped win over a reluctant Seabury, who joined the convention after a recess. Provoost, who objected to Seabury's irregular consecration and who feared his High Church program, remained in New York and thus made it possible for White to effect his moderate strategy. The church was now one, although still deeply divided in sentiment. The final constitution gave the bishops a separate house, with a modified veto over the general convention. It made obligatory the use of the new *Book of Common Prayer* (used for over a century) but did not add the Thirty-Nine Articles until several years later. The church was thus born without any doctrinal confession, except for the traditional creeds, but in a group of canons established a discipline for its clergy.

The founding convention did not eliminate all the internal bickering. Provoost was at first unwilling to join Seabury in consecrating new bishops. Others resented Seabury's dictatorial style. Fortunately for the church, in 1790 Virginia elected the scholarly James Madison as bishop-elect, and he left immediately for England. There he received his consecration (the third agreed to by Parliament) and returned to America. Reluctantly, in 1792 Provoost joined Seabury, White, and Madison in the first American consecration, since Seabury's participation was not required to make the action legitimate. Seabury's participation may have prevented the secession of the Connecticut church.

In polity, the Episcopal church was unique in America. White recognized that, outside Connecticut, American Anglicans would not accept a monarchical form of church government. He had been willing to form a church without consecrated bishops, and he used arguments similar to John Wesley's to vindicate presbyterial ordination. Thus, the Protestant Episcopal church would be episcopal in doctrine much more than in government. The new church was more of a federation than a truly national body. Until New York split into two annual conventions in 1838, the church was organized at the state level. Clergymen and laymen in each state elected their own bishop and jealously guarded this prerogative. The annual convention (closely modeled on the annual conferences of the Methodist Episcopal church), not the bishop, made policies for the church and also had jurisdiction over the clergy, with local congregations largely autonomous in selecting their pastors. Bishops served a ceremonial role – ordaining, jointly consecrating new bishops, confirming young people, and visiting parish churches – but had almost no power. Yet, through visitation and persuasion some became very powerful leaders. Bishops had no seat. They usually held, or soon gained, the pulpit of a large congregation, but on their merits and not because of their role as bishop. Not until after 1850 did the church begin using the name "cathedral," and this was not for diocesan centers but for special church buildings with a broader than local function.

The episcopacy, nonetheless, was critical to Episcopalians and particularly to the dominant early High Church faction. The three orders of clergy, and the spiritual role of bishops, distinguished the church from other Protestant bodies (except Methodists) and gave substance to its claim to being a wing of the primitive Catholic church. High Church bishops and clergymen emphasized apostolic succession. In fact, they rested the spiritual and redemptive authority of the church, and its sacraments, on such authority, which they traced back to Jesus. The most zealous High Church bishops infuriated other Protestants by denying fellowship to clergymen not ordained by apostolic bishops, and at times they came close to denying salvation to anyone not within a properly constituted and thus necessarily episcopal church.

Episcopal Decline and Recovery

The organization of an American Protestant Episcopal church did not soon arrest the relative decline of what had been in 1776 the third-largest confession in America. Of all the newly nationalized denominations in America, the Episcopal church fared worst in the years between 1790 and 1815. Before the Revolution, the Anglican church had grown to at least 480 parishes, with nearly 100 in Virginia alone. By 1815, the struggling new national church could list only 7 bishops and about 180 clergy, serving only 15,000 reported members. This was the low point. In the next fifteen years the church, blessed by able local leaders, was able to double its membership, triple its ministry, and maintain active bishops in most states east of the mountains. Its growth would be continuous from 1815 to the Civil War and even more rapid after the war. In 1865 it had approximately 150,000 members, making it the sixth- or seventh-largest confession in America (behind Methodists, Baptists, Roman Catholics, Presbyterians, Congregationalists, and possibly Universalists). By 1883 it would have 400,000 members and over 3,700 clergy in 3,000 parishes. Its rate of growth never rivaled that of Baptists and Methodists but did, after the Civil War, exceed that of Congregationalists and matched that of Presbyterians.[2]

The hard early years primarily reflected a paucity of able leadership and the lingering devastation of American Anglicanism occasioned by the Revolution. The church, from its founding convention, was divided, but the internal divisions, between High Church and evangelical factions, did not cause the slow growth before 1815. In fact, the church later grew most rapidly in the midst of intense internal conflict. If anything, the competition within led to greater proselytizing zeal on all sides.

The Protestant Episcopal church remained unique in a denominational America. It tried to remain an inclusive church and to a large extent succeeded. It included people who disagreed profoundly on beliefs and practices. Its loose governmental system, and the convergence of worship practices tied to the *Book of Common Prayer*, helped prevent major schisms. In a sense the divisions that led, elsewhere in America, to separate and competing sects or denominations played themselves out within the Episcopal church, but not without rancor and pain.

The new denomination began its work in the worst of times for a formal, non-revivalistic type of Christianity. The Methodist Episcopal church had a five-year head start on the Episcopalians and in states like Virginia captured the largest share of former Anglicans. To an extent usually unrecognized, the colonial Anglican church was a parent to two denominations, and of the two the Methodist church was easily more competitive in the American religious environment. Bishop William White recognized the past affinities, and the Methodist competitive advantages, and sought some merger of the two churches. He had serious conversations with Bishop Thomas Coke of the Methodists about some plan of union, but such a merger was unacceptable to his own High Church faction and was always opposed by Francis Asbury, the dominant Methodist bishop.

Bishop White, long revered as senior or presiding bishop, headed an active and strong church in Pennsylvania but was never a forceful organizer on the national level. Bishop Seabury ran a tight ship in Connecticut but was too authoritarian to exercise influence on the larger denomination before his death in 1796. Bishop Provoost of New York, who represented the evangelical wing and who resented Seabury, lamented the direction of the new church and resigned his see in 1801 to spend most of his time as an amateur botanist (he would, for political reasons, later briefly resume an active role). Thus, the three founding bishops did not provide the type of leadership needed by a fledgling and floundering denomination.

In theory, the church was to have a bishop in each state. This long remained an unfulfilled goal. Even as late as 1811 the church had only seven bishops. Some states did not have enough parishes to justify a bishop (Vermont had only one congregation). A few elected bishops refused to serve. For an extended period the churches in South Carolina chose to dispense with a bishop. By 1816 the church had consecrated sixteen bishops, but no more than half this many had been active at any one time. At the triennial convention of 1811, only two bishops showed up (along with twenty-five clergy), and thus the convention did not have the required three needed to consecrate two newly elected bishops. The church had strength only in urban areas, such as New York, Philadelphia, and Baltimore. It would, throughout the early nineteenth century, remain the most urbanized of Protestant denominations. By that very fact it declined in the Deep South, where it was strong only in the Charleston area, and long had no outposts at all west of Pittsburgh.

The plight of the church in Virginia epitomized the era of troubles. This had been the stronghold of colonial Anglicanism. It became a stronghold of American Methodism, but the Protestant Episcopal church barely survived. Bishop Madison, a mild, scholarly man and a professor at William and Mary, largely neglected the church throughout his huge state. The local parishes lost their glebe lands at the time of disestablishment, local parishioners resented the cost of pews or pew rents needed to finance the church, and thus many rural parishes simply collapsed. In 1805 Virginia had only fifteen clergy, and some of these were in weak or dying parishes. For almost a decade the church convened no annual conventions and sent no delegates to four successive general conventions. Many assumed the Virginia church could not recover.

A period of revival or renewal in the national church began around 1815. In part, this growth reflected the efforts of strong, new leaders. Four bishops exerted the most influence – Alexander Griswold of New England (outside Connecticut), John Henry Hobart of New York, Richard C. Moore of Virginia, and Philander Chase in Ohio and the West. That in 1811 Griswold became bishop of five states in New England testified to the weakness of the church in that domain of Congregationalists, Baptists, and Methodists. Griswold was a moderate churchman with evangelical sympathies, able to work effectively with both evangelical and High Church clergymen. He deplored party conflict. From his consecration to his death in 1843, he worked patiently to create new parishes, ordain new clergy, and create one of the first missionary boards. He was able to increase the number of parishes by fivefold, and just before or after his death his one superdiocese separated into five state conventions.

Hobart was a much more forceful and controversial bishop in New York. He became the symbol of High Church Episcopalianism in early America. Intense, forceful, dogmatic, and charismatic, he served as bishop for only nineteen years (1811–30), but before his election as bishop, he made a major impact on his denomination as minister of Trinity church in Manhattan, or what became, during his reign, the de facto cathedral of American Episcopalianism. Before consecration, he was secretary to the House of Bishops and to two general conventions, served on the board of Columbia College, took the lead in organizing the first theological seminary for the church, and helped found Sunday schools, a Bible and tract society, and a missionary organization. He wrote books on worship, became editor of the denomination's first and long its most influential periodical, *The Churchmen's Magazine*, and in 1806 published a vigorous, dogmatic defense of episcopal church government, a defense that astounded and appalled most non-episcopal Protestants and even some evangelicals within his own church. As bishop, he increased his leadership role. In only four years he doubled the clergy in New York, and he soon made New York by far the strongest diocese in the denomination, with parishes in every important city. Because of his dominant role in early publications and seminary education, his passionate preaching, and his political skill in the triennial general conventions, he gave a High Church slant to the whole denomination and helped ensure that a majority of young clergymen reflected High Church principles. During a two-year trip to England, made in behalf of improved health, he gained unexpected fame and, in immeasurable ways, contributed to the reforms that became known as the Oxford movement (see below).

Except for the passion of their preaching, John Henry Hobart and Richard C. Moore had little in common. Ordained in New York by Bishop Provoost, Moore became famous for his piety and the force of his sermons. Thus, he was elected bishop of Virginia in 1814 and pastor of the church in Richmond. He committed himself to rebuilding this all but dead convention. A warm evangelical, with much of the zeal and fervor and moral rigor of Methodists, he fit the particular needs of the southern church. He traveled the roads of his large state, confirmed children, recruited young men for the ministry, and advocated a Wesleyan standard of moral purity (no cards, no dancing, no theaters, no horse racing). Unlike Hobart, he cultivated contacts with other evangelical denominations, joining in benevolent enterprises. He turned his annual conventions into what amounted to revival meetings and encouraged extraliturgical elements in worship and in separate prayer meetings. Moore was not as forceful, not as much a leader, as Hobart. He had much less institutional impact, much less of a voice in the general convention, but he did help establish an evangelically oriented theological seminary at Alexandria, Virginia, as a counter to the General Seminary that Hobart had helped create and eventually locate in New York City. When Moore died in 1841, the formerly moribund Virginia church had nearly 100 ministers serving 170 churches, more than in the glory years before 1776.

What was painfully clear by 1820 was that the Protestant Episcopal church had all but surrendered the region west of the Appalachians to the Methodists and Baptists. Until 1818, it did not have a single convention in the West. The one person who did most to reverse this trend was a New Englander, Philander Chase. Also ordained by Bishop Provoost, he remained within the evangelical party. He always had an itch to travel, committed himself to missionary activity, and began by organizing new parishes in upstate and western New York. He was the Asbury of Episcopalianism. In 1805 he moved to New Orleans, organizing the first Episcopal church in that city. From here he moved back to Connecticut but in 1817 decided to launch a mission in Ohio. He rode horseback through much of Ohio, forming several small congregations. These were soon numerous enough to form a convention, and in turn the delegates of course elected Chase their first bishop in 1818. Consecrated in 1819, he began a frustrating effort to build the church in the West, without any real financial help from the East. In defiance of the eastern bishops, he traveled to England in 1823 to raise money for his diocese and to launch a new theological school to train needed ministers (Hobart strongly condemned such an effort). In less than a year he raised over twenty thousand dollars (a large sum in 1824) and returned to Ohio to found Kenyon College and an attached but small seminary. He eventually settled the College at Gambier (a town named after an English benefactor) but was so dictatorial in his governance of the college as to trigger a virtual revolt. His faculty won a hearing from the state convention, and a hurt Chase resigned as president and as bishop. This move helped his church, for a restless Chase soon moved on to Illinois, where he was again elected bishop in 1835. He even returned to England to win funds for his new diocese and for a new but eventually unsuccessful college. He died in 1852, the parent of two colleges and a seminary and the bishop in the first two strong western dioceses.

The Divided Soul of Episcopalians

The period from 1830 to the Civil War was a particularly turbulent one for the Protestant Episcopal church. It often seemed as if various factions were fighting for its soul. The outcome was inconclusive, and even the terms of the debate were confusing and misleading. Yet, it is hard to summarize the history of the denomination in these years without trying to unravel the issues involved in the struggle between evangelicals (their term) and advocates of a High Church (also their term). The labels easily mislead. In retrospect, a historian cannot easily fit most Episcopal bishops within ideal typical evangelical or High Church molds. Even less can one so classify the clergy or lay members. In fact, most leaders fully within the High Church party tended to exaggerate the number of evangelicals; self-proclaimed evangelicals consistently overestimated the strength of a High Church faction. More than the various alignments suggest, a large share of bishops, clergy, and lay members remained somewhere in the middle between the almost sentimental piety of Moore and the tough churchmanship of Hobart. But to clarify the issues, and to explain the conflicts, one needs ideal types.[3]

The divisions within the English church went back to its founding, in particular to the settlements under Elizabeth I. The church tried to find a middle way between Roman Catholics and pietistic reformers or Puritans. Through time, the pendulum swung back and forth – to a High Church ascendancy under Charles I and Archbishop William Laud, to Puritan dominance during the Commonwealth, to a broad High Church position after the restoration of 1660, and to a quite latitudinarian church by the eighteenth century. Because of the competitive lure of Congregationalists and Presbyterians in the American colonies, the colonial Anglican church moved toward a moderate High Church stance, except on issues of church government. The few evangelical ministers, or a visiting George White-field, faced resentment or ostracism. After the American Revolution, former Anglicans of an evangelical bent usually found a home within Methodism. These factors helped ensure that a majority of leaders in the new Protestant Evangelical church would range from a moderate to a High Church position. But to so assert is to beg definitions.

Bishop Hobart, by almost all acknowledgments, epitomized a High Church stance in America. This position was quite different from the forms of Anglo-Catholicism that would follow the impact of the Oxford movement. For Hobart, being High Church meant an emphasis on the corporate church, on the apostolic status of bishops, and on the critical role of sacraments in the drama of salvation, although he still insisted on justifying faith. He supported a formal worship, one tied rigidly to the *Book of Common Prayer*. What he rejected was more defining than what he affirmed. He would not join in cooperative endeavors with nonepiscopal Protestants, formed separate Sunday school and publishing institutions, condemned and even outlawed among his clergy all free or extemporaneous supplements to the standard worship (such as free prayers, separate prayer meetings, and sentimental hymns), and believed the ordinary path to salvation was within the church, tied both to its sacraments and to justifying faith, but not by way of a tempestuous or wild rebirth experience. He condemned popular forms of revivalism. In doctrine he was a complete Arminian, but so were some of his evangelical opponents. From his perspective he was a Protestant, since he believed in justification by faith and not in the efficacy of sacraments without faith. He was avowedly hostile to Rome, rejected the Roman Eucharist, with its symbolism of an altar sacrifice, and was not infatuated with new (or ancient) rituals. He would have rejected the convergence toward Rome, and the many liturgical innovations, supported by the Oxford movement, which was just beginning in England at his death in 1830 and which would, in America, considerably alter the tensions between evangelicals and a much more Romanist High Church party.

Few American Episcopalians were as rigidly High Church as Hobart, not even many clergymen in his own diocese. Few were as willing to defend episcopacy or to refuse any cooperation with evangelical denominations. Thus, Hobart's was a polar position, as was Moore's on the other side. What distinguished self-identified evangelicals was a bit more amorphous and more symbolic. Episcopal evangelicals were close to Methodists and Presbyterians, with whom they usually tried to form alliances. They made no exclusive claims for their episcopacy or mode of worship. They stressed the Bible as the common source of authority for all Protestants and emphasized salvation by faith alone. Thus, they emphasized the necessity of a rebirth experience (not necessarily an explosive one and not a rebirth separated from the church and its sacraments). They used revival techniques and encouraged supplements to the prescribed worship. They discounted the more formal elements of worship and rejected symbols that seemed reminiscent of Rome (Cassocks or other vestments, stone altars, candles, too many crosses, or the sign of the cross in baptism). They emphasized effective, even converting, preaching and were first to adopt hymn singing in worship. Finally, they tried to live up to a very high moral standard and were close to Methodists in the types of renunciation expected of members. Some, but not all evangelicals, insisted on a literal subscription to the Thirty-Nine Articles and thus professed a moderate Calvinism in their doctrines.

Not much remained common among the most polarized factions. At least in form, all shared a common worship experience. The fervor of preaching was dependent on the minister, not factional alignments. Hobart was as passionate as any Episcopal minister in America. The stance on social issues was not specific to faction. High Church bishops, in cities like New York, led the way toward free pews and effective ministrations to the poor. In fact, the evidence suggests that the High Church position had the broadest appeal across class lines. Both sides launched mission efforts, but in time through separate organizations, even as seminaries tended to reflect one side or another. By 1850, when the evangelicals were most ascendant in the larger denomination, the church was close to a complete dual system of institutions, all loosely grouped under the General Convention, which by then had become a debating forum for contending factions.

The catalyst for more intense conflict and competition was the influence of the English tractarians. In the late 1820s, a group of concerned Anglicans at Oxford began to work toward reform or revitalization within a lax Anglican establishment. They wanted to restore a strong and effective church. To foster these goals, they began to explore the history of the primitive church, or what they would refer to as the early or old Catholic church. Their study led them to an accommodating stance toward the church of Rome and to a criticism of the more divisive innovations of Luther and Calvin. A young man, John Henry Newman, became the intellectual of the movement, but he was supported by such revered and older churchmen as Edward B. Pusey, then regius professor of history at Oxford. In America, many Episcopalians referred to the movement as Puseyism. Newman, in an 1834 "Tract for the Times," issued a manifesto for the movement. In the next decade he moved ever closer to Rome and converted in 1845, becoming a cardinal and possibly the most influential English intellectual in modern Roman Catholic history. Pusey remained in the English church but helped launch what became known as Anglo-Catholicism, a stance as close as possible to Rome without an open break with the Anglican confession. Before conversion to Rome, Newman had argued, against what seemed overwhelming evidence to the contrary, that almost all the Roman Catholic tradition was consistent with the confession of the Anglican church. In Britain the movement created deep controversies (a vast majority of Anglicans rejected Anglo-Catholicism), led to the defection to Rome of hundreds of Anglican clergy, and remained a source of division into the twentieth century.

Although Hobart may have had some influence on the young men he met at Oxford, the movement soon moved away from, or in new directions from, his version of High Church Episcopalianism. To the tractarians, liturgy was often a more important factor than doctrine. Out of the Oxford movement would come major liturgical changes in the English church, including finally an authorized hymnbook that drew on primitive church music. The tractarians placed great emphasis on church tradition and by this fact less on scripture. They found appealing many Roman practices without biblical precedents. They took a Roman view of the sacraments and their efficacy, instituted weekly communion and revived daily offices, formed monastic orders, revered the saints, and practically worshiped Mary. They moved the Eucharist back toward the sacrificial interpretation of Rome and revived such practices as priests facing altars in the administration of the elements. They embraced elaborate priestly vestments, used crosses and statuary freely, celebrated Gothic architecture, and in many ways endorsed a widespread romantic infatuation with all aspects of medievalism.

The Oxford tracks circulated almost immediately in America, and an American edition of the heretofore completed tracts appeared in 1839. Such was the intellectual dependence of the American church on its English parent that doctrinal or liturgical developments in England directly influenced Americans, particularly those involved in seminaries and publications. Yet, Americans were more detached from the new innovations than English churchmen. They could read the tracts, easily pick and choose among the recommendations, in part because they were not so involved in the controversies that shook and divided England. Few American churchmen embraced the extreme views of a Newman, but several High Church bishops (at least five), and dozens of clergy, found inspiration in the tracts and began introducing some of the doctrinal and liturgical themes into their own teaching or worship. As one would have expected, the most receptive audience was in the greater New York area, in the dioceses earlier influenced by Bishop Hobart. His successor in New York, Benjamin T. Onderdonk, was also the head of the still largest and most influential of three seminaries, the General Seminary in New York City. He was already the symbol of High Church orthodoxy, and, at least from the critical perspective of evangelicals, he capitulated to Oxford. Bishops George W. Doane of New Jersey, William DeLancey of western New York, and Onderdonk's brother, Henry, of Pennsylvania led the new High Church party, ably supported by Samuel Seabury, the grandson of the founding bishop and editor of the most distinguished journal in the denomination, *The Churchman.*

The Oxford influence led to an ever greater diversity of belief and practice within the American church. But it was not as disruptive as in England. For example, not nearly as large a proportion of American clergy converted to Rome (no more than twenty-nine in all and some of those not because of tractarian convictions). At least in the decades of the 1840s and 1850s, the controversy embarrassed the High Church party, led to a massive and successful evangelical counterattack, and by the Civil War had allowed the evangelicals to gain a balancing or even majority strength in the larger denomination. After 1840, a majority of new bishops would be moderate or evangelical in conviction.

Bishop Charles P. McIlvaine of Ohio, the successor bishop to Philander Chase, became the intellectual leader of the evangelicals. In intellect and in polemical skills he had no peer among the High Church party. In his opposition to the tractarians, and to Romanism, he clearly spoke for a vast majority of Episcopalian laypeople. In 1840 he published a sweeping critique of the tractarians, *Oxford Divinity Compared with That of the Romanist and Anglican Churches.* For the next two decades he continued his polemical battles with High Church leaders, and in most cases he won at least respect, if not dominance, for evangelical views.

Much of the controversy involved symbols. Episcopalians fought over clerical dress, the shape of altars, the role of rituals, the types of bread (plain or unleavened) and wine (ordinary or cut with water as in the primitive church), the frequency of communion, the use of crucifixes and signs of the cross, the elevation of the Host (introduced by High Church extremists), prayers to saints, vested choirs, and on and on with what seemed to evangelicals to be a hundred Romanist practices. In retrospect, some of the battles now seem slightly ridiculous. One evangelical clergyman had to stand trial (he was exonerated) because he ignored his High Church bishop and preached in a Methodist church. On the other side, Bishop McIlvaine forced a young, Oxford-enthused priest in his diocese to replace a stone altar with a plain table (according to one story, the High Churchman simply knocked out the sides of his altar and thus created a table).

Some of the contested issues went to the heart of church doctrine (for an understanding of the theological issues at stake in liturgical controversies, see chapter 6 on worship). The church had to refight old battles between those who emphasized justification by faith and who viewed the sacraments as confirming ordinances and those who believed that one attained justification through obedience and devotion within the church, particularly through the redemptive function of the sacraments. The Oxford devotees all emphasized the efficacy of the sacraments and at times refused even to accept infant baptism by converts from Methodism or Presbyterianism, on the grounds that the infants had received baptism from a lay minister (from priests not ordained by successors of the apostles). The issue of baptismal regeneration best focused this very fundamental division. In fact, the English church had finessed the issue from the seventeenth century. The Thirty-Nine Articles, now the refuge of evangelicals, clearly expressed a Calvinist view on justification. But in the more inclusive and accommodating *Book of Common Prayer,* the baptismal ritual included a reference to the newly baptized infant as "regenerate," or what became the proof text for the High Church party. Obviously, these issues remained unresolved as the larger church successfully contained both sides.

Within the Oxford movement was a type of piety largely unfamiliar to most American Protestants, although it made up one theme of John Wesley's. This involved a rich, continuous devotional life within the church, or a form of individual and communal devotion, often blended with types of mysticism, that had it highest expression in monasticism and in disciplined, daily forms of prayer and meditation. The extreme manifestation of this in America grew out of devotions, and missionary plans, by a group of former seminarians, most from the General Seminary. Led by James Lloyd Breck, William Adams, and James Henry Hobart (son of the former bishop), a group of young, idealistic men formed their own monastic order, with an early commitment to celibacy, a community of goods, poverty, and strict obedience. They were able to gain support, and land, from the bishop of Wisconsin, Jackson Kemper, and thus established their community and school on a beautiful lake in eastern Wisconsin, Nashotah. From here they rode on mission circuits, trying to form new congregations. The struggling community survived as an educational center, as a unique Episcopal institution, but the idealistic founders all eventually left, some to marry, some to move on to new missions (Breck), and six to convert to Roman Catholicism, a relatively minor shift because they were already Anglo-Catholics in both doctrines and rituals.

Unfortunately, the depth and sincerity of convictions on both sides soon became camouflaged by a series of highly public, and much publicized, confrontations. In these, the evangelicals won, and the High Church party suffered several embarrassments. The evangelicals correctly identified Bishop Onderdonk of New York as their strongest opponent and recognized that the General Seminary, in both faculty and students, leaned toward the Oxford views. In fact, the evangelicals, particularly in the South and the West, developed an almost sinister view of all the evils and the conspiracies at work in the Northeast, blending populist or antimetropolitan sentiments with doctrinal issues. The evangelical counterattack began with the trial of a very sensitive, almost ascetic seminary student, Arthur Carey. This was only a prelude to what was to follow.

The Carey case began when he, as a seminarian, applied for ordination in the congregation where he already taught Sunday school. The pastor, Hugh Smith, who was one of two evangelically inclined clergymen in New York City, refused to sign a required certificate recommending him to Bishop Onderdonk for orders, on the grounds of Carey's Romanist and Oxfordian convictions. When Onderdonk's congregation, Trinity, granted Carey the certificate, his offended pastor and another evangelical minister challenged his impending ordination, demanding a hearing on his doctrines. This extraordinary hearing before the bishop, with seven examining ministers, took place in June 1843 and soon took on much more significance than the issues warranted. The examiners, by a vote of five to two, approved Carey for ordination, and subsequently Onderdonk ordained Carey, but at the ordination the two dissenting evangelicals and former examiners challenged the ordination from the floor, which allowed them to air all over again, and gain newspaper publicity for, the same issues that had dominated Carey's hearing. The two evangelical examiners also subsequently published damaging tracks describing and evaluating Carey's response to the questions.[4]

Carey, a sensitive, almost mystical young man, seemed evasive to his evangelical examiners. As a gesture of balance, the questions included not only ones related to Romanism but also others on predestination and high Calvinist positions now generally rejected in the church. Carey easily gave correct responses to these, but not to heavily loaded questions posed by the evangelicals. He did not affirm, but would not deny, the doctrines enunciated at Trent. He said he did not hold to transubstantiation but did not find the doctrine repugnant to scripture. He believed both the Anglican and the Roman churches to be in the church of Christ and assessed blame on both for the schism that led to a separate English church. In these, and other leading questions, Carey followed Newman in a very loose interpretation of the Thirty-Nine Articles and in the broadest possible conception of what was allowable within an inclusive church, thus in effect adopting positions that seemed expressly condemned by the articles. His acquittal, and subsequent ordination, scandalized evangelicals and led to their subsequent crusade to clean up the General Seminary and block further inroads from Oxford. Incidentally, Carey died within a year of his ordination, becoming a martyr to his like-minded seminarians, many of whom subsequently converted to Roman Catholicism. One of the two assisting bishops at his ordination, Levi S. Ives of North Carolina, subsequently converted, the only American bishop to defect to Rome during the Oxford controversies.

The evangelicals, defeated on Carey's ordination, now had a clear target in the General Seminary and in Bishop Onderdonk. In the annual New York convention of 1843, the two protesting ministers, joined by other evangelical delegates, tried but failed to gain new rules that would have required a candidate such as Carey, when opposed by two clergymen, to stand trial before a church court. But they did gain support from the house of bishops at the next general convention for an inquiry into the General Seminary itself, or what some considered a little Oxford, completely given over to tractarianism. Actually, some members of the faculty were open to the tractarian cause and were willing to protect students with leanings toward Rome, but none were tractarians, and two or three were moderate or broad church. Onderdonk, as head of the General Seminary, was able to guide, or deflect, the formal inquiry, which amounted to a series of specific questions about the seminary. But the fate of the seminary was, by then (1844), tied all too closely to the character of Onderdonk.

In 1843 and early 1844, Onderdonk had prevailed in all the controversies. He was not as commanding a leader as Hobart, but he was a politically skilled old Dutchman, head of the nation's largest diocese, and pastor to some of the most prominent families in America. Unknown to the public, even to most of his parishioners, he had a weakness. Several years before the Carey examination, he had on several occasion made unwanted sexual advances to women in his congregation. Today, these might amount to sexual harassment in a legal sense. The episodes occurred in public, at social occasions, when the good bishop had imbibed too much wine. The incidents were either verbal or what some described as pawing or petting. They led to nothing. As far as the evidence goes, he was faithful to his wife. Other ministers knew of these embarrassing episodes but heretofore had not chosen to charge him with the type of indiscretions that would jeopardize his status as bishop. Now, with all the controversy in the church, it was almost inevitable that some of his opponents would press morals charges against him, which they did in June 1844 in the form of a memorial to the presiding bishop, William Meade of Virginia, an evangelical who had succeeded Moore. By then, rumors were widespread in the church as a whole.

The bishops had no alternative but an investigation and what turned out to be a highly publicized trial, for this was the Watergate of High Church Episcopalianism. All was public. Half the most prominent citizens of New York were involved on one side or the other. Many witnesses had observed the abusive incidents, and the women who had been targets reluctantly provided affidavits as to the facts. Such was the seriousness of the trial that both sides hired counsel. The trial dominated New York newspapers for weeks and gained a national audience. The facts were reasonably clear; all had to concede a measure of guilt, some sadly, some evangelicals gladly. The divisive issue was the severity of punishment. Philander Chase, the oldest bishop, presided over a jury of twenty-three bishops, the leadership of the whole church. The evidence was strong on nine charges, although one young woman absolutely refused to appear and testify. The trial took twenty-four days, lasting into early January 1845. The bishops at first disagreed on appropriate punishment. Eventually they agreed on suspension (not removal) from office, and thus until his death in 1861 Onderdonk remained a suspended bishop (his replacement took the title of provisional bishop). Onderdonk subsequently appealed unsuccessfully for reinstatement, and to some of the High Church faction he seemed to be a martyr to the cause.

Embarrassments for the High Church party followed one after another. None gained the publicity of Onderdonk's trial. Sadly though, his brother, Henry, a High Church bishop in Pennsylvania who barely gained election because of evangelical opposition, faced charges of intemperance, and even though he voluntarily confessed and resigned as bishop, his convention refused to accept his resignation, almost forcing the House of Bishops to suspend him from his office. In this case, evangelical zeal may have forced the issue, but the weakness was all too clear, a family affliction. To add insult to injury, Bishop Doane of New Jersey turned out to be a completely inept, irresponsible administrator of funds for an academy and went to trial in 1852 for mismanagement. He failed of conviction by only one vote. Meanwhile, the fall of Bishop Benjamin Onderdonk and investigations of the faculty had demoralized the General Seminary. By 1846 it seemed close to closing, and in reaction to all the outside pressures the faculty was heavy-handed in investigating its own students. Apparently, some of the students had plotted ways of moving the seminary, or even the church, back to Rome. One student suffered expulsion, rumors of a Romanist conspiracy abounded, and the indignities of the internal purge helped spur the early defection of nine seminarians to Rome.

After 1850, moderate and evangelical leaders held a dominating position in the church. But by then new trends were visible. The most lasting effect of tractarianism would be liturgical changes, changes adopted by many ministers for their esthetic value and for enhancement of the worship experience, not from any sympathy for Rome. On the other side, the evangelicals experienced growing internal rifts, with a small, Methodist-like minority becoming ever more alienated from the church. After the Civil War, this faction became more and more isolated and, under the leadership of Bishop George D. Cummins of Kentucky, separated in 1873 to form the small Reformed Episcopal church (only ten thousand members in 1900). Notably, it resurrected the original prayer book drafted by the 1785 convention, defended the episcopal system on practical and not obligatory scriptural grounds, rejected altars and sacramental salvation, and claimed a close fellowship with other Protestant Christians. The new denomination veered toward Methodist holiness and would later become a part of what some called American fundamentalism. A vast majority of evangelicals remained in the church and competed successfully for position and policy until after the Civil War. The very fact of schism in 1873 motivated the next general convention to adopt an even broader and more inclusive policy on the Eucharist, meaning that Episcopalians could adopt positions as far apart as Zwinglian symbolism and real presence.

The issues that had so divided evangelicals and High Church advocates before the war were already shifting by 1865. Even during the Oxford controversies, a group of moderate bishops had tried to find a middle way in the church. Very significant was the ministry of William A. Mühlenberg in New York City after 1846. Mühlenberg was a great-grandson of the virtual founder of American Lutheranism. He reflected what would later be known as a broad church position. He welcomed liturgical innovations and thus seemed to some evangelicals to be a tractarian. He was not. He had a functional view of liturgical elements and simply wanted a more broadly appealing form of worship. Unlike the traditional High Church advocates, Mühlenberg wanted to broaden cooperation with other Christians, and he drafted the first major ecumenical proposal for the church. He envisioned an Episcopal church that was both evangelical and catholic, a church that would be willing to be so flexible on its liturgy as to accommodate other Christians with different worshiping traditions. He was also unusually open to the new challenges of biblical criticism and the natural sciences. Finally, in his urban parish he launched an early version of a social gospel, insisting on free pews, founding St. Luke's Hospital, sponsoring a nursing sisterhood, and experimenting with a communal colony. His work provided a model for a more open, socially involved, doctrinally liberal, liturgically rich, and ecumenical Episcopalianism that gained increased support by the late nineteenth century, when the old High Church party seemed irrelevant and the few nonaccommodating evangelicals had split from the church.

The majority of continuing evangelicals proved responsive to liberal doctrinal trends in the wake of Darwin, much as did New School Presbyterians and Congregationalists. They kept their emphasis on personal experience, on cooperation with other evangelical denominations, and some on social reform. Gradually, most accepted liturgical reforms. After 1873, it made little sense to speak of an evangelical party, although the broad and inclusive church would continue to accommodate an identifiable spiritualistic, or today even charismatic, element.

Unique among major American denomination, slavery and even the Civil War did not really divide many Episcopalians. This fact, so consoling for church leaders at the time, has become a bit of an embarrassment for later, socially active Episcopalians. In 1860 the Episcopal church was a predominantly northern denomination. By then it had organized conventions in all the southern states, but except in Virginia and South Carolina these were very weak conventions (no more than sixteen hundred members in all of Alabama). In the South the Episcopal church had greatest appeal for larger farmers or planters and even more for professional and commercial classes in the cities (even in a largely rural South, up to half its membership was in cities). This meant that a small and hardly competitive denomination had a disproportionate share of politically influential members, almost all committed to a defense of slavery. Many blacks were members of congregations controlled by their masters (nearly half the members in South Carolina were slaves), but they had no autonomous role (unlike the Methodists and Baptists, the Episcopalians had no black ministers or exhorters). What requires explanation, therefore, is not the position of the southern church toward slavery but the virtual refusal of the northern state conventions, or the general convention, to take any public stand. More than any other major denomination, Episcopalians refused, in their corporate capacity, to become involved in any way in the slavery controversy (not a single action by a general convention).

A few of the more evangelical Episcopal clergy joined in antislavery causes, but it is hard to find even any of them or many prominent laymen among the abolitionists (Samuel Seward and Salmon Chase were prominent antislavery, but not abolitionist, laymen). In the High Church faction, the dominating opinion seems to have been sympathy for the South and acceptance of slavery as an institution. Samuel Seabury, editor and professor at the General Seminary, wrote a major book in defense of southern slavery in 1861. Several northern bishops were at least sympathetic to the South. They were able to keep slavery out of the agenda of general conventions, leaving a situation in which Episcopalians fought highly publicized battles over rituals but all but ignored the most divisive moral issue in American history. Even with war, and the separation of the southern conventions, the High Church bishops and clergy North and South retained a high regard for each other and thus easily reunited after the war. Only among evangelicals was the sectional split one of moral and religious import. The more evangelical bishops in the North, led by McIlvaine, strongly supported the Union cause, with McIlvaine serving President Abraham Lincoln as a special delegate to London. Evangelicals in the South, of course, supported the Confederacy and rationalized slavery.

With secession, the southern state conventions had no alternative but to seek a separate national church. This fit the normal pattern for all Anglican confessions. Two southern bishops called a meeting in July 1861 in Montgomery. Representatives of six state conventions attended, and appointed a committee to draft a new constitution for a southern church. Lay and clerical delegates from eight conventions met in October 1861 in Columbia, South Carolina, to approve this constitution. Ratification by seven conventions occurred in September 1862, creating the Protestant Episcopal Church in the Confederate States of America. This church approved more than one revised version of the *Book of Common Prayer*, consecrated one new bishop, and prepared special literature for soldiers. One southern bishop, Leonidas Polk, became a Confederate general. Because of the disruptions of war, the southern church never really united all eleven Confederate state conventions in a triennial meeting, which it called a council rather than a convention. The council met only once during the war (November 1862) and then a second time to dissolve itself at the war's end. Union occupation prevented a ratification of the constitution in Louisiana and Tennessee and long delayed it in Florida.[5]

What was unusual was not the separation of the southern church but the attitudes toward the secessionists by the church in the North. In the fall of 1862 the first wartime general convention met in New York City. Presiding was Bishop John Henry Hopkins of Vermont, who had been a strong apologist for southern slavery. The conservatives wanted no resolution at all respecting the departed southern brethren. Many evangelicals wanted a harsh condemnation for such sins as rebellion and sedition. The moderates negotiated a mild set of resolutions, authorizing support for their nation in time of war and approving prayers for the president and Congress, but refused any words of condemnation or reproach for the separating southern churchmen. Instead, they bowed in humiliation before their common Father in heaven for the sins that brought such judgment on America. The convention did not acknowledge any schism in the church. It acted as if the southern bishops and clergy were temporarily absent. The convention called the roll of southern conventions as always.

The next general convention came after the war, in the fall of 1865. Hopkins wrote the southern bishops inviting their attendance. The bishops of North Carolina and Arkansas (a convention founded by the southern church) plus lay delegates attended and were accepted as if nothing had happened. Lay delegates also attended from Texas. In its second and final council meeting in Augusta, Georgia, in November 1865, the remnants of the Confederate church dissolved, and the various state conventions all voted to renew their membership in the national church. The northern bishops not only welcomed back their absent brethren but accepted the one bishop consecrated by the southern church. Never had reunion been so easy, although some sectional frictions developed during the Reconstruction era. All the southern conventions sent representatives to the general convention of 1868. In the South, the church gradually lost a majority of its black members, leaving such a small nucleus that black Episcopalians never formed a separate denomination. The church began ordaining black clergy just after the war, and those served in a scattering of all-black congregations, many in the North. In 1884 the church established a small seminary for blacks but ordained only seventeen black clergymen before 1880. The social and class profile of white Episcopalians in the South did not change.

Reconciliation between North and South facilitated a period of rapid growth for Episcopalianism in the two decades after the war. The growth came despite continuing internal tensions. Membership almost tripled in the period from 1860 to 1890, from approximately 150,000 to 500,000. The rate of growth was almost double that of the national population. Many trends in the larger society supported such growth. A nonconfessional, doctrinally inclusive, and richly liturgical church had broad appeal, particularly among business and professional people in the larger cities. The gradual shift of the American population toward cities, the expansion of commercial and manufacturing industries, and the rapid growth of entrepreneurial and professional classes all expanded the constituency to which the church appealed. In addition, Episcopalianism continued to have a disproportionate appeal to more affluent Americans, a fact that was a source of embarrassment to many leaders in the church; this appeal meant that, even apart from religious motives, the church provided an inviting option to upwardly mobile professionals (membership was fashionable, less demanding than in more evangelical churches, and a source of excellent social and business contacts).

Yet, the growth proved self-limiting. At no time did the Episcopal church pose many threats to more evangelical denominations. From the mid-eighteenth century, when evangelically oriented Anglicans in Virginia moved to the Presbyterian church, the tradition had suffered a steady drain of membership from the bottom, climaxing in the small evangelical schism of 1873. This was always a more dangerous temptation than any exodus to Rome. The Oxford movement appealed primarily to clergy, not laypeople. Given the American context, and the social status of the Roman Catholic church, one can understand why few Episcopalians, unless moved by intense doctrinal motives, would convert to Catholicism.

The church gained as much as it lost. Up to half its clergy in the mid-nineteenth century had moved from other Protestant bodies, some attracted by the greater doctrinal latitude within the church, some to the richer forms of worship. In the late nineteenth century, with the battles raging over religious liberalism in the evangelical denominations, the Episcopal church avoided any heresy trials and slowly, with some internal opposition, so broadened its fellowship as to accommodate liberalism and modernism. In fact, its most famous and eloquent preacher, Phillips Brooks, was a religious liberal. Thus, after 1870, the church had ever wider appeal to diverse Americans, but largely those of British ancestry and of middle- or upper-class status. It had a unique niche within Protestantism, or what many Episcopalians identified as a middle way between Catholicism and Protestantism. Many in the church were increasingly unwilling to identify with the Reformed tradition or were unhappy with the Protestant label in its name (in 1967 the church adopted the now generally used alternative "Episcopal Church," without "Protestant").

In the pluralistic mix of American Christianity, most nineteenth-century denominations appealed to members either on the basis of a distinctive set of doctrines or because of an emphasis on spiritual and moral purity or holiness. The Episcopal church, in effect, had no confession and accepted members with widely varying beliefs. It never demanded a nonworldly moral standard. Thus, worship has remained the greatest single key to its identity. It is appropriate that, in the twentieth century, the deepest divisions within the church have not involved doctrine but revisions in the prayer book or divisions over such social issues as ordination of women or tolerance for homosexuals.

The German Reformed Church and the Mercersburg Theology

For many reasons, the two surviving branches of continental Reformed Christianity in America tended toward the conservative and formal spectrum best represented by the Protestant Episcopal church. In the colonial period, the Anglican church absorbed the American members of Calvin's own church (French Reformed or Huguenot) and, as the names of famous Episcopalians demonstrate (Roosevelt, Onderdonk), a share of the Dutch Reformed along the Hudson River. In the period before the Oxford movement, Episcopalians shared much with these conservative continental Christians, as is clear from the history of the German and Dutch confessions in America.

Despite heavy German immigration by the 1850s, the German Reformed church remained a small denomination in America. It had only about 1,200 congregations and 100,000 members by the Civil War, a third less than the then more rapidly growing Episcopal church. Even this number represented considerable growth from the formation of an independent American church in 1793, when the denomination had only about 15,000 members (the same as the Episcopalians). In the larger history of American Protestantism, this small denomination is better known for two of its seminary professors than for all its other achievements. These two men – John W. Nevin and Philip Schaff – were the architects of what became known as the Mercersburg theology, a theological posture that had direct impact on Lutherans and Dutch Reformed and that challenged Presbyterian and Congregational theologians. But such theological innovations deeply divided the Reformed church, at least temporarily blocked merger possibilities with either Presbyterians or Dutch Reformed, and probably retarded its growth.[6]

In 1800 the Reformed church (correctly, *Der Synod der Reformierten Hoch Deutschen Kirch in den Vereinigten Staaten von America*) remained a largely German-speaking sect. It gradually lessened its earlier ties to the Dutch Reformed church even as it increased links to German Lutherans. The Germans revered their broadly Calvinistic Heidelberg Catechism and rejected the more dogmatic confessions of the Dutch church. But much as the colonial Dutch, the German Reformed had moved toward a pietistic or evangelical style of church life. Worship was informal, with no common liturgy. Most ministers supported revivals. The church was open to various types of denominational cooperation and in the early nineteenth century sought some basis of merger with the Dutch church, with the Lutheran Pennsylvania Ministerium, later with the Lutheran General Synod, and even with Presbyterians. In eastern Pennsylvania, Lutherans and Reformed often utilized the same church building and long talked of a common seminary. The commonality of language overcame doctrinal and liturgical differences.

At first, the independent synod of 1793 had remarkably little contact with Reformed churches in Germany. Language, more than any other issue, agitated the synod early in the new century. The synod had limited authority. It ordained ministers and worked for years to develop a seminary and college (it had no further supply of ministers from Holland or Germany). Until after 1820, various clergymen trained the young ministers, either individually or in what amounted to home-based seminaries. With growth, the synod helped found local or regional classes (comparable to presbyteries) and because of protracted fights over a seminary suffered the defection of a schismatic Free Synod in 1822 (it rejoined the parent synod in 1837) and in 1825 an enduring schism led by an ultra-evangelical minister, John Winebrenner. His Church of God (the first so called in America) was closer to the Methodists than to any of the continental Reformed confessions. In 1824 the classis in Ohio, frustrated by the distance its ministerial candidates had to travel for ordination, and much more open to the use of English in worship, declared independence and formed the Ohio Synod, a separate denomination until 1863 when the Eastern and Ohio synods merged in a new General Synod.

For ten years the Eastern Synod struggled with its fledgling seminary, first formed at Carlisle, Pennsylvania, in 1825 (tied to Dickinson College) and then moved to York. Because of local promotion, and offers of financial aid, the synod moved its classical school (Marshall College) in 1836, and its seminary in 1838, to Mercersburg. The college would merge with Franklin College in Lancaster in 1853, and the seminary moved there in 1871. The seminary's glory years, in terms of national distinction or notoriety, were from roughly 1840 to 1853. But even before the appointment of John Nevin as professor of theology in 1840, the seminary, despite its poverty and limited enrollment, had already engaged an unusually qualified professor, Frederick Augustus Rauch. This small denomination, because of its ties to Germany and its continued use of the German language, could recruit professors in Germany with academic qualifications that exceeded even those of professors at Harvard, Yale, Andover, or Princeton. Rauch had his Ph.D. from Marburg University and additional studies in philosophy at Gissen. He became a disciple of Hegel and an expert on Goethe but had to flee Gissen because of his outspoken political views after the revolutions of 1830. He tried to learn English, joined the Reformed church, and won a professorship at the Reformed Seminary (then at York) in 1832. He published works both on ecclesiastical history and in psychology. A European scholar in the wilds of America, he first spread the new German philosophy to his American seminarians but never really mastered the English language. Just before he died at Mercersburg in 1841 while still a young man, he was joined by the new professor of theology, Nevin, and would be succeeded as historian by Philip Schaff.

Nevin seemed a strange appointment at Mercersburg. He was an American of

Scotch-Irish descent and an orthodox, Calvinistic Presbyterian. Converted during his college years in New York, he entered Princeton Theological Seminary in 1823. Here he worked with the first theologians in that seminary, Archibald Alexander and Charles Hodge, and taught temporarily for two years at Princeton while Hodge was studying in Germany. He then moved to the new Western Seminary outside Pittsburgh. All his publications in these years reveal an orthodox Presbyterian, one caught up in several evangelical causes. His position seemed almost identical to his friend and mentor Charles Hodge, although he was perhaps more influenced by the New England theologians and, in the years before 1840, by his reading of the German church historian, Augustus Neander. The 1837 New School–Old School schism saddened him, as did all forms of sectarianism in America. He apparently offered a qualified resignation of his professorship (Western met his terms), and this became known at Mercersburg, leading to an offer in 1840. At the time of his move, or in a sense his escape from a divided Presbyterianism, he had had only limited contact with German scholarship, was as virulently anti-Catholic as most evangelicals, and had publicly condemned the Oxford movement in England. Within the next five years he matured a whole set of new convictions as he tried to understand the history of his new church and later as he conversed with a new colleague, Schaff.

Philip Schaff also did not grow up in the Reformed church. He was born in Switzerland, confirmed in a pietistic Lutheran church in Würtemberg, and began his university work at Tübingen, with later work at Halle and Berlin. He took courses from half the great German scholars, including the historians F. C. Bauer and Augustus Neander. He immersed himself in the philosophy of the now deceased Hegel and the theology of Schleiermacher. In fellowship he was a member of the United or Evangelical church in Germany (this resulted from a forced merger of Lutheran and Reformed churches in Prussia) and would later, in America, reclaim this allegiance while at Union Theological Seminary, where he became the most distinguished church historian in America. He came to Mercersburg at the age of twenty-five, already with the consuming interests in church history that would absorb him for the rest of his career. By 1845 no one in America was as familiar with German historical scholarship as Schaff. But what distinguished Schaff and Nevin was not the depth or breadth of their scholarship but the use they made of it. Out of their mutual study and debate came the Mercersburg theology. Such was the power of their minds, the persuasiveness of their essays, that they weathered the resulting divisions in their own denomination, survived some near-trials for heresy, and were able to pull their adopted church in an unexpected new direction – back toward Rome.

It is impossible, in a brief survey, to do justice to the thought of Nevin and

Schaff. They launched a major campaign against what they saw as the distortions within a developed Protestantism, particularly in the mainstream American churches. In a sense their dialectical effort led, in ways that such near-Hegelians could appreciate, to an antithesis that, by the early 1850s, verged on a complete capitulation to Rome or, for Nevin at least, serious considerations of converting to the Roman church.[7]

The most apt comparison of Nevin and Schaff would be with the Oxford movement in England, a movement with which they overtly sympathized. Nevin and Schaff wanted to restore the corporate church to the center of Christianity and thus counter an overly individualistic, sectarian, and revivalistic Protestantism. This meant, to them, a reappreciation of the history and traditions of the Western church, a restoration of the sacraments as the main and continuing medium of God's grace, the reform of public worship through the recovery of lost liturgical forms, and an upgrading of the status and role of the clergy. They did not emphasize formal confessions, which were simply another source of divisive sectarianism. Instead, they wanted to replace detailed confessions and catechisms with the early, unifying creeds, particularly the Apostles' Creed. Their ecumenism, and their openness to new scholarship and theological innovations, decisively separated them from conservative Lutherans. Their Reformed church, even though it never understood or adopted even half their proposals, would, much as the Protestant Episcopal church, combine a moderately High Church style with an accommodating stance toward new ideas, making the later church theologically liberal, liturgical, and inclusive. In the twentieth century it was able to merge first with the closely related Evangelical Synod and then eventually with the Congregational Christian church to form the present United Church of Christ.

The historical perspective, as shared by Nevin and Schaff, involved much that is now commonplace. Schaff was a student of the whole history of Christianity. In the light of that history, as reclaimed by German scholars, the Protestant Reformation was not the sharp, sudden break or watershed that American evangelicals too easily assumed. The commonalities, including the early doctrinal settlements, the great creeds, and the ministry and sacraments, much outweighed the differences. Thus, Schaff saw Luther and Calvin as reformers of the Catholic church, as men who, in a type of dialectical movement in the historic church, developed a fuller and more adequate understanding of salvation (soteriology). He and Nevin wanted to force Americans, caught up in sectarian strife or blinded by the later and overly scholastic formulations of Calvinist and Lutheran doctrines, to look carefully at the original Reformation context, at the issues in controversy, and at the original response to them by Luther and Calvin. In particular, Nevin wanted to recover the sacramental emphasis of both reformers and at least leaven the later, unendurable emphasis on divine decrees (he later rejected any strong version of predestination).

An ecumenical concern pervaded this historical outlook. Schaff and Nevin revered the church, the body of Christ. Nevin, much influenced by his reading of Schleiermacher, used, or at times seemed almost coerced by, organic metaphors. The church was one, not many. He rejected the prevalent Protestant idea that the church of Rome was the Antichrist, and instead he made modern sectarian divisiveness the Antichrist. When Nevin and Schaff talked of a truly catholic church, they referred not just to the invisible body of believers affirmed by Protestants but to a visible and real church, a divinely ordained institution, with a special ministry and a source of grace for humans, largely through its sacraments. In fact, the Roman church, much more than Protestant sects, maintained the idea of a unified or catholic church, whatever the excesses or distortions within its ecclesiastical institutions. They wanted their own small Reformed church to affirm this catholicity, to acknowledge its heritage, which traced back through the reformers to medieval Catholicism and beyond that to the age of the patristic fathers. Nevin, at low periods in his somewhat chaotic mental life, almost despaired of ever engrafting such a churchly view on any Protestants and thus considered moving to the Roman Catholic church. American Catholics celebrated his writings and waited, breathlessly but as it turned out in vain, for his final capitulation.

Much of this emphasis was not completely original in America, although it was shocking to evangelicals in the very decade of anti-Catholic crusades. Even Charles Hodge at Princeton, so resistant to most aspects of the Mercersburg theology, was enough of a church historian to recognize the historical continuities, to grant that Roman Catholics were often good Christians and within the church. Many confessional Lutherans and Old School Presbyterians moved toward a high view of the institutional church and its sacraments. For Schaff, the historical continuities pointed toward further historical developments in the church or toward some synthesis of the truths present in both Roman Catholicism and Protestantism. Such an envisioned unity involved much more than sectarian mergers; it meant a repudiation of sectarianism and a broader, internalized understanding of what it meant to be a participant in the body of Christ. Short of such an understanding, ecumenism would remain partial, often itself a testimony to the sin of sectarianism.

Nevin first advertised a distinctive outlook at Mercersburg with his devastating analysis of the new revival methods of Charles Finney, particularly the anxious bench. He followed this by a short treatise, and a series of essays, on the mystical presence of the body and blood of the Christ in the Eucharist. This was his opening salvo in behalf of a sacramental Christianity. He eventually went much further, including a defense of the objective, remitting role of baptism. But his views about the Eucharist occasioned the most controversy. The subtleties forbid a full expli-cation. In brief, Nevin insisted that almost all Protestants had forgotten, or ig-nored, the sacramentalism of Luther and Calvin. Since he wrote for a Reformed church, he explored in most detail the sacramental beliefs of Calvin and claimed that Calvin had believed in the real presence of the Christ (in body and not just in spirit) in the communion service. By the judgment of later Calvinist scholars, he pushed Calvin too far toward a sacramental conception of grace and placed too little emphasis on the role of the Word but was generally correct in his inter-pretation of spiritual presence in at least many of Calvin's writings. Calvin did believe that the Christ was present in the elements, but present not by the miracu-lous transformation of the elements (Roman Catholic) or by the ubiquity of the body of Christ and thus its miraculous presence with the elements (Lutheran), but through the mysterious work of the Holy Spirit. In one image, Calvin even talked of spiritual radiations from heaven, communicating the body to the recipi-ent. In this emphasis on the strongest possible meaning for "spiritual presence," Nevin at least was closer to Calvin than subsequent understandings within his, or other, Reformed churches (most often they viewed the supper simply as a memorial).

Critical to Nevin was the real presence, not the various ways of explaining such a presence. He defended spiritual presence because that was the tradition of his church. One feels that he would have been quite satisfied with either the Lutheran or Roman Catholic explanations and that such explanations were almost inciden-tal to the central, and to him unifying, fact: Jesus, in his fullest human traits, was present in the sacrament.

Nevin's larger purpose went well beyond the mysteries of how Christ could be present in the Eucharist. He wanted to reestablish the sacraments as central in the life of Christians and to make them the main channel of divine grace. This moved him very close to Rome. Implied was a diminished significance for any regenera-tive experience, any crisis-like conversion. Nevin believed the normal path of sal-vation was within the church, beginning with baptism. The big, divisive issue was thus the old one of the original Reformation. Were the sacraments efficacious in themselves? Did the church have the keys to the kingdom? In some sense, Nevin answered yes, but not without qualification and some degree of ambivalence. His critics believed he had crossed a critical line and had deserted the Protestant po-sition that faith is the sole condition of salvation and that the sacraments are efficacious only when conjoined with faith, not in themselves. Closely bound up with this issue was the status and role of the institutional church and of its clergy. By 1850 Nevin had moved closest to the Catholic view. He could not understand salvation outside the ministrations of the church, without sacraments and or-dained clergy to administer them, although, in some sense, he still affirmed the necessity of faith. Nevin was not a philosophical theologian; he did not always clarify the logical implications of his beliefs and in fact was not even sympathetic with an overly systematic, dogmatic development of church doctrine. This, again, explained his devotion to the ancient, comprehensive, inclusive, but not rigorously logical creeds or to the historic and traditional practices of the church.

One implication of such a High Church version of Protestantism was a more formal, richer worship, keyed more to creeds, sacraments, and song than to preaching. Mercersburg led the way in liturgical reforms, although not without strenuous resistance within the Reformed church. Before 1850, the German Reformed church usually ignored the traditional forms utilized by its parent congregations in Europe, particularly for Sunday worship. It had accepted the free style of most evangelicals, with no set prayers, no congregational response, and except in singing, no participation. Nevin's church was, in these respects, even less liturgical than Methodists. The sermon remained central; a conversion experience was climactic. Just as the doctrinal controversies over the Mercersburg theology began to abate about 1853 (Nevin retired from his theological professorship), the Reformed church began two decades of arguments over a liturgy, with Schaff very active in working for a formal, High Church style.

After 1847 the Eastern Synod began almost annual discussions of a common liturgy and invited committee suggestions. The movement had greatest support in eastern Pennsylvania, in those classes most under the sway of Mercersburg. It was most resisted in a few very small southern classes and by the whole Ohio Synod. Progress toward a common liturgy awaited Schaff's 1855 return from a sojourn in Germany. He took the lead in a committee (formerly chaired by Nevin) that prepared, after ten years of work, a provisional liturgy, one so sweeping in its implication for Sunday worship that the committee did not dare do more than to call it provisional, even as the synod never did more than commend the work of the committee and offer it to congregations as an acceptable option. Schaff, the major author of this liturgy (it contained some options), drew most directly from the *Book of Common Prayer*. The most formal recommendations structured almost all the worship service as well as all special or sacramental services. It included a yearly calendar of scripture readings, set prayers and litanies, confessions and absolution, and several types of congregational response. Its clear purpose was to diminish or eliminate extemporaneous prayers and subordinate the role of sermons. It would never be adopted by the synod and led to years of controversy. To many who had been leery of Romanism at Mercersburg, this simply seemed another bit of evidence of a conspiracy against the Reformed tradition. The classis of South Carolina even, briefly as it turned out, broke from the synod.

The liturgical battles, along with theological ones, dominated synod debates until well after the Civil War. These combined, at times, with an emphasis, by

Nevin and others, on something close to apostolic succession in the clergy and even to a few isolated recommendations for ordained bishops. In 1864 the now-unified General Synod appointed a new committee to revise the Provisional Liturgy of 1857, one adopted in only a minority of congregations and never used within the Ohio Synod. The committee submitted a revised liturgy in 1866, one not formally adopted by the synod but recommended as a replacement of the earlier version, again for congregations or classes that opted to use it. Only in 1883 did the General Synod gain approval for an official directory of worship, one that represented a compromise between Low Church and High Church factions. It included two forms, one largely free, the other almost as formal as desired by Schaff and Nevin, or a remarkable parallel to the contemporaneous development of broad church inclusiveness within the Episcopal church. By then the Mercersburg controversies had paled, replaced by such new issues as Darwinism and the status of scripture.

The influence of Mercersburg extended far beyond the small Reformed church. The views of Nevin and Schaff were at the center of theological controversy among many Lutherans and Presbyterians. The controversies led to the defection of some of the Reformed church's most evangelical ministers to the Dutch church, retarded merger efforts, created temporary schisms, and delayed the merger of the Eastern and Ohio synods. On the other side, up to a dozen Reformed ministers converted either to Roman Catholicism or to the Protestant Episcopal church. In the larger history of American Christianity, the Mercersburg theologians proved prophetic. They began a larger ecumenical effort, one that included Roman Catholicism (and, by implication, the Eastern Orthodox confessions). They first clarified Protestant commonalities with Catholicism and anticipated by a century movements toward convergence. They led, at least among Calvinist confessions, the first movement toward liturgical reform. In the short term, they won few converts to their more extreme High Church position and did not win over even a majority of congregations in their own denomination. But they at least posed an option, to many evangelicals a shocking option: a truly catholic form of Protestantism, a Christianity that, in Nevin's words, so followed the Apostles' Creed that its theology was objective, historical, and churchly and its worship sacramental and liturgical.

The Dutch Reformed Church

The Dutch Reformed church did not follow the Mercersburg High Church pattern. It remained moderately evangelical in commitment but at the same time fully loyal to orthodox doctrine and historical confessions. Most of its ministers repudiated the Mercersburg theologians and for this reason broke off promising efforts at merger with its German sister. This was the last real chance for merger of two confessions with a common parentage in Holland and western Germany, since in the late nineteenth century the German church became too liberal in doctrine, too ecumenical in outlook, to appeal to the more conservative Dutch. The German church also retained fewer ethnic and linguistic traditions.[8]

The Dutch church has retained its ethnic heritage. Unlike other Reformed bodies, it has as yet not joined in any mergers. But it did suffer one major schism, one closely related to new Dutch immigration and to divisions back in the Netherlands. The first, very tiny breaks came in 1822 and 1857. From these would derive the later, intensely confessional, rigorously orthodox Christian Reformed church, a denomination that is almost as large today as the older Reformed Church in America.

In 1772 the Dutch church in effect declared its independence from European control and formed its own independent coetis. Then, after the revolution, it, along with at least seven other America confessions, established an independent denomination. Its 1792 constitution (Standards) united approximately one hundred congregations in New York and New Jersey as the Reformed Protestant Dutch Church in North America.

In the new century the new denomination faced the same problem as other ethnic sects – how to resist, or properly assimilate, the dominant, British-born evangelicalism that surrounded it. Its original tactics resembled that of the German Reformed church. To a large extent it capitulated. The most influential father of the new, national church was American-born John H. Livingston, a Yale graduate with his subsequent doctorate from the University of Utrecht. He long served as pastor of the prestigious Collegiate Reformed congregation in New York City and helped found both Queen's College (now Rutgers) and the New Brunswick Theological Seminary (in 1784, the first seminary in America), where he became the first professor of theology. He was moderately evangelical in outlook, much influenced by New England theology, but rejected the wilder forms of revivalism. He tried to build bridges with other evangelicals but adhered rigorously to the historic confessions of his church. He helped make New Brunswick a junior version of Princeton.

In the new century the Dutch church was both confessional and evangelical. It faced many of the same tensions as the Presbyterians and came close to a schism remarkably similar to that which led to the New School and Old School division in 1837. The polarization never clearly involved any doctrinal differences, only the rigor by which the church interpreted the confessions, particularly Dort. The divisions involved the more northern congregations, in the Albany area, in competition with the even larger cluster in New Jersey and New York City. The Albany Synod, which often resisted new revival techniques, had a few ministers who sympathized with Nevin at Mercersburg and many who worked out close contacts with New England Congregationalists. One of their ministers, Taylor Lewis, wrote an important book on Christian evolution (*The Six Days of Creation*) just four years before Charles Darwin published his *Origin of Species*. Notably, he combined his accommodation of newer scientific knowledge with a strong antislavery position and a preference for a High Church, sacramental form of worship. The Albany men tended to be more ecumenical, more flexible in their interpretation of Dort or in their understanding of election. Ironically, their receptivity to the theological system of Samuel Hopkins became the center of controversy, with the southern clergymen of the church complaining that Hopkins had moved away from pure Calvinism, particularly on the doctrines of election and limited atonement. At least one minister faced, and survived, a heresy trial on charges of being a Hopkinsian.

The southern congregations, although still evangelical in style, remained rigid on confessional issues and soon established their links to the Princeton theology of Hodge. In a sense they made up an Old School faction – confessional but not liturgical. They kept their seminary at New Brunswick in the conservative camp. Joseph Berg, the ablest evangelical opponent of the Mercersburg theology in the German Reformed church, moved to the more conservative Dutch church and became theology professor at New Brunswick, making him the Charles Hodge of that seminary.

The still small, still ethnically pure denomination survived such doctrinal conflict with only one, seemingly minor schism. In 1822 Solomon Froeligh, a pastor in Schraalenburgh, New Jersey, convened a small group of rebels at his church. He was convinced that the larger denomination, all the way down to its seminary, had capitulated to Hopkinsian tendencies (not really true) and that the church had become lax in doctrine, in the administration of sacraments, and in the exercise of church discipline (true, at least by his rigorous standards). The new group, which had no more than ten congregations by the Civil War, called itself the True Reformed Dutch church. It was minuscule in comparison with the mother church, which by 1845 had 274 congregations and over 30,000 members. Its enduring significance related to events that began in that year, with the resumption of a steady but small stream of Dutch immigration. Religious events in Holland help explain some of the necessary conditions for this migration and for the type of religious life that developed among the new Dutch colonists.

From the time of Arminius and the remonstrants, the Dutch church had been schismatic. One of the largest schisms began in 1834, when over a hundred congregations seceded from the national Church of the Netherlands. The seceders were typical pietists or puritans, distressed with laxity and coldness and with compromises in doctrine and in devotion within the necessarily inclusive established church. They were similar to the Moravians of a century earlier in Saxony. The secessionists were, in turn, characteristically schismatic among themselves, with some stressing doctrinal orthodoxy and others a type of near Wesleyan holiness.

The new Dutch migration to America did not at all compare to the massive German one (only four thousand or so Dutch each year), but it cut across all sectors of Dutch life. Several new Dutch Catholic congregations date from this migration. In total, in the 1845–50 migration, the largest number of settlers came from the national church and either joined existing Reformed congregations in New York or New Jersey or became part of the larger, clustered Dutch colonies in Michigan and Iowa or the more scattered and smaller settlements in Wisconsin, Illinois, or Indiana, where a few isolated congregations converted to Old School Presbyterianism. Both because of religious reasons and because of greater economic deprivation, a disproportionate number of seceders came, in some years making up nearly half the migration. Even more important, the leaders of the two largest and, culturally and religiously, the most influential colonies were seceders.

One colony leader, whose disciples began gathering in St. Louis in 1845, was an extreme pietist, Dendrick Scholte. Untypically, he was not so concerned with doctrinal orthodoxy as with personal holiness. He led his small group of "purists" in 1846 to what became Pella, Iowa, forming the heart of a Dutch colony in that brand-new state. Here he organized a primitive type of Christian church, on the Apostolic model, with ten new articles of faith and great revivals and rigorous moral scrutiny and discipline. It was, in a sense, another fascinating intentional community, but it did not spawn an enduring religious sect. Many settlers, who did not aspire to Scholte's rigor, soon formed a rival Reformed church. Eventually, the remnants of Scholte's colony filtered into either Reformed or Christian Reformed congregations.

The second, larger, and in time more influential colony (*der Kolony*) was planted by one of the abler secessionist leaders, Albertus van Raalte. In 1847 he led a mere handful of settlers to western Michigan, beginning the colony and also founding the town of Holland. In the next five years other immigrants formed a circle of Dutch towns in the Holland and Grand Rapids area, forming what amounted to a little Netherlands in America. The early communities always involved congregations in the more doctrinaire secessionist tradition represented by Raalte, who gathered their new congregations in a classis in 1848, one with less than one thousand members and only four pastors. The Reformed church, still clustered in New York and New Jersey, had both welcomed and assisted these new immigrants. It clearly expected to absorb them and thus expand the denomination to the west, creating a truly national although still ethnically based denomination. Except in the South, it succeeded, but not without a very small splinter movement in 1857, which, because of later events, was in an excellent position to compete for the much larger wave of Dutch immigrants who began to arrive in 1880.

In 1849 the pastor of the Albany Reformed Church, Isaac N. Wyckoff, came to Michigan to effect an alliance or merger with the new classis. He wanted to absorb it into the older Dutch church in America. Although he spoke fluent Dutch, he represented eastern congregations that had gradually accepted English, even in most of their worship services. Raalte was won over by his kindness, and in 1850 the new classis in Michigan joined the Albany Synod. The merger by these rigorous and schismatic colonists reflected their belief that the American church, unlike the national church in Holland, had remained orthodox and at least reasonably pure, a judgment backed up by the history of the American church. For the most part, and for a vast majority of Reformed Christians in Michigan, the merger was successful. Among other benefits, it brought generous financial help from the eastern brethren, help that enabled the western colony to begin Hope College in 1850.

The merger did not long satisfy a scattering of disaffected minsters and laymen in the Michigan settlements. In 1857 three congregations, and a faction from another in Grand Rapids, withdrew from the Reformed Classis. The reasons were local and often personal, but the separatists soon justified the break by accusations of lax doctrines and practices in the eastern congregations, some of which these settlers had visited on the way west. In fact, no clear confessional issue divided the two groups, since both sides adhered to Dort. But, according to the charges of the rebels, the eastern congregations had failed to preach election and limited atonement, had opened their communion to other denominations, had used the wrong hymns, had neglected the catechism, and worst of all, had admitted the adherents of the Masonic Order to membership. Symbolically important were such issues as the Albany Synod's use of the English language, its lack of rigor in doctrine and discipline, and its accommodation with the outside world. As far as the records reveal, the rebels did not raise or debate narrow points of theology.[9]

This schism was tiny. Dozens of other comparable local rebellions, in other denominations, would never even catch the attention of later scholars. The early rebels had only five congregations and less than two hundred communicants when they joined in a new classis in the fall of 1857. Only in 1859 did they take the name Holland Reformed church, to which they subsequently added the prefix "True." Through the Civil War the number of congregations remained under ten. Expansion afterward was slow, with eventual congregations in New Jersey and in Pella, Iowa, as well as in the Grand Rapids region. By 1879 the church had divided into four classes, with thirty-four congregations and twelve thousand members. Able new leadership from Holland had helped strengthen the movement, and a small seminary (1861) and academy in Grand Rapids (today Calvin College and Seminary) helped train new ministers. In 1880 the church took the name, one much used back in the Secession in Holland, of Holland Christian Reformed church. In 1890 it absorbed the thirteen congregations of the old, 1822 True Protestant Dutch Church and dropped "Holland." More important, in the wave of new immigration in the 1880s, it was able to compete equally with the Reformed church, in part because of endorsements back in Holland by kindred groups, in part because of a Calvinist theological revival launched in Holland by Abraham Kuyper, and in part because of the failure of the Reformed church to adopt a definitive prohibition against the Masonic Order. In other words, after 1880 this new, rigorously Calvinistic, separatist sect (it asked all congregations to build separate Christian schools) began to grow toward equality with the older Dutch church, gaining nearly total equality by the last decade of the twentieth century but not without some deep and very complex internal tensions.

In one sense, the Christian Reformed leaders were correct. The older Reformed church had accommodated, for it was within, although a conservative wing of, mainstream American evangelical Protestantism. It has so remained, but as a part of the mainstream it has joined in cooperative activities (the National and World Councils of Churches and ecumenical discussions). In its assimilationist stance, and its acceptance of additional aspects of modernity, the Reformed Church has drawn much more clearly than in 1880 the wide cultural and religious gap between it and the more rigorous, confessional, and culturally separatist Christian Reformed denomination. Yet, conservative factions within the Reformed church have resisted such accommodation, whereas "progressive" factions within the Christian Reformed church have resisted its more extreme separatism.

To an extent, the Episcopal and the two continental Reformed confessions reflected a right wing within American Reformed Christianity – but not clearly or neatly. Each always included evangelical minorities, and the Dutch church probably included an evangelical majority. The strongly confessional, rigidly Calvinist, but antirevivalistic factions within Old School and southern Presbyterianism, when linked to the Christian Reformed church, might also qualify as a conservative or right wing of Reformed Christianity. Thus, in Episcopalianism, and in the Mercersburg movement, one meets a form of liturgical and ecclesiastical conservatism, often joined with theological openness, a hostility to narrow confessions, and a recognized affinity to Roman Catholicism. In Old School Presbyterianism and in the Christian Reformed church, one confronts something very different, a confessional and rigidly doctrinal and anti-Catholic form of conservatism. These two conservative wings of Reformed Christianity in America rarely overlapped and thus reflect two very different traditions joined only by their hostility to the more innovative aspects of the new evangelicalism. We will confront confessional and doctrinal conservatism in subsequent chapters, which include a summary of the theological views of Charles Hodge and a brief history of the origins of Old School Presbyterianism.

CHAPTER 6

Reformed Worship

*E*xcept for the Episcopal church, the Reformed denominations in America generally moved to a free or open style of corporate worship. For millions of Americans this style seemed normal, for they were unaware of how exceptional it was in the perspective of the total history of the Western church. If at all perceptive, they were at least aware of more formal types of worship in Roman Catholicism, in most Lutheran denominations in America, and in the Protestant Episcopal church.

Early Protestant Worship

In America, early worship forms reflected the patterns brought by migrants from European Protestant confessions and by English Catholics in Maryland. In time, these changed in ways not always duplicated back in Europe, although it makes little sense to talk of any distinctive American liturgies except among the new Christian sects that originated in America. The most important roots of American worship were in the British churches – Anglican, Scottish, and Independent (or Puritan). These reflected variants on the Reformed worship that began with Zwingli and Calvin. The lines of influence were more often from Calvin; the patterns of worship that developed among Presbyterians, American Congregationalists, and most American Baptists were closest to Zwingli, but not because of his direct influence.[1]

As much as on matters of doctrine, post-Reformation Christians would eventually disagree quite radically as to what was proper worship. The battles continue today. But in the wake of the major liturgical changes in Roman Catholicism that derive from Vatican II, and after a century of convergent liturgical innovations among Protestants, it is easy to forget how deep, and how basic, were these differences in the wake of the Reformation and Counter-Reformation.

In most respects, the liturgical revisions begun by Luther, Zwingli, and Calvin reached their climax in America, particularly in the heyday of evangelicalism in the early nineteenth century. At that point, the worship style and forms favored by a vast majority of Protestants in America diverged further from Roman Catholic patterns than ever before, or ever again. For American Protestants, this was a mark of success, an indication that they had recovered the simple and free worship of the New Testament church. It is perhaps most significant that their worship only infrequently involved the Lord's Supper or Eucharist and was centered on scripture reading, extemporaneous rather than set prayers, hymns, and above all on a teaching and convicting form of preaching.

The reformers wanted to take worship back in its essentials to the New Testament pattern, although neither Luther nor Calvin were opposed to all subsequent innovations. Roman Catholics insisted that their worship was scriptural in all essentials, with later innovations complementing what they admitted were much more simple beginnings. Since so much scholarship has been devoted to this topic, no one can lightly choose a winner. The contested issues are now much broader than Catholic versus Protestant. The greatest division today is that between those who find, even in the New Testament, the basis of a quite formal and Eucharistic mode of worship and those who find the basis of a simple, free, informal, and largely nonsacramental form.

Unfortunately, those who find in the New Testament or in the primitive church the beginnings of set forms refer to theirs as the "liturgical" tradition. The word *liturgy* bears a heavy burden in these debates. In its simplest meaning, the word refers to the degree of lay or popular participation in worship; if the people are much involved, then worship is by that fact liturgical. This means that modern, Pentecostal services are possibly the most liturgical of all, even though most elements are extemporaneous or even spontaneous. Others typically use *liturgy* to refer to set forms of worship, those ordained by ecclesiastical authority and uniform within a national church or a given confession, and thus worship that has little room for extemporizing. This usually means written prayers, confessions, and litanies, with each step in worship often prescribed in a prayer book or manual. Such patterned or repetitive worship usually, but not of necessity, accompanies rich, highly symbolic, colorful, or artistic worship (beautiful buildings, colorful clerical dress, plenteous visual supports, elaborate processions or ceremonies, and trained choirs) and parallels a central emphasis on the Eucharist along with a relative demotion of the role of the sermon.

The sharp, often embittering conflict among the major reformers over matters of doctrine or liturgy too easily camouflages the large area of commonality. Beginning with Luther, all the reformers repudiated the Catholic Mass. This meant a repudiation not only of transubstantiation but also of the heavily sacrificial motifs that accompanied it as well as the priestly roles that this entailed. Only Zwingli intentionally displaced the Lord's Supper from its former centrality in worship. Both Luther and Calvin wanted to restore communion to the people and to ensure that it fulfilled the ends of the gospel (thus, they introduced the vernacular, had the people partake of both bread and wine, and condemned any "performed" communion by ministers in front of a congregation). Both preferred weekly communion. In almost none of their churches did they prevail on this point, for such meant a radical shift in lay patterns of participation and faced magisterial opposition. Communion in most Lutheran and Reformed confessions would be no more frequent than monthly and in time rarely more than quarterly. For laypeople, this still meant more frequent participation in communion than had been customary under medieval Roman Catholicism. The major shift, therefore, was away from the "performed" weekly Eucharist. Without it as the core of worship, the new Protestant pattern, as Zwingli had foreseen, would be a non-Eucharistic form of worship. What had been the pre-Eucharistic elements of Roman Catholic worship now became the norm for Protestant services, with the sermon soon central and most lengthy except among Anglicans, where prayers and responses often overbalanced the sermon.

Despite convergent elements, Protestant worship soon varied from place to place and from confession to confession. It is all too easy to generalize. For example, one could argue that Lutherans remained closest to Roman Catholicism in the content of worship, if not in form; that Anglicans remained closest in form but not in content; that continental Reformed churches and Scottish Presbyterians moved away from Rome in both content and form; and that varied pietistic or independent sects moved beyond any form at all. Such generalizations require careful qualifications, which becomes evident if one looks at the major Protestant worshiping traditions.

In America, liturgical issues, and liturgical differences, have been more important among Lutherans than in the churches of the Reformed tradition. Yet, even the Reformed churches drew on the earliest reforms of Luther, who decisively changed the meaning of traditional liturgies. In doctrine he was often radical. But he was very reluctant to change existing forms. In his own city of Wittenberg, and in his home country of Saxony, he helped ease the transition from the old church to the new. For the masses of laypeople, changes in their churches often came not because of lay demands but because of princely edict. It was all so confusing, particularly in city-states that switched religious allegiances more than once. Most resistant to reforms were patterns of popular devotion and worship. Luther recognized this and was willing to keep the old bottles if only he could fill them with new wine.

Luther loved much in traditional worship. Thus, he at first continued to refer to the Mass, even though with a quite different conception of its meaning, and kept the Latin in his first liturgical guide. He wanted to retain the Eucharist as the core of worship. His strong doctrine of consubstantiation and objective presence, and of sacraments as a medium of grace, supported such centrality. He also continued a form of confession and penance close to that of the Roman church. He retained a high estimate of the role of an ordained clergy, stressed the objective and remitting merit of baptism, and kept most of the visible ceremonies that had been part of Catholic worship (baptismal symbolism and the sign of the cross, church weddings, major festivals although no saint days, a lectionary, clerical vestments, a simple confirmation for children, and even, for a period, the elevation of the bread in the Eucharist). Lutherans made few changes in the former Catholic churches and cathedrals, thus preserving their artwork. Above all, Luther stressed preaching and music. He wanted careful instruction of his flock and stressed the duty of his clergy to develop preaching skills, so lacking in most priests of his day. He loved song and music. He composed hymns and introduced congregational hymn singing as a vital part of worship, thus making his single most influential contribution to Protestant worship.

It is more difficult to characterize Reformed worship than Lutheran. The various Reformed confessions adopted at least slightly different worship forms, meaning that one cannot specify a typical service. Even Calvin did not expect the widely influential church order he helped develop in Geneva to fit churches in other parts of Europe. He was as open as Luther to variation on nonessentials, and for Calvin this entailed a rather broad array of differences in polity (from episcopal to congregational) and in liturgy (from quite formal to very spontaneous).

One generalization is helpful and fits most Reformed worship. Except for Anglicans, almost all the Reformed confessions adopted what one might call an unfilled, rather than a filled, order of worship. All Reformed churches, including congregational ones, opted for an ordered, familiar, predictable progression in worship. In fact, quite often, congregational or free church Calvinists, such as the Puritans in New England, were more uniform in practice, more predictable in worship patterns, than those under some form of ecclesiastical authority. Familiar rituals are part of any worshiping tradition.

Roman Catholics, Anglicans, and most Lutherans had "filled" liturgies. They honored customary or published orders of worship that not only prescribed the order of prayer, scripture, teaching, and song but actually included the content of at least some of the prayers, prescribed the daily and weekly scriptures (the lection), honored an annual calendar with major festivals such as Advent and Lent, included responsive confessions and litanies, and determined the appropriate psalms or hymns. This could mean a prior determination of every detail of the service except the content of the sermon, and in some Anglican worship illtrained or lazy ministers often read "canned" or published sermons, meaning no room for any extemporaneous content at all. In largely preliterate societies, the priests alone had written guides to worship and simply followed them to the edification of the audience. In the Anglican reforms, and for the first time, all aspects of prayer-book worship were in the hands of increasingly literate lay participants.

Such filled liturgies had certain obvious advantages – uniformity of worship, compensation for ill-trained or unskilled clergy, a rational progression in the use and study of scripture, and a level of eloquence or artistry befitting acts of piety.

In non-Anglican confessions, much more of the liturgy remained open. The people knew what would take place at each step during a worship service but did not know the content. They knew when prayers would occur, but those who prayed did not always or even typically follow set forms, adapting their language to the time, the occasion, or even to the guidance of the Spirit. Such prayers, as much as the sermon, were extemporaneous. This does not mean that the sermon or prayers were spontaneous, unprepared, or unwritten but only that the content was open to the one leading or guiding the worship. Such an unfilled plan of worship placed a much larger burden of careful preparation, and composition, on ministers, and thus one characteristic of Reformed practice would be carefully trained as well as "called" ministers and carefully written, at times even scholarly, sermons. Another implication was that the minister would be the final architect of worship; he had great leeway in the choice of scripture and songs – to fit the occasion, to respond to the needs of a congregation, to adapt to crises or times of joy, or to reflect the sincere and moving spiritual concerns that a minister felt on a given Sunday. This all entailed a free, extemporaneous, but ordered and carefully prepared worship. In most Reformed confessions occasional or nonworship procedures (baptism, admission of members, ordaining of clergy or elders, catechismal instruction of children, and marriage) did follow a set and filled order or discipline (in popular language, the preacher did this "by the book").

John Calvin had more impact on worship in America than any other single individual. This is because of his influence on the English church, an even more intimidating influence on John Knox and the Scottish church, and his often more indirect but powerful sway over those English Puritans who came to New England, there to found the largest confession in colonial America. Calvin, as much as Luther, and contrary to Zwingli, wanted to keep the Eucharist at the heart of worship but failed to persuade his magistrates in Geneva to allow it each week. He had a strong sense of the real spiritual presence in the elements and saw the communion experience as essential in the life of Christians, a special divine gift that enabled them to grow toward a sanctified life. In an often ignored but, because of its influence on Scotland, significant tactic to overcome magisterial and popular resistance, Calvin so scheduled the quarterly communion services in the small Republic of Geneva that, at least once a month, one congregation would have communion, open to anyone in the larger fellowship (Geneva was legally one parish). In Scotland this led, much later, to a tradition of large, extended communion seasons of an intercongregational type, which provided the first and most important precedent for extended periods of revival in America.

Calvin was not a puritan, out to change all worship traditions or return to the simple New Testament example. He included set prayers and responses in his service (the long pastoral prayer, soon a distinctive mark of Reformed worship, was extemporaneous), allowed a simple form of confirmation (actually, more nearly a confession of faith by formerly instructed children), kept weddings and funerals under church supervision, allowed academic gowns for ministers, provided communion services for the sick, and did not in all cases condemn rings in marriage or the sign of the cross as part of baptism. These elements from traditional liturgies, plus his strong sense of spiritual presence in the Lord's Supper, provided the basis of liturgical renewal efforts in the nineteenth and twentieth centuries among some Reformed confessions, such as the German Reformed church in the United States.

Such continuities are not as significant as what Calvin tried to change. For the communion services, he substituted a simple table in the front of churches in place of an altar and had communicants come and stand or kneel at such tables. Instead of the elaborate prayers of consecration, he substituted a brief institution and a simple prayer. Since he was allowed only infrequent communions, he tried to enhance the seriousness with which parishioners approached communion, leading to some important and enduring Calvinist innovations. In the week before communion Sunday, Christians were supposed to submit to careful self-examination (they did this all the time, but communion made it even more imperative). In time, as in Scotland, this often became a standard period of fasting and prayer, practices that led, indirectly, to such later evangelical institutions as society or prayer meetings. Such preparations also led in Scotland to a special examination of prospective communicants on the Saturday before communion (a homologue of Catholic confession) and the granting of a leaden token to the worthy, which admitted them to the table on Sunday. Beginning in Geneva, ministers preceded the communion with special exhortations, often tied to the Ten Commandments, which stressed the sincerity and moral purity that allowed one to commune without fear of divine wrath (eventually called the fencing of the table). In these ways, Reformed churches made the communion a powerful tool of moral discipline, a way of forcing people to examine their deepest motives, to be truly penitent. Whereas Catholics had viewed the Eucharist as a means of grace, a sacrament of forgiveness, Calvinists reserved the table and its ineffable joys for the godly.

Penitential and confessional motifs dominated Genevan worship. The minister opened the worship service with a confession, one written and read by himself but intended for the edification of the audience. Next to the sermon, the most extended portion of the service was the pastoral prayer, in which the minister could further confess congregational sins or warn congregants of the temptations of the world. Before the reading of scripture, Reformed ministers invoked the guidance of the Holy Spirit, a distinctive way of emphasizing worship as the human response to the Word. The sermon, the heart of Reformed worship, was often a detailed explication, and application, of some scriptural passage or text. Thus, the worship as a whole reinforced the disciplinary rigor of Geneva and the types of monitoring and supervision and examination carried out by the Consistory (the elders). This penitent and introspective element and the expository and cerebral aspects of the learned sermon do not mean that Reformed worship was joyless and gloomy. This was not the issue. The worship was oriented toward a high level of righteousness, but it celebrated the gift of grace and the joys of communion. The aspects of thanks and joy dominated the congregational psalm singing.

Calvinists, from Geneva on, emphasized a serious, intelligent, sincere, and spiritual form of worship. Just as the Word and the Spirit provided the means of grace, so the Word and the Spirit were to be the dominant presences in worship. Nothing else should divert from their centrality. This led to the so-called ascetic rigor of Geneva. Although they kept the old churches, Calvinists stripped them of all images. They would suffer no artificial aids, no sensual diversions. They still noted truly Christian events (Easter) but downgraded their significance and insisted on the equal importance of each Lord's Day, or what they often referred to as the Christian Sabbath. They of course repudiated saint's days and would allow no lectionaries but did follow a logical progression through the scriptures. Even formal worship was not enough; it was so planned and conducted as to offer guidance for what Christians had to do daily – read scripture, pray, meditate – in morning devotions, before meals, in the evening, and even at the place of their vocation or calling.

Worship in the British Churches

Reformation innovations in worship reached America largely through the Protestant churches of England and Scotland. The story of worship in Britain was enormously complex and was at the heart of the seventeenth-century civil wars. At times issues of worship, of liturgical forms and practices, were a more divisive issue than differences in doctrine. The story began with the reform of the English and Scottish churches (see chapter 1).[2]

With the consolidation of reform in England, at the end of the reign of Henry VIII and under the boy king Edward, the English church made an enduring commitment. It moved, doctrinally, to a clearly Calvinist position, a position expressed in what, after revisions under Elizabeth, became the Thirty-Nine Articles. At the same time, in a country deeply divided among Catholics, moderate reformers, and radical reformers, it seemed important to develop a uniform plan of worship, one that would mediate among the contending factions. Archbishop Thomas Cranmer guided the creation of the first *Book of Common Prayer* (*BCP*) in 1549 and its much more significant, and protestant, revision in 1552. This second prayer book was a daring enterprise, unprecedented in church history. What the church adopted was a simple guide to all aspects of church life, not only plans for Sunday worship but also forms for daily worship and for all the less frequent ceremonies of the church (baptism, communion, marriage, burial, confirmation, ordination). Even Catholics had to stand in envy, for they had at least four different guides to serve the same ends. Revised in 1559 and at the Restoration in 1662, this prayer book has remained the one unifying element in an otherwise fractured English church. Even at the 1549 beginnings, Cranmer committed the English church to a "filled" or quite detailed liturgy, for the *BCP* contained all the prayers and litanies needed in the life of the church. It did not preclude supplementary items in worship, and it left room for free expression in the sermon, but for most congregations it would remain the sole guide to worship for four centuries.

In form, the 1552 prayer book adapted the ancient worship tradition of the church in Britain (the Sarum rites) but in simplified form and with clearly Protestant or Reformed content. Even Cranmer conceded the failure of the 1549 expectation of weekly, or even daily, communion, which meant that Anglican worship would normally include only the traditional items that prepared people for communion proper, now required of members only three times a year. Otherwise, the Anglican communion was, in form and purpose, fully Reformed. Ministers could not celebrate communion separate from the people, the altar became a table, and the officiating minister faced the people, who came forward to take communion at the table while kneeling. Even this posture offended many rigorous reformers and led to a special rubric (often called black) to defend the kneeling and in the process prove that it had nothing to do with a priestly sacrifice or any miraculous transformation of the elements. Prayer, scripture, various litanies, and at times the sermon became central in Anglican worship, with public prayer more important than in any other Christian confession.

In what turned out to be enduringly popular, the *BCP* included daily services of morning (Matin) and evening (Evensong) prayers. Since daily attendance was often mandatory for Sunday morning prayers, this service became, in effect, the opening part of Sunday worship, in time forming the major part of worship on Sundays without the Eucharist. The Matin had opening prayers of confession and absolution, the Lord's Prayer, the Gloria and psalms, Old and New Testament readings, the creeds, Kyries, and several daily prayers (collects), plus some other minor responses, in a pattern very close to earlier Catholic pre-Eucharistic worship. For non-Eucharist Sundays, the morning prayers were supplemented with other precommunion rites, such as an offertory and a litany, and ended with a sermon. The service could be very long. The fact that it rarely eventuated in an actual communion led later liturgical reformers, and Anglo-Catholics, to demand a return to the weekly Eucharist. Because of the length and richness of what proceeded, sermons were often short, mere homilies.

The *BCP* followed a lectionary, one that honored major Christian festivals, with stress on Lent and Advent. It provided prayers and even a communion service for the sick, allowed marriages with a ring, and included an often controversial sign of the cross in baptism. Anglicans kept the old church buildings, but reformers removed most of the imagery. The church made provision for a confirmation of youth (virtually a graduation exercise for the instructed) by the bishop. In all these ways it kept much of the form of the traditional worship, a move intended to ease the transition to Protestantism and appease those of High Church or even Roman sympathies.

In Scotland the influence of Geneva prevailed. John Knox, the most important but far from the only reformer in Scotland, had spent exile years in Geneva, as a colleague of Calvin's and in effect pastor of an English-language minority. Here he worked out an English service book, one that in 1564 he revised as the liturgical guide for the Church of Scotland (it would soon be known as the *Book of Common Order*). In a few ways Knox deviated from Geneva – more encouragement of extemporaneous prayers, communion at tables with the participants sitting (an innovation followed by some Puritans in England), and no appeal to the Holy Spirit in the consecration prayer. Unlike the *BCP*, this guide was never slavishly followed by independent-minded ministers and thus functioned as a model more than a prescribed liturgy.

In 1603 James VI of Scotland became James I of the United Kingdom. Instead of being a boom to the Church of Scotland, this union led to a century of strife and confusion (see chapter 1). The hope of James, and even more his successor, Charles I, was a uniform church for the whole kingdom. This led, first of all, to much more authority for bishops in Scotland, the source of much local congregational resistance. Then, without the permission of the Scottish church, or even consultation, Charles I in 1637 imposed on Scotland a new and Catholic-leaning *BCP*, one largely composed by his High Church archbishop, William Laud. This led to a revolt in Scotland. The Scots deposed their bishops and returned to a pure presbyterial system and restored their old liturgy. In England, the Long Parliament, in a developing civil war, and in order to buy Scottish help, accepted a presbyterian polity and convened the Westminster Assembly in 1643 to work out a new church order and both a new confession and a new *Directory of Public Worship*, which was for England, Scotland, and Ulster.

The *Directory* in effect created a much more conventional Reformed standard of worship for Britain. It had little lasting impact on the English church, since it was in use only briefly and most traditional congregations did not use it. But it became the official, although in many cases locally ignored, standard for Scottish Presbyterians, including those in Ulster and in colonial America. It also provided guidelines for English Presbyterians and for many liturgical reformers in England who remained outside the national church after the Restoration in 1660. The *Directory* met most of the demands of English Puritans and was much closer to the Presbyterian pattern than to the *BCP*. It discontinued vestments, the sign of the cross, marriage rings, private baptisms, and the administration of communion for the sick; it prescribed tables for communion so that people could sit (it did not expressly condemn the kneeling required under Laud, but this was clearly implied). It gave careful directions to ministers, included topics for prayers, kept a scriptural lection, and invoked the Holy Spirit in the consecration prayer. In place of the old church calendar, it recommended specially designated days of thanksgiving or of fasting, humiliation, and prayer as events or circumstances required. It was, perhaps, as good a compromise as possible among so many contending factions.

This leads to the confusing issue of Puritan worship. The label "Puritan" was never precise; it referred to various factions in the English church, those who demanded a more complete reform of polity, doctrines, and worship and the elimination of all remnants of papist or nonscriptural practices. As historians now use the slippery label, it refers to those who were thoroughly Calvinist in doctrine, who wanted greater degrees of local control over worship without rejecting a state church, and who wanted a fully scriptural form of worship. Such Puritans ranged from moderates to radicals and, thus, differed in the rigor with which they wanted to purify the church. Many joined English and Scotch Presbyterians in supporting the reforms implemented in the *Directory*. The more radical rejected the *Directory* as a flawed compromise.

Almost all "Puritans" wanted church order but believed that local congregations should have a say in that order. They also rejected the degree of guidance (the filled aspects) of the *BCP*. Soon even small issues became highly symbolic and suspect – vestments, wafers instead of real bread in communion, the ring in marriage or even solemnized marriages or burials, the sign of the cross in baptism, kneeling for communion, godparents in christening, imagery in church buildings, and holy days (Easter and Lent, Christmas and Advent) rather than the Lord's Day. Only in clandestine ways could the more radical Puritans practice the type of worship they preferred. Thus, the movement of Puritans to Massachusetts after 1630 allowed them, for the first time, to exemplify what they believed to be a scriptural form of worship. Here their nominal ties to the Church of England gave way to an overt congregational polity, but at first with a reasonably uniform Sunday worship. They initially had no separate church buildings, formed their congregations around a bond of union or covenant, and set up long morning and afternoon services on Sunday. These involved largely three elements – psalm singing, extemporaneous prayers, and very long sermons. On occasion they baptized children or adults, admitted adults to membership after a type of personalized confession, honored or renewed their congregational covenants, and in some congregations encouraged a lay response to sermons (this could involve a challenge to the minister). They took very seriously their infrequent communion services, asked for the same soul-searching self-examination as Presbyterians for those who received the elements (not at tables but seated in pews), and rigorously excluded those they deemed unprepared. They were not against guides for worship, such as the *Directory*, but viewed all such as advisory, not prescriptive.[3]

After the Restoration of 1660, and the reestablishment of the traditional English church with its *BCP*, the uncompromising Puritan congregations, including English Presbyterians, became often persecuted dissenters. After 1689, and the Act of Toleration, Congregationalists were able to organize and support independent congregations. English Presbyterians would decline in time, with the majority of members moving toward a rational or Arian position by the eighteenth century. They kept a free style of worship, one even less ordered than in Scotland. The Independents largely followed the model of their New England brethren, although in time they fragmented in several directions. More radical sects also gained at least a degree of toleration in 1689, including earlier Separatists, many of whom had fled to Holland and then to the Plymouth Colony in America. They, plus early Baptists, all accepted the free worship tradition, with complete congregational control.

Of great importance in America was the work of John and Charles Wesley. Without quite intending it, they effected a liturgical revolution in the English church. John Wesley loved the *BCP* and the formal, structured worship service it prescribed. He took communion at least weekly and wanted his converts to celebrate the supper frequently in a parish church. His Methodist movement was not a liturgical movement. It was a supplemental movement, dedicated to saving souls, to nourishing Christians in living a holy life, and to restoring the warmth and spirituality (literally the role of the Holy Spirit) that was so rarely present in Anglican parishes. It was in the context of his Methodist societies that Wesley made his most significant contribution to English worship – a tradition of hymn singing (see below).

Wesley remained in the English church until his death in 1791. Thus, he never developed a separate liturgy for his Methodist societies in Britain but in 1784 did revise the *BCP* to fit the needs of the new Methodist Episcopal church in the United States. Meanwhile, as part of his societies in England, he helped revive some primitive practices of the church, not as components of Sunday worship but as part of a rich devotional life. His Moravian colleagues influenced many of these, including vigils or watch-night services (all-night services, particularly for the new year), love feasts or agape (a communal meal with bread and water), and the class system with its almost monastic level of mutual support and fellowship. As Methodist society meetings became, for many, the de facto replacement for the Anglican service, Wesley retained traditional liturgical elements that were taboo to Puritans, such as kneeling at the altar for communion, adhering to the major holy days and to Advent and Lent, and retaining many fixed prayers.

Ironically, Wesley's liturgy for the new American church would have most of its impact back in England. When, after his death, the Methodist societies effected a final separation from the English church, many adopted this simplified liturgy. In America almost none of the Methodist societies used his liturgy, except for the forms for special services, which were soon included in the discipline for ministers. An informal, free style of worship was already too habitual in America. The liturgy survived and had a brief revival before the Civil War in Nashville at the publishing center of the Methodist Episcopal Church, South, only because of the influences there of Thomas O. Summers, an immigrant from Britain who was already familiar with more formal Methodist worship. It has had a revival of sorts among some twentieth-century American churches, those concerned with Methodist sources for a liturgical revival or ecumenical cooperation.

Wesley's *Sunday Service of the Methodists in North America* was close, in spirit, to the *Directory* of 1645. In the context of ordered worship he reduced the feast days, eliminated rings in marriage, simplified ordination rites, eliminated formal confirmations, did away with the sign of the cross in baptism, and left room in his service for extemporaneous prayers. But what was most distinctive in Methodism was not his via media Sunday worship but the multitude of other devotional services, in all of which laypeople prayed and sang and confessed with great joy.

Early Worship in America

All the major liturgical traditions in Europe eventually found a home in America. Lutherans and continental Reformed churches came, following for a time the same form of worship as they had left behind. Roman Catholics came to Maryland and there exemplified a highly sacramental approach to worship. The Anglicans in America remained a part of the English church, with the same *BCP*. Presbyterians came from England, Scotland, and in largest numbers from Ulster and in America developed free forms of worship that were all but indistinguishable from those of New England Puritans. That is, they opted for ordered services but left most of the content to ministers. Both the Particular Baptists, who immigrated from England but followed Presbyterian worship patterns, and the Separating Baptists in eighteenth-century New England were distinguished largely by adult baptism and the institutions that grew up around this practice.[4]

Except for Anglicans, the Reformed confessions in America converged toward a common, free worship pattern. The Presbyterians rarely followed their *Directory*. Methodists quickly put away Wesley's liturgy. At least before 1840, German and Dutch Reformed also moved close to the Congregational-Presbyterian model, with less and less adherence to traditional forms. Thus, worship for most American evangelical Christians by the early nineteenth century was remarkably uniform. The sermon dominated. Prayers were mostly or entirely extemporaneous. Active lay participation was limited to psalm or hymn singing. Communion services were rarely more frequent than quarterly and, although still vital and significant, were only an occasional and exceptional part of worship. Ministers, in whatever denomination, had great leeway in the planning and execution of worship.

All was not static. Changes came through subtle shifts in the content and meaning of free worship. As a whole, revival services came to constitute a supplement to Sunday worship. They had their origins in Wesleyan field preaching, in outdoor preaching in conjunction with the great Scottish communion festivals, and in new types of often invasive itinerancy during George Whitefield's revivals after 1740. Whether held in meetinghouses or in outdoor camps or retreat centers, revivals became the accepted times of harvest, the means to convert children and adults. They inspired new preaching styles, new ministerial roles, and new types of singing. Their central purpose – conviction and conversion – contrasted with the penitential, celebratory, or instructional purposes of traditional Reformed worship. Inevitably, such revival styles influenced public worship, particularly in those denominations most affected by revivals, most notably Methodists and Baptists and more selectively or with considerable resistance among almost all other Reformed denominations. What this meant is that the content of even worship services was keyed more and more, among some Baptist and Methodist congregations, to conversion or to an intense, highly emotional experience. This meant less structure, unwritten as well as warmer and more exhortatory sermons, more sentimental or more rousing hymns, and the introduction of some of the methods of revival into worship – invitational hymns, pleas addressed to sinners, even the anxious bench.

In a sense, such revival motifs made worship more participatory and, in the purest meaning of the word, more liturgical. Laypeople had a more active role – in leading prayers, in more fervent expressions of approval during sermons (amens and other expression of agreement), in a much more involving type of song, and in the introduction of personal confessions or personal persuasion of sinners into the actual worship service. Such innovations horrified traditionalists. Yet, such innovations proved very popular with laypeople and almost always won out against more formal services. Significantly, this form of worship appealed to a majority of American blacks and has remained dominant in black worship. Such worship, although not Pentecostal in the sense of spiritual gifts, certainly prepared the way for types of Pentecostalism in the twentieth century.

More spontaneous and more revivalistic worship helped trigger a dialectical response. Among American Episcopalians the seemingly disordered or enthusiastic style of church life in America demanded a traditional, ordered, and more esthetic alternative. In the middle were the traditional Reformed denominations, with their heritage of ordered but free worship. Revivals, revival techniques, and shifts in public worship occasioned by revivals all led to internal tensions and divisions among Presbyterians, Congregationalists, and some northern Baptists.

Such a survey of worship practices illustrates one point: almost every conceivable approach to worship found support in America. What it so easily conceals is the actual facts of Sunday worship for most Americans up through the nineteenth century. Americans mostly lived in rural areas. Outside of New England they were ill-served by ministers. A majority of rural congregations, in whatever denomination, could not have a weekly worship service, at least not one conducted by a minister. Many intensely religious individuals thirsted for worship experience; some found it only rarely, perhaps then in a summer camp or at a meeting of a church conference, convention, presbytery, or association. Methodists tried to cope with this through the class system and circuit preachers. Baptists enlisted untrained laymen to conduct their worship. Presbyterians borrowed ministers away from home congregations for weeks or months to visit new congregations without ministers or without any early opportunity of procuring any.

In such a context of ministerial scarcity, local congregations developed substitutes. In time, the most important would be the Sunday school, an institution that soon included adults as well as children in the more evangelical congregations. Lay superintendents and lay teachers assumed many of the roles normally held by ministers. Assemblies before or after classes – with scripture, prayer, and song – became a substitute for traditional worship, actually a new form of worship, one without sacrament or sermon. A preacher might come once a month and add a sermon, but in time this could seem more peripheral than central. Periodically, he would hold communion, possibly a very special occasion for some but not a vital part of religious practice. Once a year the congregation might host or join neighbors in a revival meeting, but this was apart from weekly worship, however vital to the recruitment of new members or the maintenance of morale on the part of old ones.

Even in these most attenuated forms of worship, functional homologies remained. The human experiences that undergird worship – guilt and a need for forgiveness, fear of forces beyond one's control and a need to assuage them, loneliness and a craving for fellowship and community – are close to universal. In evangelical America the revival season had some of the special intensity of Advent or Lent, potluck suppers or dinners on the ground had some of the fellowship of agape or even the early Eucharist, the traditional holy days and saint's days were simply replaced by such American originals as Thanksgiving, Memorial or Decoration Sunday, and church homecomings. The familiar and repetitious themes of a pastoral prayer could be as predictable and consoling as the cadences of a prayer book. The international Sunday school lesson plan eventually became the great lectionary of American Protestantism. New and almost always public rituals of conversion replaced older initiation rites. Fervent amens from elders in the "Amen corner" took the place of Kyries, whereas the responsive readings of Sunday school lessons or even the golden text replaced older litanies. Religiously based camping replaced medieval retreats. Enthusiastic handshakes, and the greeting of sisters and brothers, took the place of the ancient holy kiss. Annual trips to the meetings of presbyteries, conventions, associations, or conferences replaced ancient pilgrimages. Thus, the more things changed, the more they remained the same.

Music in Reformed Churches

Music has always been a vital part of Christian worship in America. It has also been a source of conflict and schism. Deep divisions over the propriety of hymn singing (in place of psalms) plagued most of the Reformed churches in Britain and America for over a century. The most conservative Presbyterian bodies rejected all hymns into the twentieth century. Individual congregations split over the introduction of instrumental music throughout the early nineteenth century.[5]

Song and music both extend back to early Jewish history. In I and II Samuel, the most ancient window we have on the early Jewish religion – before the temple or synagogues, before the great festivals, before the centrality of the Sabbath, before the codification of the Mosaic law, before any prophetic reforms – we have a record of young David playing his harp and composing hymns. In I Chronicles, a book written after the exile and informed by the major religious innovations made by the prophets, an unknown author offers a retrospective history of the early temple, as built and staffed by the then legendary King Solomon. According to this story, David, before his death, assigned various Levites, the priestly tribe, to their duties as servants to the already planned new House of the Lord. In this all-too-neat account, of 24,000 Levites who were to serve the temple, 4,000 were to praise the Lord on musical instruments that David had invented. This author also refers to a select group of these musicians who were to offer inspired prophecy to the accompaniment of harps, lutes, and cymbals, the types of instruments made by David. These "trained singers of the Lord" (282 skilled musicians) served directly under the king. This suggests that a type of musical prophecy involved poetic compositions set to music, one of the earliest references to what became religious hymns.

The Jews soon developed their songbooks. Later they would bind up to five of these together to constitute the present Book of Psalms, a book that eventually gained canonical status in the Jewish Bible. Such psalms became a vital part of synagogue worship. Jesus was familiar with the psalms, sang them in synagogues, and made frequent allusions to their content. According to the first gospel writer, Mark, as repeated verbatim in Matthew but not in Luke, Jesus and his disciples sang a Passover hymn before leaving the upper room after the final supper, thus giving a direct scriptural sanction for the use of song in later Eucharistic worship. This is the common, uncontested background for singing in all types of Christian worship.

What about the New Testament churches? The descriptions of worship by Paul, and by the author of the book of Acts, all include song. Paul notes psalms, hymns, and spiritual songs, but it is unclear how he defined hymns and songs. It certainly seems likely that he was not being redundant, that he described types of singing that went beyond the scriptural psalms. One natural assumption, by later Christians, is that the early Christians incorporated references to Jesus into their singing and that some of their songs had texts that were distinctively Christian in content. It is important to remember that they most likely still followed the synagogue pattern of chanting both scripture and prayers, meaning that the boundaries between prayers and song might have been unclear. Nowhere does the New Testament identify musical accompaniment to Christian singing. This does not mean that early Christians did not follow the Jewish pattern and use such instruments or that, if they did not have access to such in their simple home-based congregations, they were opposed to them in principle.

That song continued to be a vital part of Christian worship is beyond doubt. What is not clear for the church of the first three centuries is what types of music and song prevailed. In all likelihood this varied from region to region. The dominant tradition would have been the singing of scriptural psalms. The open issue is whether Christians adopted metrical poetry to music and used it in worship services or, in other terms, whether they sang hymns. After the church gained recognition, the influential Ambrose of Milan, the bishop who converted Augustine, became one of the first identifiable hymn writers. He convinced Augustine of the value of hymns and of the antiphonal singing of them. This singing was not clearly intended for Eucharistic worship but for private devotions and for the type of scheduled, daily group devotions (offices) that became part of monastic orders.

Ambrose was only the first of a series of poets who composed devotional hymns, many of which survived in the guides to daily worship (breviaries) followed mainly by priests in monastic orders but also open at times to laypeople. This repertoire of Latin hymns was familiar to, and loved by, that devout monk Martin Luther. He wanted to preserve such hymns, translate them into the vernacular, and thus make them a part of public praise in his reformed congregations. Such "office music" thus had a direct impact on Protestant hymnody.

Metrical Latin hymns did not become an authorized part of Eucharistic worship (service music) in the Roman church until after the twelfth century. Instead, priests or choirs chanted or sang psalms, canticles drawn from other parts of the scripture, and Christian anthems. These were usually not metrical (thus they reflected a variety of plainsong, such as the Gregorian chant), and the congregation did not participate except for prescribed responses. In the twelfth century, three able hymn writers added to a growing repertoire of Latin hymns – Abelard, Bernard of Clairvaux, and Bernard of Cluny. Abelard compiled a book of Latin hymns. Yet, the use of such hymns was usually restricted to priests and choirs, or else they became a part of daily offices. When Luther developed his first German hymnbooks, he adapted Latin hymns from as far back as Ambrose.

Of most direct impact on American worship would be the Reformation response to music. Two traditions had the most influence on Reformed churches in America – the tradition initiated by Calvin at Geneva, for a long time the controlling influence in Britain, and the Wesleyan or Methodist tradition. In a sense, John Wesley, influenced by the Moravians, returned to the Lutheran heritage. Luther had made congregational singing a vital part of worship, and hymn singing became a vital part of almost all Protestant worship in Germany.

The Reformed musical heritage is complex. Zwingli did not emphasize music in his Reformed worship. Calvin did. He was as eager as Luther to introduce vernacular singing. Without intending any mandate for all churches, but in a negative reaction largely to French popular songs and to the Catholic Latin hymns used for daily offices, he chose to restrict singing at Geneva to the psalms and a few other scriptural sources, such as the Ten Commandments. His direct inspiration was a metrical rendition of the psalms used at Strasbourg (arguably the first modern psalter), where he had served as a minister and had helped develop such a book. He wanted hearty singing on the part of the people and thus supported good poetic renditions of the psalms into French and solicited the ablest composers to write needed tunes. His Geneva Psalter of 1542, with later revisions, became a model for most Reformed churches and for literally hundreds of psalters published over the next two centuries, many by enterprising printers. Note that such metrical paraphrasing of the psalms is itself a departure from their direct use in the form of chants. The next steps would lead through a much more free para-phrase, to the mixture of psalm passages with new poetry, and on to Christian hymns that did not imitate any scriptural passages.

Calvin's influence proved decisive in both England and Scotland. Despite some early sympathy for Luther's reforms, both the English and the Scottish churches rejected hymns for worship and thus relied on English versions of the psalter. Unfortunately, these involved overly literal paraphrases of poor poetic quality, adapted to one metrical form (called common), all set to a very few familiar tunes. It is true that several early English psalters (the 1562 one by Thomas Sternhold and John Hopkins became the norm), and also Scottish psalters, contained a few traditional hymns (less than twenty), but these were primarily for private or family devotional use. In any case, they did not become part of public worship in either state church. It was this heritage of metrical psalms as the only music al-lowed in Sunday worship that both Anglicans and Puritans brought to America. Sternhold and Hopkins's psalter became the psalter of American Anglicans, with the so-called Bay Psalm Book of 1640 the standard in New England (revised edi-tions of this famous psalter appeared into the early nineteenth century). In it the New England Puritans tried to gain a more literal but still metrical version of the original Hebrew songs. The awkwardness of some of the wording did not prevent some improvements on Sternhold and Hopkins in literary gracefulness.

By and large, all the British churches throughout the seventeenth century, in-cluding those in the American colonies, remained loyal to their soon traditional or "old" psalters (English, Scottish, and Bay). Anglicans, Presbyterians, and Pur-itans were equally resistant to minority efforts at reform in church music by critics who have left us a very dismal image of song in British Christianity. In that century most congregations moved to a "modern" innovation – the lining out of psalms by the clerk or appointed presenter. This leader of the singing faced the con-gregation and sang (or in some cases read) each line before the congregation re-peated it. This facilitated singing in the limited sense that those who did not have books or who were illiterate could take part. Abler presenters could present the words not only rapidly but in tune, thus helping reduce what observers so often deplored – congregations singing out of tune and even out of unison. But it dis-rupted the continuity of singing and allowed presenters to skip or even recast lines. To add to the desultory nature of psalmody, the meter was monotonous, the few familiar tunes were limited in range, and the singing was typically very slow, with each syllable at least a full note and often more, as the audience tended to stretch out the words. Finally, the content often seemed inappropriate. These an-cient Hebrew songs of praise allowed Christians to praise their God but, as some lamented, not their Savior. When limited to psalms, Christians, in effect, had no distinctively Christian music at all. This was one belated, unanticipated, and actually unjustified consequence of John Calvin's rejection of the Latin hymns of the old church.

The eighteenth century was a century of musical reform, innovation, and intense controversy for the Reformed confessions of Britain and America. In broad terms, English independents or evangelicals took the lead in reform, closely followed by more evangelical (warmer, more spiritual, and more revivalistic) Congregationalists and New Side Presbyterians in America. Most resistant to reform were the English and Scottish churches.

The most influential reformer, by common acclaim, was Isaac Watts, the English independent minister and hymn writer. His impact on American church music would be greater than that even of John and Charles Wesley. But he did not originate the moves for reform; he was simply much more successful than his predecessors. As Louis F. Benson, the first major scholar of English hymnody, has demonstrated, a series of British reformers in the mid and late seventeen century tried several innovations. Some tried to gain acceptance of a freer, or more selective, or more graceful rendition of psalms. This led to one daring book that introduced the name of Jesus, and New Testament themes, into the psalms. Several printers and musical reformers added hymns – some from traditional sources, some new compositions – to editions of both the English and the Scottish psalters, but these had limited impact on public worship. Laypeople widely used these in private worship, thereby helping create a familiarity with hymn singing (particularly Christmas carols) and a dissatisfaction with a much less absorbing and meaningful type of song in church. Many congregations at least stopped trying to sing through all the psalms, then starting over again, and began adapting only those most suitable for worship. Finally, the king approved for optional use in Anglican churches a new and, from every esthetic standpoint, a vastly improved 1696 psalter, by Nahum Tate and Nicholas Brady. This new version won broad acceptance only in the London area and incited almost violent opposition in conservative rural parishes. Despite all its esthetic problems, the Sternhold and Hopkins psalter (the old version) had gained a type of canonicity among the English people. It is thus doubtful that Tate and Brady had any impact on Anglican worship in the American colonies. The first evidence we have of musical reform was that by John and Charles Wesley in Georgia in 1745.

This was the rather dismal setting for the revolution instigated by Watts. Born in an English dissenting or Puritan family in 1674, before the Act of Toleration (his father was twice jailed), young Isaac revealed an early poetic genius. He grew up detesting the horrible verse in the standard psalters of his day. His own congregation, at Southampton, sang his first hymn when he was only eighteen. He became an Independent minister, although illness kept him from the pulpit during the latter half of his life. In the new eighteenth century at least some of the

Independent congregations of Britain offered a receptive environment for innovations. Although a moderate Calvinist who was careful to avoid narrow doctrinal issues in his hymns, Watts in later life aligned himself with a near Arian faction among the Independents, congregations that in later years would move on to Unitarianism (few of his admirers among evangelicals were even aware of this "heresy," since many of his hymns contained what seemed to be orthodox trinitarian content). More than most hymn writers, Watts was able to appeal across most doctrinal and sectarian boundaries.

In 1707, at age thirty-three, Watts published the first of a series of hymnbooks and the single most important one in the history of British Christianity – *Hymns and Spiritual Songs*. Note the Pauline language. His first grouping of hymns in the book contained largely paraphrases of scripture, particularly from the New Testament. This was least offensive to traditionalists, for others had already incorporated such broader scriptures into some psalters. Next came 110 hymns on divine subjects (religious poetry not drawn directly from scripture) and a limited number of hymns, some with ancient roots, for use with the Lord's Supper. In later editions Watts added more hymns and eventually published a songbook for children. He still loved many of the psalms but lamented their English form in the old psalters. Thus, in 1719 he published his *Psalms of David*, which became enormously popular. He did not include all the psalms, and he so recast the psalms as virtually to turn them into Christian hymns. He freely introduced New Testament language and themes. His strongest appeal in behalf of both hymns and freely recast psalms was the need for a truly Christian, or evangelical, songbook. His psalm renditions were not very different from, and reflected the same poetic sensitivity and skill as, his hymns. But in the complicated battles over his innovations, some congregations used his psalms yet rejected his hymns.

In the beginning only three or four hundred Independent congregations adopted Watts's hymnal. In fact, Watts soon gained a monopoly among freer or more liberal Independent congregations in Britain, including many English Presbyterian churches and later English Unitarian congregations. Concomitant with this, several English Baptist groups began using their own versions of hymns. All the established churches held back or openly condemned Watts. At first, most New England Puritans were horrified at such human subversions of scripture. But time was on Watts's side. His psalms and hymns were eloquent, were varied in meter, and were acclaimed by recognized poets and literary critics. They were serious, lofty in spirit, keyed largely to praise and thanksgiving, and most important of all, delightful to sing. They were so immensely popular that almost all Christians used them outside the churches even when ecclesiastical authorities forbade their use within. The Wesley brothers admired Watts, used his hymns within their Methodist societies, and began developing their own special Methodist hymns. This provided a challenge to the church, although many conservative Anglicans so identified hymn singing with Methodism and enthusiasm that the widespread evangelical endorsement impeded acceptance of hymns within many Anglican parishes (some delayed the use of hymns in worship until well into the nineteenth century). Thus, for decades, Watts seemed a heretic to Presbyterians, an enthusiast to Anglicans.

Except among Wesleyans and a few other evangelicals, the English church never really accepted Watts. But his success eventually forced the church to create and sing its own hymns. In the nineteenth century this often meant efforts to revive the hymns of the early church, including its Eastern branch. In the eighteenth century the episcopacy never approved any hymnbook but at the same time was unwilling to discipline congregations that adopted hymns. The first hymnbook designed for Anglican worship was one compiled by the poet William Cowper and a minister, John Newton, in 1771, but it had no official endorsement. It and several successors had an evangelical tone, as did a hymnal compiled by an ex-Moravian minister. The first Anglican hymnal to win diocesan approval appeared in 1820; the first official hymnbook of the Anglican church, inspired in part by the Oxford movement, was *Hymns Ancient and Modern,* published in 1861. Long before this, hymn singing was customary in Anglican worship, and several locally approved hymnbooks had competed for acceptance. In America, the evangelical impact on Anglicans made hymn singing more acceptable at an earlier date. After their first post-Revolution convention in 1785, orphaned American Anglicans completed their first revision of the *BCP* and appended to it, for optional use in worship, fifty-one hymns, twelve by Watts. The English bishops disallowed this revision, but the adopted prayer book of the American Episcopal church, in 1790, contained twenty-seven hymns. Individual parishes were not always in agreement, but from its beginnings, the Protestant Episcopal church was open to a wide variety of musical forms and also to the use of organs and other forms of accompaniment.

For Anglicans, the problem of music tended to be one of style or taste as well as principle. In Scotland, it was always a matter of principle. Thus, the issue of hymn singing, or musical accompaniment, aggravated Presbyterians for a century. The old Covenanters (Reformed Presbyterians), who adhered rigidly to the Solemn League and Covenant, never accepted hymns or even a free paraphrase of psalms, let alone musical accompaniment. The eighteenth-century Seceders (Associate Synod) resisted hymns well into the nineteenth century. In America the combined Seceders and Covenanters (the Associate Reformed Synod) used only lined psalms in worship, and the Reformed Presbytery, a product of schism, never accepted hymns. But the established Presbyterian Church of Scotland was not so unrelenting. Many of its ministers and congregations moved far toward rationalist or latitudinarian positions in the century of enlightenment. Thus, liberal and very evangelical congregations used Watts's hymnbook almost from its first publication. But just as many congregations resisted as accommodated, and in all areas of Scotland local congregations split over music. Throughout the century the general assembly tried to evade ruling about music. It did not exclude, but never authorized, a 1745 worship guide that included scriptural hymns, some by Watts (hymns that closely paraphrased scripture texts). A powerful minority opposed such dangerous innovations. Several private hymnbooks competed for congregational acceptance, and in 1781 the general assembly finally endorsed such paraphrases as part of its directory of worship and submitted them, plus a few hymns, to local presbyteries, many of which rejected them. Individual congregations tore the hymns out of their books. Gradually, in the new century, almost all kirks finally began to sing hymns even as they stopped lining hymns, began to add the notes to the songs, and introduced choirs and organs.

In America, Watts posed essentially the same challenge to both Presbyterians and New England Congregationalists. The response was close to that in Scotland, with progressives, usually in the revivalistic or evangelical wing, rather quickly adopting Watts's hymnbook and with traditionalists, primarily Old Side Presbyterians or old Calvinists in New England, resisting. In New England Benjamin Franklin printed and sold a Watts's hymnal in 1729, but few bought it. Another publisher printed a later edition in 1739, and by then the book was winning acceptance, although primarily for singing outside worship, such as at socials or prayer meetings or even burials. During the revivals that followed Whitefield's visit in 1740 (he loved Watts's hymns), congregations began splitting over hymn singing. Many had an intense loyalty to their Bay Psalm Book. These local struggles continued until after the Revolution, when few holdouts remained in New England. By 1800 the influential Timothy Dwight, at Yale, was at work on a major book of recast psalms (he added the ones left out by Watts) and hymns, both by now generally accepted in Connecticut congregations. This general capitulation accompanied the entrepreneurial publication of several hymnbooks, with a rich hymnody developing among the liberals and later Unitarians. Also, in the new century the New England churches began numerous singing schools, introduced a much more varied repertoire of tunes, ended lined singing, and very gradually introduced choirs.[6]

American Presbyterians lagged just a bit in adopting Watts's hymnal, possibly because their congregations learned about his work later. Even at the end of the New Side–Old Side split in 1763, the church had no official psalm book, with congregations using either the Scottish or the Bay psalter. By then the combined synod received frequent queries about what to do about Watts. This resulted from the fact that many congregations were already singing his hymns in worship. The most influential advocate for Watts was Samuel Davies, the father of southern Presbyterianism. He helped form several congregations in the area around Richmond, led a revival in the 1750s, took the lead in proselytizing among blacks, loved hymn singing, and even wrote one enduring hymn. He used hymns at the ordination of John Todd in 1752. Todd became a pastor of a church at which half the members were blacks. Davies rejoiced at the musical abilities of slaves, tried to teach those in his congregations how to read, and requested copies of Watts's hymnbook from Britain to circulate among his appreciative "Negroes." The battle over hymns, and later to a less degree over organs, occurred at the local, or at the least the presbyterial, level (it completely split the Abingdon Presbytery in southwestern Virginia). Until after the Revolution a minority of Presbyterians resisted hymns, and several congregations split off from the main body to find refuge in the Associate Synod. The most polemical defender of psalms only, Adam Rankin, fomented a major schism in the Transylvania Presbytery in central Kentucky in the last decade of the eighteenth century. But the progressives were dominant before this. At Princeton, hymn singing was normal after Davies became president. Before him, Jonathan Edwards had welcomed a mixture of hymns and psalms in worship, as did almost all the New Divinity ministers who followed him. In 1788 the newly reorganized Presbyterian Church in the United States of America included hymns in a new *Directory of Worship*.

While Reformed Christians fought over hymn singing, the early Methodists in America made it central in their worship. Thus, the final musical tradition in Protestant America derived from the work of John and Charles Wesley. In fact, while in Savannah, Georgia, the two Wesleys compiled the first hymnbook ever used within an Anglican church and published it at Charles Town (Charleston) in 1737. The Moravian influence and example was critical at this point. Back in England, in 1738, Wesley issued a second songbook, one that contained English versions of several Moravian hymns, since at that time he was identified with a Moravian congregation. Eventually Wesley would publish fifty-six varied hymnbooks and four tune books, with an increasing proportion of the hymns composed by Charles (John wrote only a few hymns), who wrote over six thousand hymns (some estimates go as high as nine thousand) in his lifetime. Charles, John, and another brother all wrote hymns, as had their father. Charles was a gifted poet, although the subject, and context, of many hymns ensured their ephemerality. He wrote in over thirty different meters, and he and John adapted his poems to over one hundred tunes, thus adding a variety not present even in Watts. Leading composers, such as George Handel, contributed tunes.

The Wesleys appreciated Watts and always used some of his hymns. But they wanted a different type of hymns, in sentiment and style, than those used by English Independents. From the Moravians they absorbed a very sentimental approach to Jesus and to hymns about Jesus. Charles wrote hymns for all occasions, including those connected with the life of Jesus. John, in his theology, placed the greatest possible emphasis on the atonement, and thus Methodist hymns included sacrificial motifs that are reminiscent of Catholic Eucharistic hymns. Charles wrote hymns that directly responded to events, that incorporated distinctively Methodist doctrines (free grace and Christian perfection and the continuing role of the Holy Spirit), that fit special Methodist celebrations (watch nights and love feasts), and that had a heavy confessional content drawn from his own religious experience. These motifs, and the much greater variety of tunes, some drawn from popular ballads, led to distinctive hymns and a rousing style of singing. Charles Wesley's hymns were not as ecumenical, not as elegant, not as magisterial as those of Watts. John Wesley, in directions for congregational singing, prefaced his more detailed admonitions with the following famous rules: "Sing all, sing lustily, sing modestly, sing in tune, and, above all, sing spiritually."

By 1800, despite a few reactionary holdouts, hymn singing had largely replaced the use of psalms in American worship. In most Protestant services hymns became the only major part of worship that involved overt congregational participation (of course, silently and intellectually, worshipers were supposed to participate in sermons and ministerial prayers). The normal pattern of free worship involved from three to five or more congregational hymns each Sunday. Sunday schools incorporated singing, either in an opening assembly or as openings for instruction. Even American public schools usually began with assemblies, most of which featured Protestant hymns.

Early in the nineteenth century American Protestants rarely sang with organs or pianos. For most, this was primarily a matter of cost or lack of any tradition. For others it was a matter of principle. Roman Catholics, Lutherans, and most Episcopalians never had qualms about organs and procured them as soon as they could afford them. Methodists were divided, leery but not on principle opposed to music in churches. At least three large Methodist societies in England had organs before Wesley died, but his inclination was against such artificial devices. Some Methodist societies had used other, less expensive musical instruments in revivals, an anticipation of later Salvation Army bands. In the wake of Wesley's death, the annual conferences in 1796 and 1808 refused permission for additional organs. When Methodist societies begin to introduce organs, it led to a schism in Leeds and to a small Protestant Methodist church. In America the issue lost most of it divisiveness by the time individual Methodist congregations, in the mid-nineteenth century, could afford organs.

Congregationalists, Presbyterians, and Calvinist Baptists usually had doubts about organs or overtly opposed them. Their opposition had been uniform in the seventeenth century, was pervasive in the eighteenth, and gradually relaxed in the nineteenth. This issue divided local congregations but rarely whole denominations. The story of change is one tied to regions and to local congregations. By 1900, the only holdouts for a cappella singing were the small Covenanter sects and a major faction within the restoration movement, the present Churches of Christ.

In the nineteenth century, each major denomination eventually authorized or even published hymnals. Unfortunately, many congregations could not afford such books for all worshipers, resulting in a rather narrow repertoire of memorized hymns and tunes for worship. Until the mid-nineteenth century, most hymnbooks did not contain interlaced tunes or notes, making sight singing all but impossible. Such restrictions meant less local variety than the often lengthy hymnbooks would suggest.

The nineteenth century was a great age of hymn writing, with the impetus often tied to the imperatives of book publishing. From the beginnings by Davies and Dwight, dozens of American poets or versifiers, including such members of the New England renaissance as John Greenleaf Whittier, James Russell Lowell, and Ralph Waldo Emerson, contributed poems that became hymns. But of all nineteenth-century American hymn writers, the most prolific was Fanny Crosby (Frances Crosby Van Alstyne). Blinded soon after birth in 1823, she early began composing verse but began writing hymns only when forty-one. Before her death in 1915 she had composed over six thousand hymns, approximately the same number as Charles Wesley. In one active period she committed herself to provide a publisher three hymns a week. She well reflected the sentimental and evangelical motifs of so many nineteenth-century hymns and was for a time closely identified with the work of Dwight L. Moody. Her hymns were uneven in quality, but over a dozen still appear in most Protestant hymnals, including "Safe in the Arms of Jesus."

In several respects, nineteenth-century Americans made important innovations in church music. The new forms of revival meeting, or camp meeting, not only featured hymn singing but led to new types of hymns (those intended to convict or lure sinners to the anxious bench) and to new, inexpensive pocket hymnals. Already, Methodists had adapted folk tunes to their newly composed hymns. In the revivals, people craved ever more simple, or repetitious, phrasing and often used familiar folk tunes, some formerly used for purely secular or even bawdy singing. The new gospel hymns often utilized a simple refrain or chorus, which everyone could quickly learn. Even if only part of the congregation sang the main verses, with their more developed narrative, the whole congregation could join in the chorus. Early in the nineteenth century, enterprising collectors and publishers, or singing teachers, began transcribing the popular songs and tunes, leading to longer and longer gospel-like collections, with most of the content limited to folk tunes and often simplified texts.

In the South, the most enduringly popular collection of such church music was Benjamin Franklin White's *The Sacred Harp*, which went through many editions and inspired many imitators. In some rural churches, and among an even larger number of folklorists, sacred harp singing remains popular, with the old tunes and melodies set to the type of shaped notes used by singing masters in the early nineteenth century. It was this type of singing that black converts first learned in Baptist and Methodist congregations of the Deep South. To the older tunes, many of English and Scotch origin, they added their own improvisations. Above all, they further simplified and adapted the wording, until in some cases they repeated only a few phrases. Drawing on patterns that they probably brought from Africa, and from work songs, they introduced a call-and-response type of singing, or what at times seemed close to a chant. When later formalized and written down, these songs of field and church became the famous "Negro spirituals."

SUCH A SWEEPING and brief survey of corporate worship is only half the story of worship in the Reformed tradition in America. It is the easy half to describe. Correlative to it was family and private worship or devotion. In form, this varied enormously. But in several respects, Christians most often converge at the level of private devotion and meditation. In fact, the human needs that underlie private devotions transcend Christianity. Not only the Semitic religions but even the enlightenment-oriented or nontheistic Eastern religions find much that is common at the level of meditation or prayer.

What happens in the private religious experience of individuals is very resistant to historical scrutiny. The richest sources we have in American history, or at least those most often used so far by scholars, involve the diary-writing, intensely introspective Puritans of New England. And these sources reveal types of private experience not clearly different from those suffered, and enjoyed, by devout Roman Catholics. Thus, devotional guides tend to have greater universality that other formal aids used by Christians. At the very least, they do not vary that much from one Protestant denomination to another, as documented by a perusal of the vast array of devotional works available in modern bookstores.

All Christian confessions have tried to integrate corporate worship and private devotions. Some of the characteristics of one help shape the other. The confessional, penitential, and moralistic themes of Calvinist worship complemented an intensely introspective devotional life. The Wesleyan emphasis on the Holy Spirit and the very familiar and loving relationship with Jesus complemented the type of spirituality, of a sense of closeness and mutuality, that was normative among more sentimental Methodists. But to assert this is to confess that I have told one-half of the story – that of corporate worship – without attempting the almost impossible task of filling in the other half, the part that for many Christians may have been more important than what they did on a Sunday morning.

CHAPTER 7

Reformed Theology at Maturity:

Taylor, Hodge, and Bushnell

*T*he first golden age of American Reformed theology climaxed just before the Civil War. This period represented a transition between the earlier concerns of the New Divinity theologians and the diverse response to new scholarship and new natural science after the Civil War. In these middle years, perceptive American theologians did indeed react to both scholarship and science, but as yet the challenge in each case seemed either remote or manageable. Thus, the focus remained on the intramural conflicts among latter-day Calvinists and Arminians.[1]

The task remained one of offering a proper understanding, and a persuasive defense, of the Pauline scheme of salvation, still the central concern of evangelical Protestants. Whatever the developing intellectual challenges to the Bible, to text or to canon, the most influential American theologians still worked within the re7ceived biblical tradition. The challenges required a response but as yet suggested no despair or no retreat to some other basis of authority. At the same time, new advances in astronomy and in geology, as well as early evolutionary theories in biology, remained dark and threatening clouds on the horizon. As of yet they did not seem to offer a fatal threat to Semitic cosmology, at least not to most American theologians. Thus the old cosmology and the unique Christian foreground both remained intact, although not as securely as in the past.

The doctrinal debates of the period implicated theological issues. But the context of denominational competition rarely allows a full development of theological views. My earlier treatment of High Church positions within Episcopalianism and my summary view of Mercersburg theology in the German Reformed church exemplify some of the difficulties. Thus, one way of bringing some of the substance of theology into this story is to develop, in some detail, the views of the most influential American theologians who spoke for the Reformed tradition. I happen to believe that of all American theologians who matured their theological outlook before Darwin published his *Origin of Species*, three rank slightly ahead of all the others because of a combination of influence and ability – Nathaniel Taylor, Charles Hodge, and Horace Bushnell.

Only one – Hodge – adhered rigidly to a scholastic form of Calvinism. Taylor and Bushnell still wanted to uphold the Calvinist tradition but, in order to do so, felt they had to reinterpret and thus transform it. Their unconventional and original insights are what made them so significant. In my estimation, Hodge was the ablest scholar of the three, developed the most coherent system, and best illustrated the merit of a reactionary position; Taylor epitomized those theologians who have always tried to so amend a received tradition as to make it believable for new generations; whereas Bushnell, with the innocence and brilliance of an amateur, placed theology in such a new perspective that most of the old questions became meaningless. Of the three, I think Bushnell was the most innovative and would have the greatest impact on theology in America.

Nathaniel Taylor

Nathaniel Taylor had enormous influence in his own time. He taught Bushnell and was older than Hodge. Born in 1786, he spent his life in Connecticut, mostly at Yale College. As a Yale undergraduate, he became a friend and disciple, almost an adopted son, of President Timothy Dwight and then served Dwight as a recording secretary for nearly four years after his graduation. It was Dwight who preached Taylor's ordination sermon when he became minister of the First Church in New Haven in 1812. He served in this post for ten years, meanwhile becoming very close friends with Lyman Beecher, the leader of the more revivalistic faction among the Congregational ministers in Connecticut. In these years as a minister, Taylor first developed some of the main themes of his later theology. Although in the Edwardian tradition, he tried, without significant philosophical success, to refute the arguments that Jonathan Edwards had offered in *Freedom of the Will*. He joined Beecher in advocating a warmer, more revival-friendly version of orthodoxy than that which prevailed in the Andover Seminary.[2]

After the death of Dwight in 1817, local New Haven evangelicals began raising funds for a Yale divinity school. They could draw on three professors already teaching in the college but agreed to establish a new professorship in didactic theology. It was only natural that Yale select for this Dwight Professorship the old president's most loyal disciple, and thus Taylor proudly assumed the position as the school opened in 1822. Taylor would retain this chair until a year before his death in 1858. His early task was not an easy one. He wanted to preserve a type of Calvinist orthodoxy, to refute the views of the Unitarians, and to provide a theological outlook congenial to the revivalism espoused by his closest friend, Beecher. He recognized that this theology would have to moderate the seemingly deterministic and antihumanistic bent of the older Calvinism, of the moral determinism of the latter-day disciples of Edwards. What was needed was a new understanding of Calvinism, one that would defang the older views of human depravity, and thus a recasting that could take the sting out of Arminian and Unitarian attacks on an impossibly harsh form of orthodoxy. In other words, he sought a middle way between an older Calvinism and more humanistic and rational forms of Christianity.

Taylor's recast Calvinism, or what became known as the New Haven theology, became the center of numerous controversies. It would be a critical issue in the New School–Old School split among Presbyterians, and it even shaped divisions within the Dutch Reformed church. It also had major impact because of the number of students Taylor taught at Yale. More than anyone else, he headed a new theological movement in New England, the most important since the heyday of the New Divinity in the late eighteenth century.

The central motif of all Taylor's theology was God's role as the perfect moral governor of his creation. This was not at all a new theme. He borrowed most of this emphasis from Samuel Hopkins and other New Divinity predecessors, but most of all from Nathaniel Emmons, who anticipated a large share of his doctrines. Taylor was distinctive only in the degree of emphasis he gave to moral government. No one ever took governmental theory quite so far.

Taylor began with the all-important question: Why did God create the type of universe that he did, and in particular why did he create humans as they are? His confident answer was that God gained the greatest possible glory and happiness not in creating creatures directly under his control but in choosing to create moral agents to inhabit this world and possibly other, unknown worlds. Only creatures with freedom, with the ability to choose and pursue ends, could render to a god the type of love that was necessary for his fullest glory and happiness. Thus the foundational assumption of Taylor's system was that God had a compelling reason to create the world we live in and that he made it perfect, in the sense that just such a world most glorifies its creator. No other world would do.

Having created such a world, God then had to govern it. Again, Taylor assumed that God is a perfect governor in all respects. This involved him in continuous circular arguments. He appealed to a form of natural theology – one that moved from the purported evidence of perfect moral government to a belief in God (this parallels an argument based on the perfect design of organisms in nature). But he often used his undoubted belief in a perfect God to prove, deductively, that God's government was perfect. For humans, who are moral agents, the government is a moral system, one of divine laws with appropriate, even though usually postponed, rewards and punishments. The all-controlling law is one of benevolence. Here Taylor was never very explicit and too easily imitated Edwards and his immediate disciples. Briefly, the highest demand of God is that moral agents exhibit benevolence, or full consent to being, in all their choices. When humans reveal such benevolence, such selfless and God-oriented love, they reap the full benefit in the form of the maximum possible welfare or fulfillment or happiness. When they violate this law, when they are self-serving in their choices, then they reap the maximum of suffering or misery. In this, and in so much of his language, Taylor borrowed from British natural theologians such as William Paley. In a sense, his was an almost utilitarian scheme, one which he largely created through speculation but which he attributed to God and occasionally supported with scripture.

Implicit in this way of understanding God's providence was a very popular theodicy, one shared by most of the New Divinity theologians and by many of Taylor's contemporaries. It is conceivable that an all-powerful God (Taylor assigned all the traditional attributes to God) would choose not to create any worlds at all, although Taylor could scarcely admit even this. But it certainly did not seem consistent with God's nature that he would create a world and not govern it in the best possible way. Once having committed himself to having worlds inhabited by moral agents, God then had to accept the implications of such worlds. Literally, if God was to be a perfect governor of moral agents, then he could not do certain things. This is to say only that God cannot involve himself in contradictions. He cannot will a world of moral agents and, at the same time, will a block universe with no room for individual choice. Choice is essential to moral agency.

For Taylor, the existing world is, in a sense, perfect. The total system is conducive to the ends of creation – the greatest possible amount of benevolence and happiness. Such a system requires both natural and moral evil. Such evil is incidental to the system, not an end of the system. God had to permit it if he was to have a moral system. But he permitted just as much evil as was necessary to the system and to its end, not one bit more or less. Of course, Taylor confirmed this not on the basis of any empirical evidence but only because he accepted, on other grounds, the perfection of God. As his arguments about natural evil attested, he tried to use empirical evidence as at least a suggestive support for his grand system.

Natural evil (such as the pain and suffering endured by animals and humans) serves as a legal sanction. It helps establish and sustain the authority of a governor and helps teach certain virtues to moral agents. Taylor speculated that our world contains the highest degree of natural good possible if the system is to provide perfect happiness for obedient agents and perfect misery for disobedient ones. As a possible escape clause in his argument, Taylor was willing to concede that the amount of natural and moral evil on earth might be inconsistent with the greatest possible happiness of humans but consistent with a total system that contains other worlds and other agents. That is, some evil on earth might exceed that needed for instructive purposes here but yet serve such purposes for other worlds.

Given such qualifications, it would seem that no possible argument, based on human experience, could challenge or even touch Taylor's contention. The other trick in his argument involved postponed outcomes – the result of moral government. The future glory of God, or the happiness of humans, could vindicate almost any conceivable but always contributory, and thus necessary, evil in the present. In fact, Taylor's major "proof" of human immortality was its necessity to uphold God's perfect moral government. Without the promise of immortality, and future blessings, one could not argue that this is the best possible world.

For Taylor, the empirical evidence all supported the correctness of his belief in God as a perfect moral governor. Taylor appealed to such evidence and to good logic much more than to scriptures. He easily reflected the natural theology of the pre-Darwinian early nineteenth century. Taylor believed God's work in nature was proof of his overall benevolence. That is, of course, the age-old design argument. It was relatively easy, a la Paley or even a later Darwin, to demonstrate that what seems evil, such as the undeserved suffering of animals, is not evil within the total system. This suffering subsumes such goals as population control or the best possible adaptation to an environment. It contributes to the greatest good. Even the suffering of innocent human children seems to instruct them, or their parents, in needed duties. And for adults, natural afflictions have a variety of instructional or reformatory purposes, including the understanding of God's sovereignty. The seeming injustice of such natural afflictions (they inflict the righteous as well as the sinful) is an illusion based on shortsightedness. In the total system they are necessary and beneficial, and for those who seem to suffer unjustly, the final outcome will make it all right.

Taylor believed moral evil to be equally incidental, and thus necessary, to the system of moral government. It is impossible for even God to create moral agents without, at the same time, making possible disobedience or sin and the misery that results from sin. Like any benevolent governor, God desires that all his subjects do good. He wants only the best for them. But such is not possible in a moral system. God, by choosing a moral system, chose the evil incident to it. He wanted a system that allows sin. He did not want anyone to sin. But he foresaw that moral agents would in fact disobey, even when such disobedience warred against their own highest interest. In this sense God both foresaw and intended sin. Perfect right prevails only in the end, not in the interim. But Taylor believed that God permitted the exact amount of sin consistent with his moral government. And, contrary to most Calvinists, he argued that people do at heart understand what is conducive to happiness. Their deepest nature inclines them toward obedience. Their dominant tendency is to do good. Sin is aberrant and against a person's nature and interest. In fact, it is difficult, in reading Taylor, to grasp why people ever sin. It is almost as if people sin because God's system requires them to do so as a testimony to human freedom and responsibility. Everyone should, in this sense, be thankful for sinners.

A perfect governor is just. He gives people what they deserve. Thus, God, even to uphold standards, must punish disobedience and punish it appropriately. The sanction is complete misery. This line of argument led to some dark implications. No humans are perfectly obedient. All humans sin. This means that justice would require that they all suffer complete misery. No person deserves perfect happiness. If God relented and allowed undeserving humans to gain happiness, then he would seem to deny justice and destroy any respect for his law. Taylor thus added a particular Christian twist to his speculative model of perfect moral government, what he called the "economy of grace." God is merciful to some undeserving humans. Ordinarily, such mercy would undermine both justice and good government, for it would allow people to get by with their disobedience. The lesson would be clear – sin with impunity. God had to provide punishment equivalent to evil or risk losing his governmental authority. For God to show mercy to disobedient humans, he had to find another way of upholding justice. Thus, grace required a substitutionary atonement. Only a sacrifice of a divine being, with suffering sufficient to absorb the guilt of all humans, could allow undeserved mercy toward them and, at the same time, reveal God's awful abhorrence for sin and his just desire to punish it in full. In fact, grace and the atonement so modified Taylor's model of moral government as to strip it of any logical coherence and reduce it to a form of special pleading.

In the nineteenth-century context, Taylor developed his theology of moral government for conservative ends. In New England he tried to use it to repudiate the Unitarians and to preserve what he saw as the heart themes of the Reformation. For intelligent folk, for sensible thinkers, the old Calvinist system had become unbelievable. Taylor tried to so recast, or update, it as to make it believable. For example, his governmental system, paired with his economy of grace (he liked to borrow terms from political economists), required an atoning savior. And such was the burden of human guilt, and the need to uphold God's governmental sanctions, that only a divine being could become the sacrificial offering. A purely human Messiah could not, and thus Taylor's governmental system required adherence to the traditional trinity formulas, as least as they relate to Jesus. He used this argument against Unitarians. Here, as on other issues, Taylor utilized a type of systems analysis to arrive at correct doctrines or, as he admitted, to gain a correct understanding of the often confusing language of scripture. For instructional reasons, much of the Bible is necessarily allegorical. One cannot take it literally. Therefore, instead of careful textual exegesis, Taylor preferred to interpret the

Bible in light of the logical necessities involved in perfect government. Again, he went in circles but gradually developed a complex, at times ingenuously argued, model of how God relates to human subjects.

This governmental version of Calvinism meant a new understanding of all the old, defining doctrines – complete depravity, election, irresistible grace, limited atonement, and perseverance. When Taylor completed his refurbishing of such doctrines, critics wondered whether he had not thrown out the baby with the bathwater. Others believed that Taylor capitulated completely to Arminianism without admitting it, using verbal sophistries to keep up the fiction of adherence to the older confessions.

Taylor initially gained notoriety for his unique approach to human depravity. He first enunciated this in an invited sermon before the gathered Connecticut clergy in 1828, the annual *Concio ad Clerum* (Advice to the Clergy). He adhered to his position for the rest of his life. On no other issue was Taylor more equivocal or elusive, more anxious to have the best of all worlds.

Taylor admitted that all humans, given their weakness and the circumstances of their lives, are certain to sin. It is inevitable. They have weaknesses that lead them to choose other than God. Although not equally wicked, none are wholly good. Thus, without grace, all deserve perfect misery. But Taylor conceded no more than this to the traditional doctrine of complete depravity. He denied that humans are, by nature, sinful. They do not sin necessarily but only inevitably. This position could be consistent with almost all forms of orthodoxy. Theologians from all camps had always acknowledged the goodness of the creation, and thus the goodness of humans, in substance if not in deed. It was only their will or their affections or their developed moral character that merited such a strong term as *depravity*. What distinguished Taylor from this orthodox view was his belief that the intrinsic tendency of humans, their usually strongest affection, was one of benevolence leading in time to happiness. Under appropriate circumstances, the constituted propensities of humans, their innermost appetites, which normally lead to good choices, did lead them to morally bad choices or to sin. But such bad choices never reflected their innermost nature.

Unlike traditional Calvinists, but like Methodists, Taylor usually used the word *sin* in a moral sense. It meant disobedience of God's law. He focused on the act, not on the disposition behind it. For Taylor, sin began with the first knowing act of disobedience. He was sure that all humans, if certain opportunities offered, would in fact disobey. But for him the correct meaning of original sin was not a corruptness of nature but the first sin that a person actually committed ("original" meant "first"). Until then, individuals were in no sense guilty. Infants, until they could discern right or wrong, were not yet moral agents capable of sin. This was a position shared by Pelagians and Anabaptists.

What Taylor most emphatically rejected were all versions of sin as the imputed guilt of Adam or as inherent corruption. By subtle distinctions, one can define dozens of versions of imputation. In the Westminster Confession, English and Scottish Calvinists adopted one very extreme version – that God imputes the sin and guilt of Adam to all humans in the same sense as he imputes the righteousness of the Christ to all humans elected to salvation. In this symmetrical version, humans are sinful in God's eyes totally apart from what they choose or prior to any choice. This is literally a corruption by nature. Now, in fact, most Calvinists also believed humans are sinful not only by birth but also because they have the same character or prideful dispositions as Adam. Jonathan Edwards and the New Divinity theologians, as well as John Calvin, usually focused on the character shared by both Adam and his descendants, on their common identity. Humans are sinful, and guilty, because of their pride or their rebellious nature, because they are at one in nature with Adam, not just because of what Adam did. Taylor rejected even this milder understanding. He found nothing in the disposition of humans that necessitated sin but only those traits that made it an option. Before actual disobedience, nothing in humans is corrupt or sinful. Only in sinning do humans become sinners. As to why they sin, Taylor could point to the powerful allurements of the world (circumstances) and to the power of certain appetites in humans, appetites that are in themselves good and which humans are free to direct toward good ends (hunger does not necessitate gluttony). It is certain that all humans, with such appetites, with their limited understanding, in the presence of certain circumstances, will choose the world above God. It is, in a conventional sense of the word, quite natural that they do so, but they do not do so by necessity of any corrupt nature. Despite all his qualifications and distinctions, orthodox Calvinists believed that Taylor, in these views, was simply a clever Arminian.

Taylor confessed complete adherence to the doctrine of election or predestination. Despite some subtle differences, he probably remained closer to traditional Calvinists on this than on any other traditional doctrine. He conceded that God had eternally proposed to renew and save only a certain part of humankind. Grace is essential for salvation. God saves those whom he chooses, not because of any foreseen merit or faith on their part (of course he does foresee their faith) but simply because he chooses them for salvation. Taylor thus rejected the most familiar Arminian way of understanding divine election.

Having professed his commitment to orthodoxy, Taylor then offered his own unique and eccentric understanding. The Christ died for all, elect and nonelect. God saves all who repent and believe, and all people are in some sense free to do this. What prevents such a happy choice is their own perverseness. This is good Calvinism. But Taylor deviated from the received view in affirming that people are by nature able to choose God even without grace, although they in fact never do so. Their problem is not any essential inability. Also, God truly wants all to repent and believe. He takes no pleasure in the death or the punishment of the wicked.

One may then ask, why does God bestow saving grace on some and not on all humans? Taylor's answer was simple, expected – to do so would be to subvert his system of moral government. To save everyone, he would have to coerce repentance, not sway it by moral means, as he does within his gracious system. Consistent with his moral government, God saves all humans that he can and yearns to save more. In a sense God is frustrated, even sad, because of the requirements of moral government, but the larger goals of the system still justify God's choice of it. God has elected as many humans as possible. If he were to bestow his grace on even one additional human, the system might crumble, for either here or in other worlds this change might undermine the sanctions of the law and the certainty of punishment. Then, many more might rebel and be lost in the end. In the cosmic juggling act, God does all he can. Why could anyone ask more? In a sense, the damnation of some people is necessary for God's government to work. In echoes of Samuel Hopkins, some people have to be damned, not directly for God's glory (he does not enjoy the damnation of anyone) but to uphold moral government and the greatest happiness for the greatest number.

The one unanswered, and unanswerable, question is why, since no one deserves grace, God selects the people he does for salvation. Why does he choose to deny grace to those whom he damns (a problem that earlier had haunted Samuel Hopkins)? Those who suffer complete misery may, retrospectively at least (they do not now contemplate their fate), ask: why me? This issue – an old one for Calvinists – bothered Taylor and led him, eventually, to his most clearly heterodox position. Taylor never argued that any human deserved salvation. In this sense, God selects some of the undeserving and damns others. But as a good governor, he is rational rather than arbitrary. Taylor speculated that God chooses those persons who have treated his gospel with the greatest respect. He finds less offense in them, or he believes he can do more with them. Some people are simply more useful in his kingdom or in his designs. He needs them (Samuel Hopkins had anticipated this view). God passes over those who are least useful or those who have the most scorn and contempt for his law of benevolence. None deserve grace. But a good governor still can use his own selective and governmental criteria in choosing his elect. In this line of speculation, Taylor's governmental method, and mode of thinking, made Jehovah reasonable in a human sense and, short of making grace something earned or deserved, nonetheless indicated the type of sinners most likely to gain grace. In effect, some sinners are better than others and, even without fully deserving salvation, are in some sense more deserving of God's favor than are other sinners. Implied in such speculations was a doctrine of works – of striving and of effort. It was only a short additional step to a fully moralized Christianity.

In most respects Taylor remained orthodox in his conception of grace. The Holy Spirit alone enabled errant humans to respond to God in love. The work of the Spirit was irresistible in a moral sense – he (it) always succeeds in effecting conversion, but never by coercion. The Spirit has a supernatural (not miraculous) impact on ordinary human faculties. It enables people to do what they could do all along but what, in the circumstances of the world, they never actually did – obey God. Characteristically, Taylor described conversion in governmental and moral terms – it is a change from disobedience to obedience, from reckless behavior to doing one's duty, from irrational to rational action. One now chooses consistent with one's highest nature and one's best interest. The Spirit works through normal faculties. God simply wins the assent or trust of humans by this means. Beyond this impact on human affections, Taylor gave no other role to the Spirit and in particular rejected any tangible, indwelling, or miraculous Spirit. Since the role of the Holy Spirit is persuasive and not coercive, Taylor rejected the word *irresistible* and preferred to talk of the "unresisting" human response to God's initiative. In a sense, humans have the power to resist the spirit but not the will to do so. Again, as in so much of his theology, he granted the inevitability of human capitulation to the Spirit but not any inherent necessity for such.

Two Calvinist doctrines – partial atonement and the perseverance of saints – remained intact in Taylor. Since God cannot, consistent with his moral government, save all people, a partial or particular atonement is a necessary doctrine. Only such could be consistent with moral government. Having conceded this, Taylor tried, as always, to diffuse it of its more troublesome connotations. At the very least, God leaves to their deserved fate only as many as necessary for his moral government to attain its proper ends. No one, except God, knows how many this will be. But Taylor was optimistic. Like Samuel Hopkins, he believed the number to be a small percentage of the whole human race, a position that moved him toward the very appealing doctrine of the Universalists. In any case, even God could not do more. And for those who responded to his grace inevitably but not necessarily, salvation was permanently ensured, but not any early sanctification. The elect persevere, but they move toward a habitual benevolence at varying paces. Conversion is more of a beginning than an ending. Christians continue to sin, but they are assured that they will not die in sin. God keeps his own. Again, Taylor insisted that perseverance is not by necessity (Christians have the power to fall away) but is nonetheless certain, and in this rare case Taylor used scripture, and the idea of a covenant, to support this solacing doctrine.

It is somewhat ironic that Taylor's theology, which he viewed as a new orthodox counter to Unitarianism and transcendentalism, became a "liberal" alternative among Congregationalists and Presbyterians. Taylor had skirted the boundaries of Arminianism. Others crossed that boundary. For example, Charles Finney, the famed revivalist, adopted Taylor's method – logical system building – but in working out his theology, he overtly rejected Calvinist doctrines and added a Methodist-like doctrine of perfection.

Taylor's attempt to refortify the ramparts of Calvinism failed. He persuaded few Unitarians. And he dismayed traditional Calvinists, such as Hodge, from whom he received a devastating barrage of criticism and even ridicule. A conservative Congregationalist, Bennet Tyler, for a time president of Dartmouth, also fought a running battle with Taylor. Taylor's fate proved prophetic. He was an appealing man – open, generous, humane, full of goodwill, and in his sense very pious, a person who well exemplified the Edwardian benevolence he made normative for Christians. Like later and more open liberals, he wanted, almost desperately, to hold on to the only religion he knew, one that was emotionally bound up with his deepest hopes. He wanted to so share it as to make it broadly appealing. He wanted the Congregational and Presbyterian churches to thrive, but he watched in despair as they lost ground, numerically, decade after decade, to Arminian Methodists and Disciples, to crudely Calvinistic Baptists, or to a spectrum of bizarre new sects. Moderate Congregationalism also seemed to be losing intellectual ground each decade to Unitarians or to almost pantheistic idealists or transcendentalists. He thus tried to reoutfit the received religion. In fact he could scarcely understand the old formulas. They had lost meaning for him. Unless he could recast the doctrines, in all honesty he would have had to leave his church.

His fate would be the same as that of most theological trimmers – those who compromise old principles but reject a complete break, who struggle to have the best of all possible worlds. Taylor's influence proved ephemeral. With the shifting fashions in theology, his wonderfully circular system soon became only a footnote in American theology. His arguments, perhaps because so timely, proved also so mortal. It was his system, so circular, so intelligent, and so presumptuous, that quickly fell into disuse, and not the logically more coherent system of Edwards or the much more innovative theology of Bushnell. Today only intellectual historians read Taylor. Generation after generation, serious theologians read, and gain inspiration, from Edwards and Bushnell.

Charles Hodge

Charles Hodge, at the Princeton Seminary, became the most astute critic of Taylor and other compromisers within the Calvinist camp. Hodge seemed to live forever. He was in all respects a professional, constantly involved with theological controversies and gifted in needed foreign languages, and was a very able, at times almost arrogantly self-confident dialectician. He was both a polemicist, with dozens of long, complex, devastating essays in the *Princeton Review*, and a serious although not very original theologian (he titled his final, multivolume magnum opus of 1873 simply *Systematic Theology*). He stood at the barricades of traditional Reformed thought, as reflected in the early confessions, and tried to fight off every dangerous innovation. He was not narrowly Presbyterian, acknowledged points of agreement even with Roman Catholics, and dedicated much of his theological labors to a defense of the central doctrines of the Western church, as first developed by the great councils. Often overlooked in evaluations of his theology was his warmth, his devotion to his family, and his personal, experiential piety.[3]

Hodge was, in some ways, a provincial. Born in Philadelphia in 1797, he eventually enrolled in the College of New Jersey, there experienced conversion during a revival, and committed himself to the ministry. He moved to the almost new Princeton Seminary in 1819, to study under its chair and founder, Archibald Alexander. He then assumed a teaching role in the seminary but soon realized his scholarly inadequacies. Thus, in an all-important decision in 1826, he moved to Germany for two years of graduate work (his temporary replacement at Princeton was a former classmate, John Nevin), there developing a critical appreciation of the work of biblical scholars and theologians, including those at Halle (the product of German pietism but also one of the springs of careful and daring biblical scholarship). Here he studied the theology of Schleiermacher and gained a firsthand knowledge of the types of theology that he would spend the rest of his life not necessarily refuting (the new theology was very appealing) but trying to prove that it was not really Christian.

Hodge usually labeled his own developing theology as Augustinian, occasionally as Pauline or Calvinist. Like his mentor, Alexander, he often turned back to the seventeenth-century apologists of Genevan Calvinism, most notably to François Turretin. Much of his interest centered on a scheme of salvation, the one revived and taught by Luther and Calvin. In the mid-nineteenth century it seemed to be under siege from all directions. Hodge was very skeptical of speculative systems of any type and particularly of those developed by professional philosophers. In a very loose sense he reflected the outlook of Scottish common sense, but none of the influential spokesmen for this philosophy (Dugald Stewart, Thomas Reid, William Hamilton) were nearly orthodox enough to please Hodge. Even the last great spokesman for, and historian of, this tradition, James McCosh, made too many doctrinal concessions to please Hodge, who was horrified by his numerous compromises on Darwinism. McCosh came from Northern Ireland in 1868 to assume the presidency of the College of New Jersey (elevated to Princeton University in 1886).

Hodge's theological system was not philosophical. He developed it through his years as a seminary professor and an acute critic of most religious innovations of the century. He first stated it in often highly polemical form in the *Princeton Review*, which was practically his personal organ. In effect, Hodge tried to work out a comprehensive and coherent body of doctrine, what he believed to be the normative beliefs of a universal church. His method was straightforward – a consideration of all the central doctrines from a foundational theism to eschatology. But the challenges to his tradition mostly involved the scheme of salvation, and thus he devoted almost half of his climactic three-volume masterpiece to soteriology. For each doctrine, he clarified the issues and summarized, with some attempt at descriptive clarity, the positions held by the major Western confessions (Roman Catholic, Lutheran, Anglican, Wesleyan, and his own Reformed). He gladly acknowledged areas of consensus but in each case carefully analyzed errors, even minute ones, at points of conflict. On no critical issues did he depart from the Westminster Confession. For him, the protest of the Dutch remonstrants remained a historic turning point, the opening of the great apostasy in the Reformed churches and even in the modern world. He talked about Arminius as if he were a contemporary, as if he still battled with him for the soul of the church and of humanity.

In the mid-nineteenth century Hodge faced new enemies. He felt most beleaguered, and threatened, by a new German theology rooted in idealistic or what he always called pantheistic philosophies. He recognized a formidable enemy. Some of the German theologians were pious and persuasive. Hodge could respond to their spirituality. But he insisted that the new theologians, who joined biblical scholars in launching a major revolution in Christian thought, were neither Christian nor biblical, however sincerely religious. The idealist flank presented the most imminent danger to orthodoxy, in part because it shared so many common symbols and verbal affirmations. At the other extreme, and possibly most dangerous in the long term, was naturalism and positivism in philosophy and an emerging humanism in religion. These non-Christian beliefs gained support from the increasingly prestigious natural sciences and particularly from geology and biology. Thus, after 1859, Hodge even used his more technical theological essays to launch side attacks against Darwinism.

Hodge was not against scientific inquiry. He always claimed that theology was a proper science, with its own methods and its own truths. It was the Germans who pulled the cognitive props from under theology and relegated it to the area of feeling. Scientists, if they properly understood their task, worked to understand God as revealed in the facts of nature and in the secondary causes that prevailed in nature (even Jonathan Edwards, in Hodge's view, had opened the door to heresy by denying such secondary causes and by affirming the moment-by-moment dependence of events on God's immediate agency). Hodge professed an openness to any findings by scientists, as expressed in verified facts, and faulted scientists, like Darwin, only for speculative theories that went beyond the facts. He thus agreed that, as the sciences progressed, Christians would necessarily go back to parts of the Bible and understand its accounts of natural events in new ways. We now know the earth circles the sun. We differently, and better, understand Old Testament events that, in the telling, reflected a now antiquated heliocentric outlook. Hodge would not challenge what he believed to be established facts. He was almost convinced of the great antiquity of the earth and thus noted that, should this be proven, Christians would have to understand the reference to days of creation in Genesis to mean geological ages. This would also entail the past extinction of species and the later emergence of new ones and thus a type of evolution, but one that Hodge of course would always attribute to divine agency. Each new and fixed species reflected a creative act by God. By Hodge's death, such defensive strategies were clearly strained. For his peace of mind it is good that he died in 1878.

God even more directly revealed himself in the Word. The Christian Bible (or really the Protestant version of the Bible) was, to Hodge, a huge, internally consistent, enormously rich repository of facts and thus was comparable to nature. And these facts were many times over more important to humans, for they contained a plan of salvation. In many respects Hodge proved himself most defensive, at times most inconsistent or most blind to threatening evidence, in his own "science." He claimed to begin with biblical facts and then to classify and systematize these facts before deducing from them the central and fully authoritative doctrines of the church. This was his "scientific" vocation. The knowledge that resulted was as empirical as that in the natural sciences, provided the theologian did his work well.

Hodge was not rigorous, or at times even honest, in his efforts to establish the credentials of the received Bible. He lived into the era of very careful and very unsettling biblical scholarship, most based in Germany. He read it all. But he either rejected or ignored much of it, at least when it challenged his own beliefs. He was most apologetic, even hypocritical, in his attempts to justify both the plenary inspiration of every part of the Bible and the apparent inspiration of those who established authoritative canons for the Jewish scriptures and then for a Christian New Testament. He was, at best, cavalier in dealing with canon issues and was almost always either circular or obviously selective in dealing with textual issues. His ability to see the whole Bible as without serious internal discrepancies (he admitted hundreds of trivial or unimportant discrepancies or contradictions), and completely harmonious in what it taught, rested more on wistful thinking, or on deductions from the nature of God (often established by scriptural proofs, and thus the circularity), than on careful biblical scholarship. In ways that he never acknowledged, he picked and chose among biblical texts and in some cases effectively dismissed whole sections even of the New Testament (such as the eschatology of Revelation, including a millennium and two judgments, an earthly kingdom, and the New Jerusalem). Even as he condemned other theologians for either going beyond the Bible or taking parts of it out of context, his own system involved plenty of extra-biblical assumptions and imposed on the Bible an interpretative pattern that had no more evidential validity than any of a dozen other theological systems.

Hodge placed a creator God at the heart of his theology. Here he was most sensitive to German idealists. He deplored their tendency to merge God and humanity in some absolute mind and to make the material universe a reflection of, or effulgence from, the absolute. Against such a monistic system Hodge posed what he saw as the traditional, commonsense view – that God was an eternal, personal, willful spirit, fully distinct from created matter, which makes up another substance with its own attributes. Without any probing philosophical analysis, Hodge simply affirmed the existence of both spirit and matter, a type of philosophical dualism. He never tried to work out all the theoretical problems that attend their interaction. He surveyed various arguments for the existence of a god and was most responsive to the design argument. But he never rested his belief on any rational proofs. He argued, with a stubborn blindness to facts, that every person had an innate knowledge of God and thus believed in some god or gods. On this issue as on a hundred others, he rested his case finally on the common consent of humans. The existence of God was self-evident, intuitive, and thus beyond argument. He reluctantly acknowledged that a few people, through ignorance or when confused by speculative philosophers, might deny God's existence, but he confidently asserted that none would be able to maintain such doubts at the time of death.

Knowledge of God is only the starting point. It, in itself, is not sufficient for salvation. Saving knowledge of the one true God depends on revelation and thus on an informed knowledge of the Bible. But why believe the Bible is the revelation of the one true God? Once again, Hodge had to go in circles. Ultimately, only the guidance of the Holy Spirit could anchor such faith in the scriptures, and thus God had to provide the final assurance. Note that for Hodge, as for most theologians, the knowledge that humans could gain about God extended only to certain of his attributes, and to his revealed will, but not to his innermost nature.

For Christians, the unitary God confronts them as three distinct persons. Hodge saw the whole church, Roman Catholics and Protestants, as unified in their conception of the Trinity. As always, he completely ignored small sects that dissented from the doctrinal settlements of the great church councils, and unlike New England theologians, he was never much involved in the Unitarian controversy. He simply dismissed such extreme heretics and thus did not engage them in argument. Hodge accepted the trinity formulas that derive from Nicea and Constantinople. The three persons of the Trinity are distinct personalities, not modes or expressions of God. They share a common nature and thus collectively make up the Godhead. In certain contexts, the Son displays appropriate expressions of deference and subordination, but in his nature he is one with the Father. Hodge could not offer a rational explanation of all the conundrums tied up with the three and one, and thus he was willing, ultimately, to confess the limitations of human reason. On this and countless other issues he denied any divine truth that was irrational but believed almost all important truths were, at one point or another, beyond full human comprehension.

Hodge's conception of humans was, deliberately, conventional or common-sense. A person has both a body and a soul, thus participating in two distinct substances. A person, by possession of a spirit or soul or self-conscious mind, was in the image of God, distinct from animals. God created each form of life and endowed it with fixed or specific characteristics. Not surprisingly, Hodge's later descriptions of the human species almost always led him to an often bitter denunciation of Darwinism. Like a dog with a superficially appealing but bitter-tasting bone, Hodge could not leave the subject of specific evolution alone. He came back to it over and over again, eventually writing a whole book to explore the fullest, and to him, most appalling implications of not only Darwin's natural selection but any naturalistic account of the origin either of life or of new species. All such explanations denied the causal agency of God and were, in effect, forms of atheism.

Hodge did not caricature such evolutionary theories but offered insightful summaries of each competing naturalistic theory. He grasped the full implications of each and had little more than contempt for Christians who were naive enough to believe that, somehow, they could find a way to make Darwinism consistent with the biblical accounts. He did not want to whitewash Darwinism but to reveal it in its most shocking colors. Clearly, Hodge was threatened by the new ideas, threatened because he understood them and even at times responded to the persuasive elements in Darwin. On this as on no other issue, he usually was shrill, caustic, and denunciatory. His whole worldview was at stake – his belief that all people believe in a god, that the Bible is inspired and true (in all its teachings if not in incidental detail), and that such theistic foundations lie behind all human understanding and underwrite all moral standards. Thus, to him, the proof that Darwinism was unbiblical and naturalistic was sufficient reason to reject it (it did not cohere with any of the basic truths that anchored his worldview or that of any Christian, beliefs that were for him simply beyond question).

An understanding of humanity was only a preface to the plan of salvation. The critical condition of humans – their separation from the will and purpose of God, or their depravity – overbalanced their substantive goodness (as creatures of God, humans are in their being one of the glories of the creation, but they are corrupt in their will). This implicates the doctrine of the fall, the first of a dozen key doctrines that have divided Christians. Hodge insisted that the Genesis account of the fall of Adam and Eve was literal, not allegory. In the larger sense he also admitted that God had ordained their fall, which in ways not clear to humans had to contribute to God's glory. Such arguments, as well as most that followed, were anchored in undoubted assumptions about God's perfection. They were, in a sense, analytical deductions from the nature of God. Almost all Christians shared in a certain understanding of the fall – that Adam and Eve disobeyed God, that they suffered mortality as a penalty for such disobedience, and that in some sense God had promised a plan of salvation that would allow at least some humans to escape the curse attendant on the fall. It was in the details that Christians disagreed. Almost all conceptions of human redemption implicate certain nuances of belief about the fall. Hodge knew this and thus carefully developed his orthodox Presbyterian version.

In the spectrum of Christian versions of the fall, and doctrines about original sin, Hodge was at one extreme, at what most of his critics saw as an impossibly harsh extreme. He thought his not only the one true account but the one that best accorded with human experience. He saw Adam as the federal head of the race, a true representative of all people. Adam's disobedience infected all his descendants. They suffered his guilt, which God imputed to them. This was a more extreme doctrine than one that sees humans as similar to Adam, with his nature, and thus always ready to repeat his disobedience. God imputes such guilt totally apart from the character of Adam's children, although Hodge readily admitted that such children share his nature. But the corruptness of one's nature is a product of such original sinfulness. The corruption is indeed complete, involving understanding as well as will. One's inherent guilt is from Adam. God holds all his children fully responsible for the sins of a distant ancestor. Hodge saw no injustice in this. Humans are also recipients of all the benefits of the righteousness of ancestors and above all of the imputed righteousness of the Christ. In some human sense this may seem unfair, but this is, without doubt, how God deals with humans in their various covenants, as biblical history confirms over and over again. Since it is God's method, it cannot be unjust. And "all humans" agree that such corporate guilt is true to their experience and to history. As always, such typically Hodgean finalities end the argument, even though critics may see only circularity and bogus authorities.

The result of the fall, and of the penalties and guilt that follow it, is complete spiritual death. Humans have no ability to cure the curse. They have no ability to do good, in the sense of acts predicated on belief in and love of God. Thus, Hodge spent much time trying to refute all other views, with Pelagianism at the far extreme – the belief that humans retain their full ability to choose the good, although they usually do not so choose, a belief that, in effect, denies any original sin or depravity at all (to Hodge, Nathaniel Taylor came close to such a Pelagian view). But all Christians until the various Anabaptist Brethren (Hodge completely ignored the nearby Mennonites) had repudiated Pelagianism. Thus, his real battle, which involved a thousand subtle distinctions, was with those whom he referred to as semi-Pelagians.

This very large and error-inflicted multitude included Roman Catholics, the Remonstrants (Arminians), Wesleyans, and to a very limited extent most Lutherans. Each, without denying some form of original sinfulness, nonetheless left humans with some ability, if only the ability to resist God's grace. Indeed, most did not leave humans with any natural competence to choose the good, let along redeem themselves, but most, including Roman Catholics, so involved humans in the process of regeneration as to make them at least minor partners with God. And at the level of moral attainment, all conceded to unregenerate persons some ability to do good, to obey God. In Calvinist terms, all these so-called Christians rejected the keystone doctrine of complete depravity. In his detailed analysis of the exact contours of denial, Hodge glimpsed an embryonic humanism that would, when fully developed, destroy a God-centered Christianity. It is no wonder he attended to these heresies so closely, for even the slightest deviation here ensured a subsequent subversion of all elements of the Pauline scheme of redemption. To deny the fullest and most consistent doctrine of depravity was, in effect, to opt for a religion of works, not of faith through grace.

Almost all the issues that separated Hodge from other Christians of the nineteenth century involved the scheme of salvation. He at times felt beleaguered, almost deserted, in the defense of orthodoxy. A vast majority of Christians, beginning with Roman Catholics (except for the Jansenists) and including in fact if not in formal confession most Protestants, had already rejected the Pauline scheme, not excluding many rowdy American revivalists who still exploited its symbols but betrayed its inner logic. By the mid-nineteenth century the best-known German theologians had, in effect, finessed all the issues and had led sentimental Christians into an appealing, solacing new religion, one neither biblical nor even essentially Christian. And the appeal of naturalistic theories, buttressed by Darwin, threatened to lead others into atheism. In such hard times what most distressed Hodge was that professed Calvinists, such as Taylor and Bushnell, had compromised the faith. It was not clear that even a majority of American Presbyterians still kept up the faith. Most New School Presbyterians had bought into some of the compromises, most originating in New England.

Hodge tried to give a systematic defense of what he called the Augustinian scheme. His effort deserves commendation on several grounds. It was vastly informed. No other American theologian, not even any church historian except Schaff, knew quite so much about the doctrinal developments in the church. A lifetime of learning went into Hodge's *Systematic Theology*. Dogmatic, even arrogant, and at times almost deliberately blind in ignoring counterevidence, Hodge was at least willing to describe opposing points of view fairly, as a prelude to a devastating critique. He did not battle straw people. He was a thorough scholar. His citations were in several languages and involved all the major confessions and the major theological systems of Western Christianity. His background knowledge at times almost intimidated critical readers. No one else knew so much. For each critical element in the plan of salvation, he typically aired up to five or six contending views, explored even the smallest differences, and always ended up defending his own Calvinism. He welcomed areas of consensus and used this as a weapon. He might use Roman Catholic authorities against a Pelagian.

Hodge's views on Roman Catholicism were complex. On a majority of basic doctrines he was at one with at least major Catholic spokesmen. As he tried to steer his path between pantheism and naturalism, he at least had a growing appreciation that, in the battles to come, Roman Catholics might be needed allies more often than enemies. Yet, on the traditional cleavages of the Reformation, he was a harsh critic of Roman Catholic corruptions. But it is important to note that Hodge always believed that a majority of the members of the church of Rome were redeemed Christians, as were those involved in various Protestant heresies. His theology was a theology for the great, Catholic, holy church, not just for Presbyterians. And, in every case, his final, clinching argument for the traditional Reformed position was both the Bible and common sense (often stated as the received wisdom of ordinary people).

Hodge tried to give a simplified version of the Augustinian view as a prelude to all the subtle disagreements. In his formulation, the correct understanding of human salvation required acceptance of the following almost axiomatic beliefs: that the end of the whole creation and of history is the glory of God, and no other; that God is the sole creator of the universe and the sole author of a plan of salvation; that such was the penalty of the sin of Adam and Eve that no human is able to deliver himself from sin; that God, even before the foundation of the world, had elected a certain number of humans for salvation and left the rest to suffer the just consequences of their sinfulness; that God chose his elect according to his good favor, not on the basis of any foreknowledge of their future character or belief (none deserve salvation); that Jesus, the Son of God, became incarnate, assumed the form of man, and obeyed and suffered and died as a sacrifice for his elect; that his sacrifice served as a full satisfaction before God for the guilt of the elect; that the Holy Spirit, in his saving role, is a gift only to the elect; that the elect will in time come to a full knowledge of the truth and to belief and trust (sanctification); and that they will persevere in the faith.

Most of these doctrines involved subtle differences of emphasis even within the orthodox Reformed tradition. For example, on many issues Hodge took exception to Jonathan Edwards and his New Divinity successors, but this did not mean that Edwards had rejected the Augustinian scheme. The larger disputes involved those who rejected or modified any part of this scheme. In fact, logic required that rejection of one part almost inevitably meant rejection of all. And behind the more numerous citations of essential doctrines, what Hodge defended was the proclamations of Dort and Westminster. Most of his points fit within the five canons of Dort, or the famous TULIP (Total depravity, Unconditional election, Limited atonement, Irresistible grace, and the Perseverance of the saints) of scholastic Calvinism. And his main targeted enemies were either Roman Catholics or Arminians. Toward Lutherans his disagreements were more sad than angry. Lutherans were so close to the mark and had compromised so rarely that Hodge wanted to include them in his synthesis as much as possible, even as he still regretted the failure of Lutherans and Reformed to find a consensus in the intermediate aftermath of the Reformation. But because of this loving dissent, no other American theologian ever drew as carefully all the subtle points of difference between the Reformed and the later Lutheran views, some embodied in confessions. On two issues – the presence of the Christ in the Lord's Supper and the remitting role of baptism – his explication was almost definitive.

In almost all discussions of Christian salvation, the doctrine of the atonement is central. Hodge spent his career trying to chart all the subtle distinctions that had to accompany any correct understanding of the atonement (regeneration, fortunately, did not depend on such an understanding). For Hodge, the justice of God required the sacrifice of the Son, for nothing less would have upheld divine justice or permitted God to forgive the sins of the elect. In this sense, the sacrifice had to be fully sufficient for the effect. For those of faith, those whom God has chosen for salvation, the sacrifice not only removed the penalty for original sin but also provided a vicarious righteousness. In this sense, God imputes the righteousness of the Christ to the elect even as he imputes the sin of Adam to all humankind. Of course, the atonement is conditional. In a sense, the sacrifice was sufficient for all humankind had all humankind the requisite faith. But it was conditional on faith, and in turn faith was conditional on election and on the active work of the Holy Spirit in regeneration. The ability to respond to God in faith awaited an initiative from God, the informing of the Word by the Spirit, and thus a special, saving grace.

Hodge preferred the word *regeneration* for the moment when God claimed his elect, when he effectively imputed to them the righteousness of the Son. This rebirth is, by definition, instantaneous, although the recipient of grace may not be able to identify the exact moment. Hodge often used the word *conversion* to encompass not only regeneration but the whole period of repentance and remorse that normally preceded rebirth. Hodge was an avowed enemy of the new revivalism, particularly the techniques popularized by Charles Finney, such as tearful appeals or the use of the anxious bench. Such revival tactics created an artificial emotional climate, subverted an intellectual as well as an affectional response to the Word and Spirit, minimized the role of nurture within the church, and almost inevitably led, as in Finney, to some form of Arminianism and to a repudiation of the doctrine of irresistible grace. Human means tended to replace God's means, and the scheme of salvation became overly sentimental, humanistic, and moralistic.

For Hodge, regeneration involved all the means appointed and ordinarily used by God, such as the preaching of the gospel, but the chief actor in the drama of salvation was the Holy Spirit. Given this "evangelical" outlook, Hodge spent an enormous amount of time refuting any sacramental version of Christianity. He believed that regeneration was possible without baptism, and thus he rejected even mild, Lutheran versions of baptismal remission. He also rejected Baptist claims that baptism was the first act of obedience for the new convert and thus a rite only for regenerated adults. His defense of infant baptism, and of sprinkling or pouring as acceptable modes of baptism, forced him into indirect and forced readings of scriptures or into strained analogies (baptism as the Christian version of circumcision). It led him, in his own way, to place a great deal more reliance on tradition, and revered congregational practices, than he could ever admit. Yet, on the long-debated problem about admission of infants to baptism, he cited the Presbyterian practice (only children presented by parents who were within the church) but was open to other policies, including those that so broadened the privilege as to include the children of nonmembers.

For Hodge, regeneration reoriented one's beliefs and affections but did not lead to any type of perfection. For him, regeneration gave the full assurance of ultimate sanctification, but no human could attain this until after death. Saving grace did open the possibility of truly good works, those that not only adhered to moral standards but also reflected in motives a sincere love of God. The only perfection that pertained to earthly humans was that of Jesus, a perfection they benefited from by imputation, not by complete imitation. Thus, the Christian life remained one of struggle to overcome the surviving effects of sinfulness, or a life that could move toward full sanctification. For Hodge, the sacraments, not tied necessarily to regeneration, were avenues of divine help that enabled a Christian to become more saint-like. These joined with the scriptures and prayer as part of a devout life in the church. The memory and significance of baptism had a continuing role in the life of Christians, but it was the Lord's Supper that provided a frequent, vital avenue of grace. Hodge explored, in minute detail, the varied Lutheran and Reformed interpretations of the supper. On this one issue he was not dogmatic. He found all manner of problems in the Lutheran doctrine of consubstantiation, for in order to have the body and blood of the Christ present with the bread and wine, Lutherans had to believe in a diffuse body of the Christ, one that was with the Father in the heavens and, at the same time, present also at various points on earth. Thus, Hodge opted for the traditional Reformed doctrine of spiritual presence but recognized, and tolerated, a range of specific interpretations of what this spiritual presence meant. He saw, among most Reformed Christians, a retreat from Calvin's belief in the real, objective presence of body and blood as communicated by the Spirit to those who, in faith, took the sacrament. He thus found acceptable a range of views, from real, miraculous presence to a symbolic meal, one in remembrance of the original supper and of Christ's sacrifice. In the context of nineteenth-century revivalism, he leaned toward a greater emphasis not only on the church but also on a more sacramentally oriented form of worship.

A defender of the great church, Hodge nonetheless deplored state churches. He wanted a church more inclusive than that of early Puritanism, yet not a church that baptized and admitted to membership every person. For the local congregation, membership should include all professing adults and their children (those baptized and within the covenant). The terms of admission should be a profession of faith, whether sincere or not (only God knows), and an acceptable level of moral attainment. He wanted no congregational inquiries into the experiential aspects of faith. Thus, a church would always contain regenerated Christians, other adults who falsely confessed a faith not theirs, and baptized children who might, or might not, later confirm the presence of a saving faith. Hodge, unlike many Calvinists, had no doubt that infants who died before they could understand the meaning of salvation were among God's elect. He thus consoled parents with baptized infants but at times argued that such mercy extended to all infants. All were born with the taint of original sin, but Hodge believed that God, in his providence, had chosen such infants as objects of mercy. This generosity toward infants revealed a humanistic bias on the part of Hodge. He was continuously pained by assaults on Calvinism as harsh and cruel. He could never banish the central dilemma – that God had chosen some but not all humans, even though all were equally undeserving of salvation. In old age, he once speculated that this seemingly harsh fact might be alleviated somewhat by the likelihood that the number unsaved would be relatively small, a position that tended toward Universalism and that matched the positions of Hopkins and Taylor. In fact, it may surprise most people who share popular stereotypes of Calvinism to learn that almost all the ablest Calvinist theologians in America have believed that the elect contained not a small minority of humans but the vast majority.

Consistent with all his other doctrines, Hodge believed not only that God would take the initiative in the regeneration of his elect but that he would ensure their final salvation. Whatever the momentary lapses in behavior, whatever doubts along the way, the elect would persevere. The covenant of grace thus carried with it full assurances of salvation. Just as one's merit in the eyes of God rested not on any achievement of the person but on the imputed righteousness of the Christ, so one's hope of salvation rested not on one's own abilities but on a divine promise. All true and faithful Christians, in whatever confession they lived, despite any corruptions of doctrine and practice in that confession, or despite their innocent misunderstanding of doctrines, would attain salvation after death.

Hodge was least specific in doctrines about life after death. He also seemed here least willing to struggle with specific New Testament passages. He all too easily dismissed much of Revelation as too obscure for confident interpretation and as a result simply ignored much of it. In no area was he more conventional, more resistant to sectarian views. He not only practically ignored Adventists but also dismissed with near contempt a corporealist version of eschatology (no survival of the soul after death, and a literal resurrection to live in an earthly kingdom ruled by the Christ). He affirmed, on somewhat tenuous scriptural grounds, the immortality of the human soul and affirmed, on almost no scriptural grounds, an Old Testament Jewish belief in a resurrection or even, more improbable, in immortality (this involved him in what was, by 1870, an almost dishonest dating of the book of Daniel from the time of the Babylonian captivity). Between death and the promised resurrection, the human spirit lived on, with Christians enjoying a type of happiness or bliss. He detested the Catholic doctrine of purgatory, which he viewed as nonscriptural and the fruit of a semi-Pelagian religion of good works. In the future, the Christ would return to earth to initiate the final events of world history. Hodge did not take seriously any millennial age and saw the advent as an immediate prelude to a final judgment, a destruction of the old earth and the inauguration of the final kingdom. He would not go much further into details and lamented too concrete speculations about events leading up to the advent. Hell, the fate of the damned, was possibly a state of being and not a place. The Bible promised not extinction but eternal punishment, but this might be largely a separation from God. He was not sure where the final kingdom would be, in heavenly realms or on a completely cleansed earth.

To so summarize Hodge's doctrines is to be unfair to him. After all, his beliefs represented simply a late, fully conventional version of Calvinism. He wanted to affirm no more than this. But he brought unusual scholarly gifts to his task and did as much as any other American to draw clearly every point of disagreement that separated Calvinists from all other Christians. Yet, in reading Hodge, one senses a type of futility. He was defending a fortress long since bypassed by the major contending armies. Few enemies would engage him or even take him seriously. His system had the strength of internal coherence. It at least had biblical support at every point, although Hodge was least persuasive in his claim to have drawn all the essential doctrines of the church directly from the Bible, as if there were no room for disagreement at any point or as if the Bible were so much an organic whole, so internally consistent, as to support no other interpretation.

Hodge had enormous influence, but not in what was becoming the theological mainstream in America. His perspective was too rigid to gain acceptance among liberal theologians. Who could still believe that scripture and common sense supported only one doctrinal system? The naive realism of common sense, the almost blind defense of a unitary and inspired Bible, or even a fully rational defense of theology as a science, with its own methods and truth, were generally out of style by the time Hodge died. But his ideas were not out of style with his successors at Princeton, who dominated the seminary until the 1920s. His immediate successors, Benjamin B. Warfield and his son A. A. Hodge, preserved the tradition into the twentieth century, when their student and disciple, J. Gresham Machen, fought to maintain the tradition at Princeton. When he failed, he and his supporters seceded to found Westminster Seminary in 1929.

The scholarly, scientific, and philosophical challenges that faced Hodge were all but overwhelming. However knowledgeable or brilliant, he never had all the defensive weapons he needed. Horace Bushnell, more than any other mid-nineteenth-century theologian, did have the needed weapons, but as Hodge was so aware, Bushnell and other innovative theologians risked throwing the baby out with the bathwater when they tried to so amend and correct received doctrines as to make them consistent with the latest products of the scientific and philosophical workshops. They might defend a wonderfully appealing religion, but not biblical Christianity. As Hodge admitted, almost anyone could cook up a religion that better appealed to modern humans, that seemed more kind and merciful and helpful, than historic Christianity. He therefore defended such Christianity as true, not indulgent, as consistent with the realities of human experience, not with our fondest wishes and fancies.

Horace Bushnell

Of all nineteenth-century American theologians, Horace Bushnell was the most innovative. He drew on several intellectual traditions – on Edwards and the New Divinity, on Samuel Coleridge and Victor Cousin and thus on a new idealism or transcendentalism, on Ralph Waldo Emerson and especially on Theodore Parker, on Friedrich Schleiermacher and on several German scholars, on the new Western knowledge of the Brahmin religion of ancient India, on recent theories about language, on Neoplatonism, on the governmental theories of his mentor Nathaniel Taylor, and even on types of mid-nineteenth-century spiritualism. He was not an academic theologian. He matured most of his insights in sermons, many delivered to his congregation, others to fellow Congregational ministers. He was not systematic in the presentation of his views or apparently in the development of them. He was the brilliant amateur, continuously involved in theological investigations, able to think problems through for himself. His central purpose, one that he could not achieve, was to mediate all the doctrinal conflicts that divided the churches of New England. In pursuit of this goal, he recast doctrines in completely new ways, leading critics to charge him with a fatal bent for novelty. Finally, to an unusual extent, his theological reflections grew out of his own devotional life.[4]

Bushnell came belatedly to theology. Born in Litchfield County, Connecticut, in 1802, and an eldest son, he was able to prepare somewhat belatedly for Yale, but with no clear early vocational goals. As he grew up he was not especially devout and apparently indulged some youthful infidelity. Only at Yale did he formally join the church but did not long remain a faithful member. On graduation from Yale in 1825 he taught and then became a tutor at the college. His plans involved the law, not the ministry. But the wayward young man returned to the church during a revival at the college in 1831. He then moved to the Divinity School; there he imbibed the governmental theology of Taylor. On graduation he won the pulpit at the North Church in Hartford, remaining in this position until health forced his retirement nearly three decades later. His was an abundantly successful ministry; however much his views scandalized fellow ministers, he was able to win and retain the fullest loyalty of his largely affluent and socially prominent flock. But, as he later remembered it, his early devotional life did not yet match what he recommended to his own congregation. After family misfortune (the death of a son) and a controversy over his first major publication (two essays on Christian nurture), he had a vital religious experience in February 1848. It transformed his life and informed what began almost immediately – a continuous rethinking of all the major doctrines of his church. This rethinking accompanied a series of powerful sermons and his first effort to communicate his developing insights to his colleagues. His insights were deeply personal and often completely novel in the New England setting. By most interpretations, they were heterodox if not dangerously heretical.

Bushnell, in most respects, reflected the beliefs and values of his social class. He opposed slavery but long resisted the platform of abolitionists. He accepted the racial superiority of Anglo-Saxons, wrote a book against female suffrage, and in early life nourished irenic hopes of continued progress toward something approaching a millennial age. His sermons were often prophetic, but as a whole he did little to oppose the existing economic order. However much his theology related to later "liberal" themes, he was in no way the founder of any social gospel.

Just after Bushnell's intensely personal religious experience in 1848, he received three invitations to offer important public lectures – at Yale, Harvard, and Andover. These institutions bridged the spectrum of New England doctrinal controversy, with the Unitarian Harvard at an opposite extreme from the strictly orthodox or Calvinist Andover and with New Haven in between. Bushnell accepted all offers, again with the hope that he could find a mediating position that all could accept. These three powerful lectures (the first, at Yale, was the prestigious *Concio ad Clerum* delivered each year before the General Association of Connecticut) made up the heart of his first theological book, entitled *God in Christ.* He prefaced the three lectures with a dissertation on language, one that outlined his method and helped clarify his arguments. Rather than bridging differences, or aiding unity, the book almost immediately became a subject of bitter condemnation. In 1849 the Fairfield West Association (or consociation or synod) denounced his doctrines in resolutions and asked for discipline by the associations of Connecticut. This began an embittered four-year effort by the more orthodox ministers in Connecticut to bring Bushnell to trial. They failed. A committee in his own association voted three-to-two against a local hearing. The General Association had no authority to move against him but in various actions did stigmatize his doctrines. His congregation supported him all the way, but the harassment and conflict may have contributed to Bushnell's deteriorating health and his early retirement from the pulpit (1859).

At times, one wonders why Bushnell entered the theological jungle. He never quite fit. His bent was as close to George Fox as to John Calvin. He believed that religion was first and foremost experiential and that no verbal formulas could ever do justice to it. In fact, often with wonderfully subtle and logical arguments, Bushnell tried to reduce doctrines, dogmas, and theological disputations to a bundle of contradictions or to sheer nonsense. Verbal formulas are always inexact. As much as Edwards, but in language borrowed from Schleiermacher, he lamented a cold, rational religion, one tied to schools and creeds, to formulas and catechisms. Frenzied, carefully contrived, even manufactured revivals were not the solution. These were as artificial as verbal formulas. A true faith is a matter of spirit and life and not rationalizations or doctrines, of Christ received and not dogmas affirmed.

In 1848 Bushnell was naive enough, or inspired enough, to believe his appeal to a Christ-centered and spiritual religion would dissipate the verbal controversies. He challenged such men as Charles Hodge (a perennial antagonist in print), those who mistakenly believed that theology was a science, that concepts and evidence fit the subject. Intellect cannot conquer what is highest in God. The gospel, full of paradoxes and even logical contradictions, is a work of art, not science. It requires esthetic sensitivity for interpretation. The subject is very different from nature. And the Bible is not a simple, unified source of religious knowledge, not a source of proof texts or even of correct doctrines. It is a vast repository of perspectives on divinity, full of contraries, but in the very midst of these are the various figures that give one a living sense of God. Christian truths are not expressible in the niggardly forms of a science or in articles of school divinity. But, at a secondary level, Bushnell granted some uses for doctrine – as a teaching tool for the young, as an outlet for our desire for order and system ("it is the alphabet in which nature begins to stammer"), as a weapon against unbelief and skepticism, as a means for Christians to make peace with science and philosophy rather than act like fools out of ignorance, and as a check to fanaticism.

Bushnell began theological speculation with a theory of language, of what it is and what it can do. He traced the origins of language to proper names and showed how class terms or symbolic meanings developed. Thus, our words all originated in direct contact with sensual objects, with what we can point to. Other subjects are not immediately experienced. We cannot point to them. But, according to Bushnell, our words for such phenomena as life, thought, or what he denominated spiritual things, still have their origin in experienced objects. Even laws of grammar derive from the relation of things in nature. Thus, the word *spirit* is tied to breath and is, in its proper reference, always figurative. We talk quite literally about physical objects but only figuratively about spirits and gods or about ideas and emotions. Theologians, mistakenly, often think they have a literal language about subjects that we do not directly experience. Such a fatal mistake leads to a spectrum of theological opinions or systems, each taken literally by adherents, and thus out of the resulting babel comes all the sectarian strife that has marked the history of Christianity. Even physical terms are less than fully representational, for they reduce particularities to classes or types. Figurative descriptions of spirit are even less representative, less a mirror of things. We hope that our spiritual language, the language about how we experience, will suggest some near-identical images in the mind of the hearer. But given their inherent ambiguity, such words will inevitably suggest slightly different images in any two minds. This means that we must not take the words literally. Even more important, we should rejoice in the sheer excess of description, even in what seems contradictory descriptions.

At times, Bushnell joined transcendentalists, such as Emerson, in viewing the vast panorama of nature primarily as a source of the images needed to express divine ideas. Given that language is necessarily figurative and is rooted in nature, excess and paradox in spiritual matters are not only inevitable but desirable. These insights reinforced Bushnell's antipathy to any literal interpretation of scriptures.

On the most important issues the writers of the Bible had to use highly figurative, inexact, expressive language. In any literal sense, most that they wrote was false or even absurd. Bushnell loved to describe the Bible as poetic or to point out that Jesus never resorted to definitions, logic, or arguments. The Bible supports no one set of doctrines, no dogmatism. Dogmas always reveal the human source, are partial, simply one way of "seeing." Scripture is the poetic clothing of religious truth. Because of the necessity of figuration, the Bible is richer than any literal description in the physical sciences. And since an understanding of the Bible involves an engagement with varied perspectives, an appreciation of all manner of paradoxes, then esthetic skills are more important than logical ones in absorbing its truth (he called the Gospel of John one of the most contradictory books in the world and, by that very fact, the most truthful).

As if to rub salt into the wounds of the orthodox, Bushnell professed to like almost all creeds, as if the more the merrier. In their plurality they might lead one up the mountain, to the point of intuitive insight or truth. The best creeds were the most concrete and particular, those closer to the experience of people. No one has any tool for adjudicating creedal differences. Instead of affirming any one formula, Bushnell generally conceded that all sides were in some sense correct and that each could contribute to a richer, more comprehensive Christianity. At times this toleration went to such extremes that one wonders what possible criteria, save the inner voice of the Spirit, Bushnell could use to make any doctrinal judgments at all. He seemed to undercut any cognitive standing for theological language, any possible basis for arbitrating disputes. He belied this untenable position by some of his own firmly held and carefully argued theological views.

Bushnell began his theology with a plunge into the heart issues, particularly in the New England context – the nature of the Christ and the doctrine of the Trinity. But in any brief, and necessarily simplified, explication of his theology, it makes better sense to fit his beliefs into an overall plan, even if this means skipping among essays written at quite different stages of his career. The logical starting point was his conception of God and his account of the creation and fall.

Only with great reluctance did Bushnell wade into ontological issues. He preferred to work within the range of human experience. Thus, his central concern was God as revealed, not God in his inner nature. Talk of God was not only necessarily figurative but also, even in figuration, inadequate, in some sense even impious, when applied to God as the ultimate ground of being. Influenced by the Brahmin religions, the precursors of a polytheistic Hinduism, Bushnell in effect argued that any predication about the ultimate being is misplaced, always misleading, and demeaning. No physical or human traits, no spatial or chronological limits, ever fit an infinite god. Thus, any statement about the characteristics of the infinite are false, for all such limit and constrain God. The Unitarians, particularly

William Ellery Channing, admitted the inexact nature of all such attributions but felt that we had no alternative but to attribute to God all human virtues, with the further assumption that they were perfected in a unitary god. Such an anthropo-morphized theology seemed impious to Bushnell, as well as abstract. Yet, having foreclosed description, even talk, about such an elusive god, Bushnell always af-firmed, as a Christian, the fact of a unitary, infinite, omnipotent god, although a god beyond description or understanding. In a sense, his ultimate or absolute god was close to the infinite one of Plotinus, so far beyond conceptualization as to invite only the silence appropriate when one tries to think about the unthink-able. In his theological battles, Bushnell used this insight as a powerful tool of argument. When Unitarians pointed out the irrationality of trinity theories, Bush-nell gladly accepted the cogency of their logic but then impaled them on their own logic – their conceptions of a unitary and humane god, often imaged as a loving father, were equally absurd from a logical or semantic perspective. They were impiously projecting their own identity, and moral values, on the ultimate mystery.

This ultimate, and hidden, God had chosen to reveal himself. Bushnell recog-nized the verbal traps he entered even by this simple assertion. For example, call-ing God a he, attributing gender to the ultimate, was arbitrary and perhaps im-pious. Bushnell noted this, but as a creature of time and place he thought that nothing would be more shocking than to attribute feminine traits to divinity and that no effort would do more to discredit God in the eyes of nonbelievers. Neither did he reject personal pronouns for God, and in this he simply reflected the per-sonalism of all Semitic forms of theism. Thus, even his minimal confession – that a unitary god created the universe and various personalities in it – was loaded with unwarranted assumptions. In all such cases, Bushnell acknowledged that he was affirming a central doctrine of his church and of Christianity itself, not a logically impregnable philosophical position. The roots of such affirmations lay in experience, in the prompting of the Holy Spirit, and thus in the language of the alter and of Christian worship. It was not that he doubted that the ultimate one had extended "himself" outward (he preferred such Neoplatonic imagery), that he had created and now governed the natural universe, but that such beliefs im-posed on God all manner of human limitations.

In his first overtly theological book (not a collection of essays or sermons), Bushnell defended a form of supernaturalism. Nature, as Bushnell defined it, is a system with its own laws, one that reveals regularities or causal series. He used the term *force* to designate its internal dynamic or self-determining aspects. By impli-cation, such a natural order is not one, coimplicative, mechanical whole but rather a diversity of relatively but not fully isolated subsystems. Thus, nature does not require, but is susceptible to, outside influences. Any phenomenon that is not part of the causal sequences of nature, that is exempt from the system of cause and effect, is supernatural in Bushnell's terminology. He called such self-caused, or nonmaterial, entities "powers," what most people call "mind." This means that humans are supernatural in their capacity as agents, in their mental activities, in their self-consciousness. They can, in pursuit of chosen goals, intervene in nature and redirect natural energies. Such supernatural interventions drastically change the course of nature. Angels and gods are also supernatural beings, or powers, and have the same ability to intrude into and influence natural events, not by violating or suppressing natural laws but by redirecting such laws (again, this implies an element of nondetermination in the interaction of such laws). Humans are incapable of certain drastic interventions into nature, such as introducing new forms of life. Gods have greater power and can do what seems miraculous to humans. But such superhuman interventions are of the same type as human interventions and are in each case supernatural.

The most impressive such external interventions in natural history was the insertion (creation) of new species by God at the beginning of each geologic age. For Bushnell, a devout student of Louis Agassiz and his theory of multiple creation, this historically repeated creation of species was the most persuasive argument for the existence of divine agency in the world. Until his death in 1876, he allied with Agassiz to fight against Darwinian natural selection, for such a naturalistic explanation of new species reinforced other assaults on supernaturalism itself and thus on the possibilities of any powers above nature. That such powers are real, and that humans are perfect examples of such powers, was at the heart of Bushnell's theology. The reality of mind, of self-consciousness, of language and thought, or of phenomena not controlled by the causal laws of nature, seemed self-evident.

Since the arena of powers, of will and self-determination, is a higher realm than nature (it can control and direct nature), Bushnell saw nature as an effect of will, as a created order. It is, as such, the first revelation of God. He assumed (he knew that proof in these matters is impossible) that God first created a completely harmonious natural order, a perfectly ordered Eden. Here he followed Jonathan Edwards and made esthetic criteria (harmony, consent, symmetry, order, balance), or a type of beauty, the criteria of both divine and natural excellence. Since God, in creating the material universe, did not have to deal with other powers (minds, spirits), he could make it perfect, informed by his own perfect ideas, or what Bushnell often referred to as the Logos or the divine and informing ideas of God, a concept he would tie to the Son image in his doctrine of the Trinity. And, if rebellious powers had not come to inhabit the earth, or if God had not intended that they occupy it, the universe would have remained perfect forever as it followed its own self-determining laws. It was not that Bushnell observed such a world – far from it. Corruptions, disorders, and diseases abounded. Ugliness was as pervasive as beauty. The natural world was all messed up, fallen.

More than perhaps any other Christian theologian, Bushnell generalized the idea of depravity. It was an all-pervasive distortion and ugliness, visible in nature and in social life or what Bushnell referred to as the corporate realm, as well as in individuals. Thus, any full conception of redemption must mean a restoration of harmony and beauty in all areas, a type of natural and corporate redemption as much or more than individual salvation. But why did nature fall into disorder? Here Bushnell followed closely the doctrines of his mentor, Taylor, and beyond him the New Divinity theologians. He combined a theory about the origins of humans with a theodicy. God could have created fully obedient creatures, and he did so in animals. Perhaps he could have created a spiritual being, tied completely to his own will and thus fully obedient. But such spirits would not be free and thus not authentic powers at all. For hidden reasons of his own, God chose to create powers other than himself, but being powers, these were in his own image (supernatural, with mind and choice). Like Taylor, Bushnell saw in this choice – to have other powers or spirits – a subsequent limitation on God. To have free spirits is to give to such spirits the self-originating powers of a god and to leave them free to exercise choice. Here Bushnell adhered to scriptural accounts much more than did his orthodox enemies, for he accepted the existence of various powers other than humans, angels and demons and possibly even a mind attached to celestial worlds or humanlike powers on other planets. We do not know the range of such powers or the diversity of their character and ability.

The theodicy was in Bushnell's assumption – an old one – that God gained greater glory, or found greater satisfaction, in creating powers and allowing them free choice. In his infinite being, God of course knew, even in a sense willed, that they would choose wrongly as well as rightly, for such is the necessary implications of freedom. As dramatically enacted in the Genesis account of Adam and Eve, newly created humans chose to disobey God. They thereby reaped the consequence of such a choice. In a sense, God grieved at this. He did not want them to sin but wanted them free, which entailed their sinning. He did not will what they did but consented to their being able to choose it. God was not, therefore, the author of evil or of sin. In the total picture, his choice to have powers in the world, potentially or even necessarily rebellious powers, was a good choice. Here Bushnell assumed that God in the end received more glory from the voluntary consent and love of powers who had, in a long pilgrimage through rebellion and sin, reached a point where they were receptive to God's reconciling grace. Thus, they came to him in love, freely.

Human sin corrupted the earth. Humans, by their ignorant or selfish choices, messed up the pristine harmonies. Or, in anticipation of their choices, God even preestablished certain natural evils as a type of precautionary warning, to teach lessons to errant humans. Either way, the fact of natural evil, of disease and suffering, was a consequence of the fall. So were all corporate evils, such as wars and social injustice. Bushnell even speculated that humans, in their greedy exploitation of nature, might start so many fires as to consume all the oxygen and thus commit environmental suicide. But in substance, neither a degenerate earth nor sinful humans were evil. Like Taylor, Bushnell did not see humans as depraved by nature. They do not, by nature, choose evil. The temple is the same one that ultimately will stand perfected before God. Here he tried, as always, to bridge what he saw as the largely verbal differences between Calvinists and Arminians. Calvinists correctly saw that divine providence lies behind all events; Arminians rightly saw that humans were free. To describe depravity as inherent by nature is to implicate God in evil, as Arminians alleged. But to suggest that humans can, in some sense, choose to be virtuous on their own, as a consequence of such freedom, is to challenge God's omnipotence and also deny the necessity of grace. Like Taylor, Bushnell argued that humans will inevitably sin but do not sin by necessity of their being. On certain issues, such as the imputation of Adam's sin to humans, Bushnell simply assumed that such God-demeaning doctrines were no longer in vogue in New England. No liberal and fair minds entertained such cruel notions. Such doctrines were artifacts of the past, perhaps believable, if carefully worked out, but no longer a meaningful figuration of spiritual truth. Bushnell was willing to attend such traditional doctrines carefully, to flesh out their possible meaning, only when they were a vital part of popular worship, embedded in the language of the altar. Imputation did not strike him as such a doctrine.

To talk about the great drama of salvation is to impose human terms, and temporal categories, on an infinite God. They ill fit. But we have no alternative. Bushnell saw human history as a long road back from rebellion to righteousness. God led humans at what, from a human perspective, might seem a very slow pace, but of course it was not such in the timeless comprehension of God. The infinite one could not, in his aloofness or unapproachability, directly guide humans back to himself. He had to do it indirectly, through representations. The first of these was nature itself, with its natural evils and analogous lessons for humans. Next was the divine law as codified at Sinai, a tutor with its own burdens and near slavery when it had performed its function of conviction. Finally, Jesus came. He was the final, perfect, all-sufficient expression of God to humanity. The Christ was the central theme for Bushnell. No theologian was more Christocentric. Yet, none were quite as heterodox in their understanding of Jesus.

No simple summary can do justice to Bushnell's beliefs about the Christ. He believed that, until the birth of Jesus, God had not revealed himself in a direct and fully personal way. With Jesus, a new mode of self-revelation took effect. It involved not just Jesus but the whole Trinity. The three persons of the Trinity have no meaning apart from Jesus as an incarnate god. Bushnell found all trinity formulas full of contradictions or even sheer nonsense. Most involved tricks in the use of language. The Unitarian critique well expressed the problems of rationalizing three gods in one. But the Unitarian answer – the complete unity of God – removed the most vital content in Christianity. To Bushnell, the Trinity was an essential doctrine of the church, although he admitted that it was not a scriptural doctrine. In fact, the New Testament had few if any doctrines. It did have the Trinity, but not as a doctrine or even a clearly developed concept. Concepts are least useful when the Trinity is at issue.

Bushnell simply refused to engage the ontological issue, the problem of the ultimate nature of either God or the three persons who represent God to humans – the Father, Son, and Holy Spirit. Note that, until the Christ, God was not properly a Father. Thus, the unitary God, the ultimate ground, is not the Father any more than he ("it") is the Son. But God, to make his salvation known to humans, chose the best possible means – the three persons of the Trinity. These persons are presented in the scriptures, confronted in experience, but are beyond any conceptual rationalizations. God had to become incarnate to become a savior god. A god without incarnation remains as cold and aloof as Brahmin. But no incarnation can be identical to God. Neither can such incarnations be modes of God or essentially one with God. Bushnell had no good tag for his view. The three persons are, given the context and purpose, the necessary means for God to reconcile humans to himself, to bring them, and with them society and nature, back to complete harmony and beauty. Each of the three persons is necessary for the fullest revelation of God to humans, and Bushnell spent much time justifying the necessity in each case. He lamely referred to his view as an "instrumental" trinity. But, obviously, it left dangling all the traditional intellectual puzzles and was not satisfactory either to Unitarians or to traditional Congregationalists.

Never, with any confidence, would Bushnell speculate about whether the three persons of the Trinity inhered in the infinite one. The most he ever conceded to the orthodox was that it seemed to him most reasonable to assume that these persons represented an eternal form of self-expression or revelation in God. In this sense, the persons were in some figurative sense with God eternally, as if God was in a certain place. This is only to demonstrate the foolishness of trying to settle such impossible dilemmas. But given that these persons were the needed revelations of God, not essentially harder to fathom in their depths than nature as a divine revelation, Bushnell insisted on their full personhood. They were three different personalities, three substances, three powers. And they were superhuman, divine persons, with all the characteristics that humans, in their limited understanding, attribute to gods. Among such attributes of gods is a much greater power to impede or redirect natural laws or, in common language, to perform miracles. In function and effect, Bushnell believed in three proximate gods for Christians, but in some sense dependent gods. They are not the infinite one but are powers who come from God. They are very different from the absolute, solitary, unitary God that humans can affirm but never comprehend. They are gods with us, analogous to us, familiar to us, approachable. They bring God to us. Their inner nature remains mysterious, but only in degree more mysterious than the nature of angels and humans. In a functional sense, Bushnell applauded a type of polytheism and lamented the cold and forbidding aspects of any strict monotheism. Humans need three gods, in the literal sense of three quite distinctive divine personalities. But such a functional polytheism in no way, he believed, undermined the oneness of ultimate reality or the unknown God that we have to accept intellectually but who remains aloof from us until he approaches us as Father, Son, and Spirit. In this analysis, Bushnell was very close to numerous Hindu theologians, who defend the needed richness of Indian polytheism against the background of an infinite Brahmin.

Involved in this view of the Trinity seemed to be a rejection not only of all traditional trinity formulas but also of the human and divine essence of Jesus. For Bushnell, none of the prevalent views of Jesus worked. His ready response was to withdraw from the battlefield, to rest content in what is beyond our ken. But no one would let him retreat. He saw Jesus as personlike but as a divine person, not therefore similar to humans. Jesus was one person, not two. A divine person, as a person, shared much with humans, but the distinction was vital. Thus, Bushnell seemed to deny the humanity of Jesus and never quite found words to disarm those who so charged. Even to chart the overlap of divine and human traits in Jesus' inner nature required knowledge not open to humans. After all, both humans and Jesus are supernatural beings. They have a mind or soul. Jesus had one soul, not two. Bushnell ridiculed Christians who tried to partition Jesus, to attribute the temptations and growth and suffering to his human soul and the miracles to a divine Jesus. But Jesus, the divine being, the incarnate god, was the only one who suffered and performed miracles. Both acts were appropriate to his personhood, as the New Testament abundantly attested. The New Testament said nothing about two natures in one, and the early church knew nothing of such nonsense.

With his presentation of himself to humans in the Trinity, God began the final drama of reconciliation. But even in his understanding of the central doctrines of the Pauline scheme of salvation – the atonement, justification, regeneration, sanctification – Bushnell was appropriately original and heterodox, at least by the standards of most of his contemporaries. Space does not allow even an approximation of his subtle position. Once again, his analysis of such doctrines often hinged on language, on its limitations and on its figurative uses. He could not accept the traditional doctrine of a substitutional atonement. Commercial and penal images horrified him. Jesus did not suffer and die (Bushnell saw his ministry as one, with his death only a climax and not essentially different from other suffering) to ransom humans from Satan, to appease God's wrath and so to assume the burden of sinfulness and allow a just god to suspend the penalties attached to sin, to assume a debt owed to God, or to fit any of a dozen other inexact and, to Bushnell, demeaning images of God's work in salvation. On the other hand, Bushnell did not retreat into a weak version of the atonement, such as those which pictured Jesus as the example of righteousness for humans to follow. Instead, he engaged, in several essays and over many years, in a penetrating inquiry into forgiveness and the conditions of forgiveness. Jesus did bring forgiveness to humans. In this sense he atoned for them. In this sense he was a sacrifice for them.

Forgiveness is very difficult. It requires one not to repudiate righteous judgment, not to suspend esthetic repulsions at the ugly acts of others, but to seek to make brothers of sinners. It is, in a sense, a tactic of rehabilitation, but a very difficult tactic for the one who forgives. Few humans ever forgive. True forgiveness requires one to enter into the lives of others, to see the world as they do, to suffer their anguish and guilt, to identify with their wounded and beleaguered egos. To atone for another is to suffer with and for another and in this sense assume her burden. Such atonement may or may not work its intended effect. It may or may not transform another. The forgiven person may not be open to such concern and generosity on the part of another. The forgiven person may refuse to become a sister. In the case of the profound transformation involved in regeneration, Bushnell knew that no one could appropriately respond without divine help, without the prompting of the Spirit.

But note the power of such forgiveness. Like no other act, it touches the heart of another, for the sinner (one who may have wronged you in the worst possible way) may not be able to resist your suffering, for which the sinner now must take responsibility. Like nothing else, such authentic forgiveness forces people to confront themselves, to enter into agonizing self-evaluation. It may lead to true repentance. The effect of this is a transformed person, in a sense a new person. The atonement brings two estranged people together as brothers. It makes them one. It means at-one-ment.

To forgive is to solicit reconciliation. To Bushnell, forgiveness does not suspend law or do away with the penal effects of law. One forgiven, one reconciled, has gained a great deal. But the past misdeeds are not thereby erased or forgotten. Nor is one beyond continuing suffering because of those memories. In a legal system, forgiveness does not erase the proper punishment. A forgiven thief may still face a fine or imprisonment. But if the forgiveness truly reconciles and transforms, he will not steal again. In a legal sense, certain punitive laws may remain in effect only so long as they serve certain ends, such as conviction and a confessed need for help. Jesus fulfilled the old law and initiated a new law and covenant. For those who became part of this covenant, the old penalties no longer applied. For those who did not become part of the new covenant, the old penalties remained in place. In this sense, the special form of forgiveness, or atonement, reflected in Jesus' ministry did remove a legal penalty, but Bushnell was not comfortable with this type of language. He saw the long-term goal of God as reconciliation, not damnation, which was only a necessity tied to freedom. Bushnell did not want, in any way, to paint God as a being who relished punishment. The reason for punishment had been moral, not the fulfillment of some abstract conception of justice. God had several, fully integrated, and complementary attributes, with justice and mercy among them. These attributes are not of necessity in conflict, but each suits a particular occasion and purpose. In the context of effective forgiveness, and authentic reconciliation, punishment is not appropriate, except in the sense that past actions continue to haunt those who did them.

This view of atonement permeated Bushnell's understanding of the whole sequence of events involved in reconciliation. In a sense, his was a more irenic view than that of most Calvinists. But he so presented his plan of salvation as to leave both Calvinists and Arminians mystified. He was not clearly one or the other or, more exactly and by intent, both at once. He affirmed justification by faith as the heart of the gospel. But he then gave a somewhat idiosyncratic definition of both faith and justification. He always defined faith, that which justifies, as trust or consent to the Christ. One has faith when one properly perceives, and responds appropriately to, a suffering savior and a prompting spirit. For anyone who is open to the forgiveness of Jesus and to the life of understanding and suffering, even unto death, that manifested such forgiveness, then reconciliation, at-oneness, consent, trust, and love are natural responses.

It is in this sense that God's grace, as given in the forgiving Son, is irresistible. But clearly the element of irresistibility is moral and esthetic, a matter of what appeals, not what commands. Such a view is completely consistent with Calvinism. And, in the larger perspective of the infinite God, Bushnell always affirmed that any regeneration is within the providence of God. God willed it. He elected those saved. This is the only pious way to view salvation from the divine perspective. At the same time, the transformation in humans is moral, a matter of a new perception, a new sense, a new character. It is only a dramatic and vitally important example of how humans respond to experience, how they grow morally, how they accumulate a new identity. In this case they assume an identity close to that of the Christ, for they come to share in his righteousness. Arminians tried, by their inadequate confessions, to make just this point. It may be misleading, a fully unjustified use of language, to talk of a newly gained trust in the Christ as a choice. Trust may involve choices, or motivate choices, but trust in itself is not a choice. Yet the Arminians correctly identified what is true in any relationship between powers or spirits – a mutuality, a fully involved and free response one to another. Subjectively considered, the language of election and predestination is inadequate to express this fact. As always, Bushnell found truth, and limitation, in all descriptions of the Christ-human relationship. Instead of rejecting all such limited descriptions because they were limited, Bushnell affirmed all of them because they were complementary.

To be justified, Bushnell argued, is to be made righteous. Again, he rejected juristic images. Regeneration, as a response to forgiveness, means that one gains a new character. One becomes righteous or shares in the righteousness of the Christ. By a careful analysis of the root meanings of the New Testament words for *justification,* Bushnell tried to prove that justification meant "to make just" or righteous. Clearly, such an understanding subverted hard Calvinist positions, those in which justification entailed a human assumption of the righteousness of the Christ, but not by becoming righteous oneself. To Bushnell, the cross was a symbol of a ministry and a life of healing and empathetic suffering for others; it was climactic but still only one extreme example of such a ministry. It had, for him, almost no sacrificial meaning. The crucifixion was not as central to Bushnell as it has to be to anyone who sees the death of Jesus as the only soteriologically important event – a sin sacrifice, one necessary to appease God or to make it possible for him, in his justice, to forgive sinners. Bushnell's stress on the change of heart, the newly gained trust or benevolence, moves the focus away from the satisfaction of God and all but merges regeneration and sanctification. Bushnell acknowledged that regeneration, as faith or trust, was at least a full promise of sanctification or even a type of incipient sanctification. But he resisted any literal perfectionism and again remained within the increasingly fuzzy boundaries of Calvinist orthodoxy. For one in Christ, the lures of the flesh remain and ever tempt. Thus, the full attainment of the righteousness of the Christ, in deed, awaits the death of the body. But one's character, consisting of one's deepest motives, is Christlike at the time of regeneration.

Bushnell had no elaborate eschatology. In so many ways he was a representative Victorian Christian. He saw human history as progressive. Slowly, under God's prompting, and in due time, humans moved back toward reconciliation with God. It was not that Bushnell ignored all the remaining evils or that he thought corporate redemption was near. But the direction was clear, the path now upward. He hoped that the church could keep expanding, that its message of a suffering savior would win over more and more of the world's population. His very hopes betrayed his own parochialism and myopia. He too often reflected the smug assurances of race, sex, class, and nationality. He too easily made the kingdom an inevitable outcome of a historical process already aimed in the right direction.

Bushnell was perhaps most distinctive among American theologians in rejecting any purely individual salvation. Individuals were linked to society and to institutions, and these in turn were rooted in a sustaining natural order. Sin and corruption permeated all, and any meaningful redemption would involve all of these. Later Christians, concerned about environmental issues, or the overpowering role of collectivities or groups, would find Bushnell prophetic.

His corporate emphasis informed the essays that became his most famous and enduring book – *Christian Nurture*. This series of essays, most not tightly linked to his theological arguments, had an enormous impact on religious education in the nineteenth century, on the Sunday school movement, and possibly on patterns of child rearing in Christian families. In a sense, Bushnell rejected a century of developments among American evangelicals and wanted to move back to the early Puritans. Unlike the state churches of Europe, the newly arrived Puritans accepted for baptism only church members' infants. They, like most Calvinists, viewed baptism as the Christian replacement of circumcision under the Jewish covenant and as an initiation of children into the covenanted community that made up the local church. Among Reformed Christians of all types, the baptism of infants had offered some assurance to parents that their children, should they die young, were in the church and were not subject to damnation. The assurance involved assumptions about God's mercy or his likely decision to bestow saving grace on all such doomed children. Left in a much more precarious position were the unbaptized children of nonmembers.

Bushnell believed that, in time, New England Congregationalists had lost the assurance, and the commitment, involved in this sacrament for children. The explosive revivals in the mid-eighteenth century, and again early in the nineteenth, changed the way parents viewed their children. The early revivals were clearly spontaneous works of the Spirit, and Bushnell honored them as such. But soon the revivals became planned, contrived, highly emotional times of harvest, and with this everyone soon regarded conversion as an intense, crisis-like, even explosive event. This was the way one became a Christian. Parents soon accepted the fact that they would have to await such a conversion for their children and that it would most likely occur in a seasonal revival meeting. Meantime, they often accepted, as if inevitable, a turbulent adolescent period, when young people would sow their wild oats. Some even tended to correlate youthful sinfulness with a thorough conversion, as if one needed to dam up a plethora of bad deeds in order to have plenty to repent of at the time of a revival. As a parish minister, as a father who had lost a dear son, Bushnell was horrified by this mentality. He tried to correct the errors involved in it.

No one dissented from part of Bushnell's message. He emphasized the duty of parents to rear their children within the church, more by Christian example than by rigid discipline. In his practical suggestions he reflected liberal pedagogical theories of his age. What worried the orthodox was what seemed a denial of the Pauline scheme of salvation, the centrality of a regenerative experience. Bushnell, with his emphasis on the covenanted community, or the corporate dimensions of salvation, argued that properly reared children literally grow up in the church, without any memory of a time when they were in need of a special saving grace. As far back as they could remember, they had loved and trusted Jesus and had tried to be obedient to him. Bushnell believed that the children of the covenant, even at baptism, in some sense entered the church, the ark of salvation. God even so early in their life extended his grace to them. This did not mean baptismal remission, in the Roman Catholic sense, but rather baptism as a symbol of what God had promised to faithful parents and of the grace he granted their children. This view placed very high obligations on parents, and Bushnell clearly used his essays as effective sermons directed at parents in his congregation, as had Samuel Hopkins two generations earlier. He almost made them responsible for the salvation of their own children. At times, Bushnell seemed to move close to a type of inherited salvation, generation after generation, and also to a more liturgical and corporate form of church life. He clearly preferred such a normal, regular, orderly path to Christian discipleship over a disorderly conversion at revival meetings. If parents were faithful in the nurture of their children, such revivals need function only for the conversion of adults outside the church. He wanted to count baptized children as members of the church, admit them freely to the communion table, and as soon as possible, with their growth and their more sophisticated understanding of their already existing faith, confirm them and admit them to the privileges (voting) of adult members.

Bushnell continued to meditate on theological issues until his death in 1876. After his retirement in 1859, he was plagued by ill health but nonetheless completed his three most systematic books. He was by then an esteemed citizen of Hartford, much involved in civic affairs (he helped design one of its parks) and no longer viewed as a heretic. In a sense, mainstream Congregationalism had caught up with his views.

It is too tempting to classify Bushnell as the first modernist theologian in America. The label is anachronistic in his case, and not because of his determined opposition to Darwin. He rejected, as emphatically as Hodge, all forms of pantheistic idealism. Despite his flexible mode of interpreting scripture, he still affirmed the Bible as the main source of knowledge about God when the Spirit aided one's understanding. Much more than Taylor, and with more nuances than Hodge, he continuously studied the Bible and tried to fit all his doctrines to the Word.

He, like Hodge, wanted Christians to accept, and incorporate, the proven truths discovered by scientists, but in no sense did he see in scientific knowledge a second and equal source of knowledge about spiritual matters. In fact, as a near-transcendentalist, he tended to subordinate such physical knowledge to its analogical and figurative uses in probing the spiritual realm beyond nature. Beyond this, he was very much a creature of time and place, of the comfortable business elite in Hartford who came to his church, of the unwarranted optimism of his Victorian age, of the class and gender assumptions that only a Theodore Parker dared challenge.

Bushnell was a Christian spiritualist. He always sought the guidance of the Holy Spirit, much as had earlier Quakers. He was intrigued by types of popular spiritualism. Maybe mediums did contact hidden spirits. He noted, with a sense of loss, the absence of the spiritual gifts so prized by the early apostles. He believed in the reality of demonic spirits. He thought that glossolalia and even healing were possible gifts of the spirit in the modern age, and in his old age he reported something close to a spiritual healing of a close friend. In these and other ways, he was not at all "modern."

THE WORK of Taylor, Hodge, and Bushnell was at the center of doctrinal controversies during their lifetimes. Each man had tremendous influence on clerical and even lay opinion within the Calvinist tradition. Hodge helped articulate a Princeton position in theology that survived until the 1920s, a theological position that won broadest acceptance in Old School Presbyterianism and subsequently in the southern Presbyterian church. The competing positions of Hodge and Taylor were at the heart of the rancorous split between New School and Old School within Presbyterianism in 1837 (see the next chapter). Taylor's views led to an ongoing theological dialogue among Congregationalists. Bushnell's views likewise stimulated intense debate among Congregationalists, and after the Civil War he became an inspiration, or a point of reference, for dozens of ecumenically oriented, moderate evangelicals in several denominations. But even as they struggled to preserve the essential truths and consolations of the traditional faith, evangelical Christians faced frightful new challenges from both scholarship and natural science. Only Bushnell, and he obliquely, offered a possible pathway through these new challenges.

CHAPTER 8

Storm Clouds on the Evangelical Horizon

*T*he age of interdenominational cooperation, and soaring Protestant hopes, ended after 1840. The leeway for ecumenical cooperation and the authority of confessions became points of controversy within all the Reformed denominations, but most of all for Presbyterians. For most ministers and laypeople, the critical issues still involved salvation doctrine and in some sense almost always the elusive differences between Calvinists and Arminians. What was evident to perceptive observers – scholarly and intellectual challenges to the received understanding of the Bible and scientific challenges to Semitic cosmology as well as to biblical versions of history – remained small clouds on the horizon until the Civil War era. Before that, sectional division related to slavery proved most intractable.

Sectional Divisions among Methodists and Baptists

After 1830, the mainline churches splintered into several new denominations, with most separations related in some way to the divisive issue of slavery. Before the Civil War, American Presbyterians had divided into four large bodies and at least five smaller ones. The Methodists, as part of an enduring pattern, suffered the secession of small splinter groups and then separated between north and south in 1844. Baptists had never joined in any tight ecclesiastical organization, but the largest coalition of Baptists split north and south. Congregationalists, after the traumatic separation of the Unitarian minority in 1825, maintained an uneasy, doctrinally conflicted unity, largely because of regional concentration and near unanimity in opposition to slavery (but not on the proper strategy to solve the problem). Only the less evangelical Reformed confessions avoided major divisions.

In 1830 almost all Methodists were united in the largest denomination in America. It continued to grow rapidly. Methodists also had the tightest episcopal system in America. The church was national, but with a higher percentage of members from Maryland and farther south. Of all the mainstream churches, it had taken the strongest early stand against slavery. It had to compromise on the issue, but at the national level, as reflected in its quadrennial general conferences, it continued to condemn the evils of slavery even as it accepted slave owners into fellowship. Southern Methodists rarely defended slavery in principle but only as a necessary expedient, and Methodists in the South did more than any other denomination to fund and staff an effective mission to slaves.[1]

In 1843 a group of strongly antislavery, or abolitionist, Methodists in New York State insisted on agitating the issue, against the prohibition of their bishops. They separated rather than submit. They formed the small Wesleyan Methodist church (only twenty-two ministers at the split), which admitted laymen as delegates to its conferences, dropped the title of bishop, condemned membership in secret orders, and espoused the holiness doctrines of John Wesley. Later, this meant that the Wesleyans would become a part of a much larger holiness movement (based on belief in Wesleyan perfection or full sanctification). Another splinter in 1860 led to the Free Methodist church. The title had multiple meanings. The separating ministers had failed to gain several goals within the parent church – free pews, free soil, and free church government. They, like the Wesleyans, abolished the centralized hierarchy and emphasized the holiness doctrine. In their opposition to the power of bishops, these splinters reflected the spirit of the abortive Republican Methodist movement, which followed the establishment of the Methodist Episcopal church in 1784, and a small Methodist Protestant church formed in 1830.

By agitating the pew issue, the Free Methodists embarrassed not only mainstream Methodists but most American Protestants. The pew system has been all but forgotten in most churches, but in some cases as late as the early twentieth century it remained a favored method of church financing. With the disestablishment of colonial churches (as late as 1833 in Massachusetts), all congregations had to raise their own funds to build and maintain sanctuaries and to pay ministers. This proved difficult. Churches tried, with small success, to rely on appeals to members. A few, where the law allowed, even used lotteries or other games of chance. Most, with some moral qualms and frequent apologies, adopted either the older practice of selling pews or the newer and more lucrative one of renting them. The way the system worked reinforced class distinctions. The best-placed or most conspicuous pews rented for more than back pews. The location of a family pew in a church was a conspicuous symbol of social standing. Affluent and ambitious people rented pews, in some congregations even bid for choice ones when they became vacant, for quite crass social reasons. Poor people could not afford pews and often had to stand for services or sit in stigmatized free sections or galleries.

The pew system was most deeply entrenched in Episcopal and Presbyterian congregations and worked more effectively in cities than in rural areas. Of all the major denominations, the Methodists most resisted pew rentals, accepting them after 1856 with a sense of guilt (the General Conference never recommended pew rentals and only belatedly permitted such at the congregational level). The practice seemed to war completely against the egalitarian Wesleyan tradition. When the first few urban congregations began the practice, this documented for the emerging Free Methodists the degree to which some Methodists had accommodated the fashions of the larger world. Gradually, most American congregations would abolish rents, but not without financial strain (no other fund-raising system worked as well). The modern use of annual pledges is the favored substitute, but unless kept fully confidential, pledges also give status and political clout to those who are on record for their generosity. In other words, modern fund-raising techniques still appeal, in subtle ways, to human pride and the desire for power. This is why most small, egalitarian sects have resisted not only rented pews but also annual pledges or committed ministerial salaries, relying instead on free-will offerings.

The sectional break for most Methodists came at the General Conference of 1844. It would be a bitter separation, one that lasted until 1968. Technically, a group of southern annual conferences formed a new denomination in 1845 – the Methodist Episcopal Church, South, because of what had happened at the 1844 General Conference. They insisted that they did not separate in defense of slavery. But the issue underlay their decision. Bishop James Andrews hailed from Georgia (the church at that point had itinerant bishops, without a geographical assignment). He opposed slavery in principle and had worked to convert and educate slaves yet had retained ownership of a black woman who had rejected emancipation. Then, by a second marriage, he gained an unwanted relationship to slaves owned by this wife, even though he deeded these slaves to her. Because of Georgia law the family could not emancipate them, and for humane and religious reasons, Andrews would not sell them. A majority of delegates to the General Conference (ministers from each annual conference) could not accept a slave-owning bishop, despite the unique legal and moral bind that confronted Andrews. They voted to suspend him as bishop for so long as he held slaves. He offered to resign, a tactic that did not satisfy northern delegates, who wanted to establish a principle. Southern delegates also would not accept this solution and saw in the action of the majority a threat to the effectiveness of Methodist ministers in the South, who had to minister to slave owners and who could continue their ministry to slaves only through the cooperation of such owners. As a result of the impasse, the delegates accepted a plan of separation, one that seemed almost amiable at the conference.

The plan for separation, which was of questionably legality, soon led to an embittered controversy. The provisions for the division of denominational property led to friction and eventually litigation. In border areas annual conferences fought for the loyalty of individual congregations. Such was the growing disillusionment over the separation agreement in the North that at the next general conference of the Methodist Episcopal church (1848) a majority of delegates voted to void the 1844 plan of separation, an action without practical meaning but one with symbolic import. This conference even refused to accept formally the one delegate from the Methodist Episcopal Church, South, a fraternal provision of the 1844 plan. Southern Methodists were incensed and long argued that it was the suspension action against Andrews by the conference in 1844 that was illegal; on strictly legalistic grounds they were probably correct (one northern-born bishop, Joshua Soule, adhered to the southern church for procedural reasons). Notably, at the time of the split, over one-fourth of southern Methodists were black. In some conferences this proportion approached one-half.

Until after the Civil War, southern black Methodists remained in the Methodist Episcopal Church, South. But in several cities this denomination sponsored special mission efforts, leading to all-black congregations, some with black ministers but under nominal white supervision. In 1866 the southern church granted to those black members who so desired the right to join a new Colored Methodist Episcopal church, a denomination somewhat stigmatized among blacks by its paternal origins. Meanwhile, in the North two independent but very small black Methodist denominations had formed in Philadelphia and New York City. The two would later argue over priority. Richard Allen, the first black Methodist to receive the first level of ordination (a deacon), helped found an all-black congregation in Philadelphia but because of jurisdictional conflicts separated and formed the African Methodist Episcopal church in 1815–16, with himself as its first bishop. It later published the first black periodical and gained control of the first black denominational college – Wilberforce University. In New York City, a contemporaneous black congregation split in 1821 from its parent congregation to launch the African Methodist Episcopal Zion church. Both sects remained very small until after the Civil War, when they expanded among freedpeople in the South, quickly becoming the two largest black Methodist denominations, but not nearly as large as black Baptist denominations.

No significant doctrinal issues underlay the Methodist split of 1844–45. Strains aplenty existed within Methodism, but they cut across sectional boundaries. Already visible in 1844 were developing cleavages over the Wesleyan doctrine of perfection. An increasing proportion of congregations, and some bishops, all but ignored sanctification or the second step, and new Methodist hymnals referred to it less often. This evasion only reinforced the zeal of a holiness faction, which was becoming more self-conscious, and assertive, by the Civil War. Beginning in 1837, the most famous holiness leader, Phoebe Palmer, began rallying the second blessing advocates at Tuesday meetings in her home. Among the holiness faction, older practices, such as the class system and love feasts and the reliance on summer camps as tools of evangelism, remained central. Despite these internal divisions, the main southern and northern branches of Methodism avoided a holiness schism until the last decade of the nineteenth century.

One cannot talk collectively about Baptists. They came in too many flavors. But the largest American Baptist fellowship loosely united the former separating Baptists, those moderately Calvinist Baptists who separated from congregational churches during the Great Awakening in New England and whose missionaries soon recruited a large following in the South. They had no formal denominational body but united in local associations, and after 1814, congregations throughout the country sent delegates to a triennial missionary society, the General Convention. Even this much cooperation alienated many local associations, including several in the South. The mission-antimission conflict simmered for years and led to the popular appellation "Missionary Baptists" for those who participated in the General Convention. Most noncooperating associations remained independent, but a minority organized into Primitive Baptist associations, with the first in North Carolina in 1826. The Primitives took a hyper-Calvinistic and separatist position. They believed in a type of predestinarian determinism. God chose his elect, and nothing that humans could do had anything to do with salvation. Thus, they rejected human means, including mission activity or even Sunday schools, refused to join in any interdenominational activities, rejected ministerial training of any type, accepted only free-will offerings, and would not commune even with other Baptists.[2]

Baptists were not in a position for joint stands on any issue, internal or external. Most white Baptists in the South accepted slavery. A few ministers joined more able Presbyterian apologists for it. But at the local level, some Baptist associations were even more zealous in seeking black converts than the Methodists, and in rural areas they achieved some truly biracial congregations. When a majority of northern delegates to the General Convention took a strong stand against slavery (they would not admit a slave owner as a candidate for foreign mission assignments), the southerners decided to separate and form their own missionary convention, which they did in 1845. The separation was friendly, in part because the conventions were voluntary organizations without any ecclesiastical authority. Yet, at the time, Baptists recognized that this was a momentous parting of the ways, as symbolically significant as ecclesiastical splits among Methodists and Presbyterians.

Much more than in the case of the Methodists, the Baptist separation soon marked a growing divergence of style if not of doctrines. By the Civil War the General Convention was a quite distinct denomination, with no chance of any early reunification with a more rigorously orthodox and more separatist Southern Convention. The General Convention remained a loose association of northern Baptists, most of British origin, until the early twentieth century. In 1905 its affiliated associations created a more centralized Northern Baptist Convention, one modeled institutionally on the Southern Baptist Convention. It later took the name American Baptist Convention and in 1972, with a merger with some black Baptists, changed its name to American Baptist Churches in the USA. This northern Baptist denomination suffered intense conflict over fundamentalism in the 1920s but survived these as a broadly inclusive, ecumenical, and socially active denomination, one closely related to northern Presbyterians and Congregationalists.

The Southern Baptist Convention began as something more than a missionary organization. The more centralized convention established dependent boards not only for missions but also for publishing and education. Such a near-denominational structure further offended the Primitive Baptists and helped stimulate a type of Baptist restorationism eventually known as the Landmark Movement. It influenced most Southern Baptists but never captured the convention. Its most influential advocate, James R. Graves, editor of the *Tennessee Baptist*, affirmed the primitive origins of baptism and the continuous history of this true church from the age of the apostles. This gave full sanction to Baptist practices, including the purpose and method of baptism. Thus, Graves and a growing body of disciples throughout the South advocated a separatist congregationalism similar to that espoused by the later Churches of Christ. Landmarkers rejected all cooperative and ecumenical agencies, accepted to communion only those properly baptized, and would not even transfer membership from one congregation to another. Only a minority of Southern Baptists accepted such an extreme version of primitivism and localism, but the pressures from the Landmark "reformers" helped strengthen the localistic and exclusive characteristics of the southern church. One faction of Landmark Baptists, centered in Texas and Oklahoma, would form a separate denomination in 1924 (the American Baptist Association).

By the Civil War a majority of black Christians were Baptist and would remain so after emancipation. Generally, they reflected a very evangelical version of Southern Baptism. Gradually they separated into their own black congregations and local and regional associations. A northern missionary convention dated from 1840 and a national agency from 1864 – the American Baptist Missionary Convention. In 1880 black Baptists, largely in the South, organized a foreign missionary convention, followed by two additional agencies. These provided the foundation for a full denomination in 1894 – the National Baptist Convention of the United States of America. Unfortunately, this denomination split in 1915 because of controversies over publications, with the larger splinter group taking the name National Baptist Convention, USA, Incorporated. Since then, two additional schisms have created four denominations out of the National Baptist family, collectively a black Baptist empire that is second in size only to the largely white Southern Baptist Convention. Contrary to most present assumptions, the separation in the South of black congregations from white-dominated parent churches was often friendly, with white congregations remaining helpful patrons of black offshoots. But most of the educational aid in behalf of freedpeople came from northern Baptists. They had both the means and the will.

The Presbyterian and Congregational Plan of Union

For Presbyterians and Congregationalists the sectional issues mixed with doctrinal conflict. This was only appropriate for the two American denominations that still professed their complete allegiance to the reforms of John Calvin and John Knox.

In Scotland, Ireland, and then America, Presbyterians had been almost fatally schismatic. Yet, in the new American Republic at least, a majority of Presbyterians remained in the Presbyterian Church of the United States of America. All others were either in small, struggling splinter sects, including various alignments of the old Covenanters (Reformed) and Seceders (Associate Synod), or in the regionally concentrated but midsized Cumberland Presbyterian church.

The seceding churches of Scotland played a small role in American Presbyterianism. In the eighteenth century both Covenanters and Seceders migrated from Scotland and Northern Ireland and founded small congregations in America. Several divisive issues (such as burgher and antiburgher) in Britain had no meaning in America. Thus, the majority of Reformed congregations merged with the Seceders to create the Associate Reformed Presbyterian church in 1783. Divisive issues led to several schisms within this church and to a merger of several strands in 1858 in the United Presbyterian church (much later it would merge with northern Presbyterians). Unfortunately for simplicity, several splinters survived. One small cluster of Reformed congregations refused even the 1783 merger and suffered at least two schisms in the nineteenth century but continued as the Reformed Presbyterian church until a merger in 1965 united it with a small, aggressively orthodox splinter from northern Presbyterianism, Carl McIntire's Bible Presbyterian church. This denomination, the Reformed Presbyterian Church, Evangelical Synod, merged in 1982 with the Presbyterian Church in America, a 1973 splinter largely made up of conservatives in the southern Presbyterian church who resisted its move toward merger with the northern body. Reformed Presbyterians upheld a distinctive doctrinal position. In addition to rigid adherence to Westminster, they rejected hymn singing and worked for decades to get the

United States to affirm, by constitutional amendment, its status as a Christian nation. In effect, they wanted to revive the Solemn League and Covenant. Since they failed in this effort (not without widespread popular support in the nineteenth century), early Covenanters refused to vote or otherwise participate in a secular government.

Most Seceders merged into various small sects in the nineteenth century, but one small component remained independent – the Associate Reformed Presbyterian church. It resulted from a small synod in the Carolinas that rejected the merger that created the United Presbyterian church in 1858. Today the Associate Reformed Synod is conspicuous largely in North and South Carolina. The various Reformed and Associate denominations provided an occasional refuge for dissident members of the larger Presbyterian bodies, offered a rationale for rigid confessionalism, and developed rather elaborate and carefully argued critiques of popular revivalism or of hymn singing.

The Scottish dissenting sects never had broad appeal in America. Their rejection of new revival techniques, as well as their rigid adherence to Westminster and primitive forms of worship, made them a curious but ineffective minority, a minority that bears closer comparison to Primitive Baptists than to the main Presbyterian bodies. What the Presbyterian Church in the United States of America most feared was evangelical and Arminian splinters. It first suffered these, in a major way, by the defection of the Cumberland Presbytery in 1810. The Cumberlands kept what they saw as desirable in Presbyterianism, including it polity and its doctrine of perseverance, and added the major appeals of Methodism (complete atonement, the innocence of infants, a cooperative human role in regeneration) plus the evangelical tools best perfected by Methodists, such as camp meetings, the circuit system, and a confessional devotional style. In the Southwest, at every point of direct competition, the Cumberlands were able to attract more new members than the old church. The Methodists bested both denominations.

In northern Ohio, and most of all in New York State, the mainstream denomination grew most rapidly. It did so in part because many ministers in its presbyteries accepted the new revival techniques of Charles Finney, in part because it worked out a cooperative plan with New England Congregationalists, and in part because its middle-class profile and ethic appealed to generally literate farmers, artisans, and professionals in areas dominated by Yankee settlers. In both North and South, the nineteenth-century Presbyterians rose on the social and economic scale, a fact that both pleased and at times embarrassed its leadership.

Growth in the North, and among former Congregationalists, created almost uncontrollable tensions among Presbyterians. These came to a head in the 1837 split between New School and Old School, but tensions had been growing for a century. Of all the schisms in the nineteenth century, this was the best publicized in the middle period and by far the most complex and most far-reaching in its implications.

The Presbyterian crisis indirectly involved slavery, which was a necessary but far from sufficient condition for the split. The schism joined issues of doctrine, style, and polity. More than in most controversies, serious theological positions also competed. From their first synod in 1707, Presbyterians claimed a truly national church. Presbyteries soon existed in all regions of the country, although the church long retained its greatest strength in areas of heavy Scotch-Irish settlement or migration. In the eighteenth century, the New Side–Old Side schism presaged the split to come one hundred years later, for the church united some rather disparate groups. But in the eighteenth century, slavery had not yet exasperated doctrinal and stylistic differences.

The church had a dual heritage, from English Puritans who adopted a presbyterial polity and moved to America and from the overwhelming mass of Scotch-Irish migrants in the mid-eighteenth century. English Presbyterians, who at first dominated the church from New Jersey north, shared much with the New England Puritans, worked out informal alliances, drew from the same theological sources, and never wanted a rigidly confessional church. They joined in interdenominational revivals, stressed the experiential aspects of Christianity, yearned for a broader evangelical unity, and worked for the types of reform that would purify the larger society. The Scotch-Irish often, but not always, wanted full subscription to Westminster, an ordered Presbyterial polity with rigid discipline, an educated and orthodox but not necessarily a revivalistic ministry, and a rather passive but not separatist role in society. Above all, they resisted New England influences in church life, in doctrine, and in theology. They jealously guarded the distinctive attributes of the old Scottish church. Such divisions led to the New Side–Old Side split in 1743, a division not fully healed by reunification in 1858.

These divisions resurfaced during the great revivals at the beginning of the nineteenth century. It is difficult to characterize the differences, except by extreme polarities or ideal types that rarely fit individuals. From the time of the New Side split on, some ministers and congregations continued to reflect a very experiential religious style, one characterized by an arduous conversion (conviction, repentance, and finally comfort), by a warm and affectionate style of devotion and worship, and by a commitment to missions and reform. These Presbyterians turned their extended, intercongregational communion seasons into converting revivals. They welcomed alliances with other evangelical Christians, cooperated with Methodists in revivals, but above all found affinities with like-minded Congregationalists in New England. These Presbyterians remained reasonably orthodox but did not view creeds and confessions, or small nuances of doctrine, as of greatest importance. They gladly affirmed the Westminster Confession, although many did not want a formal or rigid subscription for new ministers. They gave priority to the Bible and nourished hopes of broader ecumenical cooperation, particularly in mission work. They were the puritans of Presbyterianism in the sense of high moral expectations. They tended most often to use church discipline for moral, rather than doctrinal, lapses on the part of ministers and laypeople.

It is hard to characterize the other side, if in fact there was one other side. The clearest opposite would be the Reformed and Associate synods, for they alone rejected all new revival methods, including hymn singing, adhered in every particular to Westminster, made doctrinal purity the test of membership, and rejected every form of ecumenical cooperation. Few in the main denomination went so far. But at least a minority, most from the Scotch-Irish who still dominated the denomination in the South and West, moved toward this subscriptionist, rational, confessional extreme. Of course, they claimed the label "evangelical," professed their desire for authentic (ordered and scriptural) revivals, and accepted some measure of interdenominational cooperation, particularly in the heady years of the new century. But when ecumenism seemed to threaten the distinctive traditions and rigorous Calvinism of the Scottish church, they fled back toward confessionalism. Their outlook, in most respects, matched that of old Calvinists in New England who had also opposed new revival techniques.

The more confessional and scholastic Calvinists faced an impossible dilemma with the widespread revivals from 1800 to 1805. In ways they could not control, revivalism became linked with doctrinal compromises and incipient Arminianism. As the more conservative Presbyterian ministers tried to control emotional excesses, or to counter sentimentalism or overt Arminianism, they seemed to place themselves in opposition to the great revival itself. The Kentucky Synod, through inept tactics and a complete unwillingness to compromise, practically forced the Cumberland Presbyterians to separate in 1810. In the old Southwest the church stagnated; it was stigmatized as cold, rational, and elitist by booming Cumberland Presbyterians and Methodists. In eastern Tennessee and the Carolinas, somewhat more revivalistic Presbyterians prevailed and thus averted division.

Revivals throughout New England and New York were at least more decorous than those in the South and West. Here the affinities between Presbyterians and more evangelical Congregationalists broke down most distinctions between the two traditions and allowed the soon infamous 1801 Plan of Union. Throughout the eighteenth century, Presbyterians in New York and New Jersey, and Congregationalists in Connecticut, had worked together so closely that they enjoyed a de facto merger. Ministers moved easily from one confession to another. The associational polity of Connecticut was a loose form of Presbyterianism, whereas Presbyterians of English origin in Connecticut and Long Island were only loosely confessional or wedded to the tight discipline of the Scottish church. The theological affinities were even closer. Jonathan Edwards was as much a Presbyterian as a Congregationalist in sentiment, and ended his career as president of the New Side College of New Jersey. He was a hero to almost all New Side ministers. His disciples (the New Divinity theologians) were evenly divided between Presbyterians and Congregationalists and moved freely back and forth. Jonathan Edwards, Jr., became a Presbyterian minister. The coherent theological system of Samuel Hopkins won widespread approval among Presbyterians in the northern presbyteries of the church and, through one minister, Hezekiah Balch, gained an enduring foothold in East Tennessee (Balch founded Greeneville College, the basis of the later Tusculum College, and a disciple founded Maryville College). But Hopkinsianism became a scandal for conservative Presbyterians, who had nourished profound doubts about Edwards and found in Hopkins several subversive doctrines (an underlying monistic idealism that countered their commonsense dualism, an exaggerated emphasis on benevolence, compromises on the imputation of Adam's sins to all humankind, and above all a theodicy that made God responsible for evil in the world).

The common doctrines, and past cooperation, eased the way for the seemingly sensible Plan of Union, and at first almost no Presbyterians objected to it. The purpose of the plan was to eliminate competition among Congregational and Presbyterian migrants to the West, particularly those in western New York and all of Ohio, where a scarcity of ministers plagued each denomination. The only divisive issue seemed to be polity, not the doctrines essential to salvation. According to the plan, worked out originally between the Presbyterian General Assembly and the General Association of Connecticut but later expanded to other Congregational associations in New England, the two groups would join in their mission to these western areas. The plan followed the earliest attempt by both denominations to establish a home mission agency. By the terms of the plan, congregations formed according to either of the two forms of church government were to welcome ministers from the other, creating what amounted to a joint ministerial fellowship. The congregations continued to conduct business under their own system (for Congregationalists, this meant congregational meetings and elected trustees; for Presbyterians, this meant the traditional session, composed of minister and ruling elders). The plan had some rather complicated formulas for settling conflicts that crisscrossed the two types of church government (such as when a Congregational membership pressed charges against its Presbyterian pastor). The plan also provided for mixed or hybrid congregations, in which a mixed committee administered discipline and in which accused members could, in a sense, choose their appropriate appellate court (Presbyterian members could appeal to their session or, beyond that, to their presbytery; Congregationalists could appeal to all male communicants and, beyond that, to an intercongregational council). In such appeals, committeemen, even if Congregationalists, could sit and act in the appropriate presbytery.[3]

In a strictly legal sense, the plan violated, at several points, the standard Presbyterian discipline. In the early years no one challenged it on these grounds. In practice the plan had an unexpected effect. Most congregations chose to affiliate with presbyteries, whatever the affiliation of their minister, further arresting Congregational growth outside New England. But some converted congregations retained their beloved congregational system. This meant that they elected delegates to their presbytery or synod who were trustees but not elders in the Presbyterian sense. As the more confessional Presbyterians reacted in horror to this violation of discipline, they began to advocate the formal ordination of lay or ruling elders, a practice adopted later in the Old School and southern Presbyterian denominations and eventually in the northern church. Several rapidly growing presbyteries and synods in the North, but particularly those in western New York and the Western Reserve of Ohio, were primarily composed of Congregationalists or former Presbyterians who willingly accepted the polity of Congregationalists at the local level. At least one Congregational association simply joined the Albany Synod, in effect becoming a presbytery without changing the forms of local church government. Thus, somewhat ironically, the effect of the plan was to boost Presbyterian membership in the one area of most rapid growth for the church and the one area where it still won in competition with Baptists and Methodists. At the same time, it loosened or undermined the strict Presbyterian polity and, by the judgment of its conservative critics, even rigorous Calvinist doctrine. The church had more nominal members, but were they really Presbyterians?

The plan was intended for mission areas, where settlers formed new congregations. It reflected the outlook of the most revivalistic Congregationalists, those who increasingly monopolized the label "evangelical." Just like Presbyterian critics, the most rigidly Calvinist Congregationalists were deeply suspicious of the union. But it seemed to work well and encouraged other forms of cooperation. For example, the Presbyterians chose to merge their foreign mission efforts and personnel with a mission board originally formed by Congregationalists (American Board of Commissioners for Foreign Missions) rather than form their own, and Congregationalists joined in the work of the largely Presbyterian Home Missionary Society. These joint efforts combined in the even more broadly based benevolent societies that involved both denominations. But the high point of ecumenical cooperation came in the early 1830s. After that, denominational self-consciousness tended to increase in almost every denomination, and slowly the cooperative enterprises would yield to denominational boards or agencies, with an enormous duplication of services.

The New School–Old School Controversy

Those Presbyterians who were increasingly unhappy with the Plan of Union claimed that it had been unconstitutional from the beginning. These conservatives were largely from synods stretching south from Pennsylvania, with deep divisions within Pennsylvania. By 1830, every general assembly degenerated into struggles between two polarizing factions – those who supported and those who opposed the union. But much more was at stake than polity, as both sides recognized.[4]

One divergence involved revivals. This had been a divisive issue from 1740. It took on new implications after 1820 because of the work of Charles G. Finney. Finney was born in Connecticut but grew up in upstate New York, the scene of his first revival successes. Although he was trained as a lawyer, a conversion experience in 1821 led him almost immediately into a career as a minister. His training and ordination was Presbyterian, but he later left this church either for free Presbyterian congregations, which he helped form in New York City, or for Congregationalism. A gifted preacher, with almost magnetic power over an audience, Finney began his ministerial career as a missionary in the newly settled towns of western New York. In his first year as a revivalist, 1824, he stimulated a series of well-publicized crusades, most in small towns. These featured such wild exercises, including swooning, that Finney was temporarily suspect among leading Congregational and Presbyterian evangelicals, including Lyman Beecher, who must have resented a pulpit competitor. But Finney soon tried to control excesses, met with and impressed Beecher, and began organizing evangelical campaigns in large cities, such as New York and Philadelphia. He wrote manuals on revival methods, crusaded even in Britain, and became so popular and so successful that it was difficult for evangelicals, whatever their doubts about his methods or emerging doctrines, to oppose him. Thus, Finney became the first master of a new religious vocation. Other ordained ministers had devoted most of their time to mission work. Others had locally established reputations by their ability to enflame audiences and win converts. But Finney alone gained a truly national reputation. He was the first of a series of such giants, including Dwight L. Moody, Billy Sunday, and Billy Graham. In many respects, he was also the most sophisticated, except possibly for Moody. He had enormous influence, and his revival efforts gave way later in life to theological writing, reform, and educational leadership (he was president of Oberlin College).

Finneyism became a divisive issue. His new measures were not really new, but he popularized them (extensive planning for scheduled revivals, intensive lay involvement by women as well as men, personal pleading and prayer, invitational hymns, and the clustering of people under conviction at the front of congregations for prayer and special appeals, at what he called the anxious bench, which became the prime symbol of his new methods). Finney organized the first city-wide, interdenominational crusades in America, deliberately downgraded confessional differences, and soon added a distinctively Arminian rationale for a conversion experience that he presented as something easy, rational, and voluntary. Since he moved to an overt Arminian position, stressed his own special version of Christian perfectionism, and reflected a popular form of optimism about the achievement of a perfected kingdom here on earth, Finney was beyond the pale for almost all Presbyterians and most Congregationalists. But his methods were not. Some Presbyterian ministers adopted them, often with great success. Their congregations grew. Opponents were horrified at the contrived, even mechanical aspects of Finney's revivals, as well as the form of appeal that bypassed issues of correct doctrine. Those who became Old School Presbyterians after the split in 1937 almost universally condemned the new methods. At least a large minority within the New School either affirmed them or adopted many of them.

Finney's theology was not an issue in the Presbyterian split. Neither side would defend his doctrines. What the emerging Old School indicted was doctrinal slippage (covert Arminianism) and doctrinal laxity. The northern evangelicals, they charged, simply did not take doctrinal issues very seriously. The northerners were catholic or liberal in outlook, willing to include as ministers those who interpreted the historical creeds and confessions in quite varying ways. Widespread among these "Presbygationists" of the North was admiration for the theology of Nathaniel Taylor and his colleagues at Yale. In no sense did it become the official theology of any presbytery, and some evangelicals did not agree with it but adhered to the continuing and more orthodox Hopkinsianism of the Andover Seminary, but even this was anathema to the Old School.

Taylor, above all, became the symbol of doctrinal subversion. Much of the polemical battle would involve Taylorism, not that the debates did much to clarify the issues. The Old School tried to block the appointment of a Taylorite to a church in Philadelphia, and when this failed they brought him to trial for heresy, but the general assembly eventually reversed a guilty verdict that prevailed for one year. Conservative Presbyterians also brought to trial for heresy a Pennsylvania minister who preached a sermon drawn rather specifically from Taylor. In a complicated procedure, the presbytery eventually denounced some of his doctrines but graciously continued him in his pulpit, a leniency that horrified its predominantly Old School synod, which censored the offending presbytery. When the famous Lyman Beecher resigned his Boston pulpit to accept the presidency of Lane Seminary in Cincinnati, he moved into a presbytery formed under the Plan of Union. After the local presbytery admitted him to fellowship, a rival at Lane brought charges against his doctrines, charges that, in the glare of publicity, the presbytery refused to hear. In 1834 the persistent rival prosecuted Beecher for heresy, slander, and hypocrisy before his presbytery; the heresy involved border-line Taylorite doctrines on depravity. The presbytery, and then on appeal the synod, exonerated Beecher, but the trial aired, for a national audience, the theological issues contested within the church.

This is not the place to analyze Taylor's governmental theology (see the preceding chapter). As he understood it, he remained within the boundaries of Calvinism. Few of his critics agreed. At several points his reinterpretation of Calvinism was substantial enough to warrant the claim that he was an Arminian. In so describing him, and by making the New Haven theology a symbol of northern doctrinal liberalism, the Old School chose well. No other theological tradition better expressed developing tendencies within the evangelical side of both Congregationalism and Presbyterianism, as borne out by the subsequent history of Congregationalism and New School Presbyterianism.

These issues, alone, might have eventually precipitated a Presbyterian schism, but not as early as 1837. Slavery was a final, complicating factor. Attitudes toward slavery did not mesh with the ecumenical and doctrinal differences. Many Old School Presbyterians in the North opposed slavery. But notably, few as yet wanted the church to take a stand on the issue, and few approved of abolitionists or more outspoken antislavery advocates. This is not the place to air the various religious arguments for and against slavery, but it was clear that among evangelicals, many Presbyterians had made the easiest peace with southern slavery. The last strong antislavery statement by the general assembly dated from 1818. The church then successfully avoided the issue until the assembly of 1836, one with a slight New School majority. It was by then clear that the assembly could not much longer suppress the issue. The meeting was soon bogged down with strong antislavery motions from northern synods and opposing ones from the South. When a debate over slavery threatened to split the church immediately, the assembly approved a motion for indefinite postponement. In the critical assembly of 1837, slavery was not an overt issue. But it lay behind the whole strategy of the Old School.

It is not surprising that the emerging factions disagreed on how to address the slavery issue. The New York synods, particularly Genesee, were a hotbed of abolitionism. Northern Presbyterians felt duty-bound to agitate the issue and to force such resolutions as to drive unrepentant southerners from the church. A great evil was at stake. Southern Presbyterians had often moved beyond an expedient defense of an existing and inherently evil institution, but one that allowed no easy or early solution, to an outright defense of the institution. The ablest theologian in the South, James Henley Thornwell, later chair at the strongest Presbyterian seminary in the Deep South, at Columbia, South Carolina, defended the servitude of blacks in the South as the best solution given their situation. Nothing in the Bible condemned such servitude (it did place responsibilities on both master and servant), and plenty of biblical examples seemed to provide a type of endorsement. But Thornwell really tried to convert slavery into nothing more than a form of employment and set such high standards for masters (they had to protect black marriages, teach blacks to read, and instruct them in the Christian faith) that slave owners found his strictures little better than those of abolitionists, particularly when Thornwell tried to get state laws to reflect such high moral demands.

Thornwell recognized that most northern Presbyterians would not accept even his apology for a mild form of servitude. To him, that was largely irrelevant. In theology he was close to his friend Charles Hodge at Princeton, and possibly more brilliant. But unlike Hodge he maintained a very narrow, almost impossibly narrow, conception of the institutional church. Its obligation was limited to its teaching role, to spreading the gospel. He rejected all independent boards and social agencies and did not believe that the church, in its corporate capacity, should take stands on policy issues. Such a restrictive view of the mission of the church meant that northern and southern Presbyterians could remain united, despite their personal conflicts over slavery.

In the South, Christians had two options – defend slavery as a positive good or defend its temporary continuance as a necessary evil but one preferable to all the dire results of emancipation (a position accepted by many Methodists). Christians in the North could, on general moral principles, indict slavery as a sin or they could seek specific biblical sanctions against it. In the battle of biblical exegesis the southerners had an advantage. In the battle of moral principles they were at a disadvantage, and they knew it. They could remain in a national church only if northern representatives, who honestly believed slavery to be evil, would accept them in fellowship as moral persons confronted with an intractable social problem. Increasing numbers of northern Presbyterians would not so accept them. For the conservative majority in the southern church it seemed better to force a division over other issues and thus preclude a later, nasty separation over slavery, when they would appear, to outsiders, at a disadvantage. Given the slavery issue, they could not foresee any amicable compromises on all the other differences. In this estimate they were undoubtedly correct. Yet, as they knew, separation left the slavery issue unresolved.

The victory of the Old School in 1837 proved easy, if premeditated. Old School delegates met in a convention before the convening of the assembly and there perfected their legislation. Since they had a majority in the assembly, they simply voted through their four resolutions. In the critical first resolution, the general assembly affirmed that the 1801 plan was an unconstitutional act by that assembly and had been approved by Connecticut without authority and that such an unnatural and unconstitutional union had led to much confusion and irregularity; thus it declared the Plan of Union abrogated. In two separate resolutions, the general assembly declared that four synods (Western Reserve, Utica, Geneva, and Genesee), all formed under the Plan of Union, no longer had any ecclesiastical connection with the general assembly. A final resolution declared that the operations of the American Home Missionary Society and the American Education Society were exceedingly injurious to the peace and purity of the Presbyterian church and that these organizations should cease to operate in any of its congregations. By these resolutions the Old School rid itself of the four synods with strongest abolitionist sentiment, the four most closely tied to New England Congregationalism and to the New Haven theology, the four most liberal or inclusive in their use of confessions, and the four most vitally involved in ecumenical benevolence and reform.

In the year following this coup, some Presbyterians desperately sought some means of conciliation, but without success. At the general assembly of 1838, the four outcast synods sent delegates, but they were denied seats. At this point these delegates, plus sympathizers still legally in the assembly, withdrew. They formed a new church at a meeting at Auburn and tried to defend their doctrinal orthodoxy in the Auburn Declaration, which became an unofficial bond of union in the new denomination. This separation led to two denominations with exactly the same name, distinguished only by the unofficial labels New School and Old School (legally, the Old School represented the continuing denomination). The division created two large denominations, with the New School only slightly smaller than the Old. In the Deep South only a few congregations, and one presbytery, aligned with the New School. Of course, in the targeted areas of Ohio and New York, almost all remained with the New School. But in between, the denomination split, presbytery by presbytery, congregation by congregation. In the larger South only in Tennessee did a majority of presbyteries choose the New School; most other southern New School congregations were in border states, such as the largely New School Abingdon Presbytery in southwestern Virginia. The Old School kept control of Princeton Seminary, Union at Richmond, and Columbia. The New School kept its two premier seminaries – Auburn and Union of New York – plus some fledgling seminaries in the West. In time, the theological faculty at Princeton, led by Charles Hodge, created the dominant Old School or Princeton theology – conservative, commonsense, and confessional.

Separation brought a type of fragile unity to each of the two Presbyterian bodies, although the New School still contained factions, not the least on the issue of how to deal with slavery. In New England the same doctrinal and attitudinal cleavages continued within Congregationalism, but the congregational polity and common enemy to the left, in the form of Unitarianism, kept the church together, a coalition of factions. In time a majority of Congregationalists would accept the broad, inclusive, nonconfessional outlook of the New School. By the late nineteenth century, the theology of Taylor would seem mild or even conservative.

Because of the restraint of northern Old School Presbyterians, and a general unwillingness to involve the church in political issues, this denomination remained united until the actual outbreak of war. Its leadership continued to accept biblical sanctions for types of servitude and thus to grant fellowship to southern slave owners. More important, the denomination did not believe such social issues were properly an issue for the church, although this stand led a few northern congregations to leave the denomination. At the general assembly of 1861 the issue was now inescapable. Northern delegates ultimately voted a resolution of support for the Union, leading the southern delegates to withdraw. Since the church normally organized along national lines, such a separation was inevitable. Only in December 1861 did commissioners from forty-seven southern presbyteries create the Presbyterian Church of the Confederate States of America. This was, in effect, the southern branch of the Old School.

The New School had already separated over the slavery issue. For a few years, the New School Assembly had tried to accommodate its southern synods, but the overwhelming antislavery sentiment in the church (almost half of its members were in the militant New York synods) made this impossible. Strong resolutions in 1857 led southern delegates to withdraw. They formed a very small denomination, the United Synod. After secession this synod was in a bind, without even one seminary. Thus, formally, its presbyteries voted to merge with the new Confederate church in 1864, but a few congregations resisted this merger and affiliated with the New School. The most important remnant would be in the Union areas of eastern Tennessee, where several congregations remained part of the northern church, as did two colleges. The old Hopkinsianism of early ministers, joined with strong Union allegiances, provided the New School with its one wedge into the South.

By the end of the war the reunion of Old School Presbyterians north and south was all but inconceivable. The wounds of sectional conflict were deep. Thus, the Confederate church remained intact, but reorganized as the Presbyterian Church in the United States. In the North the war brought cooperation between the New School and Old School churches. By its end, the New School seemed more confessional and less ecumenical in outlook (it had adhered fully to the Auburn Declaration), whereas the less numerous Old School, now stripped of its southern brethren, seemed less tied to a narrow confessional orthodoxy. The two reunited in 1869 as the Presbyterian Church in the United States of America, the name that both had heretofore claimed. In doctrinal purity, adherence to Westminster, opposition to ecumenism, and fear of interdenominational or even independent denominational boards, the southern church best continued the Old School tradition, but by the twentieth century it was deeply divided between liberal and conservative factions. In 1906 the northern church, after a moderate revision of its confession, welcomed back the Cumberland Presbyterians, although about a third of Cumberland presbyteries refused to accept this merger.

The Old School Presbyterians exemplified one continuing tradition in American Protestantism. Naming it poses problems. Although the adherents of this tradition claimed the label "evangelical," the word had, for them, traditional meanings that did not fit most uses in America. That is, they used it to denote the role of the Word and the Spirit but not such innovations as new revival methods or a very affectionate or sentimental devotional life, all characteristics of their enemies. The label "fundamentalist" is likewise inappropriate and anachronistic. Thus, I prefer such labels as "orthodox," "conservative," and "confessional." These reflect a continuing adherence to traditional confessions, an often quite intellectualistic and academic concern for correct doctrines and for well-trained ministers, and a philosophical objection to most aspects of modernity.

The Old School mentality supported consistency at the cost of marginality. The New School mentality supported tolerance at the cost of vagueness. The Old School made almost all the doctrines of the church, and all the Bible, authoritative and essential. The dilemma faced by the New School, and by evangelical Protestants generally, was how to draw the boundaries between the essential doctrines, or the truly binding parts of scripture, and those not essential, those on which Christians were free to disagree. This raised the old problem of authority, of the justifications for one's religious belief. Both the Bible, as the source of a particular religious tradition (Judeo-Christian), and the foundational Semitic cosmology, and thus theism itself, faced unprecedented challenges in the nineteenth century. As people learned more about the Bible – historical development, early texts, the sources and motives of authors, internal tensions and conflicts, and the complicated road to a canon – it became increasingly difficult to believe that the whole Bible, Catholic or Protestant, was true in all its historical claims, divinely inspired in all its doctrinal guidelines, or without error in the received text. As people discovered more and more about natural history, about the origins of the solar system, about existing geological features, and about varied flora and fauna, it became almost impossible to give credence to the Semitic myths about origins or to the foreshortened history of the earth as recorded in Genesis.

Biblical Scholarship

Even before the Civil War, the mainstream churches faced new intellectual challenges. In the perspective of the present, the two most important challenges involved new biblical scholarship and new forms of understanding in the natural and biological sciences. Given the internal tensions over salvation doctrines, and the moral controversies centered on slavery, it is not surprising that these challenges largely concerned a minority of ministers and theologians until after the Civil War. But they were such dark clouds on the horizon that they deserve attention even in a book focused primarily on the Reformed churches before 1865.[5]

Neither scholarly nor scientific challenges were new issues in the nineteenth century. Deists and rationalists had challenged biblical authority in the eighteenth century. Thomas Paine, in his popular *Age of Reason*, had fun ridiculing the contradictions in the Bible and lamenting the cruelty of much of the Old Testament. Joseph Priestley, a leader of British Unitarians, mined existing biblical scholarship to write a controversial book on the multiple corruptions of the church. But in the new century the most innovative and radical biblical studies all occurred in German universities. With only two exceptions, Americans reacted to such scholarship but did not add to it.

The two American scholars who gained an appreciation in Europe, and who did pioneering work in specialized scholarship, were almost more German than American. Philip Schaff, who came from Germany to the Mercersburg seminary in 1844, would eventually become America's most distinguished church historian as well as a notable theologian. He did most of his historical work only after the Civil War, during his long tenure as a professor at Union Theological Seminary. His training was in the German universities, and much of his historical work involved the church as a whole, although some of his most perceptive insights involved the unique aspects of Christianity in America.

Edward Robinson became the world's premier nineteenth-century expert on ancient Palestine, particularly its geography and sites critical to later archaeology. His meticulous fieldwork in Palestine made him famous. As he began his researches, he represented Andover Seminary, where he had earlier been an instructor in Hebrew and where, in 1830, he had assumed a chair in sacred literature. But, notably, he had already spent four years as a student in several German universities, had married the daughter of a professor at Halle, and had tried, with limited success, to publicize Germany biblical scholarship in a pioneering but unsuccessful journal, the *Biblical Repository*. In 1837, just before years of work in Palestine, he moved to the New School Presbyterian Union Seminary in New York. He published his 1841 magnum opus, *Biblical Researches in Palestine, Mount Sinai, and Arabia Petraea*, simultaneously in German and in English. Notably, the work of both Schaff and Robinson was innovative but not radical; it did not directly challenge, and in some cases it supported, conservative doctrinal and theological positions.

This was not true for critical historical studies. Such studies are almost as old as the church, with Origen arguably the first great Christian Old Testament scholar, one whose allegorical and nonliteral interpretations would offend conservative critics even today. Among Renaissance humanists, the Bible became a prime subject for scholarly effort. Erasmus completed a Greek text of the New Testament and then based a Latin translation on it. This work had doctrinal significance, for it challenged Roman Catholic understandings of both penance and the priesthood. Baruch Spinoza, the Jewish rationalist, contended that Moses did not write the Pentateuch; Ezra, he believed, wrote the first twelve books of Jewish scripture (he was right about Moses, wrong about Ezra). He argued for the late date of many of these books and noted the numerous adulterations made by later priest-editors. His views scandalized the Christian world.

At the beginning of the nineteenth century, the German expert on the gospels, J. G. Eichhorn, distinguished two types of criticism. The lower type involved Erasmus's problem of reconstituting the ancient biblical texts. The higher involved theories or explanations of what those texts contain, or the type of problems broached by Spinoza – who wrote the texts and when, who edited and adapted them, what sources lay behind the texts, and what cultural forms shaped them? – or, in the broadest sense, a series of historical questions. The purely textual issue, although at times pregnant with doctrinal significance, was a project that few Christians could renounce, whatever their doctrinal position. Thus a type of "lower" criticism became a part of any theological education and placed a premium on proficiency in the ancient languages. The "higher" criticism went beyond or behind the texts, was thus more theoretical and speculative, and on almost every issue threatened received wisdom and orthodox doctrines, including belief in an inspired or inerrant Bible.

By the seventeenth century, several components of the Bible fed critical controversies. To embarrass Protestants, Catholic scholars identified corruptions in the Hebrew text of the Old Testament. In Holland, the Remonstrants or Arminians speculated about lost, early sources for the New Testament. Thomas Hobbes, who defended corporealist and adventist doctrines, speculated about the authorship of several books. Early rationalists or deists began to discount or reject various "irrational" passages in the scriptures, and would by the early eighteenth century reject any "revealed" religion whatsoever in behalf of a natural religion. But critical scholarship would mature in Germany, not in Holland or England, and in one of many ironies, it would first develop in the most pietistic university in Germany, Halle, a university established in the late seventeenth century by one of the two founders of German pietism, A. H. Francke.

Biblical scholarship at Halle originated as a response to Spinoza and English deists. Deists, in particular, condemned the absurd and cruel content of the scriptures, particularly the historical books of the Old Testament. They were rarely careful scholars and almost always indulged presentist judgments. One counter to such external iconoclasm was careful historical scholarship – to recover the exact linguistic and cultural context that produced the sacred texts. In this context, what seemed cruel to an eighteenth-century rationalist might make perfect sense. Such an enterprise was full of dynamite. In the eighteenth century a series of Halle scholars, culminating with J. S. Semler, looked all too closely at the ancient texts. Soon the more daring scholars even had trouble within their own university. Semler and his predecessors found numerous errors of fact and history in the Old Testament. They also broke from a venerable Christian conceit – understanding the Old Testament only through New Testament perspectives and not in its own Jewish setting. The Halle critics demanded a free and critical spirit and tried to approach biblical texts like any other ancient documents, using what they would describe as a "scientific" approach. In other words, they fully historicized the Bible and, unintentionally, thereby began to lessen its authority for Christians.

The historical-critical method fully matured in the first half of the nineteenth century. The work of various scholars led to much of the biblical knowledge which is now commonplace but which seemed scandalous to the orthodox at the time. It also led to some rather wild speculation. Today, the pioneering scholars are not household names – Semler, Eichhorn, Johann Michaelis, Friedrich Schleiermacher, David Strauss, Wilhelm De Wette, and F. C. Bauer – but they were the founders of modern historical scholarship. They worked not in seminaries, not in direct dependence on the churches, but in research-oriented universities. Whatever their personal confessional position, they helped disinfect the Bible of its former sacred and authoritarian position. They opened it as a complex subject for historical understanding, as the most basic cultural text in the Western tradition.

Textual restoration gained from the discovery of three reasonably complete fifth-century New Testament manuscripts (the earliest available, although more recently discovered papyrus fragments date from as early as the second century). Because of variant textual traditions, it was never possible to restore a single, authoritative Greek text, but the soon very sophisticated effort would make possible the scholarly translations of the twentieth century. At the very least, the enduring rules of textual criticism were in place by 1850.

Most troubling to the orthodox were the new theories about the New Testament books, particularly the gospels. Scholars slowly, although never conclusively, established the priority of Mark, which provided much of the common content for Matthew and Luke. They also established the likely existence of a non-Markian source used by the other two synoptics: what scholars would soon call "Q," short for the German word for source, *Quelle.* They challenged the apostolic authorship of the gospels, documented the very different oral or documentary sources that informed the gospel attributed to John, and speculated about the date of writing for each New Testament book. They identified spurious and late books, such as the pastorals attributed to Paul, and later interpolations, such as several endings to the book of Mark. They clarified the complex, Gnostic-influenced path to a western New Testament canon. Those with a naturalistic outlook offered reasonable explanations for the miracles and in a sense denied their reality, including even the resurrection. Others, informed by the growing dominance of philosophical idealism in German universities, so spiritualized the meaning of New Testament passages as to deny any literal truth to them at all. In fact, one reason for the more daring or radical criticism in Germany was the shift, among so many theologians, away from historical and textual authorities to the inward truths lodged in human consciousness.

One result of such scholarship was a much better understanding of each component of the received Bible. Another was an awareness of the internal tensions and contradictions. Most sensitive of all were the new, competing theories about Jesus. Early critics retained a divine Jesus but divided on questions about his mission (the trend was toward a moralized or spiritualized goal and away from eschatological and apocalyptic themes) and his own self-understanding and purpose. The bombshell in such speculation came in David F. Strauss's *Das Leben Jesu* (Life of Jesus) in 1835. He was the radical of them all and was widely repudiated in Germany. Strauss went well beyond earlier naturalizing or spiritualizing interpretations. He turned most of the New Testament into mythology. Behind all the improbabilities and discrepancies of the gospels, Strauss found only a small kernel of historical truth – that Jesus did live in Palestine, was a disciple of John the Baptist, and did preach a message of a coming kingdom and looked forward to a liberating messiah. The Christ of the gospels, the Jesus who rose from the grave and ascended into heaven, was a mythical figure created by early Christians, who had compelling reasons to create such a Christ. John, the most mythological of gospels, was also the least reliable from a historical perspective. Strauss was personally devout and welcomed a religion not tied to the historical accuracy of the New Testament. The concept of incarnation and exaltation, which the disciples attributed to Jesus, properly referred to possibilities open to all people. The only proper authority for such a religion was within the human mind, not in a body of mythological legends. Few critics went so far as Strauss. His most esteemed contemporary, F. C. Bauer, still found a large kernel of historical truth in the three synoptics, although it was clear that the sources would never allow scholars to find one historical Jesus.

In Germany the more radical critics stimulated a strong conservative counterattack. It in turn abetted the rise of confessionalism in German Lutheranism, which in turn dramatically affected Lutheranism in America. In fact, in Protestantism as a whole, the most likely effect of the new criticism would be the stimulus it gave to a revived orthodoxy. In Britain both Scottish and English scholars proved most resistant to the German approach; their reaction paralleled their first response to early evolutionary theories – an emphatic but narrowly empirical approach and a denunciation of speculation of all types. Until 1860 the more radical criticism gained few disciples in Britain (Samuel Coleridge was the most eminent of the liberals), and outside textual areas British scholars made few contributions to such criticism.

In the United States the first scholar to try to imitate the Germans was the precocious Joseph S. Buckminster. He became a legend among the liberals at Harvard, where he eventually assumed a new Dexter lectureship on biblical criticism, the first such in America. He might well have become the intellectual of an emerging Unitarian movement had he not died of epilepsy at the age of twenty-eight in 1812, even as he was trying to learn German well enough to absorb the work of Semler and Eichhorn. Buckminster gathered the best biblical library in America, saw to the printing of the most recent reconstruction of a Greek New Testament, and in particular devoted more attention to the development of the New Testament canon than any prior American. He was a radical in the American and Congregational context, although he never had doubts about the integrity and divine status of the four gospels. He drew from both rationalists and scholars for his ideas. He rejected any single, unified, inspired Bible, found the path to a canon full of accidental or purely political judgments, and denied any unambiguous basis in scripture for various human creeds and confessions. The word of God was in the scriptures, but the scriptures were much more, and much less, than the word of God. As a liberal and rationalist, he believed the problem of biblical criticism was finding the Word, the gems of truth, in the ancient, human-written texts.

When Buckminster died, the New England liberals had no one qualified to replace him. William Ellery Channing, who replaced Buckminster as Dexter lecturer, was never a devoted scholar, although he was a perceptive consumer of scholarship. Two young Congregationalists, and part of the emerging Unitarian wing, Edward Everett and George Bancroft, might have distinguished themselves as biblical scholars. Both traveled to Germany for graduate work. Everett, who took Buckminster's pulpit, soon moved to Harvard as professor of Greek and in 1815 left for Germany. He was the first such American to earn his doctorate in Germany and was there able to study with Eichhorn and other eminent scholars. Yet, when he returned to Boston he quickly gave up scholarship, briefly teaching classical Greek before beginning a political career. Bancroft, a student of Everett's, absorbed his fascination with biblical scholarship and followed him to Germany as the second recipient of Harvard funds. He too studied with the masters and gained his Ph.D. in 1820. By then he had excellent credentials in the New and Old Testament, but on returning to Harvard he directed his efforts at a new high school and soon became an extremely nationalist historian and reformer. Both

Everett and Bancroft retreated from biblical scholarship, at least in part, because of the troubling implications it had for their own religious faith. Another reason was the lack of an American audience or satisfactory career possibilities for such a profession.

Two conservative Calvinists – Charles Hodge at Princeton and Moses Stuart at Andover – provided a sophisticated, informed audience for the new German scholarship. Hodge studied in Germany. Subsequently, he read and reviewed all the important books. He was open to new insights about text and context yet was horrified at the conclusions drawn or suggested by the more radical critics. Thus, he carried on a continuing debate with each author, drawing with precision his conclusions about where they had made valid contributions and where, usually through too much speculation, they had gone dangerously astray (see the preceding chapter).

Stuart was a very different observer of the German workshops. No other American was more fascinated with the product. He lived and breathed biblical scholarship and at times loved the game so much that he almost forgot his confessional allegiances. He never repudiated his orthodox Calvinism or his belief in an inspired Bible. Yet, he supported and commended every young American who embraced critical scholarship, avidly read and collected all the available books on the subject, and in the interests of scholarship formed warm personal ties to Unitarians and other "apostates" who shared his scholarly concerns.

Stuart's own scholarship remained, primarily, in the doctrinally safe areas of Hebrew and Greek grammar. He tried to keep the scholarly achievement of such Germans as Eichhorn separate from their false theological views. He also made a distinction between biblical scholarship, which should be quite separate from matters of personal belief, and confessional issues. Thus, scholars, whatever their disagreements over doctrine, should be able to move toward a consensus on issues of fact. This meant that, at times, Stuart could seem as dispassionate as any German in his studies of the Bible. Generally he defended the received view – that Moses wrote the first five books and that the whole Old Testament canon was valid because Jesus and the apostles had so conceived it. He was ingenious in finding ways of harmonizing books, especially by finding early books not erroneous but incomplete, with a fuller revelation in later books, or the doctrine of progressive revelation. He tried the impossible – to absorb and then utilize critical scholarship in behalf of orthodoxy. He wanted to capture the original meaning and intent of the scriptures, a meaning often quite different from modern understanding, but in order to sustain, not challenge, the full authority of these writings. Compared with many Unitarian scholars, who worked to defend the authority of the New Testament or at least the gospels, Stuart wanted to defend the complete integrity of the Old Testament and did this in his last book, one that reflected his usual ambivalence – an openness to many of the scholarly problems yet always the final insistence that the Old Testament still revealed a complete unity of outlook. It was almost as if he had to defend the outcome of scholarship – preserved orthodoxy – to salve his guilt over all the fun in playing the scholarly game, often on its own terms.

Harvard established the first American professorship in what amounted to biblical criticism in 1819, just before the emergence of a separate divinity faculty. Andrews Norton, minister and religious journalist and the most aggressive polemicist in behalf of a separate Unitarian fellowship, used every bit of persuasive ability to get the former Dexter lectureship upgraded to a full-time chair and to secure it for himself. He thus became the biblical authority for a whole generation of largely Unitarian ministerial candidates at Harvard. He, along with William Ellery Channing, wanted to base the Unitarian cause on scriptural authority but agreed that the scriptures had to be interpreted by use of human reason and that some parts of the received Bible were much more useful and authoritative than others. Norton remained open to most critical revelations about the Old Testament, largely because he never believed that it provided any binding authority for Christians. He would be much more resistant to radical criticism of the New Testament, particularly of the gospels.

As a teacher, Norton made it his goal to recapture the great truths in the Bible, truths subsequently corrupted by the church. This required careful study, critical thinking, and thus the linguistic and historical knowledge necessary to understand books written in the idiom of the people of biblical times. In a sense, he was a restorationist, as was Channing. Unlike the leaders of the American Restoration churches, such as Barton Stone and Alexander Campbell, Norton recognized the impossibility of using the varying biblical texts as a charter of church reform. The sources were too complex, too varied, and too full of contradictions and ambiguities. Scholarship enabled one to get behind these problems and arrive at the great truths contained in the midst of all the bad science and deceptive language. These grand truths, as Norton established them, were in fact the key doctrines of the emerging Unitarian movement – a benevolent and unitary god and Jesus as his revealed son and redeemer. Essentially, his was a religion of the gospels, and soon after assuming his new chair at Harvard he set about what became his life work – a defense of the truthfulness of the four gospels.

Ironically, Norton, who seemed heterodox to most American evangelicals, soon became the avowed enemy of the more radical German critics. He had gladly embraced their iconoclasm about the Old Testament but was horrified when they began to challenge the gospel story. Critics, even before Strauss, had rejected the miracles attributed to Jesus, had denied the apostolic authorship of the gospels, and had challenged the accuracy of the accounts of Jesus contained in even the synoptic gospels. Then Strauss went all the way with his mythologizing of the gospel stories. Norton was horrified. He had been, in a sense, a minimalist, reducing the authoritative content of the Bible largely to the gospel message. His whole religion outlook depended on what he called the genuineness of these gospels. By this, he meant that the assigned authors wrote them, that they wrote them early in the history of the church and had full apostolic authority, that despite the quite distinctive purpose and approach of the four independent writers, the four gospels were in harmony on all significant issues, and that the miraculous acts attributed to Jesus actually took place. After all, it was these miracles, climaxing in the resurrection, that attested to the fact that Jesus was the Messiah.

Norton published his magnum opus in 1837 and entitled it, descriptively, *Genuineness of the Gospels*. It appeared just after Strauss's *Life*, of which it was, in Norton's estimate, a sufficient refutation. His three-volume work won the plaudits even of Moses Stuart at Andover, although the two men disagreed on other critical issues. It was a work of scholarship, of study over two decades, and reflected considerable scholarly credentials, most self-taught. In it Norton bared some of the excesses, some of the wilder speculations, of his German antagonists, particularly Eichhorn. For the time he offered the strongest possible arguments for four early, apostolic, and essentially uncorrupted gospels (an evaluation closer to the truth than the extreme views of Strauss). It now seems almost certain (on none of these issues can anyone be fully certain) that three and possibly all four canonical gospels were written before 100 C.E., that the churches early accepted them as genuine, that the received and critically compared texts are very close to the originals, that the authors were probably directly influenced by apostles (Norton claimed more than this, of course), and that other early, competing, largely Gnostic-influenced gospels had much weaker credentials on strictly scholarly grounds. But Norton was just as frequently wrong or blind. He was not open to any scholarship that would undermine his own doctrinal position. Thus, the aging "pope" of Unitarianism became, in many respects, more rigid and doctrinaire than such orthodox critics as Stuart.

Because of a growing transcendentalist faction in his own church, Norton was also a beleaguered scholar after 1840. The basis of conflict was, at the highest level, metaphysical and only secondarily biblical. Norton still rested his faith on a historical revelation, on the scriptures as interpreted by reasonable standards of scholarship. To him, certain scriptural claims, such as the authenticity of Jesus' miracles, came to symbolize scriptural authority. Reject them and Christianity was cut loose from any principle of objective authority whatsoever. It was doomed. Of course, orthodox critics of Norton gladly pointed out that he had asked for just this, that his attempt to sift and winnow the truth out of humanly flawed scriptures had so loosened the principle of authority as to leave no effective barrier against ever more erosive claims.

Theologians who bought into the new forms of absolute idealism changed the rules of the critical game. The philosophical movement that climaxed in Hegel shifted the whole issue of religious authority from externals of any kind, from the purported lessons of nature or the purported truths of historic revelations to the facets of a divine mind immanent in the consciousness of individuals. In human reason, or what amounted to a type of intuitive insight, people came to their apprehension and always incomplete understanding of divinity. Most idealists believed in an objective or absolute mind, a type of god, and thus denied that this approach was dangerously subjective. But the path to insight was still subjective, in the sense that it involved an interpretation of one's own experience, or an introspective exploration of the rational, a priori aspects of mind. From this perspective, scriptures might have value – as examples of how inspired people in the past had tried, always inadequately, to characterize the infinite spirit. Such scriptures might inspire one's contemporary quest, but they could not control it. If they became authorities, binding on Christians, then the scriptures became idols, blocking the avenues of revelation that extend to each individual. Such a perspective on scripture meant that idealists were open to, and not threatened by, any scholarly findings about the Bible or any scientific findings about nature.

Norton gave up his chair at Harvard to complete his masterpiece. He died in 1852, after two decades of controversy, much directed at the upstart transcendentalists in his own denomination. His student and successor at Harvard, George R. Noyes, did most of his work in the field of Old Testament criticism, a relatively safe subject for a Unitarian. The years after 1840 were not propitious for biblical scholarship in America. Few scholars engaged in serious research, and over and over again events proved that such scholars had no market for their work. Sensational works, such as that of Strauss (the English novelist, Mary Ann Evans, who took the name George Eliot, did an early English translation), were widely read and reviewed in America, but the Germans retained the greatest commitment to such scholarship. Soon a flow of American seminarians traveled to Germany for graduate work. But it is important to note that they there had access to conservative as well as liberal critics and that few changed their theological orientation while in Germany. Back home, they had no career opportunities in serious biblical scholarship. Even the one American most open to the work of the more radical Germans, a convert in fact, Theodore Parker, reviewed, translated, and popularized the German harvest but was never able to become a productive scholar himself. He had the interest, the intellect, and the linguistic tools, but not the opportunity.

Parker was an early convert to Emersonian transcendentalism and soon became the most radical of Unitarian clergymen. He wrote one of the first and most favorable reviews of Strauss in 1840 and would soon be even more sympathetic. For a few years he seriously considered a career as a biblical scholar, even though he was only a parish minister. In 1843, in what turned out to be his only major excursion into criticism, he translated and rather elaborately edited and expanded on W. M. L. De Wette's epochal two-volume *Critical and Historical Introduction to the Old Testament.* Since even Norton had been open to such Old Testament criticism, Parker long planned to move from this to a more risky critical commentary on the New Testament. But few bought his De Wette, and few even reviewed it. He kept updating editions of it, largely at his own expense, and contemplated a long, comparative history of the progressive development of religions. Nothing came of these plans. Parker did not have the time or the support and died prematurely of tuberculosis. He was a busy parish minister, a beleaguered Unitarian controversalist, a reformer, and eventually an outspoken abolitionist. He had to limit himself to the popularization of biblical scholarship through sermons and essays. Because he read all the important new books out of Germany, his American audiences often misunderstood him. He tried to begin and maintain a dialogue when no one was listening.

In one sense, the impact of the new biblical scholarship, particularly of the more iconoclastic higher criticism, was very limited in pre–Civil War America. It led to an ongoing dialogue, one significant enough to involve and shape lay opinion, largely among Unitarians, or among such radical apostates from the Reformed tradition as to constitute an outside option, not an internal alternative. Even among the Unitarians, Parker gained only a handful of ministerial supporters. The denomination as a whole adhered to Norton and Noyes, to a religion still tied to the objective authority of the gospels and the miracles they reported. If the Unitarians went only this far, it is no wonder that new and daring scholarship challenged, in a few cases engaged and stimulated, but did not shake the Biblicism that was at the heart of the Reformed tradition. The bitterly divisive issues, and the most famous heresy charges and trials, involved doctrinal slippage, particularly Arminian inroads into purportedly Calvinist denominations. But despite the limited impact, the early engagement of American evangelicals with the most sophisticated forms of criticism, such as that of Stuart at Andover, had profound implications for the future.

Critical issues began to disturb the peace of the mainline evangelical denominations only after 1875. By then, the oldest American seminaries had moved toward a new level of professionalism. The issues that led to heresy trials, and major national publicity, were often peripheral or minor, showing how little biblical scholarship had gained broad acceptance in America. Professors risked expulsion from teaching posts or from the Presbyterian, Methodist, or Baptist ministry if they affirmed that Moses was not the sole author of the first five books of the Old Testament, or that the book of Isaiah, as contained in the Jewish canon, had at least two authors, or even that the book of Jonah was a parable and not the record of historical events. These issues, all involving the Old Testament, scarcely required the heavy guns of the higher criticism; for example, the "heretical" claim of multiple authors for Isaiah was clear from a commonsense reading of the text. Still beyond the pale were other minor or marginal issues, such as the increasingly weighty reasons to reject Paul's authorship of the three pastorals (Timothy and Titus), or Peter's composition of the late, thin book called II Peter, or the numerous political bargains and accidental circumstances that led to both the Jewish canon and a New Testament canon. In fact, not until the twentieth century could mainline professors openly and safely embrace new, critical findings concerning the New Testament or join in the now raging debates about a historical Jesus.

Yet, in a sense appreciated by some of his colleagues, Moses Stuart had set even the most orthodox mainline seminaries off in a fatal direction. Careful scholarship was bound, sooner or later, to undermine the conventional Protestant (and Catholic) belief in an infallible Bible. The new scholarly game would have a major impact much later in America than in Germany because of the conservatism of the ministry and of the lay membership, who continued to exercise control over denominational seminaries. Biblical professors in America had none of the protection of university scholars in Germany. Neither did they have the unique opportunities of a Theodore Parker, who was able to promote his critical views within independent congregations.

All evangelical Protestants professed the Bible as their final authority, not only on issues of faith and salvation but on all the issues of cosmology and history broached in any part of the Bible. Acceptance of this position was an implicit, and often a stated, prerequisite for any teaching position in a denominational seminary. American Protestants had no church hierarchy to resolve issues of biblical interpretation. The ministry, or more broadly the ministry and laypeople, owned the Bible and determined what it meant. Until the pastoral clergy and at least the lay leadership in congregations were willing to defer to the claims of special competence, or of "scientific" knowledge, by seminary scholars, professors or daring ministers had no leeway to embrace purportedly new and more scholarly biblical theories that in any way threatened its fully authoritative status. (Note that they could and did teach about the new scholarship in all the better seminaries but that they could not personally and publicly endorse many of the new theories.) To move into these areas, confessionally, was to move on to very sensitive and dangerous ground, more threatening than even Darwinism.

The Impact of the New Geology

Even by the late eighteenth century, new work in geology had already disturbed Christians. It cast doubt on the biblical age of the earth and on Noah's flood even as several naturalists speculated about or developed early evolutionary theories to account for what was increasingly clear in the fossil record – the extinction of past species and the emergence of new ones in each geological age. Just after 1800, Jean Lamarck published a very complex evolutionary theory, and by 1830, in America, thousands of people had already concluded that some type of organic evolution had occurred over a very long period of time. They believed this even as the evidence convinced them that uniformitarian geology, as mastered by Charles Lyell and several American disciples, was correct, meaning a very ancient age for the earth, an age not comparable to the standard biblical chronology. Most philosophical idealists, including Emerson and other American transcendentalists, embraced a processive or evolutionary metaphysics that entailed the emergence of new species through time. All types of emergence in nature illustrated the unfolding or development of a divine mind.

Not only were the challenges already in place, but if anything was clear it was that these were bound to multiply in the near future. No one was more certain of this than Theodore Parker, who insisted that Christians had to transfer their allegiance away from all types of external authority, in nature or in scripture, and to the inward authority of conscience and experience. Horace Bushnell, while trying to salvage the best of both Calvinist and Arminian forms of evangelical Christianity, emphasized the figurative or poetic nature of scripture; it was now absurd to read it literally. Also, he embraced an early, spiritualized, and Christian form of evolution, one that attributed a now quite evident series of new species to the creative work of God at the beginning of each new geological age. These strategies worked. They made Christian belief, and the promise of redemption, almost immune from any threat from science and scholarship and so subordinated, or relativized, the traditional authorities of the church as to leave, as the final anchor of the faith, only the types of experience or the aspects of divinity immanent in the human mind.

Parker and Bushnell were way ahead of American evangelicals in the pre–Civil War era. They were too radical for any but a small minority of Unitarians and Congregationalists. Mainstream Presbyterians would not move so far until the mid-twentieth century, and even then the doctrinal pluralism of the church alienated at least a large minority. For mid-nineteenth-century evangelicals, the Bible remained a fixed symbol of authority, and even those who were persuaded by uniformitarian geologists or early evolutionists rushed not to finesse the issues by denying the literal authority of scripture but to demonstrate that the Bible, correctly understood, still agreed with the proven facts of natural science. In a pattern that stretched through Asa Gray and even into the twentieth century, the most accomplished and ablest American scientists were also evangelical Christians. They worked from the other side to bridge the seemingly widening gap between biblical cosmology and the new scientific accounts.

Broadly defined, geology occasioned the first extended American debate over the challenge of the physical sciences to the received biblical cosmology. The maturation of geology in the early nineteenth century led, particularly in Britain, to a sustained controversy, not only between churchmen and natural scientists but also among geologists, all to some extent influenced by the traditional doctrines of Christianity. A huge body of polemical literature circulated in America and was reviewed in journals of opinion, but by and large Americans contributed little to the debate. The divisive controversies among American denominational leaders involved such issues as slavery, interdenominational cooperation, or the complex dialogue between Calvinists and Arminians. Pre–Civil War heresy trials did not involve, at least directly, any clerical capitulation to the new theories in geology.[6]

By 1800 geologists had a great deal to explain. Explorations had revealed, around the world, layer after layer of fossil-bearing sedimentary rocks, or what seemed to be deposits accumulated during an enormous lapse of time, one that involved hundreds of thousands of years at least but more probably millions of years. The layers also revealed what seemed to be a range of now extinct flora and fauna, with organic life varying from one level to another. As the debates took form, the new geology usually involved a few rather peripheral biblical issues – the age of the earth, the validity of the accounts of creation in Genesis, and the historical credentials of the story of Noah and the great flood. Even by 1800 almost any geologist had to concede that the earth was much older than six thousand years, the approximate age yielded by the genealogy of the Jewish scriptures, and that some universal flood, one that covered all the earth in the comparative recent past, was physically impossible. The first geologist to make this clear, in print, was a very empirical James Hutton, an Englishman who published his *System of the Earth* in 1785. Hutton wrote in opposition to geologists who posited a suspension of all surface phenomena in water and a rapid deposition of the phenomena as the water subsided, a theory that still honored old Noah (geologists, as devout Christians, were often guided to such theories by scripture). Hutton explained at least a portion of the rocks by volcanic action and clarified processes that proved the antiquity of the earth, advocating hypotheses that could not be consistent with any literal reading of several stories in Genesis.

By 1820, Hutton's basic outlook had become consensual. For at least another decade a debate raged between geologists who still accounted for the various geological ages by major catastrophes and a growing number of critics who believed that slow and gradual processes of change, most still at work, largely accounted for the present geological record. Such a uniformitarian outlook required a much greater antiquity for the earth and was less consistent with the Bible. In 1830 Charles Lyle published the first of three volumes in defense of such a uniformitarian theory and within another decade had won most naturalists to his position, among them a young Charles Darwin in England and Louis Agassiz in Switzerland (he soon immigrated to America). Actually, the catastrophic-uniformitarian duality was misleading, since aspects of both are today accepted explanations of natural history. But the controversy, in Britain, developed in part because of the ongoing debate about the threat such theories posed to the biblical accounts (in the parochial language of the day, this was often cited as a conflict between "science," which remained undefined, and "religion," by which everyone meant Christianity).

In Britain and in America, geologists on both sides remained apologists for Christianity. Almost to a person, the uniformitarians insisted that geological knowledge would change people's understanding of scripture, in some cases requiring a distinctive new interpretation, but would in no sense challenge the religious truth of the Bible. The reaction to the new geology would only replicate what had happened numerous times in the past, such as when Christians had to change their understanding of biblical references to a fixed earth and a circling sun and moon. But they were a bit disingenuous in this tact, for the new geology challenged more than a popular idiom for talking about origins. Even the uniformitarians, including Lyle, gave a backhanded acknowledgment of this when they conceded that the next step, one logically consistent with uniformitarian theory, was clearly beyond the pale: belief in some form of organic evolution that required no divine intervention. In fact, the geologists seemed so antagonistic to mutability, so hostile to evolutionary theory (that of Lamarck or the more pantheistic theory of idealists), that one suspects they recognized the fragility of their own labored apologetic, their attempts to prove not only that their empirical geology was consistent with scripture but that it offered wonderful new support for natural theology. By this, they meant that it revealed the intricate contrivances of a deity and thus begged wonder and awe. William Paley, the English natural theologian best popularized these arguments. He used the most intricate adaptation of species to demonstrate the necessity for and the wonders of divine design.

American naturalists generally followed English precedents, with Louis Agassiz making the greatest contribution and gaining the most international prestige. Ironically, he later gained notoriety for his resistance to Darwinism, but before this he had helped fill out the details within geological ages, had developed the first theories about the effect of glaciers, and had even used a theory that resembled natural selection to help explain varietal diversification within each age. Agassiz was a product of evangelical Christianity, as was perhaps the most prominent American scientist of the era, Benjamin Silliman, who as a youth was a convert of Timothy Dwight's and was thus heir to the New Divinity. At Yale, he used the same apologetic tactics of British scientists, including the day-age interpretation of creation in Genesis. His student, Edward Hitchcock, wrote not only texts on the new geology but also a series of articles and books to deny any irreligious implications in geological findings that were now so proven, so universally accepted by geologists, as to be beyond doubt for anyone honest enough to look at the evidence. He rebuked, equally, those geologists who were uninformed about the Bible or "correct" Christian doctrine, or those resistant Christians who were abysmally ignorant of a complex new science. His reconciliation of uniformitarian geology with the biblical record well exemplified a position that gained broad acceptance among "liberal" churchmen, such as Horace Bushnell, but a position that had barely gained acceptance before it had to face the shock of Charles Darwin's naturalistic explanation of how new species emerge.

Hitchcock, a Congregational minister as well as a self-taught geologist, could not reject the "unassailable" and empirical truths of geology. These made clear the great antiquity of the earth, the long geological history before the appearance of life, the absence of human remains in any of the early ages, the distinctive flora and fauna of each geologic age (he believed, incorrectly, that no species carried over from one age to the next), and the enormous length of time (he would guess at least 300,000 years) required for the deposition of such fossil-bearing layers. In his most famous apologetic, *The Religion of Geology* (1851), he began with the plan of creation, tried to deal with Noah and the flood, and then spent much of the book defending the glory of God in the creation, drawing much of his theodicy from such theologians as Nathaniel Taylor. Hitchcock rejected the day-age theory so popular among British scientists and liberal churchmen. By it, the word *day* in the two somewhat variant Genesis accounts of creation meant a vast age. Thus, roughly, the days of creation corresponded with past geological ages, with humans originating in the present age. This theory had all types of problems, including an unjustified attribution of preternatural insights to the author or authors of Genesis.

In place of the day-age solution, Hitchcock preferred another rather widespread theory (today called the "gap theory"), which had circulated in some form for centuries. He believed that eons of time elapsed between the creation of the world and the six days detailed in Genesis. He thus crammed all the vast geological history of the earth into this long interim, including the creation of life at the beginning of each age. This did not solve all the problems. He took the story in Genesis to be an account, written for untutored audiences, of how God created the flora and fauna of the present geological age. His dilemmas involved such problems as dispersion – how did regionally concentrated species move from the one place mentioned in Genesis, and how did he account for what seemed clear in the fossil record, that most plants and animals of the present age existed long before humans? Without being dogmatic, Hitchcock considered solutions to such problems. His main point was that such understanding allowed one to harmonize the biblical accounts, written in the language of and consistent with the understanding of past audiences, with any of the facts of geology.

The problem of Noah posed additional problems. For years Hitchcock had accepted the truth of the great flood and had used surging waters from the North to account for what he later had to accept as glacial effects. Thus, after a series of retreats, Hitchcock finally conceded that there was no geological evidence whatsoever for a worldwide flood. For people today, it may seem odd that old Noah figured so large in all the debates. The flood story in Genesis reflected the integration of two Jewish accounts of a legendary flood, a flood acknowledged in most of the folklore of the ancient Near East. One possible explanation for the almost universal belief in such a flood was a great flood or series of floods in the Mesopotamian valley in prehistoric times. Whatever the source of the legend, the Genesis account, in its details, was simply untenable in any literal sense (one cannot find any physical explanation for so much water, cannot imagine such a long inundation followed immediately by a resurgence of normal plant growth, cannot calculate a boat large enough to carry either seven or two of all species, and so on). For a time, the discovery of fossils on mountains gave some credence to such a great flood, but the detailed work of geologists soon disproved the flood explanation (the fossil deposits were of such depth as to have required thousands of floods, whereas uplift processes accounted for the location of skeletons on mountains). By 1851 Hitchcock had to argue that the whole idea of a worldwide flood was simply absurd, beyond the credulity of anyone who would take evidence seriously. Yet, such was the status of the story among Christians that Hitchcock could not dismiss it out of hand. He saw that such a dismissal would undermine what he stipulated in his preface as his working assumption – that the Bible is the divinely inspired, infallible source of religious truth (not scientific truth, but no scientific truth can be inconsistent with the Bible). Thus, by his assumption, the story of Noah had to be consistent with scientific facts. How could this be?

Hitchcock had an easy answer. The flood was really a local flood, but one of large enough scope to encompass all the early humans that lived on earth. Its universalist language was proper for such a valley people, for the flood destroyed all land animals and humans in the world they knew, except for the known species Noah rescued on his ark. To so account for this, Hitchcock had to accept a few troubling facts – that humans had been on the earth for only six thousand years and that all the pre-flood humans were clustered in the Mesopotamian valley. Already, these assumptions were challenged by a steady accretion of paleontological and archaeological evidence.

Hitchcock chose not to dwell on such weak accommodations but to use the new geology in a positive way – to deepen piety. The new facts required a reinterpretation of scriptures but otherwise added to the message of scripture. For example, Hitchcock argued that the new geology proved miracles. It proved that God, at the beginning of each age, created appropriate life forms, a miracle of the highest order, for by no natural means could one begin to account for the perfectly adapted organisms that appeared at the very beginning of each age. For this, and for many of his celebrations, Hitchcock simply followed Paley; for his rationalization of natural evil, he followed Taylor and Bushnell. His accommodations, and particularly his theory of a limited valley flood, would remain very popular among evangelical scientists and liberal ministers, yet relatively few Christians in America were willing to accept even Hitchcock's mild reinterpretations of the ancient Semitic cosmology.

AFTER the Civil War, Christians of all denominations had to confront the same types of problems that had plagued them before the war. Slavery, however divisive, had at least focused moral concern and had often diverted attention from other social ills that would become ever more visible as the century wound down. Christians would continue to divide, not only over the proper response to social evils but also over the proper role of the church in the world. The challenges of biblical scholarship would not go away. They became more conspicuous, and more threatening, with each decade. Likewise intractable were challenges to a belief in the cosmological foundations of Christianity, challenges reinforced in the wake of new historical and theoretical knowledge about nature, as best symbolized by the controversies over Darwinism.

Afterword

$\mathcal{T}$his book has no clear end point. No sharp breaks or momentous transitions marked the history of Reformed Christianity in the nineteenth century. In the preceding essays, I have tried to include major themes that became important before the Civil War. When it seemed appropriate, or necessary for a full understanding, I traced some of these well beyond the war. The Reformed mainstream has not only continued to the present but still makes up one of the largest segments of American Christianity. Thus, I have told only half a story. If health permits, I may someday complete the story.

I can rationalize a date around 1865 as a justified breakpoint in the story of the Reformed churches, but if pushed too far such would seem like special pleading. For example, the war was very important for the churches. It solidified the sectoral divisions that grew out of controversies over slavery. It helped shift the southern evangelical denominations – Baptists, Methodists, Presbyterians – off on a course of change, or more often resistance to change, that widened differences between North and South. The war, by emancipating slaves but leaving them legally and economically vulnerable and dependent, encouraged the development of what became large black denominations, almost all Baptist and Methodist and in each case emphatically evangelical. The story of these black denominations (six large ones today) further complicated the story of Reformed Christianity, for these churches were doctrinally close to white denominations yet different in forms of worship and religious style. By 1900, these black churches, plus new schisms within white Protestantism, increased the number of large Reformed denominations from approximately seven in 1800 to well over twenty. By then it was increasingly difficult to find the mainstream, or to give content to the word *Reformed*.

In the search for transitions, one might emphasize 1859 and the publication by Charles Darwin of his *Origin of Species*. It has, in retrospect, become a watershed event, at least in a symbolic sense. Yet, perceptive Protestant intellectuals opened the debates over specific evolution well before 1859, whereas "Darwinism" became most divisive among churches in the early twentieth century. I have tried, in this book, to anticipate the nature of later controversies over both biblical scholarship and the natural sciences. No doubt, these tensions increased after 1865. Although not a new agenda, they became a much more critical one by the last decades of the century and helped create deep divisions, particularly in the northern wings of Reformed Christianity.

With each decade, the religious mosaic in America became more complex. The number of denominations increased. The range of options grew. But even here one finds no critical turning point in the middle decades of the nineteenth century. Gradually, with each decade, the Reformed mainstream contained a smaller proportion of Christians in America. This did not, in most cases, mean any significant loss of members to older, or new, varieties of Christianity. But the Reformed denominations did face ever sharper competition for new converts and had to suffer the knowledge that the outside options often grew more rapidly than they did. Only Southern Baptists, black and white, retained a competitive edge into the twentieth century.

In a sense, the direct competition abated about 1865. In the eighteenth century, both Puritans and Anglicans lost members to the Quakers. But by 1800, as American Friends lost most of their proselytizing zeal, their movement stabilized or declined, and a majority of the remaining Quakers (the Orthodox Friends) moved much closer to the evangelical side of the mainstream. Early in the nineteenth century, the new Universalist movement had broad appeal and drew converts from the mainline churches, particularly New England Congregationalists. But for complex reasons, including a shift from an evangelical style to a more rational one, and flirtation with other doctrines almost as radical as universal salvation, the Universalists reached their peak growth by 1850 and declined even in real numbers after the war. Possibly one reason for their decline was the flood of anti-Universalist literature that poured from the evangelical press.

As the Universalists lost appeal, the new Restoration churches replaced them as effective competitors. The Restoration movement began around 1800 with three separate and local reform efforts: schismatic Republican Methodists in North Carolina and Virginia, who soon repudiated creeds, took the Bible as the whole standard of truth, and chose to call their congregations simply Christian; members of a small number of former Baptist congregations in New England, who also repudiated creeds, chose the name Christian, and flirted with Arian doctrines; and New Light or revivalistic Presbyterians in Kentucky and Ohio, who, led by Barton W. Stone and six other revivalistic ministers in the wake of the great revivals of 1801, separated from the Presbyterian church, rejected any centralized church government, and formed independent Christian congregations.

After 1810, two Seceder Presbyterians from Scotland, Thomas Campbell and his son Alexander, broke from the strict conformism of the American Associate-Reformed Synod and formed an independent congregation in western Pennsylvania. Until 1824, this congregation loosely identified with the Red Stone Baptist Association in the Pittsburgh area. In 1824, after Alexander Campbell had matured doctrines completely alien to Calvinist Baptists, he joined a new Mahoning Baptist Association centered in the Western Reserve of Ohio and soon captured it for his reforms. During these Baptist years, Alexander Campbell worked out the doctrines of a truly New Testament church, which became the Disciples of Christ with the dissolution of the Mahoning Baptist Association in 1830. Campbell defined faith as acceptance of the gospel story and required a step-by-step process leading to church membership, a process that began with repentance and confession and ended with a remitting form of baptism. It was his rejection of a crisis-like conversion, and his baptismal remission, that most set him apart from evangelicals. In 1832, Barton Stone began largely successful efforts to get most of his western Christians to merge with the new and competitive Disciples. The growing Disciples proved very appealing to Baptists and remained highly competitive with other evangelicals until after the Civil War. In time, the most liberal and ecumenical wing of the movement (today the Disciples of Christ) became so liberal and inclusive as to become, in effect, a part of the mainstream. The more exclusive, restorationist, and conservative wings (Christians and Churches of Christ, and the Churches of Christ) became more isolated from the mainstream and thus less directly competitive in the twentieth century.

No other denominations ever competed so directly as the Disciples or drew away as many potential converts. The Roman Catholic church, with its exponential growth after the massive Irish and German immigration that began around 1830, became a favorite devil of evangelicals, who did all they could to stigmatize Catholics and to isolate them culturally. Protestants suffered few losses to the Catholic church. If anything, the growing Catholic presence helped provoke cooperation among Protestants and heightened their zeal. Even as few Protestants converted to Rome, so few Roman Catholics, except in very isolated enclaves, were open to conversion. Consistently, Protestants exaggerated the danger and the number of Catholics. But, sometime after 1865, Catholic membership exceeded that of any single Protestant denomination and was on the way to its present two-fifths of all American Christians. This growth was, at least, demoralizing for Protestants and helped subvert their earlier hopes for a Reformed and Christian America.

Other new American denominations were further from the mainstream, in basic doctrines, than even Roman Catholics. Unitarians in New England were too heterodox to appeal to any but a minority of Congregationalists and too latitudinarian to do much proselytizing. New Adventist sects, with their distinctive doctrines (an early and apocalyptic advent, a denial of any immaterial substance, belief in a literal resurrection into an earthly kingdom but no immortality, and denial of any eternal torment), were simply too small to compete effectively until after the Civil War. It is true that, by the twentieth century, the two largest Adventist denominations (Seventh-Day Adventists and Jehovah's Witnesses) competed very well indeed. It is also true that premillennial doctrines would distinguish new evangelical and fundamentalist factions within the Reformed denominations by the early twentieth century. But this millennialism did not involve the unique doctrines of Adventists.

The Mormon movement was even further away, in doctrines and practices, from the mainstream. It drew plenty of condemnation but was rarely competitive with Reformed Christians. It would become so in the twentieth century and is today the sixth-largest Protestant denomination. Before the Civil War it was a struggling, much persecuted sect. The church founded by Joseph Smith had unique doctrines (a literal or polytheistic trinity, a finite deity, several gradations of glory after the advent, and possibilities for all humans to become as gods) based on his *Book of Mormon* (a purported translation of ancient plates left in America by a branch of Israel) and his prophetic visions. It also had a unique, dual priesthood and distinctive practices tied to its temples, including secret endowments, the vicarious baptism of progenitors, and marriage for eternity. Driven to Utah in 1848, the church remained beleaguered in the post–Civil War years because of its acceptance of plural marriages. Only after it repudiated this practice (not the doctrines that justified it) after 1890 did it converge toward the mainstream, improve its image, and launch very successful missionary campaigns in America and around the world.

In theory but not, as it turned out, in practice, the most appealing competitor to Reformed churches should have been their closest cousins, the Lutherans. Because of the pietistic outlook of colonial Lutherans, and the evangelical style of many eastern and indigenous Lutherans in the early nineteenth century, it seemed briefly that Reformed and Lutheran denominations might so converge as to be jointly part of a mainstream. It was not to be. Waves of immigration, first by German and then Scandinavian Lutherans, arrested the convergent tendencies. These newly arrived Lutherans tried to preserve ethnic identities, formed over twenty separate denominations, reacted negatively to the revivalistic or puritanical style of American evangelicals, and increasingly emphasized a strict adherence to their own Augsburg Confession. In their defensive reaction to a new land, they drew more clearly than anytime after the early Reformation the differences between Lutheran and Reformed and rejoiced in a type of cultural isolation, often tied to their clustered ethnic communities. This would all change by the twentieth century, with more convergent trends on both sides. But by the Civil War, the Lutherans were almost as separate, as much outside the mainstream, as Roman Catholics, although never so much resented or stigmatized by other Protestants.

The most important postwar challenge to the Reformed center – internal factionalism – does not yield to any brief description. Intimations of deep internal divisions predated the war. But they became much more significant by the end of the century. It was this internal conflict, leading to fragmentation, that eventually so subverted the mainstream denominations as to leave them, today, a distinct minority within American Christianity. The internal conflict took two separate forms.

One was primarily doctrinal, although with ramifications in polity and worship. Two of the former most emphatically Calvinist denominations (Congregationalists and northern Presbyterians) had to confront the challenges of new scholarship and new scientific discoveries. They had a tradition of intellectuality and distinguished educational institutions. Both sensitive ministers and informed laypeople had no alternative but to deal, as honestly as possible, with the new challenges to the received faith. In their seminaries, even some that had formerly been bastions of orthodoxy, they sought adequate defenses of older doctrines or explored ways of accommodating new truths. This led, before 1900, to identifiable liberal (meaning a relaxation of rigid confessional standards for membership, an openness to new understandings of the Bible, and accommodations with newer scientific findings) or modernist (an emphasis on an immanent God, on the historicity of revelation, and on the revelatory uses of scientific knowledge) beliefs and to seminaries that both stimulated and reflected such beliefs. Some liberals and modernists shifted from a former emphasis on correct doctrine and individual redemptive experience to efforts at social reform, a social gospel tied to kingdom building here on earth. The effect of such new thinking was a dilution of whatever remained of the older Calvinism in these northern confessions, as well as confessional revisions in 1903 for northern Presbyterians. Those most vulnerable, or open, to a new understanding were often those who had, all along, been in the more evangelical or revivalistic camp. To a lesser extent, these same issues divided Episcopalians and northern Baptists.

Such shifts triggered a determined counterattack by the defenders of an older orthodoxy. At a sophisticated level, this meant a theological response, best exemplified at Princeton and among those who wanted a rigid adherence to the Westminster Confession. At a more popular level, it meant a defense of the most central or fundamental doctrines of evangelical Christianity, doctrines shared by Calvinists and Arminians. By 1900 the defining doctrines had become clear and even, among some groups, almost formulaic. These included the key doctrines relating to a redemptive Christ, such as his virgin birth, miracles, and death and resurrection. They included a substitutionary view of the atonement and justification only by faith through grace. A crisis-like rebirth, an affectionate style of worship, and very rigid moral standards also identified these Christians who struggled, in what they saw as the worst of times, to retain the evangelical Protestantism of the great revivals earlier in the century.

As an authority for these traditional doctrines, latter-day evangelicals insisted, with a great deal more vehemence because more was now at stake, on an infallible Bible. In the early twentieth century, various vaguely defined evolutionary theories came to symbolize a rejection of biblical truth. Most of those determined to retain the older evangelical faith also made a type of premillennialism a test of orthodoxy. This involved a pessimistic belief in awful tribulations that will precede a literal return of the Christ to reign here on earth for a thousand years. This millennialism, often tied to a schematic version of historical epochs or dispensations, marked a rejection of optimistic hopes for human achievement and rested any hope of a future kingdom on earth directly on divine intervention. In the new century, these divisions hardened and led in the 1920s to climactic battles between liberals and moderates, on one side, and aggressive fundamentalists on the other, in northern Presbyterian and northern Baptist denominations. These controversies led to several new, schismatic, and conservative denominations that, in almost all cases, grew more rapidly than their more liberal parent churches.

Internal conflict and then fragmentation within the Wesleyan tradition took a somewhat different course. The early warning signals preceded the Civil War. In 1835, two New York sisters lamented the decline of spirituality and holiness within the Methodist church. They wanted to reaffirm and realize in their own life the perfectionist or holiness beliefs of Wesley and thus began special holiness prayer meetings on Tuesday evenings. The hostess of these meetings, which continued for half a century, was one of the two sisters, Phoebe Palmer. She remained a good Methodist, and her advocacy of holiness even helped revive a holiness faction within the church. After the Civil War the holiness faction began to develop its own separate institutions, the most important being a series of holiness periodicals and, beginning in 1869, a National Camp Meeting Association for the Promotion of Holiness. This association not only sponsored annual camps but also provided what soon became a para-church institution, one that drew support from Calvinists as well as Methodists.

By 1880, disaffected holiness advocates, unhappy with what they saw as worldly or antiperfectionist trends within both the northern and southern Methodist denominations, began to form independent congregations. Two small pre–Civil War Methodist splinters, the Wesleyan and Free Methodist churches, both continued to emphasize the holiness doctrine, thus qualifying as the first Holiness denominations. Out of the scattered and independent Holiness congregations, those associated with the Camp Meeting Association, would come several twentieth-century Holiness denominations, with the largest being the present Church of the Nazarene. All Holiness congregations emphasized the attainment of holiness, or full sanctification, as a second step in the life of a Christian, a step as transforming and climactic as an earlier experience of regeneration. These new denominations drew most, but not all, their members from the established Methodist denominations. Without ever repudiating the holiness teachings of Wesley, the mainstream Methodist churches clearly subordinated the doctrine, so that today many Methodists do not even know what the doctrine entails. The ostensible reason for the two large Methodist bodies to oppose the Holiness movement was its schismatic potential, not its emphasis on holiness. Even today, a small Holiness faction remains, as a somewhat isolated echo of the past, within the United Methodist church.

Many Holiness Christians were also concerned about doctrinal issues. A goodly number of conservative Calvinists accepted some aspects of holiness, as did the famed revivalist Dwight L. Moody. But the defining concern of Holiness Christians was experiential, a lament over the loss of the exaltation and even ecstasy that accompanied the second step. Their indictment of mainstream Methodism focused on a loss in the quality of devotional life, on a cold and unmoving type of worship. Most Holiness Christians assumed an infallible Bible. Most affirmed a standard evangelical approach to regeneration. Yet many, perhaps a majority, did not believe in a form of dispensational premillennialism, and some did not place great emphasis on an infallible Bible. This was not the focus of their concerns. Thus, the reactive evangelicals within the traditionally Calvinist denominations fought their battles against doctrinal declension and in behalf of an older orthodoxy; Holiness Methodists fought primarily to preserve the experiential aspects of an older evangelicalism. The two reactions to the inroads of modernity were often, but not always, congruent. Confessional Calvinists were often horrified at the emotional extremes of Holiness churches. Some Holiness Christians viewed orthodox Calvinists as cold and harsh. Calvinists were more likely to embrace confessional orthodoxy; Holiness advocates emphasized a warm and fulfilling experience.

In a historical perspective, the late-nineteenth-century Holiness movement now seems to have been largely transitional, one step toward something much more radical. Today, the number of Pentecostal Christians far outnumber those in Holiness denominations. And, to a large extent, Pentecostalism was an outgrowth of the Holiness movement. The history of Pentecostalism is both complex and fascinating and therefore not easily summarized here. Its roots go back to the early church. Anticipations in America date well back into the nineteenth century. One small sect, the Shakers, used ecstatic language just after the American Revolution, and both Adventists and Mormons in the pre–Civil War years had experimented with ecstatic speech. But as an organized movement, Pentecostalism dates only from the beginning of the twentieth century, when tongue speaking erupted first in Topeka and then much more explosively in Los Angeles. Some Holiness preachers had long identified the second step, or sanctification, as the baptism of the Holy Spirit, and some identified it with the Christian experience on the Day of Pentecost. If the second step was indeed the Pentecostal experience, then clearly most Holiness Christians had neglected one of the key signs of Spirit baptism, the speaking in tongues that erupted among the apostles after they received the Spirit at Pentecost.

It was such speaking that triggered a new religious movement. Soon interpretations varied. Many out of the Holiness movement, those who had long since experienced sanctification without tongue speaking, believed that the baptism of the Holy Spirit, and the resulting tongues, was a third step in the Christian life. Others, who did not come directly out of the Holiness churches, usually saw only two steps – regeneration and spirit baptism – and thus conflated holiness perfection and Spirit baptism, with tongues the one test or sign of such baptism (the largest such denomination today is the Assemblies of God). Even to this day, Pentecostals are almost equally divided between two- and three-step advocates and also divided doctrinally between the overwhelming trinitarian majority and a small but forceful unitarian or Jesus-only minority (only one God and Jesus is his name). Blacks were as much involved in early Pentecostalism as whites, and today the largest Pentecostal denomination (the Church of God in Christ) is predominantly black. After the sifting out of the early, often biracial movement, Pentecostals tended to move to racially separate denominations. But much more than in traditional denominations, early Pentecostals accepted women as clergy or even prophets.

Much as with Holiness Christians, Pentecostals tended to be conservative in their doctrines and in this sense a part of the evangelical-fundamentalist spectrum. Again, however, it was not doctrine but experience that set them apart. Above all, it was speaking in tongues. All the early Pentecostal leaders believed that, under inspiration of the Spirit, Christians spoke in various foreign languages. This is what they meant by "speaking in tongues." Even to this day, despite compelling evidence to the contrary, some still hold to this position, sometimes having recourse to the idea of angelic languages not presently spoken anywhere on earth. Early ecstatic speech, such as among the Shakers, had been a form of meaningless utterance, or glossolalia, with no linguistic counterpart. This meant that such ecstatic speech had no meaning for listeners, unless some other person had the gift of interpretation. Note that tongue speaking, or ecstatic speech, made up only one of the special gifts of the Spirit identified by Paul in I Corinthians 10–13. Prophecy and healing were very important among early Pentecostals, but most continued to make tongues the proof of Spirit baptism, thus giving it a preeminence that Paul had discouraged at Corinth.

Membership in Pentecostal denominations may now number 10 million; the membership figures reported by well over a hundred such denominations are much higher. Membership in Holiness but not Pentecostal churches is close to 4 million. Holiness and Pentecostal Christians together far outnumber the members of the present United Methodist church. In addition to separate Pentecostal denominations, after World War II a charismatic movement boomed in Roman Catholic and mainline Protestant denominations, leading to separate discussion and prayer groups and to glossolalia as the central and additive experience, mixed in at times with prayer healing. Such charismatic groups have created some tension, and much apprehension, among even the most tolerant church leaders. Only some of the evangelical, fundamentalist, or doctrinally very conservative denominations have condemned, or strongly discouraged, such a cultivation of spiritual gifts. In a sense, such mainstream spirituality has come full circle, back to the affluent and socially prominent urbanites who first attended Phoebe Palmer's Tuesday meetings back in 1835. Unlike the almost fashionable charisma at the top, the separate Pentecostal denominations have, so far, appealed largely to people at the very bottom of the economic and social order.

I have thus identified at least four major challenges to the older, Reformed mainstream – modern evangelicals, fundamentalists, Holiness advocates, and Pentecostals. By "evangelicals," I mean those who, in the late nineteenth and the twentieth centuries, have continued to affirm the salvation doctrines and other essential characteristics of early-nineteenth-century evangelicals, characteristics such as a crisis-like rebirth (born-again Christians), a warm and spontaneous worship, frequent revivals, strongly committed mission efforts, and a puritanical or antiworldly moral stance. *Fundamentalism* is now a loaded word, and scholars have never accepted any one conventional definition, leading to some needless interpretative conflicts based on verbal ambiguities. By "fundamentalists," I mean a subclass of evangelicals, a coalition of evangelical Christians who have continued to make doctrinal issues central, who have identified a range of shared doctrines that seem fundamental or essential, and who have openly and aggressively challenged what they see as modernist innovations or corruptions within the mainstream denominations and have equally aggressively challenged societal changes (in education, in legislation, in the media, in moral standards) that threaten evangelical beliefs and values. They have often entered the political realm to block what they perceive as overly secular or humanistic trends, such as in early-twentieth-century efforts to prevent the teaching of Darwinism in the schools or recent efforts to gain equal time in schools for creation theories.

In my estimation, the most important shift in the history of the Reformed mainstream, in the decades after the Civil War, was this increasingly disruptive internal factionalism. By 1900 it was difficult to locate a center or mainstream, Reformed or not. It is even more difficult today. In one form or another, the Reformed denominations of 1800 remain at the center of Protestantism in 1994 – large, respectable, but most with declining appeal and dropping membership. The

Southern Baptist Convention is now by far the largest Protestant denomination in America, and is still growing. After reunification of northern and southern wings, the United Methodist church and the Presbyterian church remain large and wealthy, still in the top ten in membership (Methodists are second among Protestants, with Presbyterians approximately seventh). The Episcopal church barely remains tenth, whereas the modern offspring of Congregationalism (the United Church of Christ, which includes the former German Reformed) is approximately thirteenth, and American Baptists (northern) are fourteenth. Even the small Reformed Church in America (Dutch) is stable and prosperous. In this sense, the mainstream of 1800 endures. But such a grouping is even more problematic and the label "mainstream" even more vague.

What about all the many denominations that have splintered off from these core denominations? In particular, what about the black Baptist and Methodist denominations? Note that, by their latest reported membership, three of these black churches are now in the top ten in membership (the National Baptist Convention, USA, Inc., the Church of God in Christ, and the National Baptist Convention of America), and a fourth (African Methodist Episcopal) is now eleventh in size among Protestants.

Today, most people use sociological criteria to define a Christian mainstream. It is made up of those denominations that retain venerable traditions, that possess strong organizational and educational resources, that appeal to middle-class families, that are broadly inclusive in membership, that have made accommodations to the modern world in doctrine and ethics, and that are open to ecumenical discussions or are members of such cooperative bodies as the National Council of Churches. By such criteria, some earlier nonmainstream churches, including those not from the Reformed tradition, have gained certification as mainstream, such as the Disciples of Christ and the present product of several mergers, the Evangelical Lutheran Church in America. Some debate whether Roman Catholics have now joined the mainstream and, if not, how close they are. At the same time, many would argue that the Southern Baptist Convention, recently so captive to aggressive evangelical and fundamentalist leadership, is no longer a part of the mainstream but rather a component of evangelical-fundamentalist reaction. For complex reasons, tied often to worship style and conservative doctrines, few place the black Methodist and Baptist denominations within the mainstream, although the African Methodist Episcopal church is close.

If one returns to 1800, the seven denominations that made up my broadly defined Reformed tradition then accounted for almost nine out of ten church members in America. How have these denominations fared? Today, the Separate Baptists of 1800 have their most direct lineage in two denominations: the northern American Baptist Churches in the USA, and the Southern Baptist Convention.

One independent denomination in 1800 (German Reformed) is now allied with Congregationalists in the United Church of Christ. The others – United Methodists, Presbyterian Church (USA), the Episcopal Church, and the small Reformed Church (Dutch) in America – are still kicking. Their total inclusive (and thus somewhat exaggerated) membership is around 33 million today and is stable, with the annual growth in the Southern Baptist Convention almost compensating for the annual decline in all the other denominations. Total church membership for the United States is very much an educated guess because of the lack of a religious census, misreporting to the annual *Yearbook* of the National Council, out-of-date statistics, and the large number of nonreporting independent congregations or noncooperative small sects. The upper total is around 150 million. If one subtracts over 57 million Roman Catholics, and at least 3 million in various Eastern Orthodox churches, the Protestant total is around 90 million. This number does not take into account several nonreporting but usually small denominations or include the full figures from some almost unbelievable recent membership reports from a few Pentecostal denominations and from four black Baptist denominations. For this reason, it is a plausible but challengeable figure. This means that the mainstream churches, in the literal sense of denominational continuity, make up just over 36 percent of Protestants and only 22 percent of all Christians. This is quite a drop from 1800, but in many ways the numbers are very misleading.

The first problem with these numbers is deciding what to do with the present Southern Baptist Convention. If one drops it from the mainstream, the total number in the center drops to 17 million, less than 19 percent of the Protestant total. On the other hand, if one adds to the 15 million Southern Baptists the four major black Baptist denominations, and much in doctrine and practice justifies this combination, then those Baptists easily exceed in number all the other mainstream and Reformed denominations. The number of black Baptists is anyone's guess these days but by any fair estimate is over 7 million (the most recent reports by four denominations, which include some overlapping counts, exceed 15 million), making 22 million in the Southern Baptist Convention and the black churches that directly descend from it. Based on sentiment, and convergent doctrines and liturgies, one has good reason to add the Disciples and Evangelical Lutherans to the other former Reformed churches. This raises the more liberal and ecumenical mainstream to over 22 million, an almost equal balance with the conservative and evangelical Baptists. This leaves over 3 million black Methodists that might fit into the mainstream total or, on the other hand, fit reasonably well with modern Holiness churches.

If one approaches the Protestant churches of today, the most revealing categories involve doctrine and style, not institutional continuities. If one wants to determine how many Protestants are still in the evangelical tradition of the early nineteenth century (rebirth, revivals, affectionate and free worship, rigid moral standards), one would find this among the contemporary Christians who cling to this evangelical heritage and, often, to the older doctrinal formulas that supported it. I know of no sure way to identify such an evangelical remnant. But the core of it would include a majority of present-day Southern Baptists, a majority of black Baptists, most black Methodists, a minority within the United Methodist church and the Presbyterian Church (USA), a large number of splinter denominations that have at various points, and in reaction to liberalizing trends, splintered from the mainstream denominations, plus a dozen or so evangelical denominations that do not have such schismatic origins. The last two categories include the 6 million Americans who belong to forty-eight denominations that have affiliated with the National Association of Evangelicals (NAE). If one adds to this the Holiness and Pentecostal denominations not in the NAE, one ends up with at least 45 million self-identified evangelical Christians, or over half of all Protestants.

Is this the true legacy of early-nineteenth-century evangelicalism? Are these Christians the main modern-day legatees of the Reformed tradition, since most, but not all, trace their roots back to this branch of the Reformation? Yes and no. They seem, on first glance, to be near-echoes of an older religious style and of older confessions that liberals have revised or ignored. But in the early nineteenth century, with the Methodists in the lead, evangelicals were the innovators, the most creative and at times most prophetic of Christians. Today's self-proclaimed evangelicals are reactive and atavistic. They are trying to reclaim, or hold on to, a tradition swamped by changes in the larger society. And they also, in ways often unrecognized, have shifted emphases. For example, the prevalence of premillennialism is something new, and the great emphasis on biblical inerrancy, although not a new doctrine, has an edge to it that makes it seem so different from the easy assumptions of earlier Christians who never had to deal with biblical scholarship or completely altered conceptions of the physical universe. What was assumed has become a defining issue, and the result is a type of defensive evangelicalism that seems very different from the early-nineteenth-century Methodist variety.

Certainly, the Holiness and Pentecostal movements have added something new to a very distinctive wing of twentieth-century evangelicalism. However much the deference to Wesley, the varied modern interpretations of holiness, and what it demands, have departed from early Methodism, whereas the gifts of the Spirit, despite the New Testament justification, place modern Pentecostals in a unique tradition, with few ties either to evangelical Protestants of the early nineteenth century or to the Reformed churches of the early Reformation. In most ways, they reflect enthusiastic or antinomian trends that drew the ire of Calvin and his successors.

Where does this leave us? What is the heritage of the Reformed mainstream, and where can one locate it today? I would argue that, in an atavistic sense, one could find it among the often militant and expansive non-Pentecostal evangelicals, particularly those who still affirm a version of Calvinism. Except for Southern Baptists, only a small minority of these are in the older denominations, but they are in new denominations that reflect, more literally than their liberal parent churches, Reformed beliefs. Institutionally, and perhaps also in certain underlying attitudes, one has to locate the Reformed mainstream where it was in the beginning, in the now often liberal or inclusive or ecumenical denominations that began in colonial America and that still enjoy wealth and a fashionable membership and, possibly because of such an establishment status, suffer a steadily declining appeal. These denominations are the modern products of gradually changing religious experience, of vast societal shifts, of ever more sophisticated religious education, and of institutional and doctrinal accommodations. Given these changes through time, colonial Reformed Christians – some evangelical, some more formal and confessional – are best identified as the progenitors of people who today defend very different beliefs and values.

Notes

CHAPTER ONE

1. The history of the English Reformation remains controversial. In *English Reformations: Religion, Politics, and Society under the Tudors* (Oxford: Clarendon Press, 1993), Christopher Haigh argues that the effective reform of the English church, at the local level, came only in the middle of Elizabeth's reign, about 1580. He stresses the strength, and the enduring appeal, of the old church and thus the limited effects of early, political reformations. This is a revision of the more traditional view, one best reflected in Arthur G. Dickens, *The English Reformation*, 2d ed. (London: B. T. Batsford, 1989). Haigh offers a brilliant examination of the historiography of the English Reformation in his edited volume *The English Reformation Revised* (Cambridge: Cambridge University Press, 1987). Another recent interpretation is in J. J. Scarisbrick, *The Reformation and the English People* (Oxford: Oxford University Press, 1984).

2. The literature on Puritanism is almost overwhelming in scope and subtlety. The central problem remains definitional: how is one to use the loaded label "Puritan"? A good introduction to the problem is in Peter Lake, *Moderate Puritans and the Elizabethan Church* (New York: Cambridge University Press, 1982). The problem of the Puritans becomes entangled with the so-called Puritan Revolution and with various attempts to understand its causes. Many of the recent controversies have revolved around at least mildly Marxist interpretations, such as Christopher Hill's classic *Intellectual Origins of the English Revolution* (Oxford: Clarendon Press, 1965). I have been content to give a sketch of events and dare not try to resolve these definitional or interpretative problems.

3. Biographies of John Knox abound. An excellent representative of these is Henry Cowan, *John Knox, the Hero of the Scottish Reformation* (New York: AMS Press, 1970). A brief but very useful history of the Scottish Reformation is by James M. Reid, *Kirk and Nation: The Story of the Reformed Church of Scotland* (London: Skeffington, 1960). A more recent account is in James Kirk, *Patterns of Reform: Continuity and Change in the Reformation Kirk* (Edinburgh: T. & T. Clark, 1989).

4. A good introduction to Ulster Presbyterianism is in Peter Brooke, *Ulster Presbyterianism: The Historical Perspective, 1610–1970* (New York: St. Martin's, 1987).

5. The most succinct history of the Anglican church in the American colonies is in Raymond W. Albright, *A History of the Protestant Episcopal Church* (New York: Macmillan, 1964). Albright has chapters on each colony and a rather detailed account of the effort to gain American bishops. More detailed histories of colonial Anglicanism exist for most colonies.

6. I cannot begin to cite sources for my brief survey of Puritans or Congregationalists in New England. Here one is simply overwhelmed by the scholarship. Very soon the number of Puritan scholars will exceed the number of seventeenth-century Puritans in New England. This explosion of scholarship began with the appreciative and probing writings of Perry Miller and Edmund Morgan on the thought and culture of Puritan New England, of

William Haller on the English Puritan background, and of Kenneth A. Lockridge on New England institutions. Perhaps no other local society has received as much attention as the early Puritans in Massachusetts Bay.

7. This survey of early Presbyterians draws directly from Leonard J. Trinterud, *The Founding of an American Tradition: A Reexamination of Colonial Presbyterianism* (Philadelphia: Westminster Press, 1949). Several paragraphs in this section roughly duplicate those in my earlier book, *Cane Ridge: America's Pentecost* (Madison: University of Wisconsin Press, 1990). Two recent books that illuminate aspects of colonial Presbyterianism are Marilyn J. Westerkamp, *Triumph of the Laity: Scots-Irish Piety and the Great Awakening, 1625–1760* (New York: Oxford University Press, 1988), and Leigh Eric Schmidt, *Holy Fairs: Scottish Communions and American Revivals in the Early Modern Period* (Princeton: Princeton University Press, 1989). A record of the role of Samuel Davies in founding southern Presbyterianism is in George W. Pilcher, *Samuel Davies: Apostle of Dissent in Colonial Virginia* (Knoxville: University of Tennessee Press, 1971).

8. The beginning point for Baptist history is Robert G. Torbet's often revised and reprinted *A History of the Baptists* (Valley Forge: Judson Press, 1950). William G. McLoughlin has illuminated almost every facet of colonial Baptism in New England, in *Isaac Backus and the American Political Tradition* (Boston: Little, Brown, 1967), in *New England Dissent: 1630–1833: The Baptists and the Separation of Church and State* (Cambridge: Harvard University Press, 1971), and in *Soul Liberty: The Baptists' Struggle in New England, 1630–1833* (Providence: Brown University Press, 1991). Baptist growth in the South is charted in several histories of individual colonies, with one of the most informative being Reuben E. Alley, *A History of Baptists in Virginia* (Richmond: Virginia Baptist General Board, 1973).

9. A brief history of the early German Reformed church is in the introductory sections of an older book: James I. Good, *History of the Reformed Church in the United States in the Nineteenth Century* (New York: Board of Publication of the Reformed Church, 1911). For the insights of the greatest single founder of the German Reformed church, read William J. Hinke, ed., *Life and Letters of the Rev. John Philip Boehm, Founder of the Reformed Church in Pennsylvania, 1683–1749* (Philadelphia: Publication and Sunday School Board of the Reformed Church, 1916).

10. The most comprehensive history of the colonial Dutch church is in Gerald Francis De Jong, *The Dutch Reformed Church in the American Colonies* (Grand Rapids: Eerdmans, 1978).

CHAPTER TWO

1. This brief biographical introduction to Wesley is so general as to encompass a story present in what is now dozens of Wesley biographies. I found the best balance in approach, and the most useful details, in Henry D. Rack, *Reasonable Enthusiast: John Wesley and the Rise of Methodism* (London: Epworth Press, 1989). The title well expresses his balanced interpretation. A very competent, but briefer, biography is Stanley E. Ayling, *John Wesley* (Cleveland: Collins, 1979).

2. For an introduction to Wesley's theology, I recommend Colin W. Williams, *John Wesley's Theology Today* (Nashville: Abingdon, 1960), and William R. Cannon, *The Theology of John Wesley, with Special Reference to the Doctrine of Justification* (Nashville: Abingdon, 1946). For a brief exploration of Wesley's theological reflections, see Robert W. Burtner and

Robert E. Chiles, eds., *A Compend of Wesley's Theology* (Nashville: Abingdon, 1954). George C. Cell, in *The Rediscovery of John Wesley* (New York: Henry Holt, 1935), offers an exaggerated Calvinistic interpretation of Wesley.

3. Leo George Cox, in *John Wesley's Concept of Perfection* (Kansas City: Beacon Hill Press, 1964), provides a running description, and apology, for almost every position Wesley ever held about perfection or complete sanctification. From my perspective, the most systematic and profound explanation and scriptural as well as psychological defense of Wesley's doctrine is in a brilliant essay by Wilbur T. Dayton: "Entire Sanctification: The Divine Purification and Perfection of Man," in Charles W. Carter, ed., *A Contemporary Wesleyan Theology: Biblical, Systematic, and Practical*, 2 vols. (Grand Rapids: Francis Asbury Press, 1983), 1:515–66.

4. The following description of Methodist institutions generally follows Rack, but for a fuller account see Rupert Davies and Gordon Rupp, eds., *A History of the Methodist Church in Great Britain*, 2 vols. (London: Epworth Press, 1965).

5. For the early history of Methodism in America, scholars have to be thankful for a major work of cooperative scholarship that remains unique among denominational histories: Emory S. Bucke, ed., *The History of American Methodism*, 3 vols. (Nashville: Abingdon, 1964). This effort involved forty-four authors, ranging from social historians to theologians, and included almost every expert then writing on American Methodism. Although sponsored by the Methodist church, it is both scholarly and critical; it is also, by its nature, uneven in quality from one essay to another. For a briefer story, and one with the advantage of a single perspective, I prefer Frederick A. Norwood, *The Story of American Methodism* (Nashville: Abingdon, 1974). Norwood also edited a useful anthology, *Sourcebook of American Methodism* (Nashville: Abingdon, 1982).

6. Anyone fascinated with early American Methodism must read Francis Asbury, *Journals and Letters*, ed. Elmer E. Clark, 3 vols. (Nashville: Abingdon, 1958). My attempts to portray the flavor of early Methodism rests almost entirely on Asbury.

7. The flavor of early-nineteenth-century Methodism is in Asbury's *Journals* and, in less accurate but more flamboyant form, in Peter Cartwright, *Autobiography of Peter Cartwright, the Backwoods Preacher* (New York: Carlton and Porter, 1857). But the detailed story is present only in numerous contemporary local histories of the booming Methodist movement, such as Albert H. Redford, *The History of Methodism in Kentucky*, 3 vols. (Nashville: Southern Methodist Publishing House, 1868).

CHAPTER THREE

1. A world of books and articles documents theological thought in America. But, as yet, we have no competent history of theology in America. The main New England stream had its first history in Frank H. Foster's *A Genetic History of the New England Theology* (Chicago: University of Chicago Press, 1907), which remains the best work on the subject. More recently, Bruce Kuklick, in *Churchmen and Philosophers: From Jonathan Edwards to John Dewey* (New Haven: Yale University Press, 1985), tried to trace continuities in New England theology, but with only the loosest and most general attention to the subtleties of theological arguments.

2. No other American theologian has received as much scholarly attention as Jonathan Edwards. A masterful edition of his works is now all but complete: *The Works of Jonathan*

Edwards (New Haven: Yale University Press, 1957–). At least fifty monographs explore every aspect of his thought. Yet, I am not aware of any biography that effectively merges his private life with an in-depth exploration of his philosophy and theology. Perhaps the best-known attempt, by Perry Miller – *Jonathan Edwards* (New York: W. Sloane, 1949) – revealed as much about Miller as Edwards. Older biographies, such as those by Ola Winslow or A. Owen Aldridge, are even more deficient on his theology. In this chapter, I drew primarily on my own scholarship and my own reading of Edwards. I have found useful the work of Conrad Cherry, *The Theology of Jonathan Edwards: A Reappraisal* (Garden City: Anchor, 1966), reissued with new reflections in 1990 (Bloomington: Indiana University Press), and the work of Douglas J. Ellwood, *The Philosophical Theology of Jonathan Edwards* (New York: Columbia University Press, 1960).

3. Edwards's successors, the New Divinity theologians, have received increasing scholarly attention. The classic that began this scholarship, and a book that helped shape my interpretation, is Joseph Haroutunian, *Piety Versus Moralism: The Passing of New England Theology* (New York: Henry Holt, 1932). The most recent book to cover much of the same ground is Allen C. Guelzo's *Edwards on the Will: A Century of American Theological Debate* (Middletown, Conn.: Wesleyan University Press, 1989). This book has a very complete bibliography on the New Divinity movement.

4. Most of this biographical material on Hopkins comes from an excellent Ph.D. dissertation that I supervised at the University of Wisconsin: Hugh Heath Knapp, "Samuel Hopkins and the New Divinity" (1971).

5. These early sermons appear in Amasa Edwards Park, ed., *The Works of Samuel Hopkins*, 5 vols. (Boston: Doctrinal Tract and Book Society, 1852).

6. My analysis of the Hopkinsian system derives entirely from my reading and study of Hopkins's *The System of Doctrines, Contained in Divine Revelation, etc.*, 2 vols. (Boston: Thomas and Andrews, 1793).

CHAPTER FOUR

1. The role of the evangelical denominations in the early Republic figures large in almost all standard histories of religion in America. Most of the more specialized studies have a contestable interpretation or thesis. Among these I would begin with Nathan O. Hatch, *The Democratization of American Christianity* (New Haven: Yale University Press, 1989). Hatch believes the dominant theme in the early nineteenth century was greater lay participation and a loss of clerical authority, conjoined with restorationist or primitive goals. His thesis perhaps best fits new religious movements but relates to the mainstream. Jon Butler, in *Awash in a Sea of Faith: Christianizing the American People* (Cambridge: Harvard University Press, 1990), relates the formal or official religion of elites to the popular beliefs or superstitions of the masses, adding a rich folk-culture perspective to the age of revivals. In a more narrow and less cogently argued book, Fred Hood, in *Reformed America: The Middle and Southern States, 1783–1837* (University: University of Alabama Press, 1980), argues that the Reformed churches, by which he means primarily Presbyterians but also German and Dutch Reformed, did more than New England Congregationalists to establish a special church-state system in America, as well as a providential or millennial sense of national identity. In a perverse, religiously insensitive book, George M. Thomas, *Revivalism and Cultural Change: Christianity, Nation Building, and the Market in the Nineteenth Century*

United States (Chicago: University of Chicago Press, 1989), tries to fit evangelical religion into a market-economic model.

2. I know of no book that explores a uniquely American type of religious pluralism and church-state relationship in the middle period. The federal role was minimal until after ratification of the Fourteenth Amendment. Peripherally related to my concerns is T. Jeremy Gunn, *A Standard for Repair: The Establishment Clause, Equality, and Natural Rights* (New York: Garland, 1992). The religious views of our leading Founding Fathers, and the origins of a type of civil religion, are surveyed in Edwin S. Gaustad, *Faith of Our Fathers: Religion and the New Nation* (San Francisco: Harper and Row, 1987).

3. Most books on middle-period Protestantism emphasize revivals. Here the literature is very rich and challenging. Most cosmic is William G. McLoughlin, *Revivals, Awakenings, and Reform: An Essay on Religion and Social Change in America, 1607–1977* (Chicago: University of Chicago Press, 1978). He fits revivals into a broader context of cultural revitalization and identifies five such cycles of revitalization in American history, not all distinctively Christian. The standard older book on revivals, and one now quite dated in interpretation, is William Warren Sweet, *Revivalism in America, Its Origin, Growth, and Decline* (New York: Scribner's, 1944). More popular and more superficial is Bernard A. Weisberger, *They Gathered at the River: The Story of the Great Revivalists and Their Impact upon Religion in America* (Boston: Little, Brown, 1958). The most insightful book on the backdrop of nineteenth-century revivalism is Leigh Eric Schmidt, *Holy Fairs: Scottish Communions and American Revivals in the Early Modern Period* (Princeton: Princeton University Press, 1989). Nancy Hardesty, in *Your Daughters Shall Prophesy: Revivalism and Feminism in the Age of Finney* (Brooklyn: Carlson Publishers, 1991), surveys, from an evangelical perspective, the new roles opened for women in Charles Finney's revivals. The following books offer a rich biographical perspective on nineteenth-century revivals: Keith Hardman, *The Spiritual Awakners: American Revivalists from Solomon Stoddard to D. L. Moody* (Chicago: Moody Press, 1983) and *Charles Grandison Finney, 1792–1875* (Syracuse: Syracuse University Press, 1987); William G. McLoughlin, *Modern Revivalism: Charles Grandison Finney to Billy Graham* (New York: Ronald Press, 1959); and James W. Fraser, *Pedagogue for God's Kingdom: Lyman Beecher and the Second Great Awakening* (Lanham, Md.: University Press of America, 1985).

4. I have relied on my recent book, *Cane Ridge: America's Pentecost* (Madison: University of Wisconsin Press, 1990), for the story of the western revivals. For an even broader perspective, see John Boles, *The Great Revival, 1787–1805* (Lexington: University Press of Kentucky, 1972).

5. My estimates of church membership and its regional distribution, and of the relative strengths of each denomination, depend on Edwin S. Gaustad, *Historical Atlas of Religion in America* (New York: Harper and Row, 1976). As Gaustad makes clear, these estimates have a very large margin of error, as is demonstrated in Roger Finke and Rodney Stark, *The Churching of America: Winners and Losers in Our Religious Economy* (New Brunswick: Rutgers University Press, 1992). Beyond some revealing statistics on membership, this book has little to recommend it: it is arrogant in its claims, simplistic in its understanding of doctrine, and even challengeable on several of its membership estimates.

6. The most detailed survey of the Cumberland schism is in two books with opposite perspectives. Robert Davidson, the noted historian of western Presbyterianism, defends the action of the Kentucky Synod in his *History of the Presbyterian Church in the State of Ken-*

tucky (New York: Carter, 1847); Franceway R. Cossitt, in *The Life and Times of Rev. Finis Ewing* (Louisville: Woods, 1853), offers an apology of Ewing and his colleagues in the former Cumberland Presbytery.

7. For the peculiar problems faced by evangelicals in the South, see the excellent study by Donald G. Mathews, *Religion in the Old South* (Chicago: University of Chicago Press, 1977).

8. Beginning in the 1950s, scholars became fascinated with the ties between evangelical religion and both social control and social reform. An early, sympathetic account was Timothy L. Smith, *Revivalism and Social Reform in Mid-Nineteenth-Century America* (Nashville: Abingdon, 1957), which complements Charles C. Cole, *The Social Ideas of the Northern Evangelists, 1826–1860* (New York: Columbia University Press, 1954). Two scholars both turned in the next few years to the role of evangelical benevolence, particularly as used by eastern elites to help control the behavior of working-class people or the benighted inhabitants of the West and South: Charles I. Foster, *An Errand of Mercy: The Evangelical United Front, 1790–1837* (Chapel Hill: University of North Carolina Press, 1960), and Clifford S. Griffin, *Their Brothers' Keepers: Moral Stewardship in the United States, 1800–1865* (New Brunswick: Rutgers University Press, 1960). More specialized studies include John R. Bodo, *The Protestant Clergy and Public Issues, 1812–1848* (Philadelphia: Porcupine Press, 1980); Victor B. Howard, *Conscience and Slavery: The Evangelistic Calvinist Domestic Missions, 1837–1861* (Kent: Kent State University Press, 1990); and Creighton Lacy, *The Word-Carrying Giant: The Growth of the American Bible Society, 1816–1966* (South Pasadena: William Carey Library, 1977).

9. Many of my comments on Sunday schools derive from my experience as a boy in rural Sunday school classes. The historical record comes, in large part, from a book written by a former graduate student: Anne M. Boylan, *Sunday School: The Formation of an American Institution* (New Haven: Yale University Press, 1988). An older, detailed history is in Edwin W. Rice, *Sunday-School Movement, 1780–1917, and the American Sunday-School Union, 1817–1917* (Philadelphia: American Sunday School Union, 1917).

CHAPTER FIVE

1. The only detailed history of the complex events leading to the formation of the Protestant Episcopal church is Clara O. Loveland, *The Critical Years: The Reconstitution of the Anglican Church in the United States of America, 1780–1789* (Greenwich, Conn.: Seabury Press, 1956). A firsthand account is in William White, *Memoirs of the Protestant Episcopal Church in the United States of America etc.* (New York: Swords, Stanford, 1836).

2. The best brief, recent, summary history of the Protestant Episcopal church is Robert W. Prichard, *A History of the Episcopal Church* (Harrisburg: Morehouse Publishers, 1991). More detailed and quite balanced are two older books: James Thayer Addison, *The Episcopal Church in the United States* (New York: Charles Scribner's Sons, 1951), and Raymond W. Albright, *A History of the Protestant Episcopal Church* (New York: Macmillan, 1964).

3. The deep divisions within the Episcopal church in the middle period still influence the interpretation of historians. Excellent in details, but serving as a High Church apology, is George E. De Mille, *The Catholic Movement in the American Episcopal Church* (Philadelphia: Church History Society, 1941). Much more balanced, and very perceptive, is a book

which I was privileged to read in manuscript: Diana H. Butler, *Standing against the Whirlwind: Evangelical Episcopalians in Nineteenth Century America* (New York: Oxford University Press, 1994). It was an indispensable source for me. Robert B. Mullin, in *Episcopal Vision/American Reality: High Church Theology and Social Thought in Evangelical America* (New Haven: Yale University Press, 1986), proves that it was often the High Church faction that led the way in social action.

4. I drew most of the details about the Carey trial, and the turbulence within the General Seminary, from the reprint of a memoir by one of the seminary students and a later convert to Catholicism, Clarence E. Walworth, *The Oxford Movement in America* (New York: United States Catholic Historical Society, 1974).

5. A brief summary of the career of the Protestant Episcopal Church in the Confederate States of America is in the introduction by William A. Clebsch, ed., *Journals of the Protestant Episcopal Church in the Confederate States of America* (Austin: Church Historical Society, 1962).

6. The Mercersburg theology has received endless scholarly attention, though not so the church that gave birth to it. The most detailed account of the German Reformed church in the nineteenth century remains an old book: James I. Good, *History of the Reformed Church in the United States in the Nineteenth Century* (New York: Board of Publications of the Reformed Church, 1911).

7. An excellent anthology of the work of Nevin and Schaff is in James S. Nichols, ed., *The Mercersburg Theology* (New York: Oxford University Press, 1966). Charles Vrigoyen, Jr., and George M. Broder have edited two anthologies: *Catholic and Reformed: Selected Theological Writings of John Williamson Nevin* (Pittsburgh: Pickwick Press, 1978) and *Catholic and Reformed: Selected Theological Writings of Philip Schaff* (Pittsburgh: Pickwick Press, 1979). The most sophisticated interpretation of Nevin's theology and its German sources is in Brian A. Gerrish, *Tradition and the Modern World: Reformed Theology in the Nineteenth Century* (Chicago: University of Chicago Press, 1978). My interpretations drew directly on Nevin's own writing, including a now joint binding of the two essays that occasioned the most controversy in America: John Nevin, *The Anxious Bench; The Mystical Presence* (New York: Garland Publishers, 1987). His more extended sacramental views are in Bard Thompson and George H. Bricher, eds., *The Mystical Presence, and Other Writings on the Eucharist* (Philadelphia: United Church Press, 1966). Of the voluminous historical writings by Philip Schaff, the one most closely tied to his Mercersburg years, and to the sources of Mercersburg theology, was his 1853 *History of the Apostolic Church, with a General Introduction to Church History*, trans. Edward O. Yeomans (New York: C. Scribner, 1856). The most recent biography of Schaff is George H. Shriver, *Philip Schaff: Christian Scholar and Ecumenical Prophet* (Macon, Ga.: Mercer University Press, 1987).

8. The history of the Dutch Reformed church is not as assessable as one might expect. The church has published a major series of bicentennial monographs, and almost every specialized aspect of the church has received historical attention. The literature on the colonial Dutch is particularly rich. Yet, I have been unable to find a single, comprehensive, scholarly history of the Dutch church in America. One of the bicentennial volume series, James W. Van Hoeven, ed., *Piety and Patriotism: Bicentennial Studies of the Reformed Church in America, 1776–1976* (Grand Rapids: Eerdmans, 1976), contains essays on the early nineteenth century. Gerald Francis De Jong, in *The Dutch Reformed Church in the American Colonies* (Grand Rapids: Eerdmans, 1978), traces the story up through the founding of a

national church. In *The Dutch in America, 1609–1974* (Boston: G. K. Hall, 1974), De Jong gives special attention to the church. Two excellent essays, by Elton J. Bruins and Herbert J. Brinks, in Robert P. Swierenga, ed., *The Dutch in America: Immigration, Settlement, and Cultural Change* (New Brunswick: Rutgers University Press, 1985), emphasize the problems of cultural assimilation on the part of Dutch Reformed immigrants.

9. The Christian Reformed church has never neglected its own history. But unfortunately almost all the scholarship has come from within the church. Much has an apologetic tone, as in Diedrich H. Kromminga, *The Christian Reformed Church: A Study in Orthodoxy* (Grand Rapids: G. R. Baker, 1949), Marian M. Schoolland, *Children of the Reformation: The Story of the Christian Reformed Church, Its Origin and Growth* (Grand Rapids: Eerdmans, 1958), and Henry Beets, *The Christian Reformed Church: Its Roots, History, Schools, and Mission Work, A.D. 1857–1946* (Grand Rapids: Baker Book House, 1946). The most critical history of this schism, and the one most helpful to me, is James D. Bratt, *Dutch Calvinism in Modern America: A History of a Conservative Subculture* (Grand Rapids: Eerdmans, 1984). Several revealing essays are in Peter De Klerk and Richard De Ridder, *Perspectives on the Christian Reformed Church: Studies in Its History, Theology, and Ecumenicity* (Grand Rapids: Baker Book House, 1983). A full chronology of the complex development of this church is in Howard B. Spaan, *Christian Reformed Church Government* (Grand Rapids: Kregel Publications, 1968).

CHAPTER SIX

1. German scholars have done the most work on the history of worship. But a few American scholars have synthesized the scholarship for American audiences and have added to this history of worship the distinctive contributions of Americans. I most of all gained insights from the work of James F. White. In *Protestant Worship: Traditions in Transition* (Louisville: Westminster/John Knox, 1989), he schematizes the major forms of worship adopted by Protestants. He also offers a broad survey in *A Brief History of Christian Worship* (Nashville: Abingdon, 1993), which I believe to be a model introduction to the subject. Other broad surveys include the work of a German scholar, Theodor Klausen, *A Short History of the Western Liturgy, an Account and Some Reflections* (New York: Oxford University Press, 1979), and Horton Davies, *Christian Worship, Its History and Meaning* (Nashville: Abingdon, 1957). Details on the very beginnings of Christian worship are in Gerhard Delling, *Worship in the New Testament* (Philadelphia: Westminster Press, 1962), Ferdnand Hahn, *The Worship of the Early Church* (Philadelphia: Fortress Press, 1973), and Ralph Martin, *Worship in the Early Church* (Grand Rapids: Eerdmans, 1973). Another leading American liturgical scholar, Paul Bradshaw, has joined Laurence A. Hoffman in editing a series of essays: *The Making of Jewish and Christian Worship* (South Bend: Notre Dame University Press, 1991). Bradshaw has also written *The Search for the Origins of Christian Worship: Sources and Methods for the Study of Early Liturgy* (London: SPCK, 1992).

2. For worship in Britain, the best survey again is in White, *Protestant Worship*. A guide to changes in Anglican worship is in G. J. Cumming, *A History of Anglican Liturgy* (London: Macmillan, 1982).

3. Horton Davies has written a history of English Puritan worship: *The Worship of the English Puritans* (Westminster: Dacre Press, 1948).

4. The literature on worship in America is extensive, with much keyed to the distinctive

styles of each denomination. Broad surveys include Paul F. Bradshaw and Laurence A. Hoffman, eds., *The Changing Face of Jewish and Christian Worship in North America* (South Bend: Notre Dame University Press, 1991), Doug Adams, *Meeting House to Camp Meeting: Toward a History of American Free Church Worship* (Saratoga: Modern Liturgy-Resource Publications, 1981), and William N. Wade, "A History of Public Worship in the Methodist Episcopal Church and the Methodist Episcopal Church, South, from 1784 to 1905" (Ph.D. diss., University of Notre Dame, 1981).

5. This essay on church music led me into unfamiliar territory. Of greatest help was a classic book by Louis F. Benson, *The English Hymn: Its Development and Use in Worship* (New York: Hodder and Stoughton, 1915). Benson surveys the many reform efforts that preceded the work of Watts and gives much attention to Watts. Supplementing Benson are Norman Victor Hope, *Isaac Watts and His Contribution to English Hymnody* (New York: Hymn Society of America, 1947), and R. Newton Flew, *The Hymns of Charles Wesley, a Study of Their Structure* (London: Epsworth Press, 1953). For serious students of musicology, the best survey is Friedrich Blume, *Protestant Church Music: A History* (New York: W. W. Norton, 1974).

6. The Benson of American church music was Henry W. Footes, who in 1940 published *Three Centuries of American Hymnody* (Cambridge: Harvard University Press, 1940). The folk and southern contribution is recorded in Buell E. Cobb, *The Sacred Harp: A Tradition and Its Music* (Athens: University of Georgia Press, 1978), and in the now famous collection of George Pullum Jackson, *Spiritual Folk Songs of Early America* (New York: J. J. Augusin, 1937). The role of blacks is surveyed by Jon Michael Spencer, *Black Hymnody: A Hymnological History of the African-American Church* (Knoxville: University of Tennessee Press, 1992). To gain insight into America's most prolific hymn writer, read Fanny J. Crosby, *Memoirs of Eighty Years etc* (Boston: J. H. Earle, 1906).

CHAPTER SEVEN

1. What is so painfully apparent to one who works on theology in the middle period is the lack of any overall history of theology in America. Perhaps no other subject of such importance has so intimidated historians. The late Sydney Ahlstrom seemed on the way to such a project but had to rest content with his magisterial *A Religious History of the American People* (New Haven: Yale University Press, 1972). He did write a short preview of such a major book, thus providing the best brief treatment of the subject: "Theology in America: A Historical Survey," in James Ward Smith, ed., *The Shaping of American Religion*, vol. 1 of *Religion in American Life* (Princeton: Princeton University Press, 1961), 232–321. H. Shelton Smith, in *Changing Conceptions of Original Sin: A Study in American Theology since 1750* (New York: Scribner's, 1955), at least surveys one of the key doctrines that involved Protestant theologians.

2. Of the three theologians presented in this chapter, Nathaniel Taylor has received the least historical attention, perhaps for good reasons. The only scholarly biography is by Sidney E. Mead, *Nathaniel William Taylor, 1786–1858: A Connecticut Liberal* (Chicago: University of Chicago Press, 1942). Taylor's work has received some recognition in most texts, and his New Haven theology merits a quite general, chapter-long overview in Bruce Kuklick, *Churchmen and Philosophers from Jonathan Edwards to John Dewey* (New Haven: Yale University Press, 1985). Thus, my evaluation of Taylor depended almost entirely on my

reading of his own work. For theology, three sources are all-important. He became controversial with one early, 1828 sermon, published as *Concio ad Clerum: A Sermon Delivered in the Chapel of Yale College, September 10, 1828* (New Haven: A. H. Maltby and Homer Hallock, 1842). After his death, his two most important lecture series were published. Most extensive was his *Lectures on the Moral Government of God*, 2 vols. (New York: Clark, Austin, and Smith, 1859), which is his nearest approximation of a systematic theology. The other series, *Essays, Lectures etc upon Select Topics in Revealed Theology* (New York: Clark, Austin, and Smith, 1859), includes extended polemical essays on the Trinity, total depravity, justification, and election. These essays are not as philosophical, but are based more directly on scripture, than are the same topics as treated in his lectures on moral government. The same publisher also collected his *Practical Sermons* (1858).

3. Charles Hodge continues to attract scholars, particularly those in the contemporary evangelical tradition. Yet, despite recent studies of aspects of his theology, we still do not have a recent biography. The details of his life are in an 1880 biography written by his son and theological disciple, Archibald Alexander Hodge, *The Life of Charles Hodge* (New York: Arno Press, 1969). His work is featured in two collective biographies: W. Andrew Hoffecker, *Piety and the Princeton Theologians: Archibald Alexander, Charles Hodge, and Benjamin Warfield* (Grand Rapids: Baker Book House, 1981), and Glenn Alden Hewitt, *Regeneration and Morality: A Study of Charles Finney, Charles Hodge, John W. Nevin, and Horace Bushnell* (Brooklyn: Carlson, 1991). In a published thesis, Jonathan Wells, *Charles Hodge's Critique of Darwinism: An Historical, Critical Analysis of Concepts Basic to the Nineteenth Century Debate* (Lewiston, N.Y.: E. Mellen Press, 1988), surveys most of what Hodge had to say about Darwinism, particularly in his book *What Is Darwinism?*.

Hodge wrote all the time. He published commentaries on Ephesians, Romans, and I and II Corinthians. He was very much involved in the politics, and polity, of the Presbyterian church, particularly at the time of the Old School–New School schism, and wrote a constitutional history of the Presbyterian church. His theological work informed his essays and reviews in the *Princeton Review* for over forty years; a good selection of the early ones is in *Essays and Reviews, Selected from the Princeton Review* (New York: R. Carter, 1857). Mark A. Noll has edited a selection of his writings: *Charles Hodge: The Way of Life* (New York: Paulist Press, 1987). But the one all-important source of his mature theology is his magisterial work *Systematic Theology*, 3 vols. (Grand Rapids: Eerdmans, 1952).

4. Horace Bushnell's reputation continues to grow. His work both on Christian education and in theology has had continuing appeal to scholars. Bushnell, so controversial in the years before the Civil War, lived on in retirement until he became rather famous in Hartford, and by then his sermons sold well. Thus, we have access to most that Bushnell wrote, including occasional essays on nonreligious topics, such as city planning and parks, and a book that he wrote to oppose women's suffrage. His first published essays were on Christian nurture, essays that grew by 1860 into his final, and now famous, version of *Christian Nurture* (New York: C. Scribner's Sons, 1916). By far his most important, and controversial, book was *God in Christ: Three Discourses etc.* (Hartford: Brown and Parsons, 1849). In defense of it, before the Hartford Convention, he wrote what became *Christ in Theology* (Hartford: Brown and Parsons, 1849). In subsequent years he wrote three theological treatises, each important for understanding his theological system: *Nature and the Supernatural as Together Constituting the One System of God* (New York: C. Scribner's Sons, 1859); *Moral Uses of Dark Things* (New York: C. Scribner and Co., 1868); and *Forgiveness*

and Law, Grounded in Principles Interpreted by Human Analogies (New York: Scribner, Armstrong and Co., 1874). The last work became, in later editions, volume two of another treatise, *The Vicarious Sacrifice, Grounded in Principles of Universal Obligation* (New York: C. Scibner and Co., 1866). Scribner's published at least two series of his sermons after his death. Anthologies include Conrad Cherry, ed., *Horace Bushnell, Sermons* (New York: Paulist Press, 1985), which includes a very helpful introduction, and H. Shelton Smith, ed., *Horace Bushnell* (New York: Oxford University Press, 1965). Bushnell deserves a new biography. The standard one is by Barbara M. Cross, *Horace Bushnell: Minister to a Changing America* (Chicago: University of Chicago Press, 1958). More theologically oriented studies include the following: Howard A. Barnes, *Horace Bushnell and the Virtuous Republic* (Metuchen, N.J.: Scarecrow Press, 1991); James O. Duke, *Horace Bushnell on the Vitality of Biblical Language* (Chicago: Scholars Press, 1984); David L. Smith, *Symbolism and Growth: The Religious Thought of Horace Bushnell* (Missoula: Scholars Press, 1980), a published dissertation; and Barbara Ella Damon, "The Development of New England Theology in Relation to Horace Bushnell's Theory of Language" (Master's thesis, Oberlin College, 1964).

CHAPTER EIGHT

1. The strongest argument about the critical role of divided churches in leading to Civil War are in C. C. Goen, *Broken Churches, Broken Nation: Denominational Schism and the Coming of the Civil War* (Macon, Ga.: Mercer University Press, 1985). The schism within Methodism receives some attention in most histories of the Methodist church in America (see the notes for chapter 2) but not nearly the detail it gained in the histories written by both sides just after the separation. I had to turn to these more proximate accounts to gain a blow-by-blow account. The perspective of the northern denomination shapes Charles Elliott, *History of the Great Secession from the Methodist Episcopal Church in the Year 1845, etc* (Cincinnati: Swormstedt and Poe, 1855). The southern perspective is clearest in Holland N. Mctyeire, *A History of Methodism etc* (Nashville: Southern Methodist Publishing House, 1884).

2. The Baptists did not suffer as much internal conflict as the Methodists. The Baptist separation is described well in a standard history: Robert G. Torbet, *A History of the Baptists*, 3d ed. (Valley Forge: Judson Press, 1963). The relationship between northern and sourthern Baptists, both before and after the separation, is detailed in Robert Andrew Baker, *Relations between Northern and Southern Baptists* (Fort Worth: N.p., 1948). Essays on these critical years, including what I consider to be the best account of the origins of black Baptist denominations, are in a series of scholarly essays edited by James E. Wood, Jr., *Baptists and the American Experience* (Valley Forge: Judson Press, 1976).

3. The 1801 Plan of Union soon attracted more than its share of polemical literature. One of the ablest opponents of the plan, and of the New School that developed out of it, was Samuel J. Baird, who wrote *A History of the New School etc.* (Philadelphia: Remsen, and Haffelfinger, 1868), which is a history of the orgins of the New School, not its subsequent development. The best recent study of the New School is George M. Marsden, *The Evangélical Mind and the New School Presbyterian Experience: A Case Study of Thought and Theology in Nineteenth-Century America* (New Haven: Yale University Press, 1970). The most recent history of the Congregational perspective is in J. William Youngs, *The Congregationalists* (New York: Greenwood Press, 1990).

4. The New School–Old School split occasioned a flood of polemical literature. To catch the flavor of the emotions aroused, one need read only the defenders of each position. The New School is defended in Zebulon Crocker, *The Catastrophe of the Presbyterian Church in 1837, etc.* (New Haven: B. and W. Noyes, 1838), and the Old School is supported in Isaac B. Brown, *A Historical Vindication of the Abrogation of the Plan of Union by the Presbyterian Church in the United States of America* (Philadelphia: W. S. and A. Martien, 1855).

5. For the story of biblical scholarship in antebellum America, I was in all ways dependent on the work of two scholars: Jerry Wayne Brown, *The Rise of Biblical Criticism in America, 1800–1870: The New England Scholars* (Middletown, Conn.: Wesleyan University Press, 1969), and Herbert Hovenkamp, *Science and Religion in America, 1800–1860* (Philadelphia: University of Pennsylvania Press, 1978). Hovenkamp includes chapters on the higher criticism as well as on the natural sciences. Without these two books, I could not have completed my section on biblical scholarship, and I cannot overstress the debt I owe to the authors. Other books were less directly related to my goals. These include Mark A. Noll, *Between Faith and Criticism: Evangelicals, Scholarship, and the Bible in America* (San Fransisco: Harper and Row, 1986), which documents early as well as later evangelical responses to the higher criticism.

6. For the controversies over the new geology, the best brief introduction is, again, Hovenkamp, *Science and Religion in America*. Also useful is Theodore D. Bozeman, *Protestants in an Age of Science: the Baconian Ideal and Ante-bellum American Religious Thought* (Chapel Hill: University of North Carolina Press, 1977). I drew extensively on Edward Hitchcock's *The Religion of Geology and Its Connected Sciences* (Boston: Phillips, Sampson, 1854). A good anthology is David C. Lindberg and Ronald L. Numbers, eds., *God and Nature: Historical Essays on the Encounter between Christianity and Science* (Berkeley: University of California Press, 1986).

Index

Apostolic and Catholic Assyrian Church of the East, 14

apostolic succession, doctrine of, 9, 109, 151

Aquinas, Thomas, 28

Arianism, 13, 14, 26, 193, 202, 287

Aristotle, 11, 28

Arius, 13

Arkansas, 134, 167

Armenia, 4

Armenian Church, 4, 15

Arminianism: Anglican acceptance of, 46–48; challenge to New England Puritans, 50–52, 54; and Cumberland Presbyterian affirmation, 132–33; in the Dutch Reformed Church, 61–63; as a foil for Jonathan Edwards, 92–94; Methodist affirmation of, 65–67, 70–71, 86; origins among Dutch remonstrants, 35–38; references to, xii, 38, 67, 98, 107, 129, 157, 212, 216, 217, 220, 230, 257, 259, 278; relationship to New Haven theology, 263–64

Arminius, 37, 67, 68, 178, 222

Asbury, Francis, 76, 77, 80–82, 84–87, 131, 137, 153, 155, 301 (nn. 5, 6)

asceticism, 75, 85

Assemblies of God, xi, 293

Associate Presbytery, 42

Associate Reformed Presbyterian Church, 256, 257

Associate Reformed Synod, 203, 287

Associate Synod, 42, 61, 148, 203, 205, 256, 259

Assyrian Church, 4, 14

astronomy, 210

Athanasian creed, 27, 46

atheism, 98, 116

Athenasius, 7, 13

atonement doctrine, 4, 16, 17, 37, 58, 68, 69, 101, 108, 133, 178, 180, 206, 215, 219, 228, 229, 243, 244, 245, 257, 290

Auburn Declaration, 266, 267

Auburn Seminary, 139, 266

Augsburg Confession, 33, 64, 67, 289

Augustine, 16–18, 21, 23, 24, 29, 30, 96, 198

Ayling, Stanley E., 300 (n. 1)

Baird, Samuel J., 309 (n. 3)

Baker, Robert Andrew, 309 (n. 2)

Balch, Hezekiah, 260

Bancroft, George, 273, 274

baptism, xii, 9, 11–13, 18, 20, 21, 28, 31, 33, 46, 52, 58, 59, 67, 68, 80, 86, 88, 103, 109, 110, 119, 134, 150, 154, 157, 160, 173, 174, 186–88, 190–92, 194, 195, 229–31, 247, 248, 255, 288, 289, 292, 293

baptism for the dead, 20

Baptist General Convention, 254

Baptists: black Baptist denominations, 255–56, 295–97; definitions of, 58; denominational growth of, 130–39; early Baptists in America, 58–59; Free Will Baptists, x, xi, 58, 291; higher education among, 139; northern Baptists, 255, 295; references to, xii, xiv, 32, 38, 43, 44, 51, 53, 57, 64, 80, 85, 86, 87, 97, 114, 117, 118, 119, 124, 127, 128, 142, 152, 155, 165, 183, 207, 220, 250, 253, 261, 286, 288, 290; revival patterns among, 121–23; and sectional divisions over slavery, 254–56; the Southern Baptist Convention, 254–55, 287, 295–96, 297, 298; worship patterns of, 193–96

Barnes, Howard A., 309 (n. 4)

Bauer, F. C., 171, 271, 272

Bay Psalm Book, 200, 204

Beecher, Lyman, 211, 262–64

Beets, Henry, 306 (n. 9)

Belgic Confession, xii, 61

Bellamy, Joseph, 91, 97, 102, 105, 113

benevolent societies, 137–38, 140

Benson, Louis F., 201, 307 (n. 5)

Berg, Joseph, 178

Bernard of Clairvaux, 199

Bernard of Cluny, 199

Bible Presbyterian Church, 256

biblical criticism, 105, 165, 223–24, 269–78

Biblical Repository, 269

Biblical Researches in Palestine, Mount Sinai and Arabia Petra (Robinson), 269

bishop, office of, 9, 10

Bishop of London, 45

Cartwright, Peter, 301 (n. 7)

Catholicism: Charles Hodge's views of, 228; early sacramental system of, 17–19; and early worship, 24–25; eclectic pre-Reformation patterns in, 28; growth of in America, 288–89; hostility to among American Protestants, 171, 173; under Mary Tudor in England, 34–35; music in, 198–99; origins of episcopal system in, 8–9; references to, x, xi, xiii, 15, 20, 23, 38, 39, 63, 78, 79, 98, 111, 115, 116, 117, 119, 120, 131, 134, 136, 141, 143, 144, 156, 157, 162, 168, 181, 183, 184, 185, 186, 188, 189, 190, 191, 194, 206, 208, 221, 224, 227, 229, 295, 296; sympathy for in Mercersburg theology, 170–76; sympathy for in Oxford movement, 158–61

Cell, George C., 301 (n. 2)

Chalcedon, Council of, 14, 15, 26

Channing, William Ellery, 238, 273, 275

charismatic gifts, 165, 294

Charles, Prince, 41

Charles I, 36–38, 40–42, 156, 191

Charles the Great, 27

Charles II, 38, 41

Chase, Philander, 154, 155–56, 160, 163

Chase, Salmon, 166

Cherry, Conrad, 302 (n. 2), 309 (n. 4)

Chiles, Robert E., 301 (n. 2)

Christ, concept of, 10, 12, 13

Christian and Missionary Alliance, xi

Christianity, defining characteristics of, 1

Christian Nurture (Bushnell), 247

Christian Reformed Church, 148, 177, 179, 181, 306 (n. 9)

Christians and Churches of Christ, xi, 288

Christian Science, xi

Christmas Conference (Methodist) of 1784, 78

church and state relationships, 51, 114, 116, 117

church as a sociological concept, 118

church buildings, 22

Churches of Christ, xi, 137, 207, 255, 288

church establishments, 52

church fathers, 6

Churchman, The, 159

church membership statistics, 130–31, 133–34, 294–96

church music, 20, 23, 159, 197–209

Church of God, Winebrenner's, 170

Church of God in Christ, 293, 295

Church of Jesus Christ of the Latter Day Saints. *See* Mormons

Church of Scotland. *See* Presbyterianism

Church of the Brethren, x, xi, 58

Church of the Nazarine, xi, 291

circuit system, 74, 82, 83, 85, 257

Civil War (United States), ix, 28, 38, 41, 82, 88, 113, 128, 131, 135, 136, 139, 146, 147, 152, 156, 159, 164, 165, 169, 175, 178, 180, 191, 194, 210, 249, 250, 253–55, 268, 269, 278, 280, 281, 285, 286, 288, 289, 291, 292, 294

Clark, Elmer E., 301 (n. 6)

Clarke, John, 58

class meetings in Methodism, 74, 75, 81, 87, 194, 196

Clebsch, William A., 305 (n. 5)

Clement of Alexandria, 7

clerical orders, 8

Cobb, Buell E., 307 (n. 6)

Coke, Thomas, 78–81, 153

Cole, Charles C., 304 (n. 8)

Coleridge, Samuel, 233, 273

College of New Jersey, 57, 139, 221, 260. *See also* Princeton

colleges, denominational, 139

Colonization movement, 143

Colored Methodist Episcopal Church, 253

Colossians (New Testament), 11

Columbia College, 139, 154

Columbia Seminary, 264, 266

commonsense philosophers, 221

communion service. *See* Eucharist

communions, Scottish, 120, 124, 125, 126

confessionalism, 259, 268, 292

confirmation, sacrament or practice of, 28, 46, 88, 136, 186, 188, 191

Congregational Christian Church, 172

congregational covenants, 36

Congregationalism: in colonial America, 48–53; in higher education, 139; and involvement in biblical scholarship, 273–77; New Divinity movement within, 90, 101–12; as part of an evangelical consensus, 114–15; Plan of Union with Presbyterians, 260–62; Puritan roots of, 35–36, 192–93; references to, x, xii, 10, 32, 43, 44, 45, 58, 61, 64, 65, 73, 74, 75, 84, 85, 86, 91, 97, 114, 115, 116, 117, 118, 119, 122, 123, 124, 128, 129, 130, 131, 132, 133, 134, 135, 136, 145, 147, 148, 152, 156, 165, 169, 172, 175, 178, 183, 186, 188, 189, 199, 201, 206, 207, 211, 220, 230, 231, 234, 242, 247, 248, 249, 250, 251, 254, 255, 256, 257, 258, 259, 262, 264, 266, 280, 283, 287, 288, 290, 295, 296; resistance to hymns, 204; support of benevolent societies, 138–43; support of missions, 139; worship patterns in, 195–96

Connecticut, 44, 45, 48, 51, 53, 101, 139, 148–51, 153, 155, 204, 211, 216, 234, 235, 259, 262

Consistory: in Geneva, 189

Constantine, 9, 13

Constantinople, First Council of, 13, 14, 225

Constantinople, Second Council of, 15

Constantinople, Third Council of, 15

consubstantiation, doctrine of, 185, 231

conversion experience, 120, 121

Coptic Church, 4, 15

Corinthians (New Testament), 20

corporealism, 111

Cossitt, Franceway R., 304 (n. 6)

Counter-Reformation, 183

Cousin, Victor, 233

Covenanters: Scottish, 41, 42, 61, 148, 203, 207, 256, 257

covenant theory, 48

Cowan, Henry, 299 (n. 3)

Cowper, William, 203

Cox, Leo George, 301 (n. 3)

Craighead, Thomas, 132, 133

Cranmer, Thomas, ix, 9, 33, 190

creationism, 294

Critical and Historical Introduction to the Old Testament (Parker), 278

Crocker, Zebulon, 310 (n. 4)

Cromwell, Oliver, 38, 41

Cromwell, Thomas, 33

Crosby, Fanny, 207, 307 (n. 6)

Cross, Barbara M., 309 (n. 4)

crusades, 27

Cumberland Presbyterians, 132, 133, 256, 257, 259, 268, 304

Cumberland revivals of 1797–1801, 124, 125

Cumming, G. J., 306 (n. 2)

Cummins, George D., 164

Dairyman's Daughter, The, 140

Damon, Barbara E., 309 (n. 4)

Daniel: in Jewish Bible, 2, 111

Dartmouth College, 139, 220

Darwin, Charles, 165, 178, 210, 214, 223, 225, 227, 248, 282, 283, 286

Darwinism, 176, 210, 221–23, 225, 239, 279, 280, 282, 285, 286, 291, 294

Das Leben Jesu (Life of Jesus) (Strauss), 272

David (Jewish king), 197

Davidson, Robert, 303 (n. 6)

Davies, Horton, 306 (nn. 1, 3)

Davies, Rupert, 301 (n. 4)

Davies, Samuel, 57, 143, 205, 207, 300 (n. 7)

day-age theory of creation, 283

Dayton, Wilbur T., 301 (n. 3)

deism, 98, 109, 269, 270

De Jong, Gerald Francis, 300 (n. 10), 305 (n. 8)

De Klerk, Peter, 306 (n. 9)

DeLancey, William, 159

Delling, Gerhard, 306 (n. 1)

De Mille, George E., 304 (n. 3)

denominationalism, 115–18, 137

depravity, doctrine of, 35, 37, 68, 99, 106–8, 110, 133, 212, 216, 217, 226, 227, 229, 240, 241, 264

De Ridder, Richard, 306 (n. 9)

De Wette, W. M. L., 271, 278

Dickens, Arthur G., 299 (n. 1)

Dickinson College, 170

Directory of Public Worship (1643), 38,
191–94, 195
Directory of Worship (1788), 205
Disciples of Christ, xi, xii, 3, 4, 6, 9, 11, 17,
21, 67, 71, 83, 84, 91, 97–99, 102, 103, 105,
113, 114, 132, 134, 137, 142, 179, 198, 211, 212,
220, 255, 260, 272, 273, 280, 288, 295, 296
Doane, George W., 159, 164
Dort, Council of, xii, 31, 36–38, 61, 133, 139,
177, 178, 180, 229
Dow, Lorenzo, 83
Drew University, 140
Duke, James O., 309 (n. 4)
Dunkards (Church of the Brethren), 115
Dutch Reformed Church: in the American
colonies, 60–61; doctrinal division
within, 178; and new Dutch migration,
178–80; patterns of growth after 1792,
176–78; references to, x, 84, 91, 101, 114,
115, 119, 128, 139, 147, 169, 195, 212, 250,
295, 296; and separation of Christian
Reformed Church, 181–82
Dwight, Timothy, 105, 113, 128, 204, 207,
211, 283

Eastern religions, 208
Ebionites, 4
ecumenical councils, 4, 9, 10–15
ecumenism, 172, 173, 181, 259, 267
Edward VI, 33, 189
Edwards, Jonathan: defense of divine sovereignty, 93–94; esthetic thought, 95–97;
idealistic ontology, 94–95; references to,
50, 57, 99, 100, 102, 103, 105–8, 110, 112,
113, 205, 211, 212, 217, 220, 222, 229, 233,
235, 239, 260; on religious experience,
92–93; theological legacy, 97–98
Edwards, Jonathan, Jr., 97, 260
Egyptian Church, 4
Eichhorn, J. G., 270, 271, 273, 274, 276
election doctrine, 35, 38, 69, 80, 93, 107,
133, 154, 163, 178, 180, 216, 217, 228, 229,
246
elevation of the Host, 24
Elizabeth I, 34, 35, 39, 156, 189, 299 (n. 2)

Elliott, Charles, 309 (n. 1)
Ellwood, Douglas J., 302 (n. 2)
Emerson, Ralph Waldo, 97, 207, 233, 236,
278, 280
Emmons, Nathaniel, 91, 212
environmentalism, 247
Ephesus, Council of, 14
Episcopalianism: Anglican roots of, 43–48;
and broad church perspectives, 164–65;
decline of before 1815, 153–54; and evangelical–High Church conflict, 156–63;
and founding of the Protestant Episcopal Church, 148–52; and growth of the
church after 1815, 154–56; impact of the
Oxford movement on, 158–61; post–
Civil War growth of, 167–68; references
to, xiii, 2, 42, 63, 84, 85, 98, 115, 119, 128,
131, 134–36, 139, 140, 144, 149, 169, 196,
206, 290; and the slavery controversy,
165–67
episcopal system, 8–10, 77
Erasmus, 270
eschatology, 18, 19, 111, 222, 224, 232, 246
Essay on Human Understanding (Locke),
94
esthetic theory, 92, 95, 96
Ethiopian church, 4, 15
Eucharist, 5, 9, 18, 19, 21–25, 33, 34, 37, 87,
157, 159, 164, 173, 174, 184–88, 190, 191,
197, 231
Evangelical Association, 83
Evangelical Church of Germany, 171
Evangelical Free Church, xi
evangelicalism: among American Methodists, 75–76, 80, 83–88; challenges to in
the mid-nineteenth century, 250, 255,
258–59, 261–64, 268, 275, 278–83, 285–90;
in colonial churches, 49–50, 55–62; as a
contending faction in Episcopalianism,
10, 43, 47, 150–68; definitions of, xii–xiii,
63–65, 114–15, 147–48; dominance of in
the middle period, 117–18; as expressed
in American revivals, 119–28; and free
worship tradition, 183, 195–97; in German and Dutch Reformed churches,

169–82; in musical expression, 201–8; and role in benevolence, 138–42; as a theme in the Reformation, 30, 33–36; twentieth century forms of, 11, 290–98; Wesleyan expression of, 66–69, 72, 73

Evangelical Lutheran Church in America, 295, 296

Evangelical Synod, 171, 172

evangelists, 119, 123–24

Evans, Mary Ann (George Eliot), 277

Everett, Edward, 273, 274

evolution. *See* Darwinism

Ewing, Finis, 133, 304 (n. 6)

Faithful Narrative (Edwards), 92

fall of Adam and Eve, 226, 241

Federal Constitution of 1787, 116

Federalist party, 118

feminism, 114, 234

fencing of the table, 188

feudalism, 27

filioque, 27

Finke, Roger, 303 (n. 5)

Finney, Charles G., 122, 123, 128, 129, 173, 220, 230, 257, 262, 263, 303 (n. 3), 308 (n. 3)

First Amendment, 116

Flew, R. Newton, 307 (n. 5)

Florida, 166

Footes, Henry W., 307 (n. 6)

foreign missions, 75

Forty-Two Articles of the English Church, 34

Foster, Charles I., 304 (n. 8)

Foster, Frank H., 301 (n. 1)

Francis II, 39

Francke, A. H., 270

Franklin, Benjamin, 54, 204

Franklin and Marshall College, 170

Fraser, James W., 303 (n. 3)

Freedom of the Will. See On the Freedom of the Will

Free Methodist Church, 88, 251, 252, 291

Free Will Baptists, x, xi, 58, 59

Frelinghuysen, Theodore, 61

French Reformed Church, x, 60, 169

Froeligh, Solomon, 178

fundamentalism, 291, 294

Furman College, 139

gap theory of creation, 283

Gasper River revival, 125

Gaustad, Edwin S., 303 (n. 2)

General Baptists, 58

General Missionary Convention, 142

General Seminary (Episcopal), 159, 161, 162, 164, 166

Genuineness of the Gospels (Norton), 276

geology, 3, 105, 210, 222, 239, 280–85

Georgia, 43, 66, 67, 124, 127, 148, 167, 252

German Brethren, 87

German Reformed Church: colonial founding of, 60; growth in nineteenth century, 169–70; liturgical reforms within, 175–76; and Mercersburg theology, 170–75; references to, x, xv, 32, 80, 84, 91, 114, 115, 119, 127, 128, 147, 177, 178, 188, 195, 210, 250, 295, 296

German Reformed Free Synod, 170

Gerrish, Brian A., 305 (n. 7)

Glorious Revolution, 38

glossolalia, 20, 87, 249, 293, 294

Gnostics, 6–8, 10, 14, 272, 276

Goen, C. C., 309 (n. 1)

Goethe, Johann, 170

Good, James I., 300 (n. 9), 305 (n. 6)

Graham, Billy, 262

Graves, James R., 255

Gray, Asa, 281

Great Awakening, 54, 60

Greek Orthodox Church, x, xx, 18, 23, 25–28, 176, 203

Greek philosophy, 10, 11

Greeneville College, 260

Gregorian chant, 199

Griffin, Clifford S., 304 (n. 8)

Griswold, Alexander, 154

Guelzo, Allen C., 302 (n. 3)

Gunn, T. Jeremy, 303 (n. 2)

Indiana, 134, 137, 179
inerrancy, doctrine of, 279, 291, 292, 297
infant baptism, 109, 110, 231, 247, 248
Institutes of the Christian Religion (Calvin),
    xii, 30, 106
instrumental music in worship, 146, 197,
    198, 206
Iowa, 179
Irenaeus, 7
irresistible grace, doctrine of, 35, 37, 95, 97,
    133, 216, 219, 229, 230
Islam, 1
itinerancy, 81, 82, 87, 121
Ives, Levi S., 162

Jackson, Andrew, 133
Jackson, George Pullen, 307 (n. 6)
Jacksonian Democrats, 118
James, New Testament book of, 7, 16
James I, 37, 40, 191
Jamestown colony, 43
James II, 38, 39, 41
Jansenists, 227
Jarratt, Devereux, 46, 76
Jefferson, Thomas, 99
Jehovah's Witnesses, xi, 289
Jeremiah, 2, 19
Jerome, 141
Jesuits, 73
Jesus: elevation to divine status in the
    Church, 1–5, 10–15
Jewish Christian sects, 4
John, the Gospel of, 11
Judaism, x, 1–4, 11, 16, 19, 143, 197, 198
Judson, Adoniram, 142
justification, doctrines about, xiii, 25, 29,
    33, 36, 87, 98, 99, 157, 160, 243, 245, 246,
    290, 297
Justinian, 15

Katherine of Aragon, 32
Kemper, Jackson, 161
Kentucky, 59, 85, 86, 124, 125, 127, 129, 132,
    134, 137, 139, 145, 164, 205, 259, 287
Kentucky Synod, 132, 133

Kenyon College, 139, 155
King, Samuel, 133
King James (Authorized) version of the
    Bible, 36, 141
Kirk, James, 299 (n. 3)
Klausen, Theodore, 306 (n. 1)
Knapp, Hugh Heath, 302 (n. 4)
Knox, John, ix, 34, 39, 187, 191, 256
Kromminga, Diedrich H., 306 (n. 9)
Kuklick, Bruce, 301 (n. 1), 307 (n. 2)
Kuyper, Abraham, 181

Lacy, Creighton, 304 (n. 8)
Lake, Peter, 299 (n. 2)
Lamarck, Jean, 280, 282
Landmark Baptists, 255
Lane Seminary, 263
language theory, 236, 237
Laud, William, 36, 37, 40, 156, 191, 192
lectionaries, 189, 191
Lewis, Taylor, 178
liberalism, religious, 290, 291
Life of Jesus (Strauss), 276
limited atonement, doctrine of, 17, 37, 58,
    178, 180, 216, 219, 229
Lincoln, Abraham, 166
Lindberg, David C., 310 (n. 6)
liturgies. *See* worship
liturgy: definition of, 184
Livingston, John H., 177
Locke, John, 94
Lockridge, Kenneth A., 300 (n. 6)
Logan County revivals, 126, 128
Log College, 54, 55
Logos doctrine, 11, 14
Long Parliament, 36, 38, 42
Louisiana, 134, 155, 166
love feast, 21, 74, 194. *See also* Agape
Loveland, Clara O., 304 (n. 1)
Lowell, James Russell, 207
Luke, the Gospel of, 6
Luther, Martin: contributions to church
    music, 199–200; evangelical emphasis,
    63, 65, 148; influence on English refor-
    mation, 32–33; references to, ix, x, xi, 1,

Otterbein, Philip, 60, 83
Oxford movement, 154, 157–62, 164, 168, 169, 171, 172, 203
Oxford University, 66, 75

Paine, Thomas, 98, 269
Paley, William, 213, 214, 282, 285
Palmer, Phoebe, 253, 291, 294
pantheism, 95, 220, 222, 248
papacy, origin of, 9
Park, Amasa Edwards, 302 (n. 5)
Parker, Theodore, 233, 277–80
Particular Baptists, 58, 59, 194
patriarchalism, 9
Paul (of the New Testament), xiv, 2–4, 6–8, 10, 11, 16, 17, 19–21, 29, 30, 96, 100, 107, 198, 272, 279, 293
Pauline scheme of salvation, 17, 47, 146, 210, 227, 243, 248
peace reform, 143
peace societies, 142
Pelagianism, 17, 68, 227
Pelagius, 17, 18
Pella colony, 179, 180
Penn, William, x, 60
Pennsylvania, x, 53, 54, 60, 76, 85, 91, 115, 116, 126, 128, 148, 150, 153, 159, 175, 262
Pennsylvania Ministerium, 169
Pentecostalism, xi, 20, 67, 71, 86, 196, 292, 293, 294, 297
Pentecost experience, 12
perfectionism, Christian, 65, 68, 70, 71, 220, 253, 263
Perkins, William, 37
perseverance doctrine, 35, 37, 69, 133, 216, 219, 229, 232, 257
Peter (of the New Testament), 4, 7, 9, 279
pew system, 146, 158, 251, 252
Philadelphia presbytery, 53
Philadelphia synod (Presbyterian), 54, 55, 57, 59
Philadelphia Synod of Particular Baptists, 58, 138
Phillip II, 34

pietism, x, 63, 64
Pilcher, George W., 300 (n. 7)
Pilgrims, 60. See also Separatists
Plan of Union, Presbyterian and Congregationalist, 3, 138, 153, 259, 256, 260–63, 265, 266
Plato, 10
Platonism, 10, 96
Plotinus, 238
Plymouth Brethren, xi
Plymouth Colony, 35, 60
political economy, 215
polity (church government), xiv, 40, 53, 73, 77
Polk, Leonidas, 166
positivism, 222
postmillennialism, 112
predestination, 31, 35, 37, 38, 48, 69, 107. See also election, doctrine of
premillennialism, 112, 289, 291, 292, 297
Presbyterian Church in America, 256
Presbyterian Church in the United States (Southern), 267
Presbyterian Church of the Confederate States of America, 267
Presbyterian Church (USA), 295, 296, 297
Presbyterianism: colonial foundations of, 53–58; and Cumberland schism, 132–33; as defended by Charles Hodge, 221–33; involvement in benevolent societies, 138–41; modern mergers within, 295–97; and New School–Old School schism, 259–67; in the Plan of Union, 256–61; reaction to hymn singing, 199–205; references to, x, xiii, xiv, 32, 35, 36, 38, 44, 45, 48, 50, 61, 63, 64, 72–91 passim, 95, 97, 101, 114, 115, 117, 120–27, 128, 134, 135, 142, 143, 144, 145, 146, 147, 148, 149, 152, 156, 157, 160, 165–85 passim, 197, 207, 212, 220, 249, 250, 251, 254, 268, 269, 279, 280, 286, 287, 290, 291; and revival institutions, 120–21; Scottish origins of, 39–42; slowed growth of in the nineteenth century, 130–31; Ulster origins of, 42–43; in western revivals, 124–27; worship pat-

terns of in America, 194–95; worship patterns of in Scotland, 191–92

Prichard, Robert W., 304 (n. 2)

Priestley, Joseph, 269

Primitive Baptists, 138, 254, 255, 257

Primitive Methodists, 83

Princeton, 57, 95, 101, 102, 113, 139, 170, 171, 173, 177, 178, 220–22, 233, 265, 266, 274, 290. *See also* College of New Jersey

Princeton Review, 221, 222

Princeton theology, 105, 113, 249, 266

prophetic tradition, 19, 197

Protestant Episcopal Church in the Confederate States of America, 166

Protestantism, ix, 34, 39, 58, 63, 64, 124, 135, 147, 168, 169, 172, 173, 175, 176, 181, 191, 197, 268, 272, 286, 290, 294

Protestant Methodist Church, 84, 88

Provoost, Samuel, 150, 151, 153, 155

Psalms of David (Watts), 202

psalters, 199–202, 204

public schools, 139, 144, 206

purgatory, doctrine of, 19, 24, 34, 232

Puritanism, xii, 36, 37, 41, 43, 44, 45, 46, 47, 56, 58, 63, 64, 65, 91, 92, 97, 104, 128, 156, 178, 183, 186, 187, 194, 200, 201, 202, 208, 232, 247, 258, 259, 287; English origins of, 35–39; and musical taste, 200; in the New England colonies, 48–53; and worship style, 192–93, 195–96. *See also* Congregationalism

Pusey, Edward B., 158

Quakers, x, xi, 8, 35, 43, 53, 75, 86, 104, 137, 144, 249, 287

Queen's College, 139, 177

Raalte, Albertus van, 179, 180

racial theories, 234

Rack, Henry D., 300 (n. 1), 301 (n. 4)

Randolph-Macon College, 139

Rankin, Adam, 205

Rankin, John, 125, 133

rationalism, 50, 97, 98, 103

Rauch, Augustus, 170

Redford, Albert H., 301

Reformed Church in America, 177

Reformed Episcopal Church, 164

Reformed Presbyterian Church, 256

Reformed Presbyterian Church, Evangelical Synod, 256

Reformed Presbyterians, 148, 203, 259

Reformed Presbytery (Covenanters), 203

Reformed Protestant Dutch Church in North America, 177

Reformed Synod (Covenanters), 42, 61

Reformed tradition, definitions of, xi

regeneration, doctrine of, 31, 68–70, 80, 102, 103, 107, 160, 227, 229, 230, 232, 243–46, 257, 291, 292, 293

Regular Baptists, 59

Reid, James M., 299 (n. 3)

Reid, Thomas, 221

religion, definition of, ix–x, l

Religion of Geology, The, (Hitchcock), 283

religious exercises, 126–28

religious journalism, 125, 128

religious liberalism, 168

Remonstrants (Dutch Arminians), 133, 178, 222, 227, 270

Republican Methodists, 84, 251, 287

Restoration movement, 127, 275, 287

resurrection doctrine, 2, 3, 4

Revelation (New Testament book), 111

revivalism: camping and revivals, 125–26; definitions of, 119–20; in the Great Awakening, 50–51, 54–59; impact of on church music, 206–8; impact of on worship in America, 195–96; as an issue in the New School–Old School Presbyterian schism, 262–63; role of Charles Finney in, 262–63; supportive Methodist institutions and, 84–89, 121–22; supportive Presbyterian institutions and, 120–22; Wesleyan influences on, 66–75; and western revivals from 1797–1805, 124–27; women and, 129–30, 135

Rhode Island, 58, 115

Rice, Edwin W., 304 (n. 9)

Robinson, Edward, 269

Roman Catholic Church. *See* Catholicism

Romans (New Testament book), 16, 17

rood screens, 24

Rupp, Gordon, 301 (n. 4)

Rush, Benjamin, 144

Rutgers College, 139, 177

Sabbatarianism, 116, 142, 143

Sabbatarian worship, 20

sacramentalism, 18, 19, 20, 21, 23, 24, 28, 29, 31, 35, 37, 55, 73, 80, 91, 119–23, 126, 128, 136, 147, 159, 160, 164, 172–76, 178, 184, 194, 230

Sacred Harp, The, 208

sacrifices, 2, 19

Salvation Army, 73, 206

sanctification, doctrine of, 18, 69–71, 73, 86, 108, 219, 229, 230, 243, 246, 251, 253, 291–93

Scarisbrick, J. J., 299 (n. 1)

Schaff, Philip, 113, 169–73, 175, 176, 228, 269, 305 (n. 7)

Schleiermacher, Friedrich, 95, 171, 173, 221, 234, 235, 271

Schmidt, Leigh Eric, 300 (n. 7), 303 (n. 3)

scholasticism, 28

Scholte, Dendrick, 179

Schoolland, Marian M., 306 (n. 9)

Schwenkfelders, x

Scotch-Irish, 39, 43, 53–57, 84, 85, 258, 259

Scottish commonsense philosophy, 221

Scottish communion, 55, 57, 86, 187, 195

Seabury, Samuel (Episcopal bishop), 149–51, 153

Seabury, Samuel (Episcopal journalist), 159, 166

Seceders (Associate Synod), 42, 61, 148, 203, 256, 257, 287

Second Great Awakening, 124, 128

sect, definitions of, 118

Semitic cosmology, xv, 99, 146, 210, 250, 268, 281, 285

Semitic religions, 1

Semler, J. S., 271, 273

Separate Baptists. *See* Baptists

Separatists, 35, 43, 193

Septuagint, 141

sermon, 22, 47, 56, 90, 102, 104, 122, 135, 175, 184–91, 195, 196, 211, 216, 263

Seventh-Day Adventists, xi, 289

Seward, Samuel, 166

sexual harassment, 163

Shakers, xi, 75, 87, 127, 132, 133, 292, 293

Shriver, George H., 305

sign of the cross in baptism, 150, 157, 186, 188, 191, 192, 194

Silliman, Benjamin, 283

Six Days of Creation, The, (Taylor), 178

Slater, Samuel, 144

slavery, 46, 57, 59, 86–88, 90, 104, 117, 118, 134, 135, 138, 143, 146, 165–67, 178, 234, 241, 250–52, 254, 258, 264–67, 269, 281, 285, 286

Smith, David L., 309 (n. 4)

Smith, H. Shelton, 307 (n. 1), 309 (n. 4)

Smith, Hugh, 161

Smith, James Ward, 307 (n. 1)

Smith, Joseph, 289

Smith, Timothy L., 304 (n. 8)

Smith, William, 149

social gospel, 165, 290

Society for the Propagation of the Gospel in Foreign Parts (SPG), 44

Society for the Suppression of Vice, 140

Solemn League and Covenant, 41, 203, 257

Solomon (King of Israel), 197

Soule, Joshua, 253

South: Christianity in, xiii, 30, 44, 45, 54, 57, 59, 84–87, 114, 115, 118, 134–36, 138–41, 143, 145, 148, 149, 153, 161, 165–67, 179, 194, 208, 250–57, 259, 262, 264–67, 286

South Carolina, 43, 44, 57, 60, 127, 148, 153, 165, 166, 175, 257, 264

Southern Baptist Convention, 254, 255, 256, 295, 296, 298. *See also* Baptists

Spaan, Howard B., 306 (n. 9)

speaking in tongues, 8, 20, 87, 249, 293, 294

Spencer, Jon Michael, 307 (n. 6)

Spener, Phillip Jacob, 64

Spinoza, 270

spiritual gifts, 20, 21

spiritualism, 234, 249

spiritual presence, doctrine of, 229, 231

Stark, Rodney, 303 (n. 5)

Sternhold, Thomas, 200

Stewart, Dugald, 221

Stiles, Ezra, 103

Stoics, 10

Stone, Barton W., 124, 127, 287, 288

Strauss, David, 271, 272, 275–78

Strawbridge, Robert, 76

Stuart, Moses, 274, 276, 278, 279

Summers, Thomas O., 194

Sunday, Billy, 262

Sunday school, xv, 87, 114, 140, 143–46, 154, 157, 161, 196, 197, 206, 247, 254

Sunday Service of the Methodists in North America, 194

supernaturalism, 238, 239

Swedenborgianism, xi

Sweet, William Warren, 303 (n. 3)

Swierenga, Robert P., 306 (n. 8)

Swiss Brethren, xi

synagogue, 2, 9, 19, 20, 198

Syrian (Jacobite) Church, 7, 15

System of Doctrines Contained in Divine Revelation (Hopkins), 90

System of the Earth (Hutton), 281

Taylor, Nathaniel: emphasis on moral government, 212–16; life of, 211; references to, 101, 102, 103, 105, 106, 108, 113, 178, 210, 227, 231, 234, 240, 241, 248, 249, 266, 267, 283, 285, 307–8 (n. 2); and reformed Calvinism, 216–20; as a symbol in the New School–Old School controversies, 263–64; theodicies of, 212–15

temperance reform, 118, 142, 143

Temperance Society, 140, 142

temple: Jewish, 19, 20

Tennent, Gilbert, 55, 56, 101, 123

Tennent, William, 54

Tennessee, 59, 85, 124, 125, 127, 132–34, 137, 139, 145, 166, 259, 260, 266, 267

Tennessee Baptist, 255

Test Act of 1704, 43

Texas, 134, 137, 167, 255

theism, 1

theodicies, 99, 102, 105–7, 213, 214, 240, 260, 283

theology, xiii, xiv, xvi, 2, 3, 4, 5, 11, 12, 17, 29, 30, 48, 63, 90–113, 169–71, 173, 175–78, 180, 181, 206, 210–49, 258, 263, 264–67, 282

Thompson, Bard, 305 (n. 7)

Thornwell, James Henley, 264–65

Todd, John, 205

Todd, Margo, xvii

Toleration Act of 1689, 39

Torbet, Robert G., 300 (n. 8), 309 (n. 2)

tract societies, 140–42

transcendentalism, 219, 233, 249, 276–78, 280

transubstantiation, doctrine of, 24, 162, 184

Transylvania College, 139

Trent, Council of, 25, 29, 141

trinity doctrines, 5, 11–15, 22, 27, 50, 92, 94, 154, 161, 215, 224, 225, 237–39, 242, 243, 289

Trinterud, Leonard J., 300 (n. 7)

True Protestant Dutch Church, 181

True Reformed Dutch Church, 178

TULIP (Calvinist doctrinal formula), 37, 216

Turretin, Francis, 221

Tusculum College, 139, 260

Tyler, Bennett, 220

Union Theological Seminary (New York), 171, 269

Union Theological Seminary (Richmond), 266

Unitarianism, xi, 4, 12, 50, 98, 104, 116, 128, 130, 148, 149, 202, 204, 211, 212, 215, 219, 220, 224, 235, 237, 238, 242, 266, 269, 273–75, 276, 277, 278, 280, 288, 293

United Brethren, 60, 83

United Church of Christ, 72, 295, 296. *See also* Congregationalism

United Methodist Church, 292, 294–97. *See also* Methodism